MEXICO

REVOLUTION TO EVOLUTION
1940 – 1960

HOWARD F. CLINE

Issued under the auspices of the
Royal Institute of International Affairs

OXFORD UNIVERSITY PRESS

NEW YORK

1963

The Royal Institute of International Affairs is an unofficial and non-political body, founded in 1920 to encourage and facilitate the scientific study of international questions. The Institute, as such, is precluded by the terms of its Royal Charter from expressing an opinion on any aspect of international affairs. Any opinions expressed in this publication are not, therefore, those of the Institute.

To Ann and Sue Cline who like
to see their names in print, and
to Mary, who does not.

Printed in U.S.A.

PREFACE

IT seems essential to say as soon as possible that the pages which follow have no 'official' blessing or character, direct or indirect. Although as Director of the Hispanic Foundation in the Library of Congress in Washington I am an officer of the United States Government, I have no authority, nor urge, to expound my Government's views on foreign policy and related matters. The present work is wholly an outgrowth of a long-standing professional concern with Mexico and Latin America, and was written at home as a 'spare time' exercise in response to an invitation by the Royal Institute of International Affairs to prepare such a study for their fine Latin American Series. I might add that it employs no sources not fully available to the scholarly public, but is based primarily on a wide range of printed materials, most of which have appeared recently.

Purposely I have chosen to confine most of the present text to the years following 1940, with marked emphasis on the past decade. With only limited space available, it seemed unwise to traverse in detail much ground covered in a somewhat similar presentation that brought the story up to about 1950, published some time ago.[1] For the most part, the present work covers matters until about the end of June 1960. The final chapters, however, extend the limits slightly to include some developments in foreign relations up to December 1960.

The difficult and thankless task of anglicizing certain Americanisms and expunging or softening some of the more vigorous expressions of the original manuscript fell to the lot of Miss Hermia Oliver at Chatham House, who performed the task admirably. To fit the particular needs of the Latin American Series and its British constituency, the first three and the last three chapters were rewritten after June 1960, in line with general suggestions furnished from the Royal Institute, but for which I am wholly responsible.

As a professional historian, I had hoped that the printed version might appear in time to be a modest but sincere contribution to the important anniversaries which 1960 marks in Mexico, commemorating important milestones in national development: Sesquicentennial of the 1810 Movement for Independence, the Centennial

[1] Howard F. Cline, *The United States and Mexico* (1953).

iii

Preface

of Liberal Reform under Benito Juárez, and the Golden Anniversary of the Mexican Revolution of 1910. Even though that intent could not be fulfilled, it is still pleasing now to reaffirm a conclusion that I had formed a decade ago: 'A salient feature of recent developments in Mexico is a clear demonstration that beneficial social and economic change *can* be brought about in so-called "underdeveloped areas" while preserving and increasing political and economic democracy as defined in the New World.'[1]

Mary W. Cline stands in the forefront of the many persons to whom I am much indebted for indispensable aid and assistance, and she has improved the work at all points. I am especially appreciative of the time and talents which Lewis and Georgia Buck lavished on the maps and diagrams. I am also grateful to General Drafting Company, Inc., Convent Station, New Jersey, for permission to use copyrighted material from their 'Humble Road Map of Mexico, 1959' which served as a helpful base and supplied important information. The 'Structure of the Official Party' [Diagram 3] has been reproduced, through generous permission of the University of Illinois Press in Urbana from Robert E. Scott's *Mexican Government in Transition* (1959).

Dr. Alfredo Navarrete and his staff at Nacional Financiera have been uniformly helpful in furnishing specific information not elsewhere easily obtainable. Friends like Dr. Ben Stephansky (U.S. Department of State) and Dr. George Wythe (U.S. Department of Commerce) similarly provided essential references and materials. From Mexico Mr. Robert C. Jones sent many needed key recent publications. Miss Jean Luft, aided by Mrs. Josephita LaRoche, carefully prepared my final typescript and checked the many tables in the text and Appendix. To these, and others, I am most grateful, and needless to say, they are absolved of any responsibility for errors and omissions. I claim these for my own.

Gratitude is also due the Royal Institute for its co-operation in this international enterprise. Mr. A. S. B. Olver, Research Secretary, and Miss Oliver, Editorial Assistant, have been especially helpful and sympathetic in seeing the work through its final stages.

Arlington, Virginia   H.F.C.
26 December 1960

---

[1] Cline, *United States and Mexico*, p. 407. cf. Cline, 'Mexico: a Matured Latin American Revolution', *A. Amer. Acad. Polit.* (Mar. 1961), pp. 84–94.

CONTENTS

Contents

Contents

THE STATE AND THE ECONOMY

THE CURRENT ECONOMIC BOOM

MEXICO ON THE WORLD SCENE

Contents

Contents

PRINCIPAL ABBREVIATIONS

A.Amer.Acad.   *Annals of the American Academy of Political and Social Science.*
Polit.

BNCE   Banco Nacional de Comercio Exterior. (*Note*: English-language titles of articles in the Bank's *Comercio exterior* refer to the English ed., Spanish to the Spanish.)

CNC   *Confederación Nacional de Campesinos* (National Farmers' Federation).

CTM   *Confederación de Trabajadores Mexicanos* (Mexican Workers' Federation).

DGE   Dirección General de Estadística.

HAHR   *Hispanic American Historical Review.*

NF   Nacional Financiera.

OAS   Organization of American States.

PAN   *Partido de Acción Nacional* (Party of National Action).

PRI   *Partido Revolucionario Institucional* (Institutional Revolutionary Party).

Rice, 'Basic Data'   U.S. Bureau of Foreign Commerce, WTIS, pt. 1, Economic Reports, No. 59–5: 'Basic Data on the Economy of Mexico' [prepared by Katherine E. Rice. Jan. 1959].

Rice, 'Economic Developments'   U.S. Bureau of Foreign Commerce, WTIS, pt. 1, Economic Reports: 'Economic Developments in Mexico' [annually, 1954–8, prepared by Katherine E. Rice]. Washington, 1955–9.

SDE   Secretaría de Economía.

SRE   Secretaría de Relaciones Exteriores.

UNAM   Universidad Nacional Autónoma de México.

USBFC   U.S. Bureau of Foreign Commerce.

WTIS   World Trade Information Service.

PERSPECTIVES AND LEGACIES

Chapter I

HERITAGES FROM THE MORE REMOTE PAST

MEXICO is one of the most important republics of Latin America. Size alone makes it significant. It is the most populous of the modern nations that developed from the Spanish colonial empire in America. Brazil, with appreciably more people and territory, stems from a distinct Portuguese tradition. Argentina, a Spanish co-heir, surpasses modern Mexico in area but neither in population nor in extent and richness of history; much of Argentina's present prominence was attained only during the past century. Mexico has held a key position in New World history from earliest times.

In the long Spanish colonial period, Mexico City, built on the earlier Aztec Indian capital of Tenochtitlán, served as the administrative centre of New Spain. Its rule embraced not only the present Republic of Mexico but also the Caribbean Islands, the Philippines, and the rest of Spanish North America, much of it now part of the United States. The corresponding capital of the Spanish viceroyalty in South America was Lima, Peru. With the Andean Highlands of Peru and Ecuador, Mexico was perhaps five millennia ago the seat of one of the oldest and most important aboriginal high civilizations of America.

It is not surprising, then, to learn that in Mexico prehistory and history make even the great Mexican Revolution, which celebrated its Golden Anniversary in 1960, seem but a moment in a long perspective.

There is no one fully agreed body of fact or interpretation about the long Mexican past, let alone the present. There is general accord on the three main periods into which the span is divided. The first of these really belongs to prehistory, the pre-Conquest, or pre-colonial era, with its testimony mainly from archaeology, and lasting until the Spanish Conquest. The arrival of Hernán Cortés in 1519 and the subsequent fall of the Aztec and other native empires opened the second, or colonial period; it was brought to a close three centuries later by movements for Mexican national independence. The achievement of Mexican nationhood in 1821 marks the beginning of a third or national period. Many Mexicans would add yet

3

another important epoch to these—the period since 1910, or what is known as the current Mexican Revolution. It indeed forms the immediate context of contemporary matters.[1]

An enormous corpus of published and manuscript material supports conclusions about the past which can also readily be drawn from even casual direct observation: within the present bounds of the Republic there still persist many ways of life strongly reminiscent of the aboriginal Indian worlds of the pre-Conquest period, of the Iberian peninsula, of Africa, and of yet other areas whose traditions were largely implanted during colonial years, then overlaid with various veneers from national times. Though these diverse traditions have blended to form the Mexican past, it is equally important to note that modern Mexico is evolving in new ways of its own at a rapid rate.

PRE-CONQUEST MEXICO, TO 1519

Man probably first drifted into what is now the Republic of Mexico about 25,000 years ago, specialists tell us. But little is known of a prehistory remarkable for its complexity until it was almost half completed. For the eons before about 12,000 B.C. a few skulls, bones, and stones reveal very little about life; it is only in about 4,000 B.C. that a more detailed archaeological record of sorts begins to unfold. The Mexican story before then is difficult to distinguish within the larger prehistory of the whole New World. In the Andean areas and in what is now part of Central America and Mexico, various groups of Neolithic peoples, seemingly hunters and gatherers, almost simultaneously around perhaps 10,000 B.C., began to make the revolutionary passage from semi-nomadic existence to become village-dwelling agriculturists, a transition nearly completed by 3,000 B.C. On this base arose the great native civilizations which the Spaniards saw in Mexico and in Peru. Because of their central and seminal position in New World prehistory, these two distinct cultural foci are generally lumped together as 'Nuclear America', separated by the less developed Indian societies of the Antilles and large parts of Central America, grouped as Circum-Caribbean cultures. These zones appear in the map on p. 5. At their margins, developments were less spectacular; the Indian groups of North America, Brazil, and the southern portions of South America did not

---

[1] Unfortunately there is in English no one brief, balanced, modern summary history of Mexico. For a helpful bibliographical survey, which includes references to standard bibliographical aids, see R. A. Humphreys, *Latin American History: a Guide to the Literature in English* (1958).

evolve the sophisticated and complex forms that characterize the high civilizations of Nuclear America.

An outline of the course of aboriginal history following *c.* 3,000 B.C. in the area of concern here, Meso-America (map on p. 6), is provided by the artefacts of this period. A slow evolution of simple, egalitarian agricultural communities seemingly gave way to a sudden acceleration of creative forces somewhere around 900 B.C., culminating in a real florescence in the sixth and fifth centuries before the Christian era.

With various phases of rise and decline, a congeries of city-states in the central and southern highlands of Mexico, in the highlands of Guatemala and adjacent tropical lowlands, especially the peninsula of Yucatán, rose, fell, and interacted. Differing in details, their basic likeness makes the whole Meso-American complex until 1519 a unit whose intricate and advanced achievements place it on a level with other highly developed contemporary societies in the Old World. Urbanism, monumental architecture, and embryonic imperial structures linking city-states in defensive and offensive alliances are some main characteristics.

The Meso-American social systems, geared to agricultural abundance, permitted the emergence of full-time specialists among artisans and quasi-professionals in government, religion, war, and commerce. Economic apparatus including formal markets and external trade to near-by areas carried on by professional traders

5

contributed to the formation of defined social classes. The upper segments controlled the means of production—land, water, labour forces. War and religion, never far apart, became highly organized as did intertwined legal and judicial organizations. The area is marked by important intellectual achievements in astronomy—including the perfection of calendar systems—mathematical and

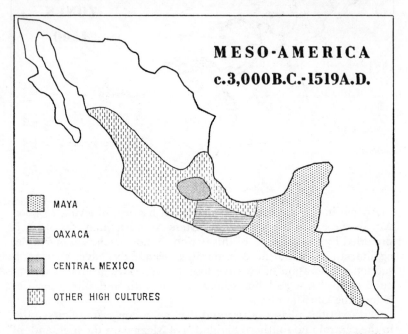

glyphic systems, an erudition usually monopolized by a small élite. Their artistic products in stone, bone, copper, gold, mosaics, and the like, command universal admiration. The masses then, as now, seemingly lived on the edge of a subsistence level. In times of famine some sold themselves into slavery.

Although many of the earlier cultural traits and activities evolved steadily from earlier times, these societies, which are exemplified by the Aztecs, showed a more decided and increasingly militaristic focus, much of the earlier eras having been theocratic in emphasis. Developments did not always proceed evenly through the myriad groups which the Spaniards encountered and pacified. Then as now, there were extremes of sophistication between the huge urban complexes and the humble hamlets they overshadowed. The opulence of Mexico City when first viewed by Spaniards astonished them as well as whetted their appetites. But there were pronounced gaps between this 'highest' native culture and various marginal or lesser Indian groups, living in isolated pockets at a different, slower pace, in older ways. Neither social stratification nor differences in regional population density are new in Mexico.

To the north of Mexico City at the time of the Conquest, for instance, still roamed untamed nomadic and semi-nomadic peoples to whom the Aztecs gave the name 'barbarians', or Chichimecs. So variegated, indeed, were the tongues and cultures that greeted the Europeans that the early Spanish Churchmen claimed that the Devil himself had purposely preceded them in Mexico to make their task of Christianizing the area nearly impossible. Many a modern student attempting to unravel the tangled strands of pre-Conquest Mexico can sympathize with this complaint.[1]

COLONIAL DAYS, 1519–1810: A GENERAL VIEW

Without warning, the flourishing chief Indian civilizations of

[1] Replacing many of the old standard summaries (Vaillant, and others) of pre-colonial Mexico is Eric R. Wolf, *Sons of the Shaking Earth* (1959), incorporating many of the specialized materials which have appeared in the past two decades; uneven but excitingly illustrated are the popular summaries by outstanding authorities in Carmen Cook de Leonard, ed., *Esplendor del México antiguo* (1959), with full bibliography. See F. Peterson, *Ancient Mexico* (1959), also summarizing recent data. Most relevant accounts down to 1952 are included in Juan Comas, *Bibliografía selectiva de las culturas indígenas de América* (1953). New finds are rapidly making earlier summaries obsolete.

Meso-America, as well as the lesser ones of the adjacent groups, underwent profound transformation when the control of their destinies passed from their own hands into those of Europeans. Suddenly in place of a land made up of native principalities and aboriginal empires, New Spain (as the area was soon named) became an extension in the New World of Western, specifically Iberian, civilization, one with quite different heritages, goals, and values.

As an overseas Spanish possession, New Spain was rapidly drawn into the Christian orbit. Previous systems of political organization, religious outlook, and leadership were remoulded to conform as nearly as possible to the unities and uniformities that underlay the continuing Spanish imperial efforts throughout Europe, parts of Asia, Africa, and the other parts of the New World not under the sway of Portugal.

The colonial period is the longest, and most complex, era of Mexican history proper. Following an initial and relatively brief military phase of conquest from 1519 to about 1525, the main story for the remainder of the sixteenth century is the transfer of European practices, necessarily adapted to Mexican conditions, by a Spanish Crown inexperienced in colonial matters yet determined to Christianize and civilize a highly developed but pagan society. Most of the chief colonial institutions for these ends were firmly established by perhaps 1580. Government and administration, economics based on European tastes and needs, and a Catholic matrix of religion and culture rather rapidly displaced previous aboriginal forms, borrowing and assimilating those elements from them that did not contravene the primary items of Iberian purposes and belief.

Most of the seventeenth century, the period of the tenth or fifteenth generation of conquerors and conquered, was undramatic. The great policy debates over the nature of the Indian and how he was to be treated had been settled a century earlier, by 1550. Spanish agricultural holdings, the great estates, had long been rooted, as had related enterprises devoted to mining, transport, and overseas commerce and trade. Missionary efforts, so crucial in the first years of contact, withered except on far-flung northern frontiers, remote from the main concerns of New Spain and linked with efforts to defend that realm from encroachments of newly risen European rivals of Spain: France and England.

The placid and opulent heartland of New Spain, the former Indian Meso-America, began slowly, then with increased pace, to change after 1700, due less to internal dynamics than as a reflection of an altered situation in Spain itself. The seemingly interminable European wars had not only exhausted the metropolitan treasury, but as result of the War of the Spanish Succession had replaced the Habsburgs by Bourbons on the throne. Viewing the colonial areas through French eyes, the latter began to tinker with and alter organs of control as well as colonial policy-making mechanisms, chiefly with fiscal goals in view. As the Enlightenment proceeded in Europe, its reflected rays opened up new perspectives in Mexico. During and following the reign of Charles III (1759-88), one of the 'Enlightened Despots' on the Spanish throne, efforts at reform were accelerated and merged imperceptibly with first stirrings of movements for independence in Mexico, in the heady atmosphere of the revolutionary late eighteenth century.

Transitional between the colonial period and national sovereignty were efforts to win first autonomy, then outright independence. Important developments began in 1810, which Mexicans hail as the date of independence. They were eventually crowned with military and political success in 1821, although the present Republic was not proclaimed until 1824.

This in briefest possible outline is the colonial background of the Mexican nation. There are few principal matters in modern Mexico, from language to law, from diet to architecture, from social structure to political boundaries, which do not have some colonial roots. In a brief space these cannot be traced in detail. The total effect of the Spanish transformation of a richly developed aboriginal land into the most important of Spain's American realms underlines the truth of an observation by E. G. Bourne that 'What Rome did for Spain, Spain did in turn for Spanish America'.[1]

COLONIAL PROBLEMS AND LEGACIES

The confrontation in 1519 of Montezuma, chief lord of the Aztecs, and Hernán Cortés, self-appointed representative of the Emperor Charles V, was momentous in the history of Mexico. The handful of Spaniards who had fought and cajoled their way from Veracruz were amazed at the barbaric magnificence of the Indian capital. However, they were appalled by the racks of human skulls of victims sacrificed to pagan deities, and were determined to add this new

[1] Edward Gaylord Bourne, *Spain in America, 1450–1580* (1904), p. 202. Modern interpretations are summarized in Charles Gibson, *The Colonial Period in Latin American History* (1958).

realm to those already ruled by Castile. Their efforts and adventures, related by Cortés himself and companions like Bernal Díaz and the Anonymous Conqueror,[1] make one of the epic tales of America, recounted in Prescott's classic, *The Conquest of Mexico*.

The success of Cortés and his band placed Mexico under Spanish control and posed many new and unprecedented problems for Europeans. As a dependency of the Crown, New Spain was locally administered by a vast and complicated network of organs that were developed after a short period of near-chaos created by the first wave of unruly Spanish adventurers. From 1535 to 1821 the King's immediate representative was a Viceroy, advised and to some degree checked by various council-courts, the audiencias. In Spain itself important policies and decisions were made by a royal Council of the Indies; hence during the long colonial span there were no real politics in New Spain, merely the evolution and workings of administrative mechanisms to carry out the will of a paternalistic absolute monarch. An enormous body of regulatory legislation, forming the background of present Mexican law, was issued and codified to cover nearly every aspect of life, individual and collective.

Spanish military and political control of the previous autonomous aboriginal regions was rather quickly established, at first utilizing the extant structures. A limited number of hereditary Indian noble families were assimilated into the European élite, then later shorn of power as the civil bureaucracy became firmly implanted. Without permitting a true feudal class of overseas Spaniards to evolve, the Spanish Crown at first rewarded conquerors and pioneer settlers by permitting them to collect royal tributes from Indian communities in return for protecting the realm and bearing the costs of Christianizing Indians under their immediate responsibility; this was the famous and complex *encomienda* system, which acted as a transitional bridge to the peonage and other systems of late colonial years, a heavy and sad legacy for the later independent Mexican nation.

In part the proclaimed exclusive rights of Spain to its portion of the New World rested on its undertaking to Christianize the vast and heterogeneous native groups. Spiritual conquest therefore went hand in hand with military pacification, for two or three generations in the hands of Mendicant Orders, the Franciscans and Dominicans. Towards the end of the sixteenth century (1572) the Jesuit Order undertook missionary work on the northern frontier and educational

---

[1] *Narrative of Some Things of New Spain* written by the Anonymous Conqueror. See Humphreys, *Guide*, no. 270.

tasks in the new Europeanized urban centres. As a nearly co-ordinate arm of government, the Church, especially through the friars, attempted to replace idolatry by the Catholic faith; to that end they learned Indian languages and recorded pagan histories and traditions, providing later generations with masses of still largely unexplored historical records.

As always, there was accommodation to local conditions. Often an Aztec or Maya deity was merged with a Catholic saint having many of the same attributes, the syncretisms often retaining a visible prehistorical cast. Because of their peculiar position as special wards, Indians were exempted from processes of the Inquisition established to maintain orthodoxy among the more Europeanized portions of the colonial population. The early friars also set up schools to train Indian upper-class youth, to 'Latinize' them, as the contemporary saying went.

The first and heroic efforts of the Orders dwindled after about 1580, although they remained a fixed feature of the colonial scene. Much of their burden was transferred to secular clergy, in the normal hierarchy headed by bishops and archbishops. The rather more subordinate role played by Orders and the Church in general during the seventeenth and eighteenth centuries coincided with a number of other main developments, perhaps the most notable of which was a halt in the almost catastrophic decline of the native population.

For a number of ill-understood reasons, among which new diseases were certainly a principal one, the native population was almost decimated from 1519 to about 1610. All such figures are controversial, but modern research suggests that an original group of perhaps 13 million at the Conquest had faded to less than 2 million by the close of the sixteenth century. Much of the human population was replaced by cattle and sheep as Spanish agricultural enterprises and estates, the haciendas of later days, became established. A scarcity of labour and the adaptation of the surviving Indian population to colonial conditions aided in establishing an equilibrium, and then a slow rise in numbers, during the eighteenth century.

Elements of technology introduced by the Spaniards included iron and steel tools, the wheel, and beasts of burden, for example. To the dietary they added major crops such as wheat. In mining, textiles, and agriculture, they revolutionized previous methods by employing European techniques. Above all, they provided a new cultural and psychological matrix that altered language, religion, art and architecture.

On their side, native contributions were not inconsiderable. Especially notable was the enrichment of European and world crop resources. Cacao, maize, tomatoes, chile peppers, and chicle (chewing gum) passed to the Old World. Many pre-Conquest handicraft skills and products persisted through the colonial years well into the present. Even within Europeanized contexts, Indian workmen gave a special and local flavour to art and architecture, especially to Mexican baroque. Often these social and cultural evolutions present a rhythm of their own, not immediately affected by political events.

In about the middle of the eighteenth century specific reforms and changes were undertaken by the Bourbon dynasty. One of the most important of these was an attempt to remodel the colonial administrative apparatus, chiefly to increase revenues. The ideas and doctrines of the Enlightenment, with their stress on reason, utility, and science, vied for acceptance with older Habsburg ways, often hallowed by two centuries of Mexican usage. For instance, the creation of a local Creole (Mexican Spanish) militia placed guns in the hands of Mexicans for the first time since Conquest, just at a time when gusts of revolutionary doctrines began to blow.

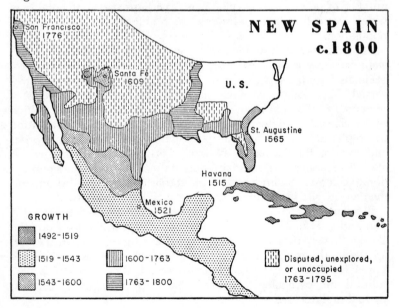

NEW SPAIN
c.1800

San Francisco 1776

Santa Fé 1609

U. S.

St. Augustine 1565

Havana 1515

Mexico 1521

GROWTH

1492-1519

1519-1543

1543-1600

1600-1763

1763-1800

Disputed, unexplored, or unoccupied 1763-1795

Under the Bourbons (1765–1800) Mexico became an even richer area, as well as a more populous one. So-called 'free' (within the Empire) trade, and other aspects of imperial reorganization revitalized economic life, and at the same time enlarged intellectual horizons. Questions, unthinkable in the seventeenth century, concerning the relation of the mother country to the colonies, such as the utility and *raison d'être* of monarchy, were inevitably raised.

The end of the colonial period in Mexico merges with the movements for political independence. Under Spain Mexico had been endowed with Western civilization and imperial splendours. Its cities, with palaces and churches, its orderly towns, its mines, ranches, roads, ports, were the more tangible legacies, while inwardly as well as outwardly the imprint of Spanish law and custom, religion and speech, marked the area off from that remote time just before the Conquest when Montezuma and his fellows had plucked the living hearts from thousands of captives not far from the site of the Cathedral on the great square of Mexico City.

In the longer view, then, the colonial period represents a constant and fascinating picture of change and interaction. Within the Spanish framework the evolution of institutions necessary to govern so vast a jurisdiction, to allocate land, labour, and opportunities, to maintain peace and justice, to collect taxes, to educate, to continue welfare services, all these and many more were important legacies to the future nation. The development of a peculiarly Mexican way of life, a synthesis of Spanish and Indian, was one of the main results of the three centuries under Spain.

THE ACHIEVEMENT OF MEXICAN INDEPENDENCE

Mexicans celebrate 16 September as Independence Day, to honour the 'Grito de Dolores'. This was the cry against bad Spanish government uttered in 1810 by Padre Miguel Hidalgo y Costilla, an 'enlightened' priest who found himself at the head of an Indian army that tried unsuccessfully to liberate Mexico. Hidalgo was captured and executed, but the ideas he voiced were, after a decade, crowned with success.

Independence was a political, and to some extent, economic movement that left the solid bases of Mexican society relatively stable for some time. Outside rather than domestic events set the stage for independence—the American and French Revolutions, commercial pressure from the expansion of European nations and the United States, and the chaos caused by European wars. The font of authority in Spain became muddied, especially when

Napoleon captured Ferdinand VII, King of Spain. A series of Juntas culminated in a revived but unauthorized Spanish Cortes which attempted to rule in Ferdinand's name during the turbulent years 1808–12. Overseas colonies, including Mexico, sent delegates to the Cortes. Their attempts to obtain redress for long-standing grievances were frustrated, and tensions heightened between Peninsular Spaniards and creoles. But viceregal authority in Mexico was sufficient to thwart an attempt to form a local Junta to rule the realm. Mexican uprisings in 1810 developed into crusades for independence, primarily in the hands of mestizo or Indian elements who were inspired by hopes of home rule and influenced by dreams of social justice. As these movements took on the aspect of caste wars, many moderates preferred to support the *status quo* as loyalists. For a decade a bitter civil war ravaged the area, with victory gradually tipping toward the loyalists.

Events in Europe proved decisive. In 1820 a liberal revolution in Spain forced Ferdinand to re-establish the Cortes and swear that he would govern the kingdom and its possessions under the Constitution of 1812, an advanced and revolutionary document. Faced with this threat to the traditional order in Mexico, conservatives and moderates determined 'to save New Spain from the dangerous innovations of Old Spain'.[1]

A young creole officer, Agustín de Iturbide, sent to quell the remnants of the independence movements of 1810, instead persuaded them to support independence under a local monarch. The combined groups declared Mexican independence from Spain on 28 September 1821, named Iturbide emperor, and attempted to reorganize the government along imperial lines. Almost immediately the Central American portions of New Spain declared their independence of the short-lived Iturbide Empire and formed the United Provinces, which in turn dissolved into separate small states.

The wars of independence had been savage civil wars, guerrilla conflicts which not only took high toll of life but also disorganized social and economic life in Mexico. Haciendas were burned, mines looted, normal food supplies reduced. Old lines of commerce were broken at independence; a flight of capital ensued. After a decade of civil strife, the new Republic did not have an auspicious start, and from the outset economic disaster was accompanied by political

---

[1] R. A. Humphreys, *The Evolution of Modern Latin America* (London, 1946), p. 40.

instability. Yet the nation had taken a major step. Henceforth sovereignty resided in Mexico, whether exercised foolishly or wisely. The colonial period had ended.[1]

[1] There is an enormous and constantly growing literature on colonial New Spain and the Empire; much of it is usefully summarized in C. H. Haring, *The Spanish Empire in America*, 2nd ed. (1952), with annual increments noted in the History sections of the *Handbook of Latin American Studies*; works in English through independence are listed in Humphreys, *Guide*, pp. 17–89 [through about 1957].

Chapter II

THE NINETEENTH-CENTURY REPUBLIC

THOUGH its culture was old and complex, the newly independent Mexican nation in 1821 was unskilled and young in the art of self-government. Contending forces within the small groups striving for leadership were relatively evenly balanced but often diametrically opposed on large and small issues, and quite unwilling or unable to compromise. The results provided Mexico with a grim and tragic history for the first fifty years following independence. Men without experience or much obvious talent groped toward solutions to the political problem of organizing a workable Government.

Excesses of the period in turn bred a quite different atmosphere in the final decades of the nineteenth century, when to maintain peace and order necessary to the economic progress most Mexicans desired, politics and political liberties atrophied under the praetorian peace imposed by Porfirio Díaz. Submerged forces held in check from earlier times, and those generated by Mexico's entrance into the modern economic world during the final years of the nineteenth century converged in 1910 to destroy much of the carefully contrived edifice erected by Díaz and his advisers. That storm, the Mexican Revolution, will be described in the following chapter.[1]

THE EARLY REPUBLIC

In 1821 the First Mexican Empire became a sovereign nation, separated politically from Spain. It was a short-lived experiment in monarchy, with Agustín I, Iturbide, unable to consolidate the coalition of republicans, moderates, and monarchists who momentarily had been able to agree only on the need to break direct ties with the motherland. Of these elements, those who favoured a republican form of government seemed dominant. They were the spiritual heirs of Padre Hidalgo and his successors such as José María Morelos and his followers who in 1814 had drawn up a constitution combining Spanish and Anglo-Saxon features to give focus to the early and abortive revolutions for independence.

Within ten months of his accession to the Mexican throne Iturbide became the victim of the first of an apparently endless series of barracks revolts. Rebellious generals packed him off to Europe, and called a constituent assembly which in November 1823 drew up a republican constitution, based largely on that of the United States. A hero of the revolutionary wars, General Guadalupe Victoria, was elected and took office in 1824 as the first President of the Republic of Mexico.

Issues in early Mexican politics were debated within a very small circle of predominantly mestizo (mixed blood) leaders, with the locus of power in the alarmingly large Mexican army. A worsening economic situation was a significant factor in the political instability. This vicious circle bred domestic and international problems that seemed insoluble. Without local industry, mining, or exportable goods, governments were forced to borrow sums abroad on the security of customs receipts. Service on these debts left the merest trickle of public revenues to carry on public business, and especially to pay the army, easily discontented when its due fell in arrears. Naturally defaults on loans raised the rates at which new ones could be obtained. It seemed for a while that the aim of generals was to put themselves in the presidency long enough to obtain such foreign

[1] Robert A. Potash, 'The Historiography of Mexico since 1821', *HAHR*, xl (Aug. 1960), 383–424, summarizes and evaluates principal writings, by periods.

loans, only to be turned out, with whatever sums they could amass, by a greedy successor, eager for the same opportunity.

Ostensibly the issues of politics split Mexico into several groups. On the one hand were the Centralists, who favoured a strongly centralized Government, with little room for state or provincial autonomy or variations; this position was in general supported by the more conservative elements of society, especially Church and army. Opposed were Federalists, really in favour of confederation, to reduce the power of Mexico City by substituting local militia for the army, and limiting the functions of the national Government to the bare minimum. Lines were not always clear, and dubious and shifting coalitions of persons and groups make the politics of the period a labyrinth in which even specialists are sometimes lost.

One feature of the period, never wholly absent from later years as well, was the great stress on personalities. Often this period of Mexican history is called 'the Age of Santa Anna' because General Antonio López de Santa Anna emerged from a welter of military men to dominate the scene, either as President, power behind the throne, or in opposition. A picturesque and picaresque figure, Santa Anna embodied Centralist principles, so far as he had any at all. In an age of Latin American *caudillos* like Rosas of Argentina, Santa Anna ranked with the best of them.

International difficulties complicated the domestic scene. Much treasure and energy poured into unsuccessful efforts to prevent the vast and underpopulated province of Texas from seceding to form the Lone Star Republic on Mexico's northern border in 1835–6. A French punitive expedition to collect debts owed a French national led in 1838 to a costly but short 'Pastry-Cook War', whose main effect was to catapult Santa Anna back to national prominence.

The most disastrous adventure of all was a war with the United States, following the latter's annexation of Texas and disputes with Mexico concerning its boundaries. This ill-starred conflict, in which the Mexicans proclaimed they would dictate a victor's peace from Washington on the basis of their superior numbers under arms, in fact cost the Republic nearly a third of its territory, then undeveloped and scantily populated. Santa Anna, when for the last time he was President of Mexico in 1853, sold to the United States some missing pieces establishing the present boundary between them.

At mid-nineteenth century Mexico was something of a shambles. Its immediate past as a republic was horrifying, and there seemed to be little prospect of improvements. However, a new generation of leaders had somehow managed to develop, and they provided the nation with its next main developments, known in local annals as La Reforma, the Liberal Reform.

REFORM AND INTERVENTION

A large group of relatively young men formed the main force which first led Mexico from the age of caudillos towards modern democracy. Melchor Ocampo and Benito Juárez are the outstanding figures who symbolize and epitomize the Liberal Reform.

In a Mexico crushed by military defeat and weary of Santa Anna's inanities, they forged a programme that, when carried into effect, transformed the neo-colonial society. The main lines of the Reform were, on the positive side, to make Mexico a true republican democracy by abolishing special privileges long held by Church and army. The latter, for instance, fought to retain ancient rights (*fueros*) that exempted them from trial in national courts. Further, the Liberals envisaged Mexico as a future land of yeoman farmers, and thus aimed at dispossessing the single largest landlord, the Catholic Church, of its vast holdings by bringing them out of mortmain through forced sales; the legal formula forbade corporations to hold property, a device which in the following decades Porfirio Díaz and others applied to landholding rural communities. The Juárez Liberals, as children of their age, also wished to assert hegemony of State over Church by legalizing civil marriage and controlling fees collectable by the clergy.

From 1853 through 1857 Mexico again experienced a cycle of destructive civil wars, won temporarily by the Liberals. To translate their military and ideological victories into more permanent form, and to provide a basis for eliminating the possibility of a new Santa Anna, they drew up the constitution of 1857. Most of its main ideological features have been retained to this day.[1]

But proclamation of this key document mobilized strong conservative resistance, whose class privileges were seemingly threatened if not obliterated. Civil war broadened into the international arena when Great Britain, Spain, and France jointly invaded Mexico ostensibly to collect debts. The first two withdrew from the enterprise when it became apparent that Napoleon III had staged it chiefly to obtain political control of Mexico. French troops finally captured Mexico City, driving President Juárez and his Republican Government outside the capital. Mexico was thus divided into those who supported the Republican Government, and those who accepted the imposed Government in Mexico City.

[1] Walter V. Scholes, *Mexican Politics during the Juárez Regime* (1957).

To provide a façade of legality to his imperial schemes, Napoleon III aided an earlier monarchist Mexican conspiratorial group, now supported by conservative elements of the country, and arranged a farcical plebiscite that brought Maximilian of Habsburg and his romantic wife Carlotta to Mexico as head of the Second Empire. The Emperor Maximilian, supported by French bayonets, was a disappointment to all: he did not govern well, and failed to provide the conservatives with desired legislation. More fatal, he split with the French. Under diplomatic and domestic political pressure, Napoleon III withdrew first the subsidies that propped up the phantom throne, then in 1867 most of the French troops. Resurgent Republican armies swept back into Mexico City. They captured Maximilian, who was shot with his chief generals, despite international pleas for mercy.

With his death another phase of Mexican history closed. The monarchists were forever discredited, and the conservatives suspect. The sombre Zapotec Indian, President Benito Juárez, believer in democracy and the rule of law, headed a relatively united people who under the pressures of intervention and Empire began truly to think of themselves as Mexicans, determined to take their own fate in their own hands. Politically this was the course for the remainder of the century, but not on the lines many had hoped.

THE RESTORED REPUBLIC AND THE PAX PORFIRIANA

Although flushed with victory over European forces that had threatened the foundations of the Republic, Benito Juárez faced enormous difficulties. For nearly seven decades Mexico had been in the throes of civil war of one sort or another. Its productive capacities, even to feed itself, had dropped to the lowest possible ebb. No rational man would invest in its apparent future, seemingly dedicated to continued chaos. Disbanded troops roamed the countryside as bandits, and most of the processes of orderly governance seemed lacking. Yet so long as Juárez lived, through personal force and mobilization of loyalties generated through the Reform and intervention periods, he was able to keep a semblance of order.

On his death in 1872, Mexico entered yet another phase of its evolution. The age of Díaz brought it into the modern economic world, laying the foundations for its present advances in that sphere, but at a social and political cost so high that the Mexican people finally rose in revolt at the injustices and oppression which the economic gains of the régime entailed.[1]

Porfirio Díaz, like Juárez, was an Indian from the state of Oaxaca. He was a strong militarist, a successful general who was inevitably drawn into politics. He led an abortive rebellion against Juárez following the eviction of the French and his own unsuccessful candidacy for President. His political and military power was still insufficient at Juárez's death to bring him to the coveted post, but by 1876 it had grown sufficiently in the midst of a still deteriorating economic and political situation to place him in the presidential chair.

He served one term (until 1880), arranged to have a faithful lieutenant succeed him, and then from 1884 continuously was re-elected until forced from office by the Mexican Revolution in 1910. Although a remarkable man, and a key figure in recent Mexican history, there are no statues to him in the land, so deeply seated are the antipathies to the régime he developed and ran for so many years. Díaz and his coterie analysed Mexico in terms now unacceptable to the majority, but in their day perhaps justifiable. From their attempts to apply rational analysis to Mexico in the Positivistic jargon of August Comte, the official circle received the name of 'Científicos' (Scientists), now a pejorative term.

They held that to progress, Mexico must be peaceful, which in turn implied that politics must decrease, administration increase. The future of Mexico, they felt, rested on rebuilding its economic base—transportation, rehabilitation of the finances, production of exportable items in mining and agriculture, and a stable currency. To achieve these ends, foreign capital was requisite, as little or none remained in the country itself. Mexico, however, was bidding for foreign capital at a time when other parts of the world, notably the United States and Africa, were also in the market for loans, hence Mexico had to offer more than equal attractions. In the longer Científico view, foreign capital would generate local resources which would eventually replace outside money.

In this competitive situation, the Díaz régime took all possible steps to reach these general goals. Through force or persuasion recalcitrant politicians were brought to heel; the country became one large, well-oiled political mechanism devoted to re-electing Díaz. To prevent unpleasant incidents that might involve foreigners,

---

[1] Daniel Cosío Villegas and others, *Historia moderna de México* (1955–) provides comprehensive coverage from *c.* 1872; this is an outstanding contribution to historiography, in progress.

and to maintain control and discipline in rural areas, an élite corps of mounted police, the Rurales, was formed to patrol the countryside; many were recruited from ex-bandits and converted to respectability by good pay and a glamorous uniform. As the backbone of the overt power of the régime, the Rurales were effective in establishing and maintaining the Pax Porfiriana.[1] The army was reduced almost to nil.

Fundamental to Díaz's outlook was an agricultural economy chiefly geared to producing export crops. To promote and protect the formation of large estates, haciendas, he permitted their owners to strip communal lands from villages, and aided them to preserve and extend the ancient peonage system, dangerously close to serfdom for the mass of Mexican countrymen or *campesinos*. Recalcitrant Indians and political nonconformists were unceremoniously shipped off to Quintana Roo or Valle Nacional to work out sentences, and usually to die, in the unhealthy areas where exportable tropical crops were grown.

A series of able, even brilliant subordinates, pushed forward other economic programmes. Among these the name of José Y. Limantour stands out as the man who finally disentangled Mexico's debt and was able to persuade European capitalists, especially French and British, to provide utilities and transportation networks in the central and southern heartland. In the northern parts, United States entrepreneurs already driving across their land just north of the border were encouraged to plan extensions of their railways south of it into Mexico. At the same time, with industrial metals keenly in demand throughout the world and especially in the United States, new foreign mining enterprises were given concessions to exploit the riches of northern Mexico.

With peace and stability, an incipient industrialization began, chiefly to furnish goods for a rather small domestic market. As might have been predicted, when the first stirrings of labour organization began to appear they were ruthlessly crushed.

It was small wonder that as the Díaz régime continued, more and more Mexicans felt that they were strangers in their own land. French culture had been given official blessing, with a corresponding disparagement of local traditions as being 'primitive—of an earlier stage' in the Científico vocabulary. As time passed, however, the chief and growing complaint was that the same, narrow circle of aging men ran the country on ideas that had outlasted their historical usefulness. In contemporary terms this was the 'Full Car' (*carro*

---

[1] Malefactors seldom came to trial. Nearly always it was claimed (and accepted) that they were shot while 'attempting to escape', the infamous 'Ley Fuga'.

completo), the loaded bus in which no room remained for new faces or suggestions. Thoughtful men of all social classes pondered these matters, but few were bold or articulate enough to formulate viable alternatives. The Mexican Establishment—a handful of mummified generals, faithful dynasties of state governors, a group of the hated local 'political chiefs', scholars cleaving to the 'official' lines, a bought and muted press—continued to give the impression that Díaz was immortal, and that all was well.

Mexico had indeed come far from the horrors of the first half of the century. Its world position seemed assured, at least in the circles where such matters are judged by stability of money and prompt debt service, together with generous concessions for new enterprises. On the domestic scene the façade of democracy, under the great Reform constitution of 1857, seemed to fulfil the dreams of the founding fathers of the Republic: Congress, the courts, all conformed outwardly to prescribed norms. Yet the system had been undermined by irresponsible power, arbitrarily wielded. Like most dictators, Díaz knew neither when to retire, nor how to prepare the succeeding generation for a peaceful transfer of the power he sincerely believed he was using patriotically. Events soon took the decision out of his hands.

In 1910 Mexico staged an impressive and internationally attended centenary jubilee to mark a century of progress since independence. Amid the celebrations could be heard the first scattered shots that heralded the Mexican Revolution, rudely shattering the Pax Porfiriana.

Chapter III

THE MEXICAN REVOLUTION, 1910–40

MODERN Mexico dates from 1910, but for fifty years the nation has been in a state of revolution and its evolution is not yet complete. Most of the present volume deals with a special phase of this unfolding process, the Institutional Revolution. The history of modern Mexico can be subdivided into several phases—the armed uprising in 1910, a quiescent period from about 1917 through 1934, and a new surge forward from 1934 through 1940. The year 1940 ushered in the Institutional Revolution, which had crystallized by 1946, the year in which President Miguel Alemán was inaugurated.

The Mexican Revolution is legitimately hailed as one of the few important social movements in twentieth-century Latin America. 'What is remarkable is not that it has achieved so little but that it has achieved so much', Professor Humphreys noted in 1946.[1] It is both a series of historical events and the name given the process designed to wipe out the imputed evils of the past.

With no important preconceived plans, the Mexicans who had launched a relatively mild political protest in 1910 ended by working out a whole new social system. They and their descendants have sought to mould their land and people to new ideals. These include many of the Liberal doctrines of the nineteenth century together with new dogmas concerning property, the role of social classes, and the obligations of the state. Hence to the conservatives and the dwindling remnants of the pre-Revolutionary élite, the Revolution is an unmitigated disaster, a view often shared by the Church and pro-clerical elements inside and outside Mexico.

But to the majority of Mexicans, their Revolution is the beginning of hope, the dawn of a new era destined to provide panaceas for the ills that chronically afflicted Mexico throughout its earlier history. Events since 1910 gave rise to a *mystique* that guides Mexican leaders and followers toward the better life which it was felt the Díaz years had denied the Mexican people.

[1] *Modern Latin America*, p. 102. A rather detailed summary of the Revolution, 1910–40, appears in Cline, *U.S. and Mexico*, pp. 113–306.

THE MADERO REVOLUTION, 1910–17

By his background and convictions Francisco I. Madero seemed most unlikely to become the 'Apostle of the Mexican Revolution', a position he holds unchallenged in the pantheon of national heroes. Coming from a wealthy northern Mexican family, and European-educated in the then current mode, he inadvertently started a movement that was to change the face of Mexican society, and even of the land. In part inspired by messages he believed came through occult channels, he first organized a very small political opposition which in 1905 unsuccessfully challenged the Díaz machine in the state of Coahuila. This was the first step in a larger destiny which he felt was his to regenerate Mexico and Latin America.

Normally this first fiasco in politics would have relegated Madero to a very minor footnote in history. But in 1908 President Porfirio Díaz somewhat inexplicably granted to James Creelman an interview that appeared in *Pearson's Magazine*. In general, the article was the normal 'puff' extolling Díaz as the 'hero of the Americas', but apparently to allay criticism that was beginning to develop abroad concerning his political methods, it was reported that Díaz stated that Mexico had reached a point in its evolution where a loyal opposition party was needed; if one appeared, he added, he would protect and guide it. The immediate and incorrect local interpretation of the statements was that Díaz would not run for re-election in 1910, and a series of small groups and nascent parties began to form.

As part of this general reawakening of political life Madero soon attracted national attention by publishing in 1908 a volume entitled *The Presidential Succession of 1910*. At first this tract assumed that Díaz would remain President and carry out recommended reforms through constitutional means, with the aid of the new party which Madero had formed, the Anti-Re-electionists. But by 1909, with support from many dissident quarters, and aggrieved when the old President did not take him seriously in a personal interview, Madero boldly announced his own candidacy, campaigning on the slogan 'Effective suffrage, no re-election'.

The elections of 1910 were held in July, coinciding with preparations for the centennial celebration to be held in September. As a precautionary measure, Díaz jailed Madero before the elections, the results of which were released in late September. Díaz, as usual, was credited with millions of votes, while Madero was allotted a total of 196. With the eighth Díaz term seemingly assured, Madero was allowed to 'escape' from prison. He immediately headed for the United States where he issued a manifesto that officially in-augurated the Mexican Revolution. Dated 5 October 1910, Madero's 'Plan of San Luis Potosí' called for nullification of the July elections as invalid. He urged the Mexican people to revolt against the tyrant Díaz, named himself provisional President, and promised that honest elections and various other reforms would follow when he became President. The dividing line between pre-Revolutionary and Revolutionary Mexico is 20 November 1910, the date designated in the Plan for a mass uprising.

Rather more than 17,000 men rallied to the Madero cause, scattered widely in the Republic. They included many names soon to be more familiar: Pancho Villa, Emiliano Zapata, Venustiano Carranza. Although 30,000 were registered as soldiers of Díaz, very few real effectives could be put into the field. Actual military operations resulted in stalemate, but in the negotiations which ensued, the Madero Revolution made most of its essential points. In May, tired of the apparently endless talking, Pancho Villa captured a main centre, Ciudad Juárez, while almost simultaneously in the south Zapata took the southern Federalist stronghold of Cuautla. These victories heartened small revolutionary bands else-where, and their gains forced an end to the first phase of the military revolution.

On 21 May 1911 Díaz and Limantour agreed to resign, and to the appointment of an interim President to hold elections. On 25 May the old man did resign, leaving Mexico for a brief exile in France. On 2 July 1915 he died in Paris, convinced to the end that he had served Mexico well and that the bloodbath through which it was passing could have been avoided if only his advice and guidance had been taken.

At this stage the chief objectives of the Revolution were exclusively political, to destroy and remodel the system developed during the Pax Porfiriana. 'Effective suffrage, no re-election' is still the official slogan of the Mexican Revolution, and closes all official correspond-ence instead of 'Yours truly'. In many ways the situation paralleled that in the wake of the revolution for independence: the old leader-ship was discredited, but there was no cadre of experienced personnel to take over the reins.

COUNTER-REVOLT

One of the saddest and darkest periods in Mexican national history is the period from 1911 through 1917. The great, often

Utopian social and economic ideals that gradually coalesced to form the ideology of the Revolution sprang from the troubled period following the military success of the Madero revolt. One feature of the Mexican Revolution is its lack of a preconceived general set of goals and ideas.

Madero, as might be expected, was elected President, together with a Congress whose experience was slight but whose plans for regeneration of the nation were grandiose. With Díaz gone, each group that had suffered repression pushed its claim for first priority, and intrigued openly for its own ends. Madero, a slight figure physically and determined to be democratic and reasonable, failed to fit the image Mexicans had come to expect of their President, a dominant power. One of the first groups to defect were the peasants, the followers of Zapata. They branded Madero as a Judas who had failed to grapple with the problem of giving land to those who tilled it, and came out in armed rebellion against his Government. Pascual Orozco, another ex-Maderista general, claimed that the 'Apostle' had sold Mexico out for 'Washington gold', and was betraying the Revolution by failing to give in to demands of the few organized workers. Bernardo Reyes, an ex-Porfirian general who had been hastily recalled from Paris to aid the Caudillo, arrived too late, but then attempted to mobilize forces for a counter-revolution; this move failed and Reyes was imprisoned, but was allowed to continue to plot. Finally, to add to the already heavy burdens Madero was carrying, Porfirio's nephew, Félix Díaz, similarly headed an abortive uprising to re-institute the Científico régime.

The month of February 1913 started with what is known as the 'Tragic Ten Days'. Suborned elements of the army released Díaz and Reyes from prison in a coup to recapture the Government, but part of the military forces remained loyal. In the first exchange of shots Reyes was killed, and Díaz barricaded himself in with rebellious troops in the Ciudadela, a few blocks from the National Palace. Madero ordered General Victoriano Huerta to oust them; he had earlier pursued Orozco in the north and had been dismissed for peculation, but Madero made the fatal error of turning to him in this crisis. For ten days Huerta and Díaz blasted each other with artillery but this was more destructive of property and innocent bystanders than of each other's forces. Later testimony indicates that some of the fighting was deliberately carried on with the purpose of decimating troops loyal to Madero. The battle came to a sudden close by the betrayal of Madero by Huerta.

In Mexican annals the name of the United States Ambassador to Mexico, Henry Lane Wilson, will ever be remembered for his important part in this affair. It does little good for historians to demonstrate that he was acting on his own, not under orders from his State Department. Wilson arranged a secret meeting between the contending generals, who came to terms whereby Huerta was to become immediate provisional President of Mexico, Díaz to succeed him when the first elections were held. The conspirators arrested Madero and his Vice-President, then publicly in the United States Embassy, before the assembled diplomatic corps, revealed their proposed arrangements. These were set down in a document, the Pact of the Embassy, which each signed. Wilson presented Huerta as the saviour of Mexico and urged all Governments to recognize him as new head of the Mexican state. His own Government would not do so.

Huerta's pledges of safe-conduct and exile for Madero were not kept. While being transferred from one prison to another Madero and Pino Suárez, his Vice-President, were killed under mysterious circumstances. This murder shocked a world somewhat unaware of events in Mexico. It also rekindled the spark of the Mexican Revolution.

THE CONSTITUTIONALIST CRUSADE

The first and most important voice raised to vindicate Madero and restore the Revolution was that of Venustiano Carranza. Governor of Coahuila, he had been in Díaz's 'full car' but had been an early convert to Madero's cause. Tough and unbending in many respects he emerged as one of the key figures of the next years, issuing in March 1913 his Plan of Guadalupe. It called for constitutional government in Mexico in accord with Madero's earlier plan, hence the Carranza group were usually called 'Constitutionalists'. He organized a politico-military coalition that included Pancho Villa and other northern regional caciques, with himself as 'First Chief'. Alvaro Obregón, of Sonora, organized a formidable force that nominally was loyal to Carranza. In the south, Zapata and his peasants were willing to co-operate, less to restore the Madero-type régime than to forward their own programmes.

Huerta, a saturnine alcoholic, had at his disposal considerable resources in money, arms, and support available from the conservative groups who had never accepted the Madero Revolution or who had become disenchanted when their suggestions had brought no response. His Government was recognized by the British. This tended to complicate matters on the international scene as Europe drifted toward the First World War. The larger context became important with the election of Woodrow Wilson as the new President of the United States, for Wilson strongly disapproved of Huerta.

However, Wilson found Huerta a slippery and wily opponent, and he discovered that Carranza was equally adamant, and unwilling to accept on Wilson's terms his various offers of help, which to Carranza merely seemed to compromise his own position and to open the door to United States' control of the Revolution, and of Mexico. Carranza succeeded in making Wilson see that more was necessary than to 'elect good men', and that the Revolution was broadening into a major socio-political movement. The two men reached a somewhat limited understanding which was inadvertently ruptured by President Wilson when his Government sent troops into Veracruz.

A number of complicated incidents led to this ill-advised move, the aim of which was to prevent German munitions from being delivered to Huerta.[1] On 21 April 1914 naval personnel and United States Marines moved into Veracruz under fire which caused casualties on both sides. It looked as though the United States and Mexico were about to go to war. Both Huerta and Carranza condemned the occupation and ordered the Americans to leave. Latin American mediation prevented hostilities, but while a conference about the incident and the organization of Mexico was going on, the Constitutionalists won a series of decisive victories, which drove Huerta from Mexico on 15 August 1914. Again the Revolution had returned to power in Mexico City.

However, the entrance of Carranza and Obregón into Mexico on 20 August was a prelude to even further anarchy. The revolutionary factions now began squabbling among themselves, and this led to unremittent civil war until 1917. Throughout the struggle, Obregón remained loyal to Carranza, and successively broke the military might of Zapata and Villa, the 'First Chief's' principal rivals. To woo support, Carranza and his advisers began to issue basic decrees incorporating the main points of the programmes promulgated by various leaders: agrarian reform, labour rights, anti-foreignism, all became campaign promises, valid if the Constitutionalists triumphed.

Defeated and irresponsible, Villa made every effort to embroil Carranza's shaky provisional (unrecognized) Government in a war

[1] Cline, *U.S. and Mexico*, pp. 155–62, summarizes official documentation.

with the United States, and nearly succeeded. Villa began killing United States' nationals, and followed this up by a raid into Columbus, New Mexico, on 9 March 1916, shooting everyone in sight. The United States ordered General John J. Pershing to head a punitive expedition into Mexico to scatter Villa's forces and put an end to such raids. When both Mexicans and Americans were killed in skirmishes within Mexican borders, each nation began again mobilizing as for war. But calmer heads prevailed, and the two states quietly emerged from what appeared to be an impasse by a diplomatic conference which terminated in January 1917.

This complicated period of the Revolution ended on 5 February 1917. On that day the great revolutionary document, the constitution of 1917, was proclaimed, embodying the goals and purposes for which fighting had been in progress almost continuously since October 1910. The remnants of the American punitive expedition withdrew. At long last national elections were held in Mexico on 11 March. Carranza was the legally elected, constitutional President of an organized Government, inaugurated on 1 May, when the new United States Ambassador, outward sign of United States' recognition, was present.

This was triumph of the Revolution, and the end of its military phase. It now had a programme, agreed to in the constitutional Constituent Assembly of 1917, and a body of battle-tested leaders. Again the cost had been high, in lives and treasure. Most Mexicans readily agree, however, that the eventual results were worth it.

THE INTER-WAR YEARS

Two world wars spanned the period of the stabilization and re-awakening of the Mexican Revolution. During the First, leaders and followers alike had been concerned primarily in establishing a new political equilibrium and working toward the eradication of some of the more obvious evils inherited from the nineteenth century. By the Second the nation, a rather thoroughly self-conscious unit whose economic and social advances in thirty years had astonished the world, was concerned with wider affairs. Mexico then was firmly established on the world scene, with an enviable record of achievement. On this solid foundation have been built the spectacular recent advances which form the main body of this study.

Mexican writers themselves draw a clear distinction between the pre-Constitutional period and the ensuing years during which the Revolution became a process rather than a series of military events.

Presidents Wilson and Carranza in 1917–18 inherited the difficulties of a post-war world, and left to their successors problems of statecraft wherein some of their major contentions were temporarily reversed. In the United States, after dashing Wilson's hope that the United States would form part of the League of Nations, the Republican Party placed President Harding in the White House. In regard to oil, the early 1920's provided an inflammable background to relations between Mexico and the United States, but both peoples, weary and disillusioned, refused to consider the possibility of war between their states. Domestic concerns in each instance far outweighed international ones.

In Mexico President Carranza still had to cope with the possibility of renewed outbreak of the military struggle which he had won so recently and by such a small margin. At the same time he had the allied problem of re-establishing orderly processes of government: collecting taxes, rehabilitating the devastated finances, and similar domestic concerns. In peace the close ties within the dynasty of northern generals who had put a stop to the military activities of other bands began to fray. When it became apparent that Carranza expected to impose as his successor a rather weak and unknown figure who would serve as his puppet, his chief supporters, Alvaro Obregón, Adolfo de la Huerta, and Plutarco Elìas Calles, engineered a barracks coup in May 1920 reminiscent of the days of Santa Anna. These generals headed the last such successful revolt.

The violent death of Carranza marked the end of the Military Revolution. General de la Huerta became interim President, and presided over the election of the acknowledged leader of the trio, Alvaro Obregón, as President in 1921. As the most powerful living Revolutionary chieftain, Obregón was able to make a start towards consolidating the Revolution and bringing its tangible benefits to the Mexican people. His term was notable, among other things, for the strong support given mass education under his great Secretary of Education, José Vasconcelos, and for the encouragement of art that gave the world the Mexican fresco school in which Diego Rivera, José Clemente Orozco, and David Siqueiros played outstanding parts. Obregón also began to tidy up some of the international aftermath of the Revolution: in conferences with the United States compromise agreements were arrived at on claims for property damages, and even oil, where Obregón took a much less radical position than had Carranza.

Claiming that Obregón had 'sold out the Revolution', de la Huerta launched a revolt in 1924, but was defeated, reducing the struggle for power to a duel between Obregón and Calles. The latter succeeded Obregón, and as a later chapter relates in more detail, it seemed that this duarchy would replace the one-man rule of Díaz. The Calles presidency, during the upward spiral of prosperity that preceded the Great Depression, was noteworthy for a number of things. Calles gave organized labour a louder voice than it had hitherto had in government, in return for political support. A small but significant start was made in agrarian reform, accompanied by the creation of organs that were in later years to have a distinguished history in irrigation and in road construction. The Revolution seemed to be gradually becoming constructive, until these developments were overshadowed by more dramatic events.

During Calles's presidency the old clerical question in Mexico flared up again. From almost the outset leaders of the Revolution had been anti-clerical, for a wide variety of reasons, not least of which was the support which the Church had given first Díaz and then Huerta. The influence of the Russian Revolution and Marxist ideology was especially strong during this period in Mexico, reinforcing the anti-Church tradition inherited from the Juárez Liberals, retained *in toto* by the 1917 constitution. Whatever else might divide the revolutionary family, it could agree on the anti-clerical issue. But this led to extremes. In some states, such as Tabasco, every church was levelled. Apparently willing to make a stand and test its power, the Church in 1926 ordered a general strike, in response to a decree by Calles that all alien priests must be deported and replaced by Mexican ones. No masses were said for three years, and the Government carried on a veritable reign of terror against clerical persons. This was partly due to the outbreak of a quasi-religious war in western Mexico which the Government believed the Church was inciting. Fanatic Catholic peasants, labelled 'Cristeros' because of their battle cry (*Cristo el Rey*—'Christ the King') attacked Federal schoolteachers as atheists and the troops sent to protect them. The atrocities on both sides, as well as propaganda issued by the world Church and Mexican government sources, kept emotion and passions high.

Relations with the United States improved during this period largely because of a change in United States policy and the appointment by Calvin Coolidge of his friend Dwight Morrow as Ambassador. Morrow genuinely tried to understand and like the Mexicans, then a most unusual ambassadorial approach. While the Morrow-Calles discussions did not definitely solve any major problems, they reached agreements which permitted a *modus vivendi* that lasted a decade. In 1929 Morrow was also instrumental in patching up a truce between the Church and the Calles Government, and in getting a peace agreement to end the Cristero War. Many responsible Mexicans date the United States' 'retreat from imperialism' in Mexico from the appearance of Dwight Morrow; others claim he had a malign influence by persuading Calles to slow down the motion of the Revolution almost to a halt.

Whatever the causes, that was the effect until 1933. The political crisis caused by Obregón's assassination after his election but before he could be inaugurated in 1929 is described below.[1] Calles, unable to succeed himself in the presidency, developed the single 'official' party through which he became the power behind the throne. As he and his cronies grew older, and richer, they also became more conservative. The expected reforms—land, labour, education—languished. The tempo of Revolution slowed down so much that the great experiment seemed to have failed, leaving Mexico with puppet Presidents, hardly distinguishable from any other Latin American country of the period.

THE CÁRDENAS REVIVAL, 1934–40

The combination of strong leadership, growing mass unrest, and a general swing of world public opinion in favour of sweeping political changes provided the setting for a sudden reawakening of the Revolution under Lázaro Cárdenas. He had been handpicked by Calles as a docile puppet to take office as President in 1934, but once in office Cárdenas steered his own notable course.

Ignoring immediate economic consequences and the reaction of the outside world, Cárdenas redistributed land at an astonishing pace, established labour in a strategic bargaining position, developed a functional official party, extended education to the remotest parts of the country, and in many other ways rekindled the sparks of hope of 'los de abajo'—the underdogs for and by whom the Revolution had initially been fought. As a climax, Cárdenas at a stroke expropriated the foreign petroleum holdings, long a symbol to Mexicans of exploitation. Expropriation Day, 18 March 1938, is revered in Mexico as the beginning of national economic independence. Less spectacular but equally important was the nationalization of the land and of the railways.

---

[1] See p. 151. The Obregón-Calles years have recently been explored in detail by J. W. F. Dulles, *Yesterday in Mexico* (1961).

Mexico, 1940–1960

The threat of the Second World War was beginning to loom over the hemisphere when President Cárdenas completed his crucial six-year term in 1940. To his successor, Manuel Avila Camacho (1940–6), fell the task of consolidating the Cárdenas gains. Camacho attempted to heal the splits and divisions created under Cárdenas, which had been held in check during his rule largely because of his personal prestige and the almost adulatory support he received from peasants, labourers, and above all, the armed forces. Many Mexicans claim that the Revolution ended in 1940 when Cárdenas, faithful to its basic political principle—'effective suffrage, no re-election'—stepped aside. But most believe that the Revolution is greater than one man, and continues, transformed but still vital as a result of Mexico's participation in the Second World War and the changes it engendered.

THE INSTITUTIONAL REVOLUTION

Certainly the history of modern Mexico and of the Revolution has taken a different course since 1940. Quietly but efficiently President Avila Camacho brought about some degree of national unity, while making Mexico an effective member of the United Nations after it had declared war on the Axis. Thus 1940 marks a significant watershed in the course of recent Mexican history.

Activities embarked upon in wartime—industrialization, improvement of communications, legislation for the readjustment of class relations, campaigns against illiteracy, the development of irrigation, and a score of other matters—did not cease with the end of the war. Many of them expanded and were given special impetus by President Miguel Alemán (1946–52), Mexico's first full-term civilian President since Madero.

'While progress in politics has not been so striking as in the economic and social life of the nation', a well-qualified observer recently wrote on the Golden Anniversary of the Revolution, 'there have been some tangible gains'.[1] In the period from 1946 through 1960 the important advances in the social and economic spheres and the leadership exercised by Miguel Alemán, Adolfo Ruíz Cortines (1952–8), and now by Adolfo López Mateos (1958–) are closely interlinked. Together they symbolize the Institutional Revolution's increasingly fruitful years.

[1] Stanley R. Ross, 'Mexico: Golden Anniversary of the Revolution', *Current History*, Mar. 1960, pp. 150–4, 180. See also his excellent *Francisco I. Madero: Apostle of Mexican Democracy* (1955) for the first stages of the Revolution.

THE ANCIENT AND MODERN
MEXICAN LAND

Chapter IV

THE CONTINENT OF MEXICO

IT is helpful to think of Mexico as a miniature continent. Its varying physical elements combine to produce a bewildering complexity of climates, resources, and geographical zones, often within a short distance. At one place or another within the Republic can be found nearly any given type of habitat, so wide is the range: from steamy tropical rain forests to areas of perpetual snow, from barren deserts to pleasant and productive oases where European fruits and grains are commonplace. One of the main charms of Mexico is its contrasts and extremes, but at the same time they are at the root of many economic, social, and even political problems.

BOUNDARIES

Political forces, not natural features, set the boundaries of modern Mexico. It has no natural frontiers in the north and south.[1] International conflict and negotiation during the nineteenth century established the northern frontier with the United States, and that in the south with the republic of Guatemala and the small colony of British Honduras. Slanting south-easterly from the United States, Mexico's rugged terrain extends between the Gulf of Mexico and the Pacific Ocean, thus providing it with an outlook towards both Europe and the East.

The Mexican-United States frontier, some 1,614 miles long, forms the base of an irregular triangle whose apex comes at the Isthmus of Tehuantepec, a narrow 140-mile strip between the seas. Beyond it to the south many features become more characteristic of Central than of North America. Across this portion of Mexico run its international boundaries with Guatemala and British Honduras, about 704 miles long. Mexico has lengthy coastlines: 1,100 miles on the Gulf, and about 2,900 miles on the Pacific (4,106 if all of Lower California is counted). Despite them, Mexico has few good harbours and has developed no major maritime traditions. Veracruz is practically its sole port. Mexican life has customarily

---

[1] César Sepúlveda, 'Historia y problemas de los límites de México', *Historia Mexicana*, viii (1958), 1–34, 145–74.

been lived inland, away from the sea, but recently it has embarked on the development of a merchant marine.[1]

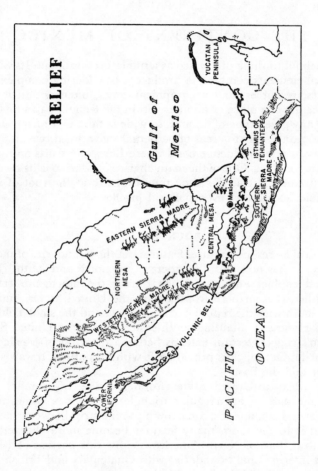

The peninsula of Lower California (Baja California) at the north-western extremity of Mexico counterbalances another distinct physical region, the peninsula of Yucatán, at the south-eastern extremity. Baja California is a continuation of the continental

[1]President López Mateos in his *2° Informe* (1 Sept. 1960) reported that the merchant marine carried 410,450 tons during 1959.

coastal range which runs southward from the west coast of the United States; after forming the peninsula, the mountains disappear below the Pacific Ocean, to reappear on the Mexican mainland as the Southern Sierra Madre. Baja California, an arid and semi-arid tongue of land, is separated from the Mexican mainland by the Gulf of California, earlier more romantically known as the Sea of Cortés.

Yucatán is a peculiar limestone shelf which thrusts into the Caribbean and Atlantic, almost touching the neighbouring island of Cuba. The seat of an important pre-Conquest native civilization, Lowland Maya, Yucatán is separated from the mainland of Mexico by a nearly impenetrable belt of tropical vegetation that until recent times defied most efforts to overcome its isolating effect. In 1953 rail connexions for the first time linked Yucatán with the mainland, at about the time that another rail link finally connected Baja California to the main body of Mexican territory.

All told, the boundaries of Mexico enclose 760,172 square miles, an area which places it among the larger modern national states. The Soviet Union, China, Canada, India, the United States, and the Sudan, outside the Latin American family, and Brazil and Argentina within it, are larger than Mexico. On the other hand Mexico is three times the area of France or Spain, eight times the United Kingdom, and fifteen times that of its small southern neighbour, Guatemala, which on occasion views Mexico as its Colossus of the North.

Since the coming of Europeans, Mexico has been variously divided for different administrative purposes. The political units have conformed largely to small cultural and economic entities that developed through the colonial years; the heterogeneous and confusing subdivisions of the colonial realm of New Spain were grouped into states when Mexico became a republic under the constitution of 1824.

This constitution set up seventeen states, many of which have retained approximately their present boundaries. Shortly afterwards, in 1826, a Federal District surrounding Mexico was first created. A number of older state units were subdivided to form new states during the first uneasy years of national existence, but after 1869 only three new units appeared: the territory of Quintana Roo (1902) and the states of Nayarit (1917) and Lower California (1951).[1] Hence with these three exceptions the present panorama of a

[1] Baja (Lower) California became a state by presidential decree, 31 Dec. 1951.

Federal District, 29 states, and two territories (Lower California, South, and Quintana Roo) has remained stable for nearly a century. Developing as they did from the accidents of geography, history, and politics, the components of the Republic vary widely in size, population, and local developments.[1]

PHYSICAL FEATURES

Mountains are a dominant physical feature of nearly the whole of Mexico except the northern mesa and the peninsula of Yucatán. Water, or lack of it, is also a critical element in its human geography. The two are closely connected, and their interconnexion is complicated by temperatures and altitudes. The most favourable conjunction of all these and other features occurs in the areas around Mexico City. Hence from earliest times a relatively restricted space has formed the core or heartland of Mexican development.

This heartland is the lower half of a V-shaped plateau near the centre of the country. The narrow portion of the V is the highest, and the plateau broadens and declines as it stretches northwards towards Texas, dropping gradually from an altitude of 6,000–8,000 feet to nearly sea-level at the northern international boundary. For descriptive purposes, this plateau is often subdivided into the Northern Mesa and the Central Mesa.

It is bounded on three sides by mountains, and lies between the Western Sierra Madre (Sierra Madre Occidental) and the Eastern Sierra Madre (Sierra Madre Oriental), leaving it open only to the north. The Western Sierra is a formidable bastion, a series of high interlocking ranges rising steeply from the Pacific shores leaving little or no coastal plain. An average width of nearly 100 miles adds to the Sierra's barrier-like qualities; major communication routes can usually only skirt it.

The Eastern Sierra fortunately is slightly less high, making access to the Gulf of Mexico possible through a few well-worn routes. Moisture-laden trade winds, although dropping much of their burden of water on its Atlantic slopes, retain some to be carried inland to the thirsty plateau. The wider eastern coastal plains, because of the usually excessive precipitation, are covered with thick tropical rain forests, shading into true jungle conditions.

A third Sierra Madre, the Southern (Sierra Madre del Sur), runs from the Pacific, near the point of the V of the plateau, to about

---

[1] Edmundo O'Gorman, *Breve historia de las divisiones territoriales* (1937). See also below, Appendix Table I.

the Isthmus of Tehuantepec through the states of Colima, Michoacán, Guerrero, and Oaxaca. Some of its peaks in Oaxaca rise to 18,000 feet before the range falls away at the Chiapas border. In the latter state yet another and lower series of mountains begins, collectively called the Sierra de Chiapas, which on a lesser scale crosses the political boundary into Guatemala, and eventually ends far to the south at the Isthmus of Panama.

Geographically distinct from the three main Sierra Madres but in fact intermingled where they meet is one of the world's most notable volcanic belts, crossing Mexico in an east–west direction from about Colima on the Pacific to Veracruz on the Atlantic, following the 19th parallel. This belt intersects the point of the V-shaped plateau at about the point where the Western and Eastern Sierras divide. The unmistakable high cones of the extinct and active volcanoes tower over age-old communities, and have poetic Indian names like Popocatepetl (17,883 ft.) and near-by Ixtaccihuatl (17,342 ft.). At the south-eastern edge of the mesa is Citaltepetl, or Orizaba Peak (18,696 ft.), one of North America's highest mountains.

Like much else connected with Mexican geography, its volcanoes are both a curse and a blessing. Constant minor tremors, with an occasional major earthquake or eruption, make life on the plateau and its associated regions an exciting matter. Some of the chief buildings in Mexico City collapsed several times before they were finally completed. From time to time a new volcano springs out of the ground, as did Paricutín or Jorullo, much to the consternation of local peasants who are driven from the slopes by hot lava. Yet volcanic soil is extremely fertile, and it is therefore not surprising that the richest agricultural regions of Mexico flank this volcanic belt.

The area within the V of the Central Plateau or Mesa, rimmed and delimited by mountain chains, is by no means a uniformly smooth and level plain like the Argentine pampa. On the contrary, its southern half is interlaced by spurs and chains of hills running outward from the Sierras. They subdivide it into a group of intramontane basins, each from 6,000–8,000 feet above sea-level, each a little enclave encircled and cut off from its cluster of neighbouring communities by overshadowing hills. The northern half of the Mesa, as it broadens and declines in altitude northwards beyond the Tropic of Cancer, loses much of its mountainous character, gradually forming a semi-arid plain, indistinguishable from landscapes of the south-western United States, part of the same zone.

Even this short sketch bears out one observer's view that of the total area of Mexico, 'mountainous terrain occupies two-thirds. The remaining third is classed as rolling, save for a scant 8 per cent. of level land'.[1] Few Mexicans indeed are born or die far from mountains.

Climate and Rainfall

The mountains which carve Mexico into small isolated clusters of communities make communications between them costly and create wide irregularities in climate and rainfall. They have confined the river systems to short steep rivers navigable only for short distances and much given to seasonal flooding. The largest rivers, in the south, flow through the least populated areas. The mountains are however vast repositories of precious and industrially important minerals; they also provide a rich and varied vegetation whose botanical richness is a principal national asset. Their altitude offsets tropical living conditions in the areas nearer the Equator.

Mexico, lying for the most part in the tropics, gets hotter as one proceeds southward toward the Equator, that is, as latitudes decrease. At the same time, the higher one gets, the cooler. Thus the lowlands are the hot lands. They are either deserts, if dry, or over-exuberant jungles, if wet. Moderate temperatures and other features making life more tolerable occur in the heights, provided by the omnipresent mountains.

Like most of tropical America, Mexico classifies its territory into three very broad zones or *tierras*, depending on altitude. Lowlands are *tierra caliente*, or hot land. Generally they lie below about 1,500 feet, with mean temperatures of 77°–82° F. Above them is *tierra templada*, or temperate land, from about 1,500 to perhaps 6,000 feet (according to latitude); in *tierra templada* the mean annual temperatures are around 70°–75°, seldom if ever falling below freezing-point. Cold land, *tierra fría*, ranges upward from about 6,000 feet, with mean temperatures around 65° and occasionally dropping much lower. Above the tree and snow line there is occasionally mentioned a *tierra helada*, or frozen land, where little will grow because of the consistently low temperatures.

Most of the population clusters in *tierra templada*. It requires special incentives to remain long in *tierra caliente* or *tierra fría*. This simple consideration explains why, instead of clinging to sea coasts, like the colonists of the United States and Canada in the temperate

---

[1] Tom Gill, *Land Hunger in Mexico* (1951), p. 20.

zone, the Europeans climbed to the plateau in Mexico, where they had long been preceded by the major native populations. The *tierra caliente* of the Gulf coastal plains facing Europe is singularly unattractive because of heat, disease, rapidly leaching soils, and other drawbacks.

Temperature, dependent in Mexico to a great degree on altitude, is not the sole criterion for good living conditions. Rainfall is equally important. In most of Mexico the rainfall is insufficient, and irritatingly irregular. For the Republic as a whole the average is about 59 inches of rain annually, but that average is made up of wide extremes. Large areas receive so little rain that its appearance is almost a miracle, and other extensive portions are frequently drenched. Even in those parts where rain is sufficient to support agriculture, its cycles are unpredictable. From one year to another the farmer wonders whether drought will wither his crop before harvest. The accompanying table indicates the rainfall zones, together with comparative percentages in the equivalent zones of the United States, Europe, Argentina, and Australia.

TABLE I

Comparative Effects of Rainfall (Moisture Regions)

MEXICO			Comparative World Areas (*percentages*)			
	Area ('000 hectares)	Per cent	U.S.	Europe	Argentina	Australia
	1,964·4	100·0	100·0	100·0	100·0	100·0
Very humid	49·4	2·5	1·9	1·0	—	—
Humid	262·1	13·4	38·3	19·0	2·7	10·0
Semi-dry	740·7	37·7	24·3	44·0	29·9	18·0
Dry ...	542·3	27·6	27·6	5·0	39·0	28·0
Very dry	369·9	18·8	6·6	1·0	24·9	44·0
Taiga/Tundra	—	—	1·3	30·0	3·5	—

Source: Armando González Santos, *La Agricultura: estructura y utilización de los recursos* (1957), tables 2, 3 and 4, rearranged by author.

Principal Zones

Mexican investigators have recently begun to divide their land into four broad zones. For each the amounts of moisture available to the agriculturalists, as well as temperatures and other conditions have been consolidated and then mapped.

These zones, shown in the map below, can be summarized briefly. The Tropical Zones lie mainly in the Gulf lowlands, relatively remote from the main centres of population and principal transport routes. They annually receive enough or more than enough regular rain to raise crops, but their very humidity, combined with high temperatures, fosters an overpowering vegetation that is a real

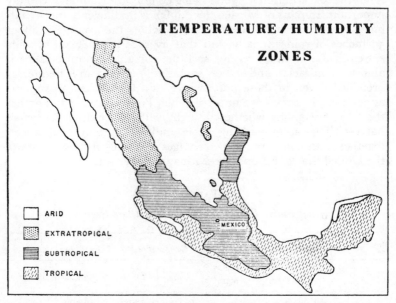

TEMPERATURE / HUMIDITY

ZONES

ARID

EXTRATROPICAL

SUBTROPICAL

TROPICAL

MEXICO

barrier to settlement and movement. Such a jungle, for instance, forms a thick insulating belt between the Mexican mainland and the peninsula of Yucatán, effectively contributing to the isolation of the latter and thus indirectly encouraging the strong separatist tendencies that marked the area in the nineteenth century. For purposes here the Tropical Zones have been grouped as a unit, although in fact there are six distinct sub-zones within them, each with habitable or exploitable patches. It is on these areas that much recent Mexican effort has been expended, to create a March to the Sea. They represent the major under-exploited habitable portions of the national territory.

The Subtropical Zone occupies much of the heavily populated area of the Republic, where optimum combinations of soils, temperatures, and rainfall occur. If and when rains come, they are adequate, but they may fail about every fourth or fifth year. Despite the fact that luck and chance constantly face the agriculturalist everywhere, the odds are more in his favour in these zones, slightly more so in the semi-humid sections than in the semi-arid ones.

The Extra-tropical Zone lies in the northern half of Mexico, constituted by mountainous areas and patches which receive enough moisture to preclude them from being considered completely arid, but in amounts normally too small and too irregular for non-irrigated agriculture.

Finally, nearly half (46·6 per cent.) of Mexico lies in the Arid or Very Arid Zones where near-desert or desert conditions prevail. Most of the land has low carrying capacity even for pastoral purposes. There are exceptions, however. Where water can be obtained, relatively rich small oases can be maintained. But in general the zone is a forlorn and uninviting one for sustained human occupancy.

Other features of Mexican geography are also significant and interesting. They may be summarized by stating that the total result of various conditioning factors severely limit the productive areas of Mexico and thus attractive human habitats. The many natural resources on which the people can draw are in general badly located in relation to each other and to the most habitable sections. The favoured spots are few.

LAND: A RESTRICTED RESOURCE

In the eighteenth century, there was a widespread belief that Mexico was a land of unlimited agricultural opportunities. This myth bewitched writers, both Mexican and foreign, throughout most of the nineteenth century.[1] The concept, never valid, came under critical attack, especially in the 1930's and 1940's, when it was common for foes of reform to overemphasize Mexico's limitations. A modified assessment, based for the first time on field data, has been developing in the past two decades. It indicates that there is a small land base which, properly employed, can feed many more Mexicans than it does today. Through careful planning and wise investment of time, money, and modern technology, the base itself can be augmented.

One Mexican estimate, based on data of about 1950, summarizes land use potentials. This view, reproduced statistically in Table 2, shows that more than 30 per cent. of Mexican land is absolutely

[1] Leonardo Martín Echevarría, 'La Leyenda dorada sobre la riqueza de México', *Investigación económica*, xiv, 231–87, provides highlights.

out of the question for agricultural utilization; about 14 per cent. is potential crop-land, much of which customarily lies fallow or unused during one or more growing seasons.

TABLE 2

Land Use Potentials, 1950

(*million hectares*)

Agricultural use potential	Area	Per cent.
Crop-lands	19·9	10·2
Pastures	67·4	34·3
Forests	38·8	19·8
Uncultivated productive lands	7·8	4·0
	133·9	68·3
Non-Agricultural		
Unproductive	11·6	5·9
Lakes and lagoons	0·3	0·2
Other (deserts, urban areas, &c.)	50·5	25·6
	62·4	31·7
TOTAL	196·3	100·0

Source: Luís Yáñez Pérez, *Mecanización de la agricultura mexicana* (1957), table 21 (p. 75), adapted.

An equally well-qualified Mexican investigator, Armando González Santos, has sifted a mass of published and unpublished material up to about 1957 in an effort to estimate the most likely ways and means of realizing the Mexican agricultural potential. His findings indicate that if maximum efforts were properly expended, Mexico would have at its disposal 30 million hectares (about 74 million acres), nearly twice the arable land under cultivation in 1957. Of these, 11·4 million hectares would be irrigated land. But the gap between actual and potential arable land closes slowly because of the high costs of irrigation projects. By 1957 only 2·7 million hectares had been irrigated. The Ruíz Cortines administration invested 3,056 million pesos to irrigate only 1·1 million hectares of land. Much work and expense lies ahead.

Professor Gonzáles, employing the temperature–humidity zones used above, hazarded an informed guess as to where potential agricultural land is to be found, and thus where developmental investment would be most productive. Through complicated but sound methods he noted the potential arable land in each zone and the area under cultivation in 1957. In simplified form his results appear in Table 3.

TABLE 3

Potential Arable Land and Percentage of Utilization, 1957

Zone	Area	Arable land	Good	Fair	Total	1957 Utilized·	Unutilized potential
	(Million hectares)				Potent. arable	Percentage	
Tropical ...	46·1	16·5	7·2	7·3	45·9	51·0	49·0
Sub-tropical ...	35·8	10·2	2·4	6·8	28·4	84·0	16·0
Extra-tropical...	23·3	2·2	0·2	1·0	6·2	78·0	22·0
Arid	91·2	7·0	3·7	2·0	19·5	96·0	4·0
Republic total	196·4	35·9	13·5	17·1	100·0	51·0	49·0

Source: González Santos, *Agricultura*, tables 11, 14; percentages by author.

This table reveals that although there are 35·9 million hectares of potential arable land, in fact only 13·5 million of them (38 per cent.) can be considered good, with another 17·1 million (48 per cent.) fair. Together they represent 30·6 million hectares, only about 15·6 per cent. of Mexico's total area. The table also suggests that the tropical areas, chiefly on the sea coasts, form the largest block of potential land. Exploitation of them partly underlies recent Mexican stress on the March to the Sea. Finally, it may be noted that at the present stage of technology the arid zone offers really few major opportunities for growth of agricultural population.

One conclusion that can be drawn is that in 1957, with a relatively small use of modernized technology, less than 14 million hectares were supporting a population of 31·4 million Mexicans with rising standards of living. Mexican planners assume that even their relatively poor land base can be made to yield sufficient food and export crops for at least double, and perhaps even triple that population with careful land management, conservation practices, and continued efforts through irrigation, drainage, sanitation of tropical zones, and other established programmes. This view purposely disregards possibly new and important technological advances, and harvests of sea and forest products whose potential cannot be estimated with any degree of certainty.

A different, but parallel study, draws many of these same conclusions. Augusto Ríos Díaz, using 1957 data, found that the 11·6 million hectares of arable land not utilized in that year formed 45·5 per cent. of the readily cultivable area, or a total of about 27 million acres of potentially arable land; he believed that there were 5·5 million hectares more than could be opened to cultivation, his figure of 32·5 millions being not far from the above estimate of 35·9 million hectares (Table 3). He noted that crop rotation, soil analyses, seed and crop selection, and above all, more intensive use of land and modernizing farming techniques need not be deferred but could be initiated immediately.[1]

Until recent times, however, decisions concerning Mexican land tenure and land use have rested more on emotion than on such objective studies. Heirs of the Revolution of 1910 have been more prone to make their points with ·30–·30 rifles than with a slide-rule. Their emotional approach now seems a luxury the nation can little afford. In the end the agronomist rather than the agrarianist may turn out to be the hero of the agrarian Revolution.

[1] Augusto Ríos Díaz, 'Agricultura', SDE, *Diagnóstico*, pp. 63–65.

Chapter V

REGIONALISM AND SECTIONALISM

THE enclaves and various physical sections into which its topography and climates have carved Mexico are paralleled by the regional and sectional subcultures which have developed historically. The main traditions of the principal regions have deep roots. At one time regional factors had more influence than at present.[1] The nationalizing and unifying influences of past decades have by no means totally obliterated regional cultures, but are transmuting them into healthy variations of an emerging national homogeneity.

THE REGIONS

The regions of Mexico are differently defined for various purposes. Here we shall employ some very broad groupings: the Metropolis, the Core, the West, the North, and the South. These serve as a useful shorthand device to group together a number of similar matters under each category. It should always be borne in mind

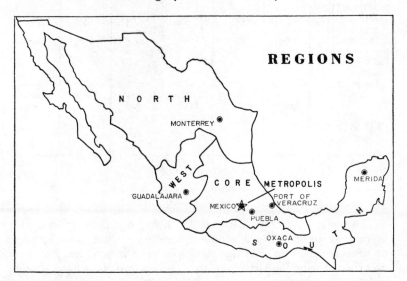

[1] Harry Bernstein, 'Some Regional Factors in the National History of Mexico', *Acta Americana*, ii (Oct.-Dec. 1944), 305–14.

that within each of these broad regions are found a number of sub-regions and localized sub-groups which do not always fit neatly into the general scheme.[1]

An overall view of the sections will emphasize some of their differences. Based on numerous criteria—aboriginal base, physical habitat, colonial and recent backgrounds, economic interests, demography, urbanization, and 'ethos'—the regions have resulted from long development and response to more recent trends. Some of those results can be represented statistically for comparative purposes, as they are in the following table and in Appendix Table II.

TABLE 4

Major Regions: Area, Population, Density, 1960

	Metro-polis	Core	West	North	South	Republic
AREA (sq. m.)						
Thousands ...	0·6	127·0	71·7	407·2	153·7	758·0
Proportion (per cent.) ...	0·1	16·7	9·5	53·4	20·3	100·0
POPULATION						
Millions ...	5·4	12·7	3·5	7·4	5·3	34·2
Proportion (per cent.) ...	15·7	37·1	10·2	21·5	15·4	100·0
DENSITY						
Persons per sq. m. ...	9,012·0	99·5	48·0	18·2	33·3	45·0
Category ...	Very heavy	Medium (Heavy)	Medium (Light)	Very light	Light	Medium (Light)
CITIES (1950)						
Over 25,000	1	17	5	24	7	54

Source: Appendix Table II

The Metropolis

The present Federal District is the 'heart' of the heartland, with an almost unbroken tradition of hegemony since pre-Conquest days. It consists of metropolitan Mexico City, which has now absorbed the smaller urban entities (Delegations) that have equally

[1] Cline, *U.S. and Mexico*, pp. 88–111, provides more extended discussion, with quantitative data summarized in table 1, pp. 404–10, and tables 3–4, pp. 411–12.

long historical traditions. As the urban centre of the nation, it is the political, economic, and cultural capital. It has far more than its 'just' proportion of people, wealth, and power, overshadowing the outlying regions and its own attached Core in nearly all respects except that of area.

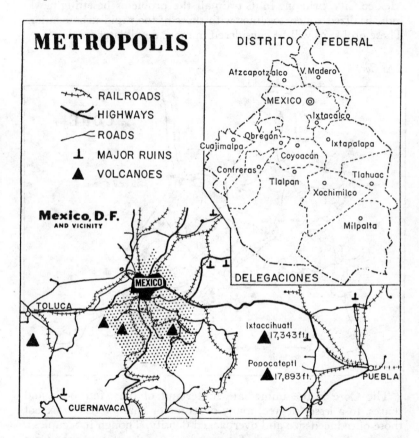

The Metropolis, accused of being hydrocephalic, is the main focal point from which change and ideas diffuse at varying pace throughout the other regions. As a cosmopolitan, sophisticated city, one of the world's great capitals, it has played a paramount role in the history of Mexico. Whatever other prizes fell to insurgent bands, their victory was of no consequence until they had shown that they could occupy and hold the capital. Control of this tiny area, now about 600 square miles, has always been the key to power over the whole land.

Recent history has added to these traditional attributes of the Metropolis its position as the chief industrial complex of a rapidly industrializing nation. This has accelerated the fantastic growth of Mexico City, bringing in its train all the problems besetting newly industrialized zones, together with those of too rapid urbanization. These problems will be considered in more detail later.[1]

The Core

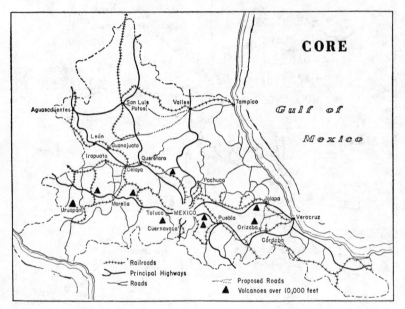

The Core is the immediate hinterland of the Metropolis and shares, to a lesser degree, many of its major characteristics, except those of reduced size and overpacked density. Though it occupies a little less than 17 per cent. of the land area of the country, the Core concentrates nearly 40 per cent. of the people and, with the addition of the Metropolis, more than half (54 per cent.). Politically the Core includes 11 states, closely interconnected with the Metropolis and with each other by rail, road, and communications networks. These states contain the major port, Veracruz, the most productive and

[1] See below, pp. 101–12.

best agricultural lands, and an almost continuous industrial corridor from the highland national capital to the port.[1]

In the shadow of the Metropolis, Puebla is the secondary main focus or regional capital of this fertile and productive hinterland. Since aboriginal days, the attractive habitats within its orbit have encouraged urbanization and high population densities. With the coming of mining under European influences, through it flowed a constant stream of wealth based on bullion, commerce, agriculture, and manufacturing, all demanding auxiliary services.

Politically the Core and the Metropolis are inseparable. Their common regional doctrine has been centralism; their inability often to distinguish between 'regional imperialism' and national ends has led to much friction. From earliest times, all other regions have been subordinate and often unwilling satellites of the Metropolis and the Core, but in the face of recent nationalizing trends in all phases of Mexican life these earlier sharp differences are slowly disappearing.

Most of the Core is well aware of the modern world and its complexities. Yet its native traditions and populations are tenacious, the juxtaposition of the two modes often providing striking contrasts. In general terms, it is the Metropolis and the Core which the tourist visits, but the panorama of modern Mexico is incomplete without a glance at other and important components of what an informed author has called 'Many Mexicos'.[2]

The West

Comparable characteristics of the Core region are found in the West, for both regions fall within the Subtropical Zone. The West is defined here as the four states of Colima, Jalisco, Nayarit, and Zacatecas. The regional capital is Guadalajara, for a long time Mexico's second city; Guadalajara was the colonial administrative centre for an enormous area of the country.[3] The West has as its geographical base a wide, relatively smooth and fruitful basin, lower and larger than the comparable intra-montane basins of the Core.

Settlement and land tenure traditions mark it off from the Core. Since there were sparse and unimportant native communities in

---

[1] States here grouped in the Core are Aguascalientes, Guanajuato, Hidalgo, México, Michoacán, Morelos, Puebla, Querétaro, San Luis Potosí, Tlaxcala, and Veracruz.

[2] Lesley B. Simpson, *Many Mexicos*, 3d ed. (1952).

[3] J. H. Parry, *The Audiencia of New Galicia in the Sixteenth Century* (1948).

the West, the Spanish colonists created a group of small to medium-sized towns there. Rather than a complex of large haciendas interspersed with landholding Indian communities as in the Core, the land tended to be divided into medium and small haciendas with a strong tendency to farm-size plots tilled by yeoman families.

The West developed a fairly large, stable, conservative middle class with few really large landholders and few landless peasants. The West also developed from early colonial times without major Indian influences. Its position on the Pacific, where trade and cultural ties with the East were weak, placed it on the margin of European trends, filtered to it through the Core. In general, the West adapted to local conditions the main elements of a relatively undiluted Spanish heritage.

Occupying about 10 per cent. of the territory, the West also contains about 10 per cent. of the population. It has a slightly disproportionate amount of arable land (15 per cent.). Moderately urbanized and strongly inclined to industrialize, the West forms part of modern Mexico.

The North

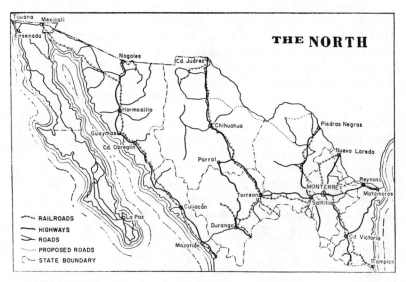

Vast, sprawling, and quite different is the North. It comprises seven states and the territory of Lower California South.[1] In fact, it would and should be even larger, as northern sections of states like San Luis Potosí and Zacatecas resemble it, but statistically they have been assigned here to the Core and to the West.

The North differs from other sections for various reasons. Its development as an integral part of the Republic is relatively recent. In colonial times its generally unfavourable characteristics attracted relatively few permanent settlers. Its main role was to act as buffer between Mexican areas and the English, Russians, and French in North America. The native population was nomadic, considered even by pre-Conquest Indians of the Core and South to be barbarians. Eighteenth-century European immigration from Spain trickled

[1] Baja California; Chihuahua; Coahuila; Durango; Nuevo León; Sinaloa; Sonora; and Tamaulipas. Parts of Zacatecas and San Luis Potosí belong to this region, but statistical rigidity makes their inclusion on a partial basis impossible.

into the area, but not until the late nineteenth century, when its industrial minerals took on sudden value, did the North come into its own. Its lands were generally of poor quality, at best useful for pasture; hence land tenure had to be based on the ownership of enormous tracts, much of them useless. Recently some portions, where irrigation could be provided, became suitable for the large-scale production of cereal grains and cotton.

The development of the United States at the northern edge influenced the region during the nineteenth and twentieth centuries. Its railways and industries began as offshoots of parallel developments in the south-western United States. From these Monterrey emerged as the main regional centre, rivalled by Saltillo. Mining, stock-raising, then early industrialism marked this frontier area, whose melting-pot also bred a less aristocratic type than the Core's élite mestizo-European.

The North is in many ways transitional between the United States and 'traditional' Mexico. This may seem paradoxical in view of the fact that the region occupies more than half (53·4 per cent.) of the national territory. However, only a fifth (21 per cent.) of the Mexican population is scattered in pockets of tolerable habitats in this enormous stretch of arid and semi-arid Extra-tropical Zone: a territory where water is a more critical commodity than land.

The South

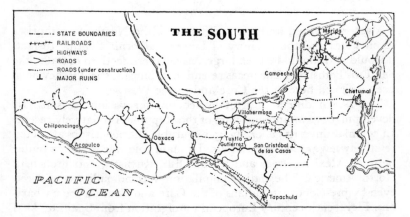

Contrasting with the North in nearly every respect is the South, in which we have included the peninsula of Yucatán and the South

Pacific states.[1] Southern Veracruz would logically form part of the South, but statistical considerations place it with the Core.

The South is Indian Mexico. It is also a congeries of small sub-regions separated from each other and from the Core by almost insurmountable geographical barriers. In 1950 more than half of the Indians who could speak only their native tongues—and there are more than fifty dialects—were grouped in small communities throughout the South.

Although the main land-tenure tradition is the small landholding Indian community, larger plantations for special crops utilizing impressed native labour also form part of the traditional regional pattern. Neither the markets, communications, capital, nor available resources combine to produce any significant modern trend toward industrialization. These elements are reflected in the general slowness of the process of urbanization. Only Mérida (Yucatán) exceeds 150,000 inhabitants among the cities of the South.

Since aboriginal days, the South has been administratively and culturally fractionalized, unified only by its heterogeneous but non-European base. Socially, economically, and politically, it is a problem area to those who wish to modernize Mexico, but it is the tourists' and anthropologists' delight. In its market-places colourful Indian costumes are still seen and the clack and buzz of ancient tongues are still heard.

Statistically the South includes about 20 per cent. of the national territory, and about 17 per cent. of the population. It shares with the Core deep-rooted native ways, but unlike the latter, these are not overlaid and engulfed in dynamic urges to change. It is profoundly rural, in the native tradition.

REGIONS AND THE NATION

The interplay of geography and history have produced the regions, and the forces generated by regional interests have constantly clashed or coincided to influence national events and developments. The nature of the problems that have beset those who would weld a single unit from its disparate components can perhaps be pointed up by analogy. Each of the regions sketched above can be compared to sizable South American republics, which each resembles in some of its main characteristics.

With Venezuela, for instance, the North shares a preponderantly

---

[1] Campeche; Chiapas; Guerrero; Oaxaca; Tabasco; Yucatán; and the Territory of Quintana Roo.

57

militaristic tradition, oil, industry, and vast tracts of almost useless land over which cowboys have roamed and fought; the North is slightly larger than Venezuela, but their total populations are exactly equal. The West and Uruguay have many common elements: their lack of Indian traditions, their pastoral base, their development in the shadow of a major metropolis (Mexico City on the one hand; Buenos Aires on the other), their agricultural productivity and interest in progress. Their areas are again equal, but the West has slightly larger numbers of people. The Indian base, the scattered nature of small settlements, the marked differences in outlook between the highland areas and those on the sea, the lack of self-conscious integration make the South and Ecuador comparable, although Ecuador is smaller both in area and population. There is really no exact parallel in South America to the Core; Peru, especially the highland-coastal-plain complex, comes nearest, with its inter-mixtures of Indian and modern ways, its deep historical roots, and its relatively compact and more nearly continuous settlements. If the useless montaña area is included, Peru is considerably larger in size, but is slightly less than the Core (not including the Federal District) in its total numbers. The following table underlines these comparisons:—

TABLE 5

Mexican Regions compared with Selected South American Republics, 1956

Comparative units	Total Area ('000 sq. m.)	Total population (millions)
NORTH	407·2	6·3
Venezuela	352·2	6·3
WEST	71·7	3·2
Uruguay	72·2	2·7
SOUTH	153·7	4·9
Ecuador	116·3	4·0
CORE	127·0	12·0
Peru...	514·0	10·2
METROPOLIS		4·5
Caracas; Montevideo; Quito; Lima ...		3·4

Without pushing the analogy too far, one might say that to integrate and to unify Mexico into one nation would be a task similar to uniting Venezuela, Uruguay, Ecuador, and Peru, all parts of the same sixteenth-century Spanish Viceroyalty, into a single republic. Other volumes in this series have exemplified the difficulties in the way even of establishing these smaller national units in South America.[1] Many, if not most, of these difficulties are applicable to the internal regional integration of each Mexican region, and in increased measure and magnitude have inhibited the rapid and easy nationalization of Mexico. It is small wonder that a *leit-motif* of its post-colonial years has been the search for a formula that would balance sectional and national needs and interests, a quest that seems now nearly ended.

The regions of Mexico, even so briefly sketched, underline some of the complexities of the Republic. If nothing else, the discussion should indicate that single, doctrinaire solutions to Mexican problems are likely to encounter passive, if not massive, regional resistance. The regions are unequal in many respects, but the Mexican nation has evolved from them all.

Speaking of recent Mexico, one able student of Mexican history and regionalism noted,

Culturally, regionalism survived most strongly in Jalisco and Yucatán . . . . But political regionalism, coupled with revolution, has declined and partially disappeared. In 1950, Mexico had gained more unity than ever before and achieved a remarkable compromise between Indianism and Europeanism, between labor and capital, and between sectionalism and centralism.[2]

[1] Edward Lieuwen, *Venezuela* (London, 1961); George Pendle, *Uruguay* 2nd ed., (London, 1957); Lilo Linke, *Ecuador* (London, 1954).
[2] Harry Bernstein, *Modern and Contemporary Latin America* (1952), p. 158; especially recommended are his chapters on Mexico, pp. 3–158.

Chapter VI

FORGING THE NATION:
COMMUNICATIONS AND TRANSPORTATION

THE varied regions of Mexico are only loosely knit into a single national unit by the transportation and communications networks that have slowly developed. Many modern highways and railways follow well-worn trails first trod by countless Indians even before the Spaniards brought in wheeled vehicles, horses, and the ubiquitous *burro*, besides continuing to use human beings as the principal carriers of goods and messages. The nineteenth century in Mexico, as elsewhere in the world, witnessed rapid acceleration and the widespread use of new inventions: the telegraph, steamship, and above all, railways. In the twentieth century communications and transportation were speeded up as motor cars, radio, air travel, and television became more commonplace. In Mexico their growth, fostered by official programmes since 1934, has accompanied the social and economic phases of the Revolution.

The urge to expand transportation and communication facilities is closely bound up with hopes of making Mexico a single nation, an economically and socially integrated entity, despite the natural obstacles in the way. The achievement of the Revolution over its fifty years has been impressive, with rather spectacular advances in the two decades since 1940. As the burden of administration increased, President López Mateos in 1958 divided the older Ministry of Communications and Public Works into two, each with Cabinet status.

RAILWAYS

The Revolution inherited from the Díaz régime the main outlines of the present railway network, created in the final quarter of the nineteenth century through British, French, and North American capital and engineering.[1] More than twenty separate branch and main lines built by them have gradually come under national government ownership, partly through expropriation in 1937 and subsequent government purchases in 1946 and 1950, leaving in

[1] Carlos Villafuerte, *Ferrocarriles* (1959), is a splendid monograph on present railways in Mexico, with bibliography.

private hands only a few hundred miles of track operated by foreign mining companies and other industrial concerns. The railway network in Yucatán, Ferrocarriles Unidos de Yucatán (FUY), is owned and operated by that state.

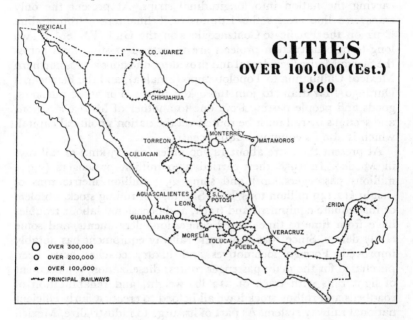

National lines nominally come under the supervision of the Ministry of Communications, but in fact are directed through semi-autonomous federal agencies. The largest and most important of these is Ferrocarriles Nacionales de México (FNdeM), controlling two-thirds of the national railways, including most of the main lines and their branches radiating from Mexico City. One of its main lines connects in the West (at Manzanillo and Guadalajara) with another independently administered network, Ferrocarril de Pacífico, which wends its way northwards along the Pacific shore before connecting with the main United States lines at Nogales. A third semi-autonomous agency, the Ferrocarril Mexicano, operates the historic line between Mexico City and the port of Veracruz, which runs parallel to the FNdeM line. The Ministry directly operates a number of smaller systems: Ferrocarril Sonora–Baja California, recently (1950) completed to link the peninsula with the mainland; and Ferrocarril de Sureste, which at about the same time linked Yucatán with the mainland by joining FNdeM lines with the state of Yucatán's network (FUY).

Geography has made railway construction costly, and to some degree unfortunately planned. The main lines run north and south, carving the nation into longitudinal strips. At present the only transverse line crosses the Isthmus of Tehuantepec, from Salina Cruz on the Pacific to Coatzacoalcos on the Gulf (FNdeM). Two long-term construction projects are to extend existing lines across the Sierra Madre Occidental and provide connexions across northern Mexico: Chihuahua to Topolobampo (Sinaloa), and the Ferrocarril Durango–Mazatlán, to join those key places. For most purposes, goods and people passing from one to another of Mexico's regions and sections by rail must be routed via the nation's political capital, which is also its communications centre.

At present there are about 14,700 miles (23,425 km.) of railways in Mexico. In 1958 they carried 27·0 million passengers (3,331 millions passengers/km.) and some 25·3 million metric tons of freight (12,149 million tons/km). Shortage of rolling stock, obsolete or inadequate equipment and track, and occasional labour troubles have from time to time caused congestion, derailments, and some costly delays. Since 1946, however, railway equipment has notably improved. Foreign locomotives and luxury coaches have been purchased for the main passenger routes; dieselization, replacement of light rails with track of 112 lb. weight, and rehabilitation of roadbeds and rolling stock have all helped to create a fairly efficient national railway system. As part of its surge to industrialize, Mexico now manufactures its own goods wagons.

Much of the revitalization of its basic means of transportation is directly traceable to efforts of the Government, through Nacional Financiera,[1] to keep pace with the expansion of Mexican society and economy. In 1959 it could be conservatively stated that 'the railroads have succeeded in carrying a steadily growing volume of freight through more efficient practices and gradual improvement in physical equipment'.[2]

Some remaining problems are capable of more rapid solution than others. Administrative consolidation of the several agencies, many believe, would help to co-ordinate efforts and cut down duplication. Continued and increased improvement of equipment is essential, the minimum cost of which is estimated at 8,200 million

---

[1] See below, p. 244.
[2] Rice, 'Basic Data', p. 16; DGE, *Compendio estadístico, 1958*, tables 207–12 (pp. 327–79).

pesos between 1958 and 1967. Closer integration between planning
of main roads and railways seems highly desirable, especially for
less-developed sections and regions, where parallelism at this stage
may be uneconomical, however politically glamorous it might
appear. Finally, the whole problem of railway labour needs re-
examination, again in relation to road haulage. These are the main
conclusions of a detailed recent Mexican study.[1]

HIGHWAYS AND MOTOR TRANSPORT

PRINCIPAL HIGHWAYS
1959

PRINCIPAL HIGHWAYS

OTHER ROADS

Like its railways, the principal highways in Mexico run mainly
north and south, connecting international frontiers with the national
capital. Unlike them, the modern highway and road networks have
come into being in the last quarter century, during the marked
upward spurt following the Second World War. In road building,
the national Government has taken the lead in creating the main
Federal highways, but has co-operated with the states, and with a
mixture of state, local, and private interests, to construct the total
system.

At present, the national aim to create the main trunk roads has

[1] Villafuerte, *Ferrocarriles,* pp. 240–71.

been nearly achieved, hence official emphasis now falls on completing the more extensive secondary roads and the feeder roads to open up hitherto isolated enclaves. Paralleling the project to connect Mazatlán and Durango by rail has been the construction of a highway; completion is near, and the road is now passable at all times. This will increase the transverse routes, which geographical obstacles had previously reduced to a minimum.

The growth of the road system has been notable, rising sharply since 1940. In 1925 there were only about 700 kilometres of passable roads in all Mexico, and in 1939 less than 10,000. Since 1948 Federal, state, and local governments have poured more than 366·8 million pesos into this essential development.[1] In 1960 the President's Annual Message (1 September) stated that recent efforts had raised the total amount of roadways to 39,298 kilometres; details are available only to the end of 1958.

TABLE 6

Growth of Mexican Road System, 1940–58
('000 km.)

	Paved	Gravel	All weather	Total	Percentage increase over 1940
1940 ...	4·8	3·5	1·6	9·9	—
1945 ...	8·2	6·8	2·4	17·4	76·0
1950 ...	13·6	6·0	1·9	21·5	117·0
1955 ...	18·4	5·9	3·0	27·3	161·0
1958 ...	23·4	6·4	2·2	32·0	223·0

Source: DGE, *Compendio estadístico, 1958*, table 194 (p. 304)

The boom in road development is closely linked with the increasing use by Mexicans of motor cars, trucks, and buses. The operation of commercial haulage and bus services is restricted to Mexican firms, who obtain concessions from the Ministry of Communications. In 1958 about 23,000 buses connected all the cities and most major towns. Equipment ranged from the latest and most comfortable models to anachronistic relics in which passengers shared accommodation with a variety of animals, vegetables, and mysterious, odd-shaped bundles.

[1] 'Highways of Mexico', USBFC, WTIS, Economic Reports, pt. 4, no. 56–13, 1956, brought up to date in Rice, 'Basic Data'. DGE, *Compendio estadístico, 1958*, tables 194, 198 (pp. 303–4, 308).

Road haulage supplements the railway freight service, and relieves the railways of a large share of their burden. Some 274,000 lorries were in use during 1958 and a national industry assembles more than 20,000 each year to replace and augment this fleet. By law, only native-born Mexicans may drive lorries on Federal highways.

Though still far from realizing the aim of having one, let alone two cars, Mexicans have taken enthusiastically to motor transport. In 1956 there were 320,429 motor cars driven by Mexicans. Cheap petrol, increasingly extended and improved highways and roads, rising standards of income, and mounting numbers of internationally standard makes of cars (17,955 in 1956) and trucks assembled in Mexico feed and maintain the trend. What Ford did for the United States, the Revolution is doing for Mexico in the field of motor transport. It is one of the fastest growing industries in an expanding economy, as is shown in the following table.

TABLE 7

Growth in Number of Vehicles, 1941–58
('000)

Year		Total	Per cent. increase over 1941	Motor Cars	Buses	Trucks
1941	...	168·2	—	106·3	11·3	50·6
1946	...	205·7	22·1	121·0	13·0	71·7
1950	...	325·7	93·5	176·3	30·1	119·3
1955	...	550·6	221·0	308·1	22·3	220·2
1958	...	675·3	300·0	378·9	22·7	273·7

Source: Cline, *U.S. and Mexico*, table 14, p. 418; DGE, *Compendio estadístico, 1958*, table 201 (p. 314). Percentages by author.

AVIATION

Since 1940 civil aviation in Mexico has greatly expanded. In that year, about 86,800 passengers travelled by air; in 1958 the comparable figure was 1,688,100. Mexico City is the main centre of a well-developed system that covers more than fifty other important Mexican cities and towns, and connects with international routes throughout the world.

The principal aircraft companies were originally subsidiaries of foreign lines, but in the past decade there has been a strong tendency to local ownership. The Compañia Mexicana de Aviación and Aeronaves de México now control most domestic passenger flights and freight. There are twenty secondary or feeder routes for short hauls. To serve this traffic, as well as the nine foreign lines and 576 private planes (1958), Mexico maintains 37 main airports, 302 aerodromes, and 453 landing fields (1958). An active segment of Mexican foreign policy is concerned with the negotiation of civil air transport agreements with the United States, Canada, France, Cuba, and a number of other nations. Air travel has not only broadened Mexican international horizons, but has also supplemented and in some cases has largely taken over the unifying influence of railways and motor transport in recent years. Even Indians are air-minded.[1]

RADIO AND TELEVISION

Mexico, a pioneer among Latin American nations in radio broadcasting, has maintained a strong interest in this field, and extended it early to television, first widely used to bring President Alemán's inauguration before the Mexican public.[2] Nearly every town and all the cities have radio broadcasting stations, 266 in all on commercial waves (as well as 20 short-wave and 2 FM). In 1956 Mexico City, Monterrey, Puebla, Orizaba, Querétaro, and several places on the Mexican side of the United States frontier boasted licensed television stations. A local industry, consisting of 38 manufacturers or assemblers of radio and television receivers, produces approximately 320,000 radio and 120,000 television sets for a seemingly inexhaustible domestic market. Whether or not one wholly approves of the mixed blessings of these mass media, the fact remains that they are playing a substantial role in nationalizing and unifying Mexico.[3]

Perhaps symbolic of changes that have occurred in the past decade is the integration of the Mexican telephone system. Old hands remember struggling, not so long ago, with two main but

[1] While among the Chinantec Indians in 1942, the writer was asked how the village of Yolox could obtain a helicopter to avoid the tortuous journeys up and down the steep canyons to reach neighbouring villages on the opposite side of the valley, only a short air distance away; cf. Cline, *U.S. and Mexico*, p. 385. See also 'Civil Aviation in Mexico', USBFC, WTIS, Economic Reports, pt. 4, no. 57 (2) (Jan. 1957).

[2] Marvin Alisky, 'Early Mexican Broadcasting', *HAHR*, xxxiv (Nov. 1954), 513–26, notes early broadcasting in 1918, with commercials starting in 1923.

[3] In 1960 a new Law of Radio and Television was approved; a National Council of Radio and Television was appointed 'to supervise and dignify' these services (*2° Informe*, 1 Sept. 1960).

distinct telephone systems in Mexico City, and the sometimes weird episodes that befell the unsuspecting traveller. These heterogeneous lines have now been consolidated, through mergers, in the hands of a single private firm, Teléfonos de México. In 1956 there were 391,358 telephones in service (269,035 subscribers), with radiotelephone connexions with various parts of the Western Hemisphere and Europe. The communications system, including telegraph and cable lines, provides a reasonably good service, but despite efforts to keep it growing, it is still far from adequate.

On the whole, however, the substantial advances in all forms of modern communications and transport are impressive. They are unifying the nation.

Chapter VII

A MODERN MEXICAN EPIC:
IRRIGATION PROGRAMMES

In Mexico's struggle to tame its sometimes wild and unfriendly habitat, partial victory over nature seems within the grasp of man. Constantly physical barriers have played a major role in separating and diversifying Mexicans from one another. Now, as in the past, the Mexican people and their Governments must expend a considerable mount of energy merely to neutralize these barriers.

These efforts to overcome geographical handicaps are a constant drain on the relatively slender resources available to Mexicans, but they are essential. As one observer has noted, 'Geographic integration has been the key to social integration, which in turn results in national political integration'.[1]

In fact, modern Mexicans determined to change the face of the land. This urge has become a permanent goal of the Revolution. After 1925 two decades of tinkering with localized irrigation works preceded the Government's recent comprehensive irrigation programme, initiated in about 1948. That programme includes not only solving the ancient problems of insufficient water in thirsty zones, and floods and an over-abundance of water in others, but such modern objectives as the development of large new habitats endowed with communications networks, schools, and other amenities of economic and social life and development. It has been successful.

THE HYDRAULIC PROGRAMMES

In 1948 President Alemán raised a previous administrative unit to Cabinet rank as the Ministry of Hydraulic Resources. It plans, supervises, and executes vast programmes in all parts of the Republic. Its work is generally divided into three main categories, partly by the nature of the activity, partly by administrative responsibility.

'Regular' work of the Ministry embraces what it calls large-scale projects, over which it retains direct control; these are paralleled by numerous small-scale programmes, often carried out in co-operation with state or local authorities under Ministry supervision. A third

[1] Robert E. Scott, *Mexican Government in Transition* (1959), p. 35.

main branch is the distinctive work of semi-autonomous Commissions, each given a broad mandate to develop large tracts, integrating local irrigation works, social agencies, transportation, and other elements in balanced fashion. President Alemán created two of these Commissions in 1948, and his successors have added to them.

The total achievement of the Ministry since 1948 is impressive. Its Annual Report for 1958 (the most recent to be published) noted that from 1926, when the Federal Government began its first efforts in the sphere of irrigation and flood-control, through 1958 a total of about 2,600,000 hectares (about 6,300,000 acres) has been reclaimed and improved. Up to 1947 previous Governments had, over a span of two decades, accounted for about 816,000 hectares of that total, about 31 per cent. The following decade of the Institutional Revolution, 1947–58, was responsible for 69 per cent. of the present improved and irrigated land, 665,500 hectares (25·2 per cent.) of it under President Alemán between 1947 and 1952, and 1,128,000 (43·8 per cent.) in the six-year presidency of Ruíz Cortines. President López Mateos set a minimum of 500,000 hectares to be brought under cultivation when he reported progress in his 1960 Message.

To obtain the results shown in Appendix Table III, a colossal investment of public funds has been required. The appropriations for the Ministry of Hydraulic Resources usually rank about third in the annual national budget, exceeded only by transportation and education, two other development programmes. From 1952 through 1958, for instance, the Ministry expended about 1·5 billion (1,542 million) pesos on large-scale, small-scale, and improvement works, to which states and municipalities added another 400 million, bringing the total outlay for 'regular' activities to nearly 2 billion. In addition to this, the Commissions required another 1·5 billion pesos of federal expenditure during the same period.

The Mexican hydraulic programme is one of the largest of its kind in the world. It is the greatest in Latin America for the creation of reclaimed and irrigated land, and serves as a training device for technicians from other 'underdeveloped' areas of the world suffering from many of the natural handicaps which the Mexicans are successfully overcoming. (See Appendix Table III.)

LARGE-SCALE AND SMALLER PROGRAMMES

An outstanding example of what the Ministry considers a regular large-scale enterprise is the construction of Falcón Dam, an

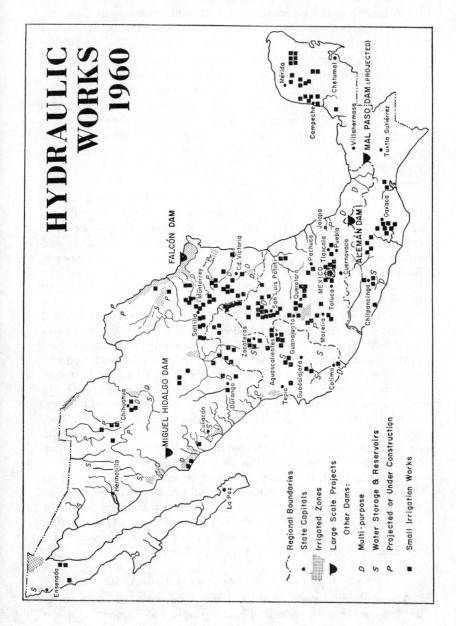

international project of benefit to both Mexico and the United States, which together share the lower Río Grande (Río Bravo). Allocation of irrigation water between the two countries, as each gradually began to exploit the hitherto useless areas on each side of the boundary, caused a number of difficulties which were amicably settled by treaty in 1944. One stipulation of that agreement authorized a joint enterprise, financed and engineered on a co-operative basis, to provide irrigation water, hydro-electric power, and interlocking communications for the Mexican and United States communities in the area stretching from Ciudad Juárez–El Paso to Matamoros–Brownsville, the zone through which the river flows into the Gulf of Mexico.

Falcón Dam

The major and central work in the project is Falcón Dam, named after Captain Blas María de la Garza Falcón who in 1750 tried unsuccessfully to canalize tributaries of the Río Bravo in order to irrigate much the same area. Construction of the dam was completed in 1953. On 19 October of that year Presidents Dwight D. Eisenhower and Adolfo Ruíz Cortines officially dedicated the enterprise; their speeches at the opening ceremony emphasized the value of the dam as a lasting and important symbol of the solid friendship and growing interdependence of their two peoples.

On the Mexican side of the border, the project has had fructifying results. In addition to the water and power derived from Falcón Dam itself, there is a related network of smaller dams and reservoirs, the last of which was completed in 1960. The Mexican authorities have designated their area the Irrigation Zone of the Lower Río Bravo, and in it have irrigated about half a million acres (220,000 hectares) of good-quality land. Running across the upper edges of the states of Nuevo León and Tamaulipas, from a new planned community, Nuevo Guerrero (near Ciudad Juárez), to Matamoros, the Zone's productivity outstrips Captain Falcón's wildest dreams.

Small-Scale Works

Although perhaps not as spectacular as Falcón Dam and other comparable large-scale works, the Ministry's work on small-scale irrigation projects is of vital local and political importance. These activities are carried on in every state and territory, usually in co-operation with the states and municipalities concerned. Steadily during the past ten years these scattered patches have grown

collectively at the rate of about 70,000 acres a year (28,200 hectares).
In parched countrysides, the appearance of engineers to survey the
problems and work out a plan is a reminder that the Revolution is
not dead. Rising from an annual expenditure of 15·5 million pesos
in 1948 to 73·4 million in 1958, the average national investment in
these localized projects has run to about 40 million pesos annually.
In addition, the constant preoccupation of the Ministry to supply
drinking-water to scattered communities is often a by-product of
its small-scale irrigation programmes. Although there had been
substantial progress up to 1958, there is still much to do; an estimated
89,000 localities still have dubious and unreliable supplies of
drinking-water.

THE REGIONAL DEVELOPMENT COMMISSIONS

In general the tasks of the Commissions combine large-scale and
small-scale works, together with social and economic development
programmes within particularly backward areas. The extensive
Commission projects, situated as they are in vast tracts of territory
isolated from the main regional capitals and centres, in places long
plagued by the problems of too much or too little water, have
contributed to the growing spirit of national unity.

The completion of schemes in these newly-developed territories not only adds important economic resources in previously lightly populated zones, but links regions and sections together by connecting their communications and markets. The map on p. 72 illustrates the siting of the two major Commission projects on regional boundaries, between the Core and the South on the one hand (Papaloapan), and between the Core and the West on the other (Tepalcatepec).

Six semi-autonomous Commissions have been established since 1947. Their work is grouped and reported separately by the Ministry of Hydraulic Resources. Although they are generally alike in administrative structure, their specific aims and procedures are in fact quite different, for they are geared to meet the pressing but quite diverse needs of six dissimilar territories. The total impact of their efforts probably exceeds the sum of the separate parts of the general Commission programme. There are such Commissions for drainage basins and river systems of the Papaloapan, the Tepalcatepec, Río Fuerte, Valley of Mexico, Yaqui (Native Zone), and the Grijalva–Usumacinta. In 1960 President López Mateos indicated that another new Commission for the Río Balsas would be authorized.

Yaqui and Valley of Mexico

Work undertaken by the Commissions for the Yaqui Native Zone and the Valley of Mexico differs chiefly only in administrative structure from the 'regular' irrigation activities of the Ministry elsewhere. These two undertakings were established as separate Commissions mainly for political rather than for technical reasons. In the case of the Yaqui Zone, the Commission, together with other interested agencies, has sponsored the irrigation by orthodox means of some 11,000 hectares of land to help to raise the standards of living of this special Indian group. This group has always been a refractory unassimilable tribe, who have long been a symbol of Díaz's repressive policies because they survived his attempts to annihilate them by military expeditions. Hence this special programme for them is part of a general political policy of unification. As such, it has a significance out of proportion to its small area and the financial investment involved.

The Valley of Mexico Commission, at the centre of the Core region, is an excellent demonstration of the work of the Ministry. From 1952 through 1958 the Government of Ruíz Cortines invested more than 112 million pesos in the undertaking, which included work on flood-control and irrigation; the result has been the creation of about 13,000 additional hectares of irrigated and improved land. Working with other agencies and groups, however, the main purpose of this Commission is to see that the metropolitan area has safe and plentiful drinking-water, a task it is manfully carrying out in spite of an unprecedented demand.

Río Fuerte

The work of the Commission for the Río Fuerte Basin is one of the really large projects. The locality is a fairly restricted area on Mexico's west coast, a sort of oasis in the Sonoran Desert and Plains, where the Fuerte river flows into the Pacific Ocean. The Commission charged with the development of this river basin has almost completed a plan not only to create 220,000 hectares of first-class irrigated land but also to provide the surrounding countryside with electricity, and to foster the construction of the necessary market roads, together with lesser programmes of social welfare.

By 1958 about 90 per cent. of the principal tasks of the Commission had been achieved. The great Miguel Hidalgo Dam had been completed in 1956, but by 1958 its three 20,000 kwa. turbines had not been fully installed. The main irrigation canal also came into operation in 1956, leaving only the subsidiary ones still to be completed; and main roads to the principal markets had been made.

Despite the relatively large national investment of capital—550·5 million pesos from 1952 through 1958 alone—the Commission estimated that the cost would be amortized in about thirteen years; from a rather low rental, 1,000 pesos per hectare of irrigated land, it was already obtaining a return of 8 million pesos per year. Drought had kept full-scale operations below capacity; the partially filled reservoirs connected with the dam could irrigate only 150,000 hectares. But the Commission had completed facilities, under more normal conditions, to irrigate 200,000 hectares, a noteworthy achievement.

Papaloapan

The mandate given to the Papaloapan Commission when it was set up in 1947 embraced a wider scope and area than that of the Río Fuerte body. The Papaloapan Commission was expected to develop totally and harmoniously all the natural resources of the Papaloapan river basin. The area, about the size of the republic of Costa Rica, included a little over 18,000 square miles (46,500 square km.) of hitherto lightly populated land where three states meet.

The territory is shared unequally by Puebla (11·9 per cent.), Veracruz (38·6 per cent.), and Oaxaca (49·5 per cent).

In 1948, when detailed planning for the several units and phases of the project was seriously undertaken, the locality was not attractive. Within the area about one-fifth of the people were monolingual Indians from more than half a dozen mutually unintelligible linguistic stocks; less than half the eligible school population from among the native children and those of the mestizos, not far removed from Indian life, were in school. More serious, life was precarious in the small and isolated hamlets, partly through unpredictable but serious recurrent floods, partly through insanitary tropical living conditions.

The Commission, therefore, faced the task of equipping this potentially useful but undeveloped territory with the apparatus of modernity. Eventually this involved a resettlement programme as well as flood-control, irrigation, hydro-electric power, communications, public health, education, and agricultural development.

The Commission's eleventh annual report in 1958 summed up the progress made in all these fields, and the State of the Nation messages by Presidents Ruíz Cortines in 1958 and Adolfo López Mateos in 1959 supplied supplementary detail. Since work began in 1948, the great Miguel Alemán Dam has been completely finished, as has its connected hydro-electric plant with a 184,000 kv. capacity; a second and somewhat smaller dam and hydro-electric unit at Temazcal, begun in 1954, is now more than 85 per cent. complete, with its first generating unit of 54,000 kv. in operation. The interconnected drainage canals, reservoirs, and pumping stations have reclaimed or irrigated more than 120,000 hectares of arable land; some 200 agricultural technicians have been advising and aiding local farmers by analysing the soils, developing and testing plants suited to each locality, carrying out experiments to improve the breeds of animals, and providing credits for co-operatives or individuals.

Accelerating its earlier efforts, the Commission between 1952 and 1958 brought electricity to most of the communities within a radius of Ciudad Alemán, a planned major community which scarcely figured in the 1950 Census, but which is beginning to take on all attributes of a provincial metropolis as the administrative centre of the project. Some nineteen airports and airstrips and 1,600 kilometres of roads, with their necessary bridges, connect the area with the regional capitals of Puebla, Oaxaca, and the national port of Veracruz and the transportation and communications networks fanning out from them.

Perhaps of special interest are some of the developments in the education and resettlement of Indians whose communities were displaced by the reservoir or other important installations. In 1948 there were about 103,000 children in schools within the Basin. By 1958 the Commission, aided by state and local authorities, had constructed a total of nearly 400 new primary schools and employed a teaching staff of about 4,100, imparting instruction to 162,568 pupils. The local system, divided into thirty-three school districts, gives instruction through secondary-school levels. Planners are now discussing the erection of a special Rural University to provide opportunities, technicians, teachers, and research related to the Basin; the Ministry reports that if these plans mature, such an institution would be the first of its kind in Mexico.

The resettlement efforts have chiefly affected Mazatec and Mixe Indians. Before their communities were inundated, they were studied and the value of compensation was assessed; the Indians were paid about 3 million pesos indemnification, and were allowed to choose, in the new localities to which their villages were transferred, parcels of land equivalent to those they had held. The new communities generally have retained the names of the original ones, prefixed by 'New' (Nuevo), and cultural continuity has been preserved, though the material conditions of the resettled communities are better than the abandoned ones.

All told, the Papaloapan Project is a successful experiment. With industry on the march, with opportunities opening on every hand, with farmers and workers with money to spend, it is not hard to discern why a new and vital spirit animates this long neglected corner of Mexico.

Tepalcatepec

Created on 11 May 1947, the Commission of Tepalcatepec follows much the same lines as the Papaloapan Commission, but on a somewhat reduced scale.[1] The eleventh annual report (1958) of the Commission gives details of its activities and achievements. In one year alone, 1957–8, local farmers produced 926,000 tons of crops, valued at 185·2 million pesos, on about 70,000 hectares of irrigated land created through the Commission's efforts. Its programme of sanitary engineering, road and bridge construction, electrification, town improvement (reconstruction of plazas, monuments, official

[1] The Basin, then on the eve of recent developments, is described and analysed in detail by Gonzalo Aguirre Beltrán, *Problemas de la población indígena de la Cuenca de Tepalcatepec* (1952).

buildings), cattle and crop improvement, and above all, education, had transformed the zone. Up to 1958, the Commission had increased the number of schools from 56 in 1948 to 354, with 751 teachers and 32,714 enrolled pupils; as in the case of the Papaloapán Project, this raised the percentage of eligible school population in schools from the 48 per cent. in 1948 to approximately 70 per cent. Again another neglected province had been added to modern Mexico.

Grijalva–Usumacinta

Finally, the Commission created in June 1951 to 'study, plan, and construct the necessary works to obtain integral development and benefits from the basin tributary to the Rivers Grijalva–Usumacinta, within national territory' deserves mention. The Basin itself actually forms part of Guatemala, but the work of the Commission is confined to the Mexican states of Tabasco and Chiapas, where the problems are not so much those of irrigation as of the need for flood-control, market roads, agricultural improvement, and social-welfare activities.

It is hoped that by bringing the vast Basin under control, the 'March to the Sea' will drain off the excess from other overpopulated regions of Mexico. To date the Commission has carried out a series of interlocking minor programmes, which have made more habitable a large tract of the southern Gulf Plain, some 267,000 hectares. Its chief work, however, lies in the future. The Commission has on the drawing boards and in its laboratories plans to construct the Mal Paso Dam. Designed for a 10,000 million cubic metre capacity, when completed it will be the largest in Latin America, and the most ambitious of the Mexican hydraulic projects. In its immediate zone of 1,600 square kilometres (about 700 sq. miles), developments similar to those in the Papaloapán Basin are scheduled. In 1959, however, the basic geological field studies and the analyses of aerial photographs necessary for detailed planning were still under way. With the solid experience of the other Commissions on which to rely, together with the knowledge which the Ministry has accumulated in its other large- and small-scale projects for over a decade, there is every reason to believe that the Grijalva–Usumacinta project will go forward as planned.[1]

---

[1] The preceding account is based primarily on the annual and special reports of the Ministry of Hydraulic Resources (RR.HH). For a similar summary, emphasizing the Grijalva–Usumacinta Project, see Karl Helbig, 'Mexiko: der Süden wird Erschlossen', *Übersee Rundschau* (Hamburg), Oct. 1959, pp. 45–49, with maps and photos. See also below, Appendix III.

THE MEXICAN PEOPLE

Chapter VIII

THE MEXICAN MELTING POT

TAKEN *en masse* the people of Mexico have been far from static. Their numbers, their ways, the places in which they have chosen to group themselves in communities, and the proportion of the several ethnic and cultural stocks within the total population have all undergone change. Just as recent activities have reduced the limitations of the physical setting and have overlaid the historical particularism of Mexico with a national veneer, so the same broad developments have affected its demography.

The principal characteristics of the population of modern Mexico can be rather simply summarized. Mexico now has a fairly large population that had expanded steadily at a fairly slow rate until the Revolution. The recent acceleration of demographic growth, common in the world and especially Latin America during very recent decades, has been little short of spectacular in Mexico. This continuing trend brings in its train undoubted benefits and very grave problems. The growth of total numbers has meant increasing densities, variable for the Republic as a whole, but favoured spots, especially towns and cities, are rapidly becoming overcrowded.

Although the flood tide of urbanization is wiping out many ancient ways and practices, it has little altered an older characteristic of the Mexican population, the dispersion of small clumps of people widely separated from one another. The magnetism that draws ranchers to villages, villagers to towns, and townsmen to cities has converged with other forces to unsettle the complex class, caste, and cultural distinctions inherited from colonial times and modified since. The Indian, as such, tends to be disappearing as an identifiable entity. But as he merges with the other elements of rural Mexico he carries with him many inherited ways, shorn of language and dress. The blurring of lines and the shifting of boundaries between one and another ethnic or cultural group has made nearly insoluble the problem of analysing the main elements of the population's composition.

POPULATION GROWTH

Population statistics are notoriously unreliable, yet those available indicate that over the past 150 years the number of Mexicans has

81

grown steadily. Figures for pre-colonial and early colonial days are highly controversial, but towards the end of the colonial régime the first attempts were made in the direction of a modern census with more rigorous counts and estimates of the number of inhabitants. The tradition of estimates flourished after independence until the first official national census was compiled in 1895,[1] which showed a total population of 12,632,427. The most recent official census figures, those of 1950, showed that the population had doubled, to a total of 25,764,366 inhabitants. Official Mexican agencies estimate relatively accurately the population on 30 June each year; their calculated figures for 1960, which will be checked by the decennial census of that year (still to be fully published), showed 34,841,011 persons. These figures are reproduced, by states, in Appendix Table I.[2]

This sizable population places Mexico demographically at the head of the Spanish-American republics. Moreover, it means that Mexico is developing the mass population base to undertake national and international programmes, which are impossible for some of the smaller Latin American states.

At the close of the colonial period, with vastly more territory, Mexico had only about one-eighth of its present population. During the first three-quarters of the nineteenth century because of civil wars, foreign intervention, political instability, and economic stagnation, the population grew very slowly. Nearly seventy years passed before the initial nucleus of 4·5 million in 1800 doubled to approximately 9 million. Mexico then shared in the general increase of population that characterized the Western world from the end of the nineteenth century to the end of the First World War. However, at that point, when the Mexican Revolution shattered the carefully contrived Porfirio Díaz system, the number of deaths exceeded that of births; the decade 1910–20 is the only one in more than 150 years of demographic history which shows a slight (5 per cent.) dip in the curve of growth (Appendix Table IV).

The restoration of order and the reorganization of political, social, and economic life resulted in a population boom that now threatens to get out of control. By 1940 the population of 1870 had doubled and the rhythm of growth is rapidly diminishing the interval between such doubling and redoubling. The seventy-year

---

[1] 'Antecedentes históricos de los censos Mexicanos', DGE, *Séptimo censo general de población, 6 de junio de 1950; parte especial* (1955), p. 16.

[2] SDE, *Diagnóstico económico regional* (1959), p. 37. Provisional results of the Census taken on 8 June 1960 recorded 34,625,903 Mexicans.

cycle is now more than halved to approximately thirty years, and at present the population increases by about one milion each year.

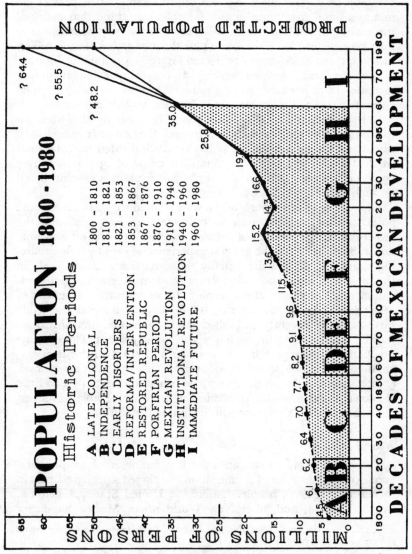

POPULATION 1800 - 1980

Historic Periods

A	LATE COLONIAL	1800 – 1810
B	INDEPENDENCE	1810 – 1821
C	EARLY DISORDERS	1821 – 1853
D	REFORMA/INTERVENTION	1853 – 1867
E	RESTORED REPUBLIC	1867 – 1876
F	PORFIRIAN PERIOD	1876 – 1910
G	MEXICAN REVOLUTION	1910 – 1940
H	INSTITUTIONAL REVOLUTION	1940 – 1960
I	IMMEDIATE FUTURE	1960 – 1980

PROJECTED POPULATION

DECADES OF MEXICAN DEVELOPMENT

MILLIONS OF PERSONS

The accompanying diagram provides a summary view of the development of the population from 1800 to the present.

What of the future? It may be premature to say more than that all students agree that the present rate of increase is likely to continue. A 1954 United Nations study attempted to predict the minimum and maximum figures for 1980, assuming that many of the main population factors will remain relatively constant over the next two decades. Taking as a base the population of 25·6 million in 1950, these investigators projected for 1980 a minimum increase of 189 per cent., to 48·2 million, and a comparable maximum increase of 252 per cent., to 64·4 million. A third, or 'medium' 1980 estimate projected a 217 per cent. increase, to 55·5 million.[1]

Renato Escamilla, in a study made in 1959 by the Mexican Ministry of Economy and the Institute of Economic Investigations, calculated the figures for 1965. His results indicated that the total would then be 39,334,301 persons, an increase of 13·5 million over 1950, i.e. nearly a million a year. Mexican plans are being based on such figures.[2]

Experience in other parts of the world would suggest that at some point in time, difficult now to estimate with any precision, the growth in the population of Mexico will tend to level off and slow down. Such has been the general experience of rapidly industrializing countries, all of which usually show massive increases early in the process of industrialization. Improvement in education, urbanization, and numerous other complex factors neutralize the effects of other programmes that decrease the death- and increase the crude birth-rates. A recently published study concludes that Mexican fertility is already starting to follow the classic pattern. There is now a significant difference between urban and rural birth-rates: 505 children per 1,000 women in towns with a population of over 50,000, compared with 689 per 1,000 in rural localities.[3] Too little is known about probable trends in the future to be able to suggest the figure at which the new equilibrium will stabilize.

Natural Increase

The population increase since the Revolution is a local phenomenon. In the past foreign immigration has played a negligible part in increasing Mexico's people. Unlike the United States, Argentina, Brazil, Canada, and other New World areas, Mexico has never

---

[1] U.N., Dept. de Asuntos Sociales, Div. de Pob., *La Población de la América Central y México en el período de 1950 a 1980* (1954), table 3 (p. 13).

[2] Renato Escamilla Andueza, 'Aspectos humanos', SDE, *Diagnóstico*, pp. 19–47.

[3] Robert G. Burnight and others, 'Differential Rural-Urban Fertility in Mexico', *American Sociological Review*, xxi (1956), 3–8.

attracted significant numbers of foreign immigrants,[1] though small groups which have on occasion appeared, such as the Spanish Republicans welcomed by President Cárdenas after 1936, have made more substantial contributions to Mexican life than their numbers suggest. The largest number of foreign immigrants entered during the colonial period, but at no time since 1900 has the foreign population reached even 1 per cent. of the Mexican total.[2] During the period following the turn of the century numbers of foreign immigrants were higher than at any previous time in Mexico's history: from 1950 through 1958 they averaged about 4,000 a year.

Thus natural increase has been the main cause of population growth. The Mexican birth-rate is at present one of the highest in the world, and seems to be climbing slowly. From the figure of 31·4 births per thousand in 1921, it seems to have stabilized itself around 45·0 per thousand since 1952 (Appendix Table V). But the rise in population is only in part attributable to an increased birth-rate; even more dramatic has been the decrease in the death-rate as programmes of the Revolution bear fruit in social and economic betterment. Sanitary campaigns, better nutrition, improved medical care, public health measures, all have contributed to reducing the crude death-rate. Since 1900 the rate has fallen from 33·6 to approximately 13 per thousand. This is still high, but a marked improvement.

As the result of a rising birth-rate and a falling death-rate, the crude natural increase (the difference between the birth- and death-rates) has multiplied more than tenfold during the present century, from 2·8 per thousand in 1900 to 34·7 in 1956. In its rate of crude natural increase, possibly the single most revealing population index for predicting future needs, Mexico is near the top of the demographic scale. In Latin America only tiny Costa Rica outranks Mexico on this score. During the same years 1946–50 the average rate of increase in Mexico was 27·7 persons per thousand, as compared with 6·3 in England and Wales, 14·3 in the United States, 13·6 in Australia, and 8 in France.

The pressure of this mounting population has put almost intolerable strains on the small and previously casually exploited natural resources of the country and has also dispersed the numerous social and cultural services which Mexicans have come to expect from the Government as tangible evidence that the Revolution is still in

---

[1] R.J.P. van Glinstre-Bleeker, 'Algunos aspectos de la emigración y la inmigración', *Investigación económica*, xiii (1953), 27–40.
[2] José E. Iturriaga, *La Estructura social y cultural de México* (1951), pp. 111–20.

progress. Schools, hospitals, roads, and trains, have all filled more rapidly than ever before. But continued growth, which seems likely to go on, also means expanding markets and sources of labour, which are essential to realize the economic dreams, equally embedded in the dogma of the Revolution. Food supplies, though for long a problem, now seem to be keeping pace and even gaining on the population increase, as will be seen below.[1]

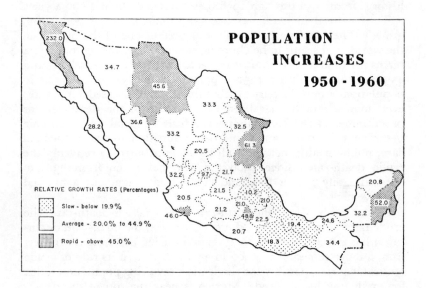

POPULATION INCREASES 1950 - 1960

POPULATION DENSITY AND DISTRIBUTION

A fairly wide variation in population density can be noted from one Mexican state to another. Appendix Table I gives details of 1960 estimates of densities, showing a range from 2·1 for Quintana Roo to the overwhelming 9,012 in the Federal District. These density figures can be roughly grouped into six broad categories from areas very lightly to those very heavily populated. Such a grouping appear in Table 8, and is illustrated by the map on p. 87. As might be expected, the highest densities cluster near the centre of the Republic, in the Core.

[1] pp. 263–4.

TABLE 8

Relative Densities, by States, 1950 and 1960

Relative Density	Persons per square mile	No. of states	
		1950	*1960*
Very light	0·0 – 19·9	10	7
Light	20·0 – 39·9	9	6
Medium (light)	40·0 – 59·9	3	6
Medium (heavy) ...	60·0 – 119·9	5	6
Heavy	120·0 – 199·9	4	3
Very heavy	Over 200	1	4

Source: Appendix Tables I, II.

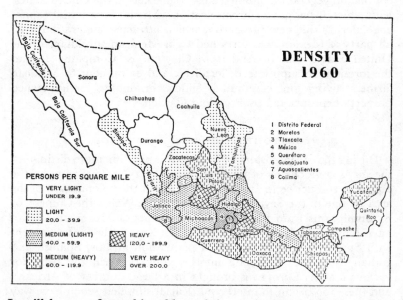

It will be seen from this table and Appendix Table II that in the decade 1950–60 all states increased their densities, some more than others. The table also demonstrates that as the total national population increased from 25·6 million to 34·2 million, the average national density also increased from 34 to 45 persons per square mile; about 864,000 more people per annum were occupying the national territory.

The population expansion of the new state of Lower California has far exceeded the national average. It made a surprising jump of

232 per cent. from 224,000 in 1950 to an estimated total of 745,000 in 1960, and its density rose from 7·7 to 26·8 persons per square mile. In the same period the Federal District also increased its already preponderant population by another 83 per cent., its density rising from 5,240 to 9,012 persons per square mile. Though the percentage increase was great in Quintana Roo—52 per cent.— it ended the decade still with only 2·1 persons to the square mile, the lowest average density in the Republic; with only 27,000 people it is the tiniest of the state and territorial units. This phenomenal population growth in Lower California reflects a boom set off by the irrigation of the triangle of territory formed by Tiajuana, Mexicali, and Ensenada. This created new agricultural land for cotton and vegetables, situated close to markets in the United States, with which it has good communications. Much of the initial capital engendering this new prosperity, which attracted emigration from all parts of Mexico, was furnished by a Mexican subsidiary of the United States firm of Anderson, Clayton, & Company. It had the foresight to supply seed, fertilizer, and equipment to Mexican farmers living on communal ejidos, originally foreign-owned property expropriated by President Cárdenas.[1]

COMPOSITION OF THE POPULATION

During the earlier history of Mexico it is not difficult to distinguish the main components of its population. In 1500, for example, the area was 100 per cent. Indian. Fables about the colonization of the area by one of the Seven Lost Tribes, or the Welsh, the Chinese, or by immigrants from the mythical continents of Mu or of Atlantis have long been discredited. For the first year or less after contact with Spain there were two main population groups, Spanish and Indian, but there was soon interbreeding between the two. For various reasons Europeans brought in a large number of Africans, and these too began to interbreed. Racial simplicity soon gave way to a confused medley. In true Hispanic fashion, the Castilian Crown attempted to codify the racial mixtures, and to assign rights and privileges according to 'purity of blood', calculated to 64 or 128 parts. But those categories underwent modification and simplification as the differences among the inhabitants of New Spain became less important than their broad likenesses. The population of 1810, after three centuries of interbreeding and cultural interchanges— euphemistically known in Spanish as *mestizaje*—has been classified

[1] 'Green Stain of Prosperity', *Time* (6 Jan. 1958), p. 26.

by competent modern researchers into three main racial stocks and three main groups of mestizos or cross-breeds. The result is shown in the following table.

TABLE 9

Composition of the Mexican Population, 1810

Ethno-cultural Groups	Persons ('000)	Per cent.
Europeans (Spanish or Creole)	15·0	0·3
African	10·0	0·2
Indian	3,676·3	60·0
Euro-mestizo	1,092·4	17·9
Afro-mestizo	624·5	10·1
Indo-mestizo	704·2	11·5
NEW SPAIN	6,122·4	100·0

Source: G. Aguirre Beltrán, *La Población negra de México, 1519–1810* (1946), table 21 (p. 236).

This table shows that possibly three-fifths of the population on the eve of independence could be identified as Indian, but of the other two parent stocks—European and African—only trace elements were present in 'pure' form. The remaining 40 per cent. was mestizo, the group nearest approaching Europeans, each constituting about 10 per cent. with less than a million persons in each group. Foreign immigration during the years following the achievement of independence has been negligible. Hence the present composition of the Mexican population is an involved mixture resulting from a century and a half of further inbreeding and cultural transfers almost exclusively among the Indian and mestizo elements already present at the beginning of the nineteenth century. It is thus not surprising that diverse and contradictory findings on the composition of the population have appeared, coloured by political and intellectual preconceptions. The Mexican Census of 1921 was the last to make any attempt towards classifying the inhabitants by 'race'. Subsequent ones disregard this emotionally-loaded category in favour of providing social and economic data from which anyone can attempt to work out his own system.

In the face of the known difficulties, a qualified Mexican scholar, José E. Iturriaga, undertook not long ago an attempt to provide a synthesis of information and opinion about the ethnic or socio-ethnic elements of the modern Mexican population. He analysed the returns from the 1940 national Census to arrive at his findings; no comparable investigation is known to have used the more recent 1950 Census data.[1] Although he does not include them in the following tabular summary, Iturriaga noted that in 1940 there still remained in Mexico a small residual group of Africans and Afro-crosses, which, he suggested, formed as much as 5 per cent. of the total population. It would be practically impossible to attempt to ferret out the lesser strains and breeds in the present population, though a prolonged search would reveal small numbers of Belgians, Germans, French, British, Lebanese, Poles, Canadians, North Americans, a few Japanese and other Orientals, and a number of modern Spaniards, but few Portuguese. In the following table a brief explanatory note on the characteristics of the five groups into which Iturriaga classes the Mexican population has been added.

TABLE 10

Ethno-Cultural Composition of Population, 1940

('000 persons)

Group	Characteristics	Persons	Percentage
Indians	Predominantly native	1,486·7	7·6
Mestindios	Native-Europeanized	1,485·4	7·4
Mestizos	Europeanized-Native	7,269·0	37·0
Creole	Mestizo-Europeanized	9,263·2	47·1
White	Europeanized ...	176·4	0·9
Total	... ...	19,653·7	100·0

Source: Iturriaga, *Estructura social,* p. 96.

Though numerically relatively insignificant, the Indian is a very special case. His presence has generated a vast body of polemical and impassioned writing since he came within the European purview in the sixteenth century. These continue unabated.[2] In deference to his historical importance and because of his emotional and symbolic significance, the following chapter is devoted to the Mexican Indian of today.

[1] Iturriaga, *Estructura social,* pp. 90–110. For other analyses of the 1940 population see Nathan L. Whetten, *Rural Mexico* (1948), Ch. 3, and Cline, *U.S. and Mexico,* pp. 74–87.

[2] Luis Villoro, *Los Grandes momentos del indigenismo en México* (1950), traces various attitudes toward Indians, citing an impressive body of literature; there is much more.

Chapter IX

THE ELUSIVE INDIAN

THE Indian still exists in present-day Mexico but is growing progressively more difficult to find. From the scientist's point of view the native population has become more and more indistinguishable from the great mass of rural Mexicans to whom his forefathers bequeathed so many every-day habits and even physical features.

With the gradual disappearance of typical native dress and customs under the constant Western impact of more than four centuries, and with the reduction—both absolute and relative—of persons who speak Indian tongues, the distinction between the Indian and the semi-modern Mexican villager is not obvious. The definition of 'Indian' depends on the immediate purpose of the inquiry.

What may appear to be native to the newly arrived tourist in a provincial market may be very 'modernized' to the trained anthropological eye and very Mexican to the national census enumerator. Thus as a point of departure, it must be emphatically stated that at present there exist no 'pure' Indians untouched by civilization comparable in every respect with those first met by Europeans in the sixteenth century. Even at the time of the Conquest, the native Mexican societies were not homogeneous in race, culture, or language, and whatever 'purity' of stock may have existed 400 years ago has long since disappeared, blending with other elements to form the present-day Mexican. Tradition and culture tend in these instances to be the distinguishing marks, not blood and race.

Yet because from the Conquest onwards the Indian has always been a major factor in the evolution of society, Mexico shares with Bolivia, Peru, Ecuador, Paraguay, and Guatemala the reputation of being an 'Indian' area within the Latin American family. This is in contrast to countries such as Argentina, Uruguay, and Costa Rica where native groups have never existed in significant numbers, nor have they had sophisticated pre-Columbian cultures comparable to that of Mexico. (See Appendix Table VI.)

This Indian 'presence' in Mexico has, without question, left a deep if indefinable impress. From the outset the European settlers attempted to absorb or assimilate the Mexican Indian within a single system developed along European lines. While never fully successful, the result has been that during much of its history since 1519 Mexico has been divided between the Indian and European worlds; at the present time nearly all observers agree that only a very small, scattered remnant of the population can be regarded as true 'Indians'.

THE INDIAN-EUROPEAN CONTINUUM

In general, most observers would agree that at present there is a continuum or spectrum of individuals and communities which share a great number of ways and practices which are believed to be peculiar and derived from indigenous backgrounds. At one end of such a spectrum, for instance, are small groups like the Lacandón Indians in Chiapas, who would clearly qualify as Indian. Though familiar with guns and axes, even with aspirin, they also retain many old Maya traits such as language, ritual, polygamy, a pantheon of pagan deities, bows and arrows for hunting, clothing from bark, &c. Less distinctively 'Indian' are several other groups of native peoples, often nominally Christian, clustered in hamlets throughout the states of Oaxaca and southern Veracruz and in small areas of north-western Mexico. Of these perhaps the most famous are the Yaqui, mentioned in connexion with the special irrigation Commission. Opinions will differ as to the classification of other groups or individuals as 'Indian'; not all cases are clear.

For instance, the Zapotec Indians in the sizable Oaxacan town of Yalalag are certainly Indian in many respects. In their community they habitually use a native idiom even though most of them can also speak Spanish, and their women wear the local native costume even when visiting the cities. Yet these same villagers have successfully entered the competitive system of the Western world as expert traders and businessmen. Many have invested their capital in urban real estate in the state capital of Oaxaca, and draw large rents from Mexican tenants. There are many such 'mixed' examples throughout Mexico.

Political and intellectual prejudices also help to determine at what point the line between Indians and non-Indians is drawn. For example, there are often wide discrepancies within short intervals of time in the national census estimates and figures. It seems clear that the criteria used by different officials and under different régimes are responsible even more than truly demographic factors for the variable proportions ascribed to 'Indian' in the national population. Table 11 tabulates these percentages.

The Elusive Indian

TABLE II

Indians in Mexico, 1900–50
(millions over 5 years of age)

		Indians			Total population	
		millions	Per cent.	Index	millions	Index
1900	...	1·79	15·37	100	11·67	100
1910	...	1·69	12·98	94	12·98	111
1921	...	1·87	15·11	104	12·37	106
1930	...	2·25	16·05	125	14·02	120
1940	...	2·49	14·85	139	16·77	144
1950	...	2·49	11·21	132	21·81	182

Source: Manuel Germán Parra, ed., Densidad de la población (1950), p. 18 (1900–40); Anselmo Marino Flores, 'Indígenas de México', América indígena, xvi (1956), 41–48.

PERSISTENCE OF ANCIENT HABITS AND TONGUES

Amid the confusion about the definitions of the Indian, there is one small area of agreement. Whatever other traits they may add, investigators generally agree that those people speaking only an Indian dialect are most probably firmly rooted in a native context. As Indian monolinguals they are excluded from the Spanish-speaking world. Language is almost as certain a diagnostic in a parallel group, who retain Indian speech but who also speak Spanish, and are thus classed as bilingual.

These linguistic traits are used in the national decennial census publications as nearly the sole criteria of 'race'. Incomplete from many points of view, they still provide some idea of the persistence of Indian speech, and by implication, of other native habits. Such information from the Census of 1940 has been reviewed by Dr. Juan Comas; a comparable summary of 1950 materials has been provided by another Mexican student, Anselmo Marino Flores.[1] Here some of their principal findings may be noted. Taking into account only those over the age of 5, census officials in both instances distinguished between monolinguals and bilinguals. Their proportion must consequently be measured against the total Mexican population above that age. In 1940 those speaking Indian languages numbered

[1] Juan Comas, 'Indígenas de México', Revista población, i (1953), 36–44. Detailed coverage for 1940 in Inst. Nacional Indigenista, Densidad de la población de habla indígena en la República Mexicana (1950). Marino Flores, 'Indígenas de México', América indígena, xvi (1956), 41–48; see also his Bibliografía lingüística de la República Mexicana (1957), with useful maps.

2·5 million, almost equally divided between monolinguals (1·257 million) and bilinguals (1·253 million); together they accounted for 14·9 per cent. of the total population over 5 years of age. In 1950 those speaking native languages still amounted to 2·5 million, but, in a total population of 21·8 million over 5 years of age, the percentage had dropped to 11·2.

In the decade there had, in fact, been a decrease of 43,000 in the number of people speaking a native language. Possibly more significant was the sharp reduction in the monolingual group to 795,000, with a corresponding rise in bilinguals to 1·652 million. If we compare the change in percentage terms, from 1940 through 1950 monolingualism dropped by over a third (36·8 per cent.) as more people learned to speak Spanish; conversely the bilingual group increased by about 400,000, or 31·8 per cent. The most important conclusions, however, are that in 1950 less than 4 per cent. (3·64 per cent.) of Mexicans over 5 years of age could speak no Spanish. Another 7 per cent. could communicate in that language but still clung to their native tongues.

For the moment, let us glance at the native dialects that have shown such staying power that nearly a million people are still using them exclusively. Represented in this group, as might be expected, are languages spoken by the major pre-Conquest culture groups and those which have survived from minor cultures in border settlements where contacts have been less frequent and powerful. Table 12 summarizes information presented in more detail in Appendix Table VII. It shows that the language of the Aztecs, Nahuatl, predominates among present-day monolingual Indians, with 212,000 people, nearly 27 per cent. of the monolingual group, speaking it; together with other highly developed languages spoken by smaller groups who shared control of Central Mexico with the Aztecs, it accounts for 45 per cent. of the existing native monolingualism.

Of the major pre-Conquest civilizations of southern Mexico, the Mixteco-Zapateco and the Mayance families together account for more than a third of the current monolinguals, with 17 and 18·5 per cent. respectively. If we add Nahuatl and the languages of other high cultures of Central Mexico to these two groups, we note that the 'empires' of 1500 still exist linguistically at the present day, with 643,000 Indians still using these imperial tongues, despite nearly five centuries of outside influence. The remaining 150,000 or so monolinguals are divided among more than sixteen small groups, of which perhaps only the Tarascans had any historical significance in native development. As Table 12 shows, more than 95 per cent. of the present monolingualism is centred in the key areas of Central and South Mexico, which in this respect have never been completely conquered.

TABLE 12

Indian Languages of Mexico, 1950: Summary

Aboriginal Area	Monolinguals over 5 years ('000)	Per cent. total monolinguals, 1950
Central	358·3	45·2
Southern	401·5	50·4
Western...	11·0	1·3
Northern	12·6	1·6
Other	11·7	1·5
TOTALS	795·1	100·0

Source: Appendix Table VII.

INDIAN MEXICO

Still using the 1950 Census data on linguistic habits, we can judge which units of modern Mexico seem more or less 'Indian'. There are two main approaches, both of which are useful. One is to concentrate on the distribution of persons speaking native tongues, whether monolinguals or bilinguals, ignoring the Spanish-speaking monolingual group as if it did not exist. This shows where the main concentrations of Indians appeared in 1950. A related, but distinct, picture is obtained by noting those states where Indians form a discernible portion of the total population. This provides some evidence as to how 'Indianized' that unit is. Results tend to be slightly different, but reinforce one another to the point where it is possible to identify and even to map Indian Mexico.

Appendix Table VIII provides the basis for such generalizations. It groups together both monolinguals and bilinguals speaking Indian languages in states where together they compose 0·1 per cent. of the total native population over 5 years old. The first thing which becomes obvious is that the present native population is centred in a few states of southern Mexico. Oaxaca, Puebla, Yucatán, and Veracruz form a nearly unbroken block in which are located 58 per

95

cent., nearly three-fifths, of those retaining native speech habits. If to these we add four more states, Chiapas, México, Hidalgo, and Guerrero, which individually have between 5 and 10 per cent. of the total native population, these eight states concentrate 86 per cent. of the natives, as is shown in Table 13. This reflects the first approach, i.e. to note distribution of native population without regard to other elements.

Table 14 below indicates the proportion of natives in the total population of any one state. It shows, for instance, that although Quintana Roo and Campeche in themselves do not have great numbers of natives, Indians form a relatively high proportion of their populations. Conversely, Puebla and Veracruz contain several thousand natives; yet in relation to the millions of non-natives, the Indians are outnumbered five or six to one. Another extreme can be found in Yucatán, where Indians outstrip the rest of the population of that state by three to two.

TABLE 13

Principal Concentrations of Natives, 1950

('000 persons)

State	Native monolinguals and bilinguals over 5 years old	Per cent. of total native population
Oaxaca	583·8	23·7
Puebla	297·5	12·1
Yucatán	279·4	11·9
Veracruz	252·7	10·3
Chiapas...	198·0	8·1
México	183·0	7·5
Hidalgo...	179·6	7·3
Guerrero	124·7	5·1
Sub-total	2,098·7	86·0
Others	348·9	14·0
TOTALS	2,447·6	100·0

Source: Appendix Table VIII.

TABLE 14

States with Highest Proportions of Natives, 1950

('000 persons over 5 years old)

State	Native speakers	Per cent. total native population	Per cent. native of state population
Yucatán	279·4	11·9	63·8
Oaxaca	583·8	23·7	48·0
Quintana Roo ...	9·6	0·4	43·7
Campeche	32·9	1·3	31·8
Chiapas	198·0	8·1	26·2
Hidalgo	179·6	7·3	25·2
Puebla	297·5	12·1	21·6
Guerrero	124·7	5·1	16·0
México	183·0	7·5	15·6
Veracruz	252·7	10·3	14·7

Source: Appendix Table VIII.

These two tables, approaching Indian Mexico from different directions, show an overlap which can be used to form one single

INDIANS 1950

HEAVILY INDIAN
INDIAN
MODERATELY INDIAN
LIGHTLY INDIAN
TRACES

presentation of 'Indian Mexico', showing the distribution of the native population as a whole, and the proportion of natives in any state. For this purpose eight units—seven states and a territory—

with negligible numbers of Indians can be disregarded.[1] The remaining twenty-four state units fall into five groupings of relative 'Indianism', which are summarized in the following table.

TABLE 15

Indian Mexico, 1950

Degree	Criteria	States
HEAVILY INDIAN ...	Over 10 per cent. total native population and Natives over 20 per cent. population	Oaxaca; Yucatán
INDIAN	Over 5 per cent. total native population and Natives over 15 per cent. state population	Chiapas; Hidalgo; Puebla
MODERATELY INDIAN	Over 1 per cent. total native population and Natives over 15 per cent. state population	Campeche; Guerrero; México
LIGHTLY INDIAN ...	Over 0·3 per cent. total native population and Natives over 10 per cent. state population	Veracruz; Quintana Roo
TRACES	Less than 1·0 per cent. total native population or Natives less than 9·9 per cent. of state population	San Luis Potosí; Michoacán; Sonora; Tabasco; Chihuahua; Tlaxcala; D.F.; Querétaro; Morelos; Sinaloa; Jalisco; Guanajuato; Nayarit; Durango

Source: Appendix Table VIII.

THE INDIAN AND SOCIETY

Nearly all students feel that linguistic criteria alone do not suffice to reveal the continuing influence of native ways in modern Mexico. They rightly point out that there is often only a slight sociological difference between communities which have only recently emerged from ancient ways of life and those which still

[1] Aguascalientes; Coahuila; Lower California; Territory of Lower California, South; Nuevo León; Tamaulipas; Zacatecas.

retain aboriginal speech. Two interesting recent attempts to provide insights and techniques for studying these complicated problems are worth brief mention.

Professor Eric R. Wolf has emphasized the difficulties of arriving at an adequate and acceptable definition of 'Indian' in Mexico.[1] He approaches the problem from the standpoint of the prevailing aims and objectives of a community at any given time, and recalls that Indian communities have always been the satellites of larger groupings in the framework of Mexican society (a matter which will be explored in the following chapter), and therefore tend to reflect, even if with less intensity, the dynamic changes in Mexican society as a whole. He argues, therefore, that during times of prosperity and general economic advance, these satellite communities tend to lose their 'Indianhood'. Positions of power and prestige, both in the local communities and in the slightly larger ones to which they act as satellites, are occupied by the more 'modern' or Westernized leaders. In times of rapid change, such as the present phase in Mexico, he argues that there is a catastrophic collapse of traditional ways as current economic aims emphasizing prestige displace the more hallowed native values. As the old emotional loyalties dwindle, those more interested in economic and social benefits either leave, or change the way of life of the community. This 'de-Indianization' process is held in abeyance and even reversed when national and international processes of change slow down. 'When the economy is depressed', Professor Wolf states, 'and political power fragmented, the middlemen lose face and position, and the relay station is again "Indianized"—that is, the provincial centres begin to rely more firmly on the agricultural and craft production of their satellite Indian communities.' This has not happened since 1940.

Another experienced observer of Mexican society, especially its native components, Professor Oscar Lewis, has developed a view that partially escapes the difficult task of definitions. After reassessing the Nahuatl-speaking community of Tepoztlán, he worked with some of its villagers who had migrated to cities, especially to the Metropolis. After working in India as well, where peasant communities act in many matters like those of Meso-America, Professor Lewis has come to the conclusion that there are more important factors than ethnic characteristics to be taken into consideration in an analysis of

[1] Eric R. Wolf, 'The Indian in Mexican Society', *Alpha Kappa Delta*, xxx (Winter 1960), 3–6.

emerging nations such as Mexico.[1] He regards poverty as far more significant than 'Indianhood', and finds remarkable similarities in what he terms 'the culture of poverty' not only between rural and urban Mexican families, but between comparable groups elsewhere in the world. He stresses the fact that Indian villages cannot be investigated apart from national culture, or even city dwellers as isolated case studies. His Foreword to a recent book states that in the face of the great current problems it seems imperative that social scientists should redirect their attention to how the universal poor really live, what they do and think, whether in isolated clusters on a Mexican mountainside or as part of a city slum.[2]

Thus in recent Mexican history the Indian has been variously defined in census statistics, but there has been general agreement that the retention of Indian languages is a reliable criterion; during boom times the Indian has been a marginal participant in national culture. Modern students tend to view him more as a part of the poorer rural group than as a separate group or ward, his position during colonial times.

Possibly in the last analysis the answer to 'Who is an Indian?' in contemporary Mexico depends on the viewpoint of the observer. Both the observer and the observed must agree that the latter is a native. Neither questions that he is a Mexican.

---

[1] Oscar Lewis, *Life in a Mexican Village* (1951); *Village Life in Northern India* (1958); 'Peasant Culture in India and Mexico', in McKim Marriott, *Village India*, (1955), pp. 145–70; 'Urbanization without Breakdown', *Scientific Monthly*, lxxv (July 1952), 31–41; 'The Culture of the *Vecinidad* in Mexico City: Two Case Studies' (mimeo., 1958).

[2] *Five Families: Mexican Case Studies in the Culture of Poverty* (1959), p. 2.

Chapter X

TWO MEXICOS: THE
PARADOXICAL URBAN REVOLUTION

THE drift citywards, which is taking place with increasing momentum in Mexico, is helping to reshape the nation. As Mexico thus grows in complexity, ties which traditionally bound families to places of origin have been loosened. The physical movement of people tips many balances in new directions, with resultant shifts in relations between urban-rural segments of society, between local centres of power and their hinterlands, and among regions. Such movement is a silent element that creates a basic revolution in Mexican ways.

PARADOX: CONCENTRATION AND DISPERSION

The speed of urbanization in recent times is shown by the obvious overcrowding of large Mexican cities, the swelling of smaller towns, and the increase in size even of hamlets. The superficial observer might be inclined to believe or even hope that Mexico is on the verge of becoming a highly urbanized nation, forsaking its immemorial traditions of small dispersed settlements. On the contrary, statistics indicate that the ancient patterns are only slowly giving way. For some time to come, the nation will retain this basic pattern of scattered, often isolated small communities.

With increasing urbanization comes modernization and Westernization. The unifying and integrating effects of communications, education, political mechanisms, and other programmes attempting to make one nation from the regions and smaller units are touching the lives of an increasing number of Mexicans. Nevertheless, the great mass of the population still resides in 'rural' places of less than 2,500 persons, the figure Mexicans use as the dividing line between 'urban' and 'rural'. In 1958 (the most recent detailed figures), of the total estimated Mexican population of 32·3 million, more than half, some 17·9 million (55·4 per cent.) were by these standards 'rural'.[1] Thus, paradoxically, while urbanization is unquestionably accelerated, the old patterns seem to remain much the same. A little patient attention and analysis of the elements involved may

[1] SDE, *Compendio estadístico, 1958*, table 20, p. 48.

resolve this paradox and at the same time reveal the structure and relationships among the various types of Mexican communities. For descriptive and statistical purposes, Mexican law recognizes about 100 different terms for populated localities. Each community falls into one of these traditional 'political categories' (*categorías políticas*). Stemming from earlier history, especially from the Spanish codes, each type once had a fixed function, size, and character, but the passage of time has blurred these minute differences and convenience has now reduced the major classes of legally defined communities to about nine. Nathan L. Whetten in 1940 provided detailed descriptions of them, together with their average populations; in the following table the number of places in the same categories in 1950 are listed, relying on his earlier figures for illustrative purposes.[1]

TABLE 16

Populated Localities, by Political Categories, 1940–50

Approximate equivalent	Category	Average no. of inhabitants 1940	Localities 1950
City	Ciudad ...	16,614	323
Small city	Villa	2,389	525
Town, village... ...	Pueblo ...	861	5,010
Cluster	Congregación	296	4,612
Hacienda	Hacienda ...	160	4,805
Rural commune ...	Ejido	219	5,582
Hamlet	Rancho ...	45	57,689
Hamlet	Ranchería ...	131	13,412
RR Station	Estación FF.CC.		561
Others	Otras ...	180	6,509

Sources Average, 1940: Whetten, *Rural Mexico*, table 7; 1950 localities: DGE, *Compendio estadístico, 1958*, table 5, pp. 13–15.

Even for these nine categories, there is now no generally specified size or clear modern definition. Cities and *villas* always tend to be larger, more important places. All the others are small, quasi- or completely rural communities. So wide is the range of population within and between most of these categories that any workable interpretation can only be based on the number of inhabitants. To a great extent, the function of a community is now directly dependent on the size of its population. Table 17 uses data from the 1950 Census which have been regrouped into units and general categories

[1] Whetten, *Rural Mexico*, pp. 40–46.

provided here by the author. These are the main components in the complicated pattern of Mexican settlements, which we shall try to summarize.

TABLE 17

Localities, by No. of Inhabitants, 1950

Class/Category	Size	No. of Localities	Total population ('000)	Average no. of inhabitants per locality
Metropolis... ...	Over 1,000,000 ...	1	2,234·7	2,234,700
Large cities ...	Over 100,000 ...	9	1,665·8	185,000
Cities	20,000 – 99,999...	57	2,304·7	40,000
URBANIZED ...	Over 20,000	67	6,205·2	92,500
Towns	2,500 – 19,999 ...	916	4,805·2	5,240
SEMI-URBAN ...	Over 2,500	916	4,805·2	5,240
Hamlets	500 – 2,499 ...	7,538	7,265·0	966
Clusters	100 – 499 ...	24,979	5,753·0	230
Isolates	1 – 99	65,090	1,772·2	27
RURAL	Under 2,499 ...	97,607	14,790·2	151
UNKNOWN ...		438		
REPUBLIC ...		99,028	25,791·0	260

This table reveals a number of significant matters. The first and most obvious is that talk of urbanization and its problems focuses on less than 1,000 of the 99,028 localities. Most Mexican communities consist of less than 500 families, or under 2,500 persons. Together the localities form a single system, a hierarchy.

THE URBAN COMPLEX

Metropolis: Mexico City

Table 18 provides the bare facts of the expansion of Mexico City over the past two decades. In 1940, at the end of the Cárdenas régime, the population was large, nearly 1·5 million, but since then it has trebled to an estimated 4·5 million, and Mexico City is now one of the world's largest national capitals and cities. It is outranked only by Tokyo (8·8 million), London (8·3 million), New York

(7·8 million), Shanghai (6·2 million), and Moscow (4·8 million). After New York it thus is the second largest metropolitan area in

CITIES
Over 25,000
1950

• OVER 25,000
◎ OVER 100,000

the New World, followed by Buenos Aires, Chicago, São Paulo, and Rio de Janeiro, in that order. All of these outstrip Paris.

TABLE 18

Growth of Mexico City, 1940–59

	1940	1950	1959 (est.)	Increases 1959 over 1940
Population ('000)	1;448·4	2,234·8	4,500·0	3,051·6
Increase (decade):				
('000)	——	786·4	2,265·2	
Per cent.	——	53·3	102·0	210·5
Per cent. of national population... ...	7·3	8·6	13·1	79·5

Source: Appendix Table I.

Two Mexicos: The Paradoxical Urban Revolution

As Mexico has grown, Mexico City has absorbed more than its share of the total national population, and dominance over the press, communications, government, industry, and most other phases of modern life seems overwhelming. This situation is underlined by the fact that in 1959 the combined population of all other Mexican cities over 100,000 inhabitants (2·8 million) barely exceeded half that of the capital.

The table shows that by 1959 some 3 million persons had been added to the population of 1·5 million in Mexico City in 1940. This influx has increased the concentration of political power and of a readily available mass market there.

The migrants as a group place enormous strains on the wisdom and resources of officials responsible for the District. Mexican economists have summarized some of the main problems: for instance, newcomers demand increased public services but pay few taxes. In general they are unskilled, low-paid labourers who have difficulty in finding steady employment. Commerce and industry, already saturated with this class of labour, cannot absorb the continuing stream; a great deal of 'hidden unemployment' thus results among this migrant group, many of whom are forced to work only part time at marginal tasks. Rising prices have multiplied their hardships. The almost intolerable burden they have placed on local food supplies has raised the cost of living in the Metropolis well above the national average. Insistent calls for housing, both by newcomers and those benefiting from the general prosperity of the city, have stimulated speculation in urban real estate, diverting much capital from more productive enterprises; high land prices have in turn aggravated acute housing problems for unskilled labour, thus generating political unrest.[1]

To recapitulate, Mexico City can be said to be the chief nerve centre of the nation. Lines of communication connect it with the main regional capitals—Monterrey (North), Guadalajara (West), Puebla (Core), and Oaxaca–Mérida (South)—as well as with the national port, Veracruz. From Mexico change moves outward. It is the main settlement, to which all others in the country are in varying degrees subordinate. Unlike Brazil, where such metropolitan hegemony is divided between Rio and São Paulo, and now Brasilia, in Mexico there is no real rival to the one metropolis.

[1] 'Population Growth in the Federal District', Banco de México, *Review of the Economic Situation in Mexico*, xxxii (Feb. 1956), 14–15.

Mexico, 1940–1960

Large Cities: Over 100,000 Inhabitants

In 1940, apart from the national capital, only three cities, Guadalajara, Monterrey, and Puebla, all regional capitals, had a population of 100,000. In the decade up to 1950, another six cities reached this figure, and estimates indicate that in the past ten years still another seven have been added, making a total of 16 in 1959. Appendix Table IX, summarized in the following table, lists the population increases in these cities.

TABLE 19

Growth of Cities of Over 100,000 Inhabitants, 1940–59
(Excluding Mexico City)

	1940	1950	1959 (est.)	Increases 1940–59
No. of cities	3	9	16	
Population (collective)				
'ooo	553·8	1,666·8	2,785·8	2,232·0
Per cent. of national	3·8	6·5	8·3	
Increases:				
'ooo	——	1,113·0	1,019·0	2,232·0
Per cent.	——	205·0	61·0	400·0

Source: Appendix Table IX.

This table shows some interesting trends. First is the increase of more than 2 million town dwellers in twenty years, but the table also suggests that the largest places have begun to mature; in 1950 all the cities except Ciudad Juárez fell below the national growth rate from 1950–9, and without exception they developed at a markedly slower tempo than in the decade 1940–50. The number of places on the northern boundary which showed rapid expansion, sharing the same trends as the United States on the other side of the border, is also notable. For this available markets and opportunities have ultimately been responsible, but it will also be recalled that Mexicali and Matamoros, as well as Culiacán, are at the confluence of Mexican government efforts in the fields of irrigation and communications. If the population estimates for 1959 have any validity, the fastest growing places at this time seem to have been relatively small in 1950. Rapidly developing into sub-regional foci, they contrast sharply with major regional capitals, which have shown the least growth during the past ten years.

These sixteen largest cities, with Mexico City at the head, form the skeleton of the Mexican nation, as the map on p. 61 suggests. Highly articulated communications networks, fanning out to the local sub-regions and to international centres, bind them together and link them to the world. Most of these larger cities are also state capitals, and they dominate their states just as Mexico City dominates the whole Republic. This subject has been studied with interesting conclusions by a Mexican economist.[1]

Cities: Over 20,000 Inhabitants

There are no 1959 estimates for the size of cities between 20,000 and 100,000 inhabitants and we must rely on the 1950 data in Table 17. Undoubtedly they too have increased in number and combined population. In general they also lie on main communications routes, are state capitals, mining or petroleum centres, and markets for small satellite areas, just as they themselves are satellites of one or more larger cities and the national capital. Like those of the larger cities, their populations are primarily non-agricultural and specialize in mainly urban occupations, but in most cases they are in considerably closer touch with their rural, chiefly agricultural, hinterlands than are the larger places.

The national capital, the large cities, and those of between 20,000 and 100,000 inhabitants together comprise a rather large proportion of 'modernized' Mexico. In 1950 it formed about one-quarter of the total population; in 1960 it is probably nearer one-third. Living in these cities are at least 10 million, possibly 12 million Mexicans, who by nearly any measure would be classed as urban. This is perhaps three times as many as in 1940. In the past two decades Mexico has become quite different in urban-rural composition, an important reason why government policies, politics, and many other matters have changed in emphasis. But there are still other marginal components of the urban complex, less central but none the less integral. These are the towns and *municipios*.

Towns and Municipios

Not as sophisticated as the inhabitants of the Metropolis, but less rustic than hamlet dwellers, are townsmen. They enjoy most of the

[1] Emilio Rodríguez Mata, 'Evolución de la población de México y de algunas entidades típicas', *Investigación económica*, xiv (1954), 385–96, analysing six states: industrial, Nuevo León, Puebla; mining, Chihuahua, Durango; agricultural, Sinaloa, Michoacán.

advantages (and disadvantages) of city living, but at a slower tempo than in the more complex centres. Many towns still retain the colonial pattern of organization, grids of narrow streets radiating from a central plaza, around which are grouped the public municipal buildings, the principal church, and the main shops. Many of the outlying streets are unpaved, and few are lit after dark. Table 17 shows that in 1950 there were nearly 5 million townsmen, in communities averaging about 1,000 families each, although the range was upward from 500 to 4,000. In large measure these towns are dependent for leadership, both commercial and political, on the cities to which they are connected by local communication networks of varying degrees of development, but in turn each town is generally the central community of a unit like a county or shire, the *municipio*.

Although it does not appear as such in Table 17, the *municipio* tends to be the smallest political unit of any significance. Within its bounds may be settlements of various sizes. In each instance, its principal city, town, or village acts as its head, its *cabecera*, with lesser dependent settlements under its jurisdiction. On 1 January 1959 there was a total of 2,352 *municipios*; a parallel arrangement (in which the unit is called a 'delegation') added twenty-four more— the Federal District (13), Lower California (7), and Quintana Roo (4)—bringing the total to 2,376. Each of the cities, together with each of the towns of 2,500 or over shown in Table 17, is generally the main community and *cabecera* of a *municipio*, which would account for 983 of them. The remaining 1,393 have as their *cabeceras* the largest villages and hamlets shown among the 7,538 in the same table.

THE RURAL COMPLEX: VILLAGES AND HAMLETS

The rural localities consist of villages and hamlets, each having less than 500 familes. Often their direct route to the nearest town is hardly more than a rutted path, suitable only for carts and donkeys. The largest of these small centres normally contains a church and a school, often a plaza and a group of municipal buildings. As a group they have drawn much attention from anthropologists, and there are a number of detailed studies of life in these small villages and their tiny dependencies.[1] As a whole these are the places in which the elusive Indian is to be found. Though usually remote, the hamlets have some ties with the nation via the towns and cities on

[1] Cline, 'Mexican Community Studies', *HAHR*, xxxii (May 1952), 212–42, discusses many in detail, with bibliography.

which as satellites they depend. Table 17 indicates that in 1950 the single largest body of Mexicans, a little over 7 million, were villagers.

Finally we come to the little dots which pepper Mexican mountain sides and valleys, places with less than 100 families. Depending on the region, they are usually known as *ranchos* or *rancherías*. They are as characteristic of rural Mexico as are the haciendas, to which

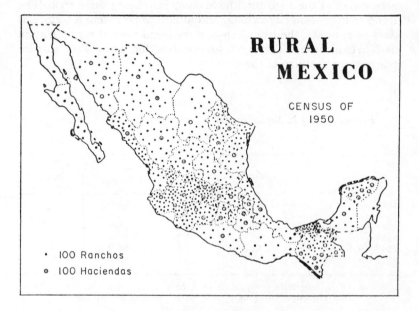

RURAL
MEXICO

CENSUS OF
1950

· 100 Ranchos
⊚ 100 Haciendas

they are sometimes attached. Normally, however, these clusters, and their even smaller counterparts having less than 100 inhabitants, have relatively weak ties with larger, more organized communities. The largest may have a chapel, visited on occasion by a priest, but stores, municipal buildings, and other signs of connexion with the nation generally are lacking. Where they are predominantly Indian in background, as is often the case, native ways in speech, dress, government, techniques, and possessions are the rule.

One principal characteristic is the inaccessibility of these settlements. They represent localities which either never were fully connected with the major currents of post-Conquest Mexico, or which were formed more recently by persons wishing to migrate for one or another reason. It is surprising to find that many of them are the creation of the Revolution.

Recent Dispersion

The number of people living in these tiny clusters and isolated groups has increased since 1900, the percentage of increase varying decade by decade. In other words, though the dispersal pattern of rural Mexico, characterized by small hamlets and clusters, is ancient, not all such present places date from aboriginal times. In fact, almost half of the 1950 total have come into being since 1900. The trend to dispersion has as long, and almost as persistent a history as does its opposite, the twentieth-century trend toward concentration and urbanization. Table 20 summarizes the growth of smaller places since the turn of the century.

TABLE 20

Persons Living in Settlements of under 500 Inhabitants, 1900–50

('000)

	Under 100	*101–500*	Total (*places*)	
			Per cent.	*Increase over 1900*
1900	31·6	17·0	48·6	
1910	45·3	19·4	64·7	32·2
1921	39·0	17·3	56·3	15·8
1930	48·1	18·5	66·6	37·0
1940	75·7	22·9	98·6	103·0
1950	57·4	24·8	82·2	69·0

Source: DGE, *Integración territorial de los Estados Unidos Mexicanos* (1952), p. 8; data regrouped and tabulated, with percentages, by author.

This table reveals a slight movement away from dispersion between 1940 and 1950. In 1940 there were 98,567 small places with under 500 inhabitants while in 1950 the Census recorded 82,237. There was also some fall in the total number of persons dwelling in these remote localities. Whether such drift to larger units is a temporary or a continuing tendency cannot be predicted. The Census of 1960 recorded 137,153 places, but details are lacking.

TWO MEXICOS: MODERN AND REMOTE

Mexican planners are thus really faced with two 'Mexicos'. The dichotomy shows clearly in Table 21, a summary of the discussion. The modern sector, which in 1950 constituted about 70 per cent. of

TABLE 21

Functional Structure of Localities, 1950

Class/Category	Localities		Population		Average no. inhabitants
	No.	*Per cent.*	*Millions*	*Per cent.*	
I. MODERN MEXICO					
Metropolis	1	–	2·2	8·5	2,000,000
Large cities	9	–	1·7	6·6	185,000
Cities	57	–	2·3	8·9	40,000
Towns	916	0·8	4·8	18·6	5,200
URBAN/SEMI-URBAN	983	0·9	11·0	42·6	11,000
Rural: hamlets... ...	7,538	7·6	7·3	28·4	966
'NATIONALIZED' ...	8,521	8·5	18·3	71·0	2,140
II. REMOTE MEXICO					
Clusters	24,979	25·8	5·8	22·5	230
Isolates	65,090	65·7	1·8	6·5	27
MARGINAL NATIONAL ...	90,069	91·5	7·6	29·0	85
UNKNOWN	438				
III. TOTALS					
REPUBLIC	99,028	100·0	25·7	100·0	260

the population, living in some 8,500 localities, extends fairly uniformly to the village or hamlet level, though it deteriorates as it spreads among the smaller communities with poorer communications. This sector includes the city dwellers, townsmen, and rural villagers within national communications and educational networks, and is the national market and the politically conscious part of the Republic. It operates within a money economy, and has at least a nominal voice in political party councils. It is, generally speaking, the dynamic group within the nation, to which 'Remote Mexico' also politically pertains, whether those who form it are always conscious of the fact or not.

'Remote Mexico' has a total population of about 8 million, scattered all over the country in little collections of huts, 'juntos pero no revueltos'—locally rendered 'near but not too scrambled'. Their 90,000 settlements make up about 90 per cent. of the total number of localities in Mexico, each with an average number of about 260 inhabitants. Without 'Remote Mexico' the average number of inhabitants in each locality would be about ten times higher. Their very remoteness places these settlements at the very edge of the national economy and its political and social life, or even outside it. With few exceptions theirs is a subsistence economy, based on simple barter or the remnants of ancient inter-community marketing traditions. Politically the group tends to be passive, if at all conscious. They thus fall outside the calculations of the national market and figure at best as minor symbols in political equations.

The paradox of rapid urbanization but at the same time the persistence of old patterns can now be re-examined. Urbanization is indeed proceeding rapidly in what we have termed 'Modern Mexico'. The Metropolis has mushroomed; cities of over 100,000 inhabitants are expanding both in number and size. Yet at the other end of the scale, in 'Remote Mexico' are still the hundreds of little places which give Mexico a characteristic pattern; these may be declining slightly in number and total population, but still contain more than a quarter of the national total. In between, cities, towns, and villages seem also to be participating in the general urbanization movement, but there are insufficient data on them to draw any real conclusions.

The differences between the two 'Mexicos' place a real burden on those who direct Mexican development. Shall plans be tipped in favour of the 70 per cent. making up 'Modern Mexico', with the greatest efforts being made in urban, progressive, industrial, and modernizing activities? Or in favour of the 30 per cent. in 'Remote Mexico', the underdogs of the Revolution, who are making little or no contribution to national life and are possibly unaware of much of it? Mexico's answer is found in a partial shift in emphasis since 1940, the Institutional Revolution. Programmes have favoured the majority, not the minority, but it is hoped that as national networks become more finely spun they will in time extend and encircle the tiny places which constitute 'Remote Mexico', and that ultimately the two Mexicos will merge.

Chapter XI

SOCIETY IN TRANSITION

THE powerful forces which are changing the settlement patterns in Mexico are equally responsible for rearranging the numbers and elements of the various strata of Mexican society. The physical movements to cities and the unprecedented growth in sheer numbers would be expected to unsettle even a stable society. In addition, the programmes of the Institutional Revolution purposely foster social change: education, industrialization, a spreading affluence all open new opportunities that larger numbers of Mexicans are grasping. Society is in flux.

SOCIAL STRATA

On the eve of the Revolution, Mexican society seemed relatively static and basically simple. It consisted of a small élite upper class which supported the régime of Porfirio Díaz; a thin layer of middle class—professional men, small businessmen, bureaucrats, and others traditionally constituting the group; and an enormous lower class comprising 90 per cent. of the population. The Revolution partly arose from the inability of the Díaz régime to accommodate the new interests which its economic policies had begun to bring into being. One of its early results was to lop off the traditional upper class, whose inherited prestige and power rested to a great extent on property in land and alliances with the Church or with foreign sources of capital. The leadership of the Revolution, drawn both from middle- and lower-class strata, was usually able to agree on the elimination of the most flagrant abuses attributed to Díaz and his closed circle, but had widely divergent views on the shape that Mexico should take once that common objective had been reached.

Both revolutionary theory and practice predicated Mexican advance towards an 'Open' society, in which caste and class lines would no longer be rigid, and in which it was hoped that every Mexican family might have the opportunity to live in personal comfort and dignity, above a mere subsistence level. Since the militant Revolution came to an end more than thirty years ago the various régimes have followed diverse paths towards these generally approved goals and their cumulative effect has made profound and lasting changes in Mexican society.

For one thing, the opening up of society has created a stratum of people who do not fit neatly into any of the orthodox three main social classes. A new upper class, different in origins and functions from its pre-Revolutionary counterpart, has come into being; and at the base of the social pyramid there is still a large mass which is now, more politely, labelled 'popular' rather than 'lower class'. Between these extremes, however, there is an important stratum whose class status is ambiguous. A large portion of this segment is, by generally accepted Western standards, unequivocally 'middle class', but there is also a substantial group remaining who do not quite fit this category, although economically and socially they have gone beyond the upper limits usually set for the 'lower class'. We propose therefore to call them collectively the 'transitional class'.

From scattered blocks of information we can reconstruct the present class system of Mexico only on the most provisional basis, both because of the ambiguity of class definitions and the absence of modern comprehensive investigations. On very general grounds, we know that in any industrializing society, social mobility leads to a relaxation of the rigid criteria between traditional groups, but the application of these general findings to the Mexican situation still awaits a great deal of further study and discussion.[1]

At the present time there is only one published analysis of contemporary Mexican society, the rapid sketch made by Professor Robert Scott, as a prelude to his discussion of political matters in his *Mexican Government in Transition* (1959). On the basis of his personal estimates and 1950 Census figures, he attempted to isolate and identify the various social strata.[2] Our own similarly tentative and subjective judgements derive principally from two distinct bodies of material: statistics of average monthly income, and of occupations. Implicit in the second is a general hierarchy based on the status and prestige attributed to various occupations and professions.[3] These data afford important clues to class structure and social organization.

[1] Seymour M. Lipset and Reinhard Bendix, *Social Mobility in Industrial Society* (Berkeley, Calif., 1959), esp. pp. 11–75 (deals directly with Japan, Great Britain, U.S.A.). Oscar Lewis, 'México desde 1940', *Investigación económica*, xviii (1958), 185–256; an extended version of a paper issued in English in mimeographed form and subsequently published as 'Mexico since Cárdenas', *Social Research*, xxvi (Spring 1958), 18–30. See also Charles Wagley and Marvin Harris, 'The Indians in Mexico', *Minorities in the New World* (1958), pp. 48–86.

[2] See Appendix Table XI, source D.

[3] Studies of special border communities and 'prestige hierarchy' appear in William V. D'Antonio, 'National Images of Business and Political Elites in two Border Cities' (unpubl. Ph.D.Diss., Michigan State University, 1958) and Orrin E. Klapp and Vincent Padgett, 'Power Structure and Decision-Making in a Mexican Border City', *Amer. J. of Sociol.*, lxv (Jan. 1960), 400–6.

INCOME LEVELS

The most complete information on average monthly incomes comes from the Census of 1950. Curiously enough, inconsistencies in the four different presentations of the Census figures make it possible to select materials to illustrate a particular thesis. Here we have tried to show the various sets of data side by side in Appendix Table X, subdividing them at common points which observers generally agree seem to mark significant levels or differences between social strata. While having little scientific validity, an average of the four different presentations of 1950 Census data tends to provide a fairly accurate picture of the total system. There remains considerable discrepancy in finer subdivisions of each of the broad levels. Table 22 summarizes the main findings given in Appendix Table XI.

TABLE 22

Income Levels and Classes, 1950

(Percentages of Economically Active Population)

Classes	Minimum monthly incomes (*pesos*)	Minimum est. %	Maximum est. %	Probable percentage
Upper	Over 1,000	1·3	4·0	2·4
Middle	300	12·6	25·5	20·3
Transitional ...	200	15·3	37·0	21·3
Popular (Lower)	1	33·5	63·9	55·7
TOTALS ...				99·7

Source: Appendix Table XI. Probable percentage is author's estimate.

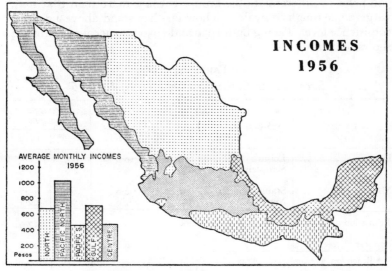

INCOMES 1956

AVERAGE MONTHLY INCOMES 1956

In 1956 the Ministry of Economy carried out an extensive study to determine income levels and buying habits of Mexican families, and their findings, using the family rather than the individual as the basic unit, are summarized in Table 23. These 1956 figures do not cover the Federal District, however, embracing a vast body of people living on low incomes in and around Mexico City, and therefore show differences from the 1950 figures.

TABLE 23

Income Levels and Classes, 1956

(Exclusive of Federal District)

Classes	Minimum average monthly income (*pesos*)	No. of families ('*000*)	Percentage of economically active families
Upper	Over 1,001	655·2	13·0
Middle	,, 300	2,389·5	48·0
Transitional	,, 200	877·0	17·5
Popular (Lower) ...	,, 1	1,079·4	21·5
TOTALS ...		5,002·1	100·0

Source: SDE, *Ingresos y egresos de la población de México, en el mes de octubre de 1956* (1958).

In both years, we note from Table XI, there existed subdivisions within each of these rather wide income groups. Most students agree that an income of 300 pesos per month is the minimum for a reasonably secure but marginal living in Mexico; if we use units of 300 pesos to differentiate the groups earning more than that sum, we get some rough equivalent of how far they stand above a general subsistence level. Taking both 1950 and 1956 into account, Table 24 shows the result.

TABLE 24

Income Levels, Classes, and Sub-Classes, 1950–6

Classes	Sub-Classes	Minimum monthly income	Times subsistence level	Percentages of population	
				*1950**	*1956*
Upper	Leisure ...	3,000	10·0	0·5	1·5
	Semi-leisure	1,000	3·3	2·8	11·5
Middle	Stable ...	600	2·0	5·1	25·7
	Marginal...	300	1·0	15·1	22·3
Transitional ...	Precarious	200	0·7	21·3	17·5
Popular		1	0·0	55·7	21·5

* Based on averages; see Appendix Table XI. Averages total 101·5 per cent.

For the moment let us assume that Table 24 is about as far as our limited information on incomes and related class levels can carry us. We are aware that at both extremes these data are suspect. High income groups are notably and especially secretive about the amount and source of their income. At the popular level, similar ingrained suspicions, illiteracy, dispersion of population, and other factors affect the results. However, despite these drawbacks, the above calculations provide one set of measures on classes. Let us look at the other.

THE OCCUPATIONAL HIERARCHY

In nearly all modern societies there is a general, if often hidden, hierarchy of roles which its members play. For Mexico, the chief data we have on such roles come from statistics of the economically active population, showing *how* they earn income, rather than how much they earn. In recent years the economically active group has represented about a third of the total national population of any given year. Thus in discussing professions and occupations, we are talking about the bread-winners, heads of households.

Taking a broad view, we must first observe that since 1950 the economically active segment of the Mexican population has increased in numbers; however, with increased population the percentage has remained about the same. That means that each year several thousand new workers are adding pressures and changes to the total system. As will be seen later, the Mexican economic system is developing equally in its rural and urban sectors with balanced emphasis on agriculture and on industry; at the same time the growth of cities and of communications have made unprecedented demands for service activities expected from Government and the semi-skilled occupations.

Taking these elements in account, we may quickly review the relative development of the economic sectors and affix to them very loose class labels. For instance agriculturalists, normally with relatively low cash incomes, belong to the popular class. In the same wide sense, service occupations, which include civil servants too, are filled by people from the transitional class; in a newly industrializing and urbanizing society, service work is the first step upward from unskilled labour for the socially mobile. Less clear-cut are the other categories reflected in Mexican statistics: industry, commerce, and transport. Each employs all strata, but in general the main groups start about the popular class, ranging upward from semi-skilled workers to directors; there is also some need for labourers. Those with relatively assured incomes from regular employment are the more fortunate members of their group.

Table 25 summarizes, in millions of persons, some directions that changes have taken from 1950 to 1958. It indicates that, in a very general way, about 60 per cent. of the gainfully employed are in 'popular' class occupations; there seems to be a slight decrease since 1950. 'Transitional' services employed many more people in 1958 than in 1950, both in absolute and relative terms; in 1958 the total was about 11 per cent. of all wage-earners. Other economic concerns have grown. Industry added nearly half a million workers since 1950. But eight years of growth has not appreciably altered the proportion of its working force. Perhaps it is important to re-emphasize that in the years under review, 2 million wage-earners were added to the increasingly evolving system, to be fitted into new slots of the social hierarchy.

TABLE 25

General Occupations and Classes, 1950–8

(Millions of employed)

Categories / Classes	1950 No.	1950 Per cent.	1956 No.	1956 Per cent.	1958 No.	1958 Per cent.	Increases 1958 vs. 1960 No.	Increases 1958 vs. 1960 Per cent.
UPPER / MIDDLE								
Industry	1·3		1·6		1·7		0·4	
Commerce ...	0·7		0·8		0·9		0·2	
Transport ...	0·2		0·2		0·3		0·1	
Sub-totals ...	2·2	28·2	2·6	27·7	2·9	28·4	0·7	31·8
TRANSITIONAL								
Services	0·8	8·9	1·0	10·4	1·1	11·1	0·3	37·5
POPULAR								
Agriculture, &c....	4·8		5·7		6·1		1·3	27·1
Semi-employed ...	0·1		0·1		0·1		0·0	0·0
Sub-totals ...	4·9	62·9	5·8	61·9	6·2	60·5	1·3	
TOTALS	7·9	100·0	9·4	100·0	10·2	100·0	2·3	29·2
Insufficiently specified ...	0·5		0·5		0·3		—	—
ECONOMICALLY ACTIVE... ...	8·3		9·9		10·5		2·2	26·5
Per cent. national	32·1		32·3		32·3		—	—

Sources: DGE, *Compendio estadístico, 1955*, table 21, pp. 43–44; 1958, tables 21–22, pp. 49–51; data classified and rearranged, percentages by author.

Fortunately, this unsatisfactory general panorama can be made slightly more specific by the income study undertaken in 1956 by the Ministry of Economy,[1] which also includes much information on professions and occupations. The sampling results given in various sections of this report are shown here in Table 26. In this instance the Federal District is included.

The Federal District, as the unique metropolitan area, is worth examining in more detail. There are two sets of data on it, slightly different but revealing, one the statistical material included in Table 26 for the nation as a whole, the other a graphic presentation, here adapted as Diagram 2, which also appears in the 1956 study on incomes; it subdivides the labour force into three broad categories, on a percentage basis. From other sources we know what that force was, and hence can provide specific figures for the percentages. Both groups of data are included in Table 27.

TABLE 26

Occupations and Classes, 1956

('000 of employed)

Categories/Classes	Number	Per cent.
UPPER		
Managerial; directors	77·4	0·7
MIDDLE/UPPER		
Professional/Technical	412·3	4·2
Office workers	905·6	9·2
Small tradesmen	1,370·1	13·8
Sub-total	2,688·0	27·2
TRANSITIONAL		
Artisans/semi-skilled	1,986·8	20·0
Miners/petroleum workers	42·2	0·4
Service employees	929·4	9·1
Sub-total	2,958·4	29·5
POPULAR		
Manual/Day labour	383·3	3·9
Agricultural	3,559·0	36·1
Semi-employed; unspecified	194·5	2·6
Sub-total	4,136·8	42·6
ECONOMICALLY ACTIVE	9,860·6	100·0

Source: SDE, *Ingresos ... 1956*, pp. 64–67, 89–91, 111–12, 132–34, 154–55, 175–76, consolidated and rearranged, percentages by author. Further occupational sub-categories are included in SDE report.

[1] See above, p. 116.

TABLE 27

Occupations and Classes, Federal District, 1956

(*'000 of employed*)

Categories/Classes	No.	SDE 1956 a		DIAGRAM 20 b	
		Per cent. D.F.	Per cent. total class	No.	Per cent.
UPPER					
Managerial/Directing ...	28·4	1·9	38·1		
MIDDLE/UPPER					
Professional/Technical ...	124·5	8·2	30·3		
Office workers	368·8	24·0	40·7		
Small tradesmen	288·4	18·8	21·0		
Sub-total	781·7	51·0	29·0	154·2	10·0
TRANSITIONAL					
Artisans/Semi-skilled ...	487·0	31·7	24·6		
Service employees	127·7	8·3	13·7		
Sub-total	614·7	40·0	20·7	632·2	41·0
POPULAR					
Manual/day labour ...	50·4	3·3	13·1		
Agricultural	17·3	1·1	0·5		
Unknown	37·3	2·7	19·5		
Sub-total	105·5	7·1	2·6	755·6	49·0
ECONOMICALLY ACTIVE	1,530·3	100·0	15·5	1,542·0	100·0

Sources: *a*: SDE, *Ingresos . . . 1956*, pp. 64–67; *b*: ibid. p. 65 (graph); *Diagnóstico económico regional*, p. 40.

This table confirms a number of earlier assertions. It shows that the Federal District contains a little over 15 per cent. of the productive labour force, with a disproportionate share of the managerial group, professional and technical specialists, office workers, and small tradesmen. It has slightly less than the proportion of service workers one might expect, who seemingly have risen to semi-skilled ranks. Figures seem low for manual labour, but there are, of course, relatively few farmers in the District. The unknown or floating population is slightly higher than the District's share of the economically active. Assuming these statistics to be representative, if not completely accurate in every respect, we can infer that more than half the metropolitan population is above the 'poverty' line, and that another 40 per cent. are not far from it on either side.

We can now attempt to place side by side the conclusions supported by our tables up to this point. For 1950 (see Table 25) and to some extent for 1956 (Tables 26 and 27) we shall have to make some informed guesses. The following summary is thus composite: statistical data provide outside limits, but between them subjective personal judgements dictate some details in specific cases.

TABLE 28

Classes and Occupations: Summary, 1950–6

Classes/Categories	Estimates, 1950			Estimates, 1956	
	No.	*Per cent.*	*Pro-portion**	*No.*	*Per cent.*
UPPER					
Managerial			All	77·4	
Professional			1/3	137·7	
Sub-total	124·5	1·5		215·1	2·0
MIDDLE					
Stable					
Professional/Technical ...			2/3	274·6	
Office Workers			1/2	452·8	
Small tradesmen			1/3	456·7	
Sub-total	830·0	10·0		1,184·1	12·0
Marginal					
Office Workers			1/2	452·8	
Small tradesmen			1/3	456·7	
Artisans			1/3	662·3	
Sub-total	1,535·5	18·5		1,571·8	16·0
Sub-total	2,365·5	28·5		2,755·9	28·0
TRANSITIONAL					
Small tradesmen			1/3	456·7	
Artisans/semi-skilled ...			2/3	1,324·5	
Miners/petroleum labour ...			All	42·2	
Service employees ...			2/3	619·6	
Sub-total	1,760·0	20·0		2,443·0	24·8
POPULAR					
Service employees			1/3	309·8	
Manual/day labour ...			All	383·8	
Agriculturalists			All	3,559·0	
Unknown, &c			All	194·0	
Sub-total	4,150·0	50·0		4,446·6	45·2
ECONOMICALLY ACTIVE	8,300·0	100·0		9,860·6	100·0

* Author's estimates

THE CHANGING SOCIAL STRUCTURE

Even the scattered figures on monthly incomes and on the numbers and kinds of jobs Mexicans held collectively suggest that changes are occurring in the social and economic system, some of them even

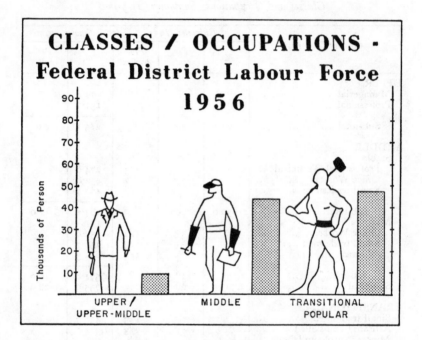

CLASSES / OCCUPATIONS -
Federal District Labour Force
1956

since 1950. We can now combine the findings on class levels from the two separate approaches: monthly incomes and occupations, and it is possible, by comparing figures for 1950 and 1956 with similar data from earlier years, to illustrate the directions of change in the social structure, and some major differences between society at the close of the nineteenth century and at the present time. The results shown in the following table in part represent subjective decisions on detail, within the general bounds set by available statistical information.

TABLE 29

Socio-Economic Classes, 1950–6

(*Percentages of gainfully employed*)

Classes & Sub-classes	Estimates, 1950			Estimates, 1956		
	Incomes (*Table 24*)	Occupations (*Table 28*)	Combined	Incomes (*Table 24*)	Occupations (*Table 28*)	Combined
UPPER						
Leisure ...	0·5	0·5	0·5	1·5	0·8	1·0
Semi-leisure	2·8	1·0	1·5	11·5	1·2	4·0
Sub-total	3·3	1·5	2·0	13·0	2·0	5·0
MIDDLE						
Stable ...	5·1	10·0	8·0	25·7	12·0	15·0
Marginal ...	15·1	18·5	17·0	22·3	16·0	15·0
Sub-total	20·2	28·5	25·0	48·0	28·0	30·0
TRANSI-TIONAL...	21·3	20·0	20·0	17·5	24·8	20·0
POPULAR ...	55·7	50·0	53·0	21·5	45·2	45·0
GAINFULLY EMPLOYED	97·7	100·0	100·0	100·0	100·0	100·0

This table shows that Mexico seems to be roughly equally divided, about half the gainfully employed being in the transitional class or above, while the other half live at a level substantially below the minimum, both economically and socially. The middle and upper classes, comprising about a quarter of the total population in 1950, had risen to about a third by 1956. The proportion of the transitional class in each of these years were about the same; they did not necessarily consist of the same families, for it would appear that there was some recruitment from the popular groups. Although perhaps the rich were getting richer, and remained entrenched in their commanding positions at the top of the social pyramid, the poor became less poor, nor were they so numerous at the end of the period reviewed.

Taking a longer view, we have some information on the Mexican class structure from 1895 to compare with 1940, 1950, and 1956 estimates. A comparative summary shows us what effects the

Revolution of 1910 has had. At the same time, we can hazard a guess as to the findings of the 1960 Census. The results are given in the following table.

TABLE 30

Changing Class Structure, 1895–1960

(Percentages, varying bases)

Classes & Sub-classes	REVOLUTION, 1910–60				
	Militant		Institutional		
	1895 a	*1940* b	*1950* c	*1956* c	*1960* (est.)
UPPER					
Leisure	0·4	0·4	0·5	1·0	1·5
Semi-leisure	1·1	2·5	1·5	4·0	5·0
Sub-total	1·5	2·9	2·0	5·0	6·5
MIDDLE					
Stable	6·1	6·1	8·0	15·0	17·0
Marginal	1·7	6·5	17·0	15·0	16·5
Sub-total	7·8	12·6	25·0	30·0	33·5
TRANSITIONAL ...	—	6·5	20·0	20·0	20·0
POPULAR	90·7	78·0	53·0	45·0	40·0

Sources: a: Iturriaga, *Estructura social,* table 6 (p. 28), adapted; *b:* Cline, *U.S. and Mexico,* p. 86, adapted; *c:* table 28 above.

It is clear from this that the trend from 1940 indicates that more and more Mexicans are enjoying the 'culture of affluence', about which so little is really known. The middle and upper classes, the productive leadership for the modernization and Westernization of Mexico, now comprise more than a third of the population. Their numbers are increasing as the various educational, economic, and social programmes of the past few years begin to show results. However, the 'underdogs' of the Revolution are still in the majority, if the transitional and popular classes are combined. Many of them have been siphoned off into the marginal middle class, where their permanence will depend on individual initiative and continued prosperity. A substantial number form the 'Remote Mexico' discussed in Chapter X.

Nearly every society for which we have any historical or presen record retains a body of underprivileged. Probably about a third c the Mexican population will so remain for many years to come But this is fewer by half than at the end of the Díaz period. Th Revolution has achieved one of its aims. Society is 'open'. I technical jargon, status is 'achieved', not ascribed; what a man does rather than who his father was, is the main determinant of status Moreover, nearly half the Mexican people have risen in the socia and economic scale since 1910, some to undreamed-of heights. Th humblest and poorest can now aspire to having a son or daughte at a university, perhaps even winning a scholarship abroad. Thi is now almost a real expectancy of the new middle class, which ha tripled under the Institutional Revolution.

Chapter XII

HUMANISTIC
RESPONSES TO FLUID SOCIETY

RALPH L. Beals and Norman D. Humphrey, studying problems which the Mexican student encounters in the United States, have drawn a succinct and penetrating view of the fluid society from which he comes. They note that 'As in thirty years Mexico has moved from pack train to motor truck to airplane, so Mexican society has moved from a feudal society toward an industrial society.' Conflicting rural-urban values, the underlying goals found in reiterated statements that Mexico must become an integrated nation, that it must maintain an independent position in international affairs, that mass education is a necessary and positive thing, and above all, that industrialization and social change are desirable, all mark Mexico off from pre-Revolutionary days. These authors conclude their sketch by reaffirming that 'Mexican culture is in transition, but the direction of its movement is not yet uniform'.[1] Puzzlement, concern, recognition that old ways are disappearing is a common theme in contemporary Mexican intellectual circles. Writers and thinkers are acutely aware of what is going on, and reflect it in their writings. They are the conscience of the Revolution.

SOCIETY IN LITERATURE

Novels and stories provide acute insights into the societies of their own times. They often furnish a missing psychological key, on a highly subjective but significant aesthetic basis. The 'social' novel flourishes in Mexico. It dates back notably to the early nineteenth century when José Joaquín Fernández de Lizardi supplied views and sketches of Mexican society shortly after independence in his *El Periquillo sarniento* (trans. as 'The Itching Parrot'). Drawing heavily on novels, past and present, María Elvira Bermúdez has attempted

[1] Ralph L. Beals and Norman D. Humphrey, *No Frontier to Learning* (1957), pp. 9–27; excerpts also appear in Lewis U. Hanke, *Modern Latin America* (1959), i. 169–74, together with interesting statements on modern Mexico by Octavio Paz, José Clemente Orozco, and a young painter, José Luis Cuevas. Mexican intellectuals also speak, generally deploring current trends, in 'The Eye of Mexico'. *Evergreen Review* (1959), 22–213, and in 'New Writing from Latin America', *New World Writing*, xiv (1958), pp. 86–181.

to recreate the everyday life of lower and transitional classes in recent times.[1] Her study provides views not found elsewhere. Two of Mexico's most able contemporary novelists, Luis Spota and Carlos Fuentes, both authors of best-sellers, have taken as themes the recent shifts in outlook and fluidity of values as the older Mexican order breaks up. Each has written 'social' novels in the great Mexican tradition, but as artists they are now beginning to drift away from this possibly overworked vein. Intellectually they are linked with an important earlier group which created the classic 'Novel of the Revolution', but their phase is the Institutional Revolution.[2]

In 1956 Luis Spota published *Casi el paraíso* (Almost Paradise), an instant success which established him as a major contemporary figure. It is a funny book, a satire on the newly-rich Mexicans who ape foreign ways, giving blind adulation to what they believe are upper-class fashions. The implicit message is 'do not negate Mexican values'. In 1959 he published another 'social novel'—*Las Horas sangrientes* (The Violent Hours), recreating a Mexican labour strike, and also in the same year a quite distinct novel, *La Sangre enemiga* (Enemy Blood). Despite its title, this is a love story, little concerned with society as such. Thus the direction he began to take with his vivid tale of the 'wetbacks' who were forced to leave Mexico because of poverty and if they survived, endured untold hardships abroad— a novel published in 1948 called *Murieron a mitad del rio* (They Died in Mid-River)—seems to be altering.

The view taken of Mexican society by Carlos Fuentes is a little less critical. His *La Región más transparente* (The Most Transparent Region), which appeared in 1958, is a best-seller. It is an excellent novel, whose locale is the Metropolis. He scans all social levels, and is disturbed by materialism, self-seeking, and loneliness in the midst of a society now able to produce surplus material goods. Like Spota, he deplores a Mexican tendency to bow to foreign values, both European and especially North American. Like him too Fuentes turned from the social scene in 1959 when he published the first volume of a four-volume work to be collectively known as *Los Nuevos* (New Ones). This first volume, *Las Buenas consciencias* (Good Consciences) depicts an internal, psychological struggle: a bourgeois youth in the provinces, wrestling with problems caused by his Catholic training.

[1] María Elvira Bermúdez, *La Vida familiar del mexicano* (1955).

[2] R. Rand Morton, *Los Novelistas de la revolución mexicana* (1949) has excellent summary account and analysis of principal novelists; slightly wider in scope, noting numerous social and popular themes is Manuel Pedro González, *Trajectoria de la novela en México* (1951).

The year 1959 is probably typical of several recent ones. Most of the outstanding novels published then had some concern with the immediate Mexican past, and more especially unsolved social problems, though few reached the level of talent displayed by Spota and Fuentes.[1] Exploration of the society which the Revolution nearly overthrew is the focus of *Una Luz en la otra orilla* (A Light on the Other Shore) by María Lombardo de Caso. Again the provinces are the scene, as she recreates the social structure of the early twentieth century, making one family and its difficulties the centre of interest. The somewhat stereotyped views of Porfirian times are enlivened by humour.

Two more excellent novels published in 1959, *La Justicia de Enero* (January Justice) by Sergio Galindo, and Luisa Josefina Hernández's *El Lugar donde crece la hierba* (The Place where the Grass Grows) were noted by Mexican critics. Galindo's theme is that justice is a subjective, never an absolute matter; he tells how honest officials become less trustworthy as their years of service increase. Even rain may have an effect on a judge's mind! Luisa Josefina Hernández's novel takes the form of a psychological monologue, part in delirium, part conscious, an 'inward' look.

Among the older figures Agustín Yáñez has an assured place; hence his newly (1959) published *La Creación* (Creation) has a special interest. The novel is about a young musician who left a small town, was trained in Europe, and returned to Mexico in the agitated 1920's and 1930's. The title symbolizes the birth of the modern Mexican Revolutionary mind. The book recreates the period of José Vasconcelos, Diego Rivera, and Dolores del Río. Critics feel that aesthetically it falls far below the standards of Yáñez's earlier works, but that it is invaluable for the social historian and those concerned with intellectual currents and trends.

PENSADORES

In the tradition of the eighteenth-century French *philosophes* are the 'thinkers' (*pensadores*) of Latin America. In Mexico too they have formed an important section of the intellectual community, bridging philosophy, history, art, and sociology.[2] Leopoldo Zea, whose views on many problems appear in *La Cultura y el hombre de nuestros días* (Culture and Man of Our Time) (1959) belongs to this

[1] Robert G. Mead, jr., 'Aspects of Mexican Literature Today', *Books Abroad*, xxxiv (Winter 1960), 5–8.

[2] W. Rex Crawford, *A Century of Latin American Thought* (1945) discusses Mexicans in Ch. 9 (pp. 247–94).

tradition. In this work he examines relationships between weak countries (like Mexico) and the powerful ones, the aims of education and government, the effects of mechanization on countries and individuals, the preservation of traditional values, and other difficult and important topics. Perhaps his main concern in this book, the companion piece of important earlier works, is the sustained role of the university as the guardian of national values. Leopoldo Zea also contributed one of three essays in *Magia y cibernética* (Magic and Cybernetics), also published in 1959. A sort of latter-day adaptation of the Ariel–Caliban contrast of Rodó's classic, these essays by three like-minded *pensadores* present a moving plea for the retention of basic humanistic values ('Magic') in the face of industrialization ('Cybernetics').

Ramon Xirau should probably be added to the group of Mexican *pensadores*. His essays, on the margins of philosophy, literature, and sociology, again are concerned with the explosive and disruptive elements altering traditional values in Mexico. In 1959 he published *El Péndulo y la espiral* (The Pendulum and the Spiral), which is concerned with the course and meaning of history for Mexico and Mexicans.

Literature has deep roots in the Mexican soil, drawing on indigenous as well as European sources, and it has matured, changed, and flourished in the recent past. It does not look abroad for inspiration, only for techniques.[1]

THE ARTS

Every epoch—pre-Conquest, Colonial, pre-Revolutionary, even the Revolution itself—has contributed to Mexico's rich and complex artistic heritage. A standard guide to Latin American art emphasizes the importance of the Revolution, stating 'Mexican art in the twentieth century is not merely the most important of the national schools; by symbolizing the aspirations and influencing the artists of

[1] On native literatures, see summary materials in Carmen Cook de Leonard, ed., *Esplendor de México antigua*, esp. pts. 2 and 3, 'El pensamiento', 'El arte'; Donald Robertson, *Mexican Codices: the Metropolitan School* (New Haven, Yale U.P., 1959), has summary discussions and full bibliography; scanty on modern matters is the standard translation, Carlos González Peña, *History of Mexican Literature* (1943), and Julio Jiménez Rueda, *Historia de la literatura mexicana*, 4th ed., (1946), to be supplemented with José Luis Martínez, *Literatura mexicana del siglo XX, 1910–1949*, and many specialized articles.

other countries it also assumes the importance of a pan-American movement'.[1]

The Mexican School, which developed one of the few original New World contributions to the general history of art, is intimately linked with the names of its three outstanding artists, Diego Rivera, José Clemente Orozco, and David A. Siqueiros. They and their lesser followers translated the ideals and forces of the Mexican Revolution into powerful frescoes, creating new techniques, symbols, and artistic liberties which exploded many of the accepted academic canons. Differing widely in individual approaches, the Mexican mural painters shared a common outlook and determination to create a Revolutionary art. Under Government contracts, they covered public buildings with huge depictions of heroes, villains, and key episodes in Mexican history. The biting qualities of good political cartoons of these works proclaimed the triumph of the class struggle, the villainy of foreigners and capitalists, and other Marxian clichés. A talent so obvious and powerful captured world attention though the original motivation was largely political and nationalistic. It was a new movement in art.

Seemingly once the creative burst that marked the years from about 1920 to about 1930 had spent its main force, Mexico continued to produce artists of smaller stature, and the aging three produced nearly as many political scandals as first-rate works. They left an indelible mark on Mexican art, linking it with the national past, the aspirations of the Revolution, and a self-confidence generated by major achievement. The Institutional Revolution has produced no comparable group.

In attempting to assess trends and activities during 1959, for instance, one writer summarized: 'Much noise, a few good kernels . . . many old faces made sudden appearance, and the "new wave" of youngsters began to rise.' Prizes in the first National Salon of Painting went to persons generally unknown to the lay public—Pedro Coronel, González Camarena, and Leonora Carrington. Large numbers of exhibitions, especially in state institutions, bore testimony to widespread interest, while Mexican shows abroad indicated that the country is still producing art and artists worthy

[1] Robert C. Smith and Elizabeth Wilder, *A Guide to the Art of Latin America* (Washington, USGPO, 1948), p. 28. Numerous bibliographical references, up to 1948, are found on pp. 394–439, 'The Contemporary Period', supplemented by continuing references in *Handbook of Latin American Studies*, 'Art'. One of the best recent general treatments is Bernard S. Myers, *Mexican Painting in Our Time* (N.Y., Oxford U.P., 1956); in Spanish the basic treatment is Justino Fernández, *Arte moderno y contemporáneo de México* (1952).

of esteem. Rufino Tamayo scored successes in Oslo, Paris, Milan, London, New York. José Luis Cuevas won acclaim and a prize in São Paulo, Brazil, where works of Orozco, Rivera, Siqueiros, and Tamayo (copy owned by the Parisian Museum of Modern Art) were exhibited. Magazines such as *Artes de México* not only dealt with Mexican art of high quality but also brought important news and views from the greater world of art within the reach of all. Art is still important in Mexico.

The creative spirit in Mexico is so rich and so Protean that it defies efforts to provide even a balanced token sample. In literature it also pervades verse and drama, and manifests itself in the plastic arts, which there is no space to describe here. And however brief, any mention of Mexican humanism must include the late Alfonso Reyes as spokesman for an earlier Revolutionary group, and Octavio Paz for the present generation—serious literary artists of world renown. They and others of lesser stature shape the dreams of modern Mexico.

GOVERNMENT
AND POLITICAL EVOLUTION

Chapter XIII

CONSTITUTIONAL CRISES, 1857 AND 1917

GOVERNMENT in Mexico, both in theory and practice, enters the lives of citizens more directly and more frequently than has been customary in Great Britain, the United States, and some other lands whose own earlier revolutions were based on the premiss that the least government was the best. Mexico's long-standing traditions have reinforced its participation in present world trends toward Big Government, endowed with social responsibilities and the powers necessary to assure minimum standards of living and to enforce real equality of opportunities for all its people.

THE CONSTITUTION OF 1917: A REVOLUTIONARY DOCUMENT

The Mexican Revolution vigorously asserted these latter principles. They are inscribed in the constitution of 1917, perhaps the single most important national document that upheaval produced. To preserve the nineteenth-century gains that had been won, often at high cost, its framers and their compatriots wholly agreed that after 1917, Government was to carry out social and economic plans and programmes, the very absence of which had been among the fundamental causes of the Revolution.

The nature and organization of Government was to remain secondary, often substantially subordinate to this central, dynamic urge. However much academic analysts deplore the demonstrable divergences between the theory and practice of Mexican federalism, the division of powers and the checks and balances to them, there are overriding considerations in favour of practice over theory.

Perhaps the most important consideration is that Mexicans fought to have this arrangement. Secondly, the governmental system fulfils many of the major aspirations currently sanctioned by the Revolution, while safeguarding individual liberties and universal civil rights.

VIEWS OF 1857 AND OF 1917

The Mexican constitution of 1917, the prime document of the Mexican Revolution, put the hopes and expectations for which the movement had been fought into the law of the land. It was by no means a wholly novel document. Rather it re-enacted nearly two-thirds of the previous constitution of 1857, preserving the main outlines of a liberal representative democracy as well as the individual guarantees which the generation of the Reforma had placed in this charter as the outcome of *their* struggles. The constitution of 1857 was itself an eclectic product, drawing on many earlier sources. Thus, as such Latin American documents go, the constitution of 1917 has a lengthy history with a continuity which even precedes independence.

Though there is an organic link between the constitutions of 1857 and 1917, there are also important differences.[1] These include different emphases on some of the matters they share, and in the new features which were imposed on the present charter by the experience of those who framed it. In very broad terms, one can say that the constitution of 1857, drawn in large part from the United States constitution of 1787, the French revolutionary constitutions, the Spanish constitution of 1812, and various constitutions growing out of the European revolutions of 1848, summed up an era that was pre-eminently political, and concerned with individual rights. It took as its corner-stone the advanced *laissez-faire* theories of its day, limiting the functions of Government, stressing private initiative, and seeking to dismantle many, if not most, of the corporative features of Mexican life inherited from the colonial era. So far as it was able, it emphasized control by the legislative branch over the executive; the generation of the Reforma had witnessed the excesses of the strong executive, symbolized by the dictator Santa Anna.

The constitution of 1917, on the other hand, was largely a reaction to the excesses of *laissez-faire* under Díaz. It avowedly strengthened the positive, active role of the state and Government, especially in social and economic spheres. Still under arms, the Constitutionalists provided for a strong President, endowed with the necessary arsenal of powers to carry out the objectives contained in the constitution. Most of its architects had never served in legislatures, and had little real experience beyond military administration, hence the constitution of 1917 tipped the balance of power sharply in favour of executive rather than legislative functions.

The attempted marriage of the old and the new in the 1917 convention involved compromise on many matters where extremist views were strong. However clear the main lines of intent, the

[1] Detailed comparison of the documents in 'The Mexican Constitution of 1917 compared with the Constitution of 1857', *A.Amer.Acad.Polit.* (May 1917), Suppl.

resultant charter is thus far from consistent at many important points, and even contradictory at others. Just as the lack of a rigid pre-existing ideology for the Revolution has in the long run been a benefit, so these ambiguities in its basic document have advantages by offering equally 'legal' alternatives as circumstances change. On numerous details there are several valid but contradictory interpretations, even among constitutional lawyers of equal competence, while on a few there is a reasonable unanimity of opinion.[1]

LAND AND LABOUR: ARTICLES 27 AND 123

Here we cannot summarize all aspects of these interesting problems, but we can note selected important ones. Of these, the novel features represented by Article 27 relating to land and sub-soil resources, and Article 123 providing a labour code, are especially significant, as are the specific grants of power given the executive and limitations of legislative functions. One cannot rely wholly on constitutional texts to understand the operation of the Mexican Government, but it is worth remarking that the dominant position which the President and his executive establishment occupies has a rather firm legal, constitutional base; it does not represent a usurpation of the constitutionally limited judicial and legislative powers.

Quite different in content, Articles 27 and 123 are closely related in several ways. Their inclusion in the new constitution was a major outcome of the convention which was called to reform the 1857 document and include the programmes of the Revolution. The same working group drafted these two important articles and the same Committee reviewed the drafts. Debate over the degree of radicalism to be left in final versions brought forth expressions of opinion from the main factions. There is a patchy, though lengthy, literature by those present, written in partisan terms. However, all authors agree on the eclectic nature of each article, and on the unanimous agreement to incorporate in the constitution vast programmes to benefit peasants and labour.[2]

The sources for each are related though not identical. The points of departure for the convention drafts were similar drafts

[1] Two standard treatments are Miguel Lanz Duret, *Derecho constitucional mexicano* (1947), and Felipe Tena Ramírez, *Derecho constitucional mexicano*, 3d ed. (1955); see also his *Leyes fundamentales de México, 1808–1957* (1957).

[2] Pastor Rouaix, *Genesis de los artículos 27 y 123 de la constitución política de 1917* (1945), seems the most documented and circumstantial; see also Félix F. Palavicini, *Historia de la constitución de 1917* (1938); Juan de Díos Bojórquez, *Crónica del constituyente* (1938), in addition to which there is a large pamphlet and periodical literature. Rouaix was Chairman of the work group which drafted the articles.

drawn up by President Carranza's advisers, based on scholarly studies of advanced social laws in other parts of the world and the presumed needs of Mexico. Thus the land legislation of New Zealand and the famous Waldeck–Rousseau labour legislation in France (1884) influenced the outcome. In addition, the various stipulations in plans of revolutionary bands, decrees of Revolutionary Governments since 1910, state constitutions, and suggestions of a host of observers who had drifted to Querétaro were considered and exploited. The personal views of the drafting group, the Committee members, and the debaters on the floor produced Articles 27 and 123 of the constitution of 1917.

Article 27 remained untouched, until amplified and reworded in 1934 and 1937; these changes were confined to Subsection VI, which was expanded and subdivided to provide a constitutional base for the Cárdenas ejido programme. Landowners whose properties he had expropriated for communal holdings were prohibited from obtaining writs of *amparo*, a device described below,[1] to slow up or prevent Federal authorities from 'restoring' lands to villages. The administrative apparatus for the ejido programme was elaborated in great detail, virtually constituting a bureaucratic set of operating regulations. The Institutional Revolution has made some changes, which are noted below.

Article 123 has been four times amended. These changes gave exclusive jurisdiction of labour legislation to the national Congress (1929), laid down minimum wage stipulations (1933), and introduced minor rewording to bring Article 123 into line with other statements in the constitution. Typically, Article 123 proposed a system of social security, but the national law (code) to make it effective was not enacted until 1943.

Mexican commentators proudly point to the international effects of their innovations in Articles 27 and 123. They claim influence on the Treaty of Versailles (1918), and on the constitutions of the Spanish Republic, Estonia, Finland, Greece, Ireland, Lithuania, Poland, Rumania, the Weimar Republic of Germany, and among the Latin American nations of Bolivia, Brazil, Chile, Costa Rica, Cuba, Guatemala, Honduras, Nicaragua, Panama, Paraguay, Uruguay, and Venezuela.[2] The novel features, then, of the constitution of 1917, which incorporated two of the principal social and economic goals of the Revolution, reforms of land and labour, have

[1] See below, p. 148.

[2] Rouaix, *Artículos 27 y 123*, quoting in part a study by Alberto Trueba Urbina, *El Artículo 123* (1943), which I have not seen.

tended to remain in principle much as originally written, and have had repercussions not only on Mexican development but also outside.

PSEUDO-FEDERALISM

The constitution declares that powers not expressly granted to the Federal Government are reserved to the states, causing Mexicans and others who read the document no further to conclude that the Republic is organized on the federal principle. Both theory and practice negate this assumption. The long nineteenth-century struggles between Centralists and Federalists may have given the latter a semantic victory, but Centralist doctrines in fact underlie the constitution of 1917 and actual practice since the Revolution.

Each of the twenty-nine states of Mexico has its own constitution, but the powers which each may exercise are circumscribed by the national constitution. Unlike the United States, where the Civil War revolved in part around the issue of which was supreme, nation or state, Mexico's constitutional doctrines clearly and early settled the matter. In the Mexican view, the nation, Iturbide's Empire, preceded the creation of states in 1824 and thereafter. States have had a certain measure of autonomy, but never any sovereignty. They were given juridical life by the nation and remain its subordinate bodies. Therefore, the troublesome problems that occasionally plague true federal systems—'secession', 'states' rights', 'interposition'—cannot occur.[1] Federal control over states has additional constitutional sanction. Congress and the President, under Article 76, are in duty bound to see that the government of each state is 'popular, representative, republican'. When the Senate finds that a state régime violates these minimum essentials—i.e. the state is recalcitrant—it can declare that the state's powers have 'disappeared', and request the President to designate a provisional state government until a regular election restores the 'disappeared' powers. Since earlier days of the Revolution this Federal intervention has been used less frequently; forty such cases transpired between 1918 and 1937, with five more to 1947, and only two from 1947 to 1958 when Alemán and Ruíz Cortines were President.

Party discipline rather than constitutional power is now the more likely device to achieve state conformity with national policies; a governor who cannot keep order in his state, or who fails to carry out his share of a national programme, will usually resign. Direct

[1] William P. Tucker, *The Mexican Government Today* (1957), pp. 73–81, 377–408, with extensive bibliography.

Federal intervention to rid a state of a troublesome local régime is on the wane.

It seems clear from even this brief examination that federalism in Mexico is a myth. Theory and practice elevate the nation far above the states. Within the national system division of powers tends also to be illusory. The President, as chief executive and principal administrator, towers above the Deputies and Senators of Congress. Circumscribed constitutionally and procedurally, the judiciary also plays an important but clearly subordinate role.

Chapter XIV

PRESIDENTIAL GOVERNMENT: A REVOLUTIONARY INSTRUMENT

ONCE it is understood that the formal prescriptions of the 1917 constitution have been modified by Mexican practice, the main lines of formal governmental apparatus are rather simply outlined. Mexico is a federally organized republic composed of twenty-nine states, two territories, and a Federal District. The 1917 constitution, fifth of a series of such written documents (1824, 1836, 1837, 1857), divides responsibilities into executive, legislative, and judicial powers, of which the executive is purposely the most powerful and independent.

EXECUTIVE POWER

The President is elected every six years, after which he is ineligible for re-election. The executive powers of Government are constitutionally vested in him.

Though he wields power many a dictator might envy, the President of Mexico can nearly always point to a constitutional provision that justifies nearly any public act he wishes to perform. Every President since Carranza has had these mandates, but events in Mexico since 1917 indicate that constitutional prerogatives alone do not determine the course of policy, although this must remain within constitutional bounds.[1] The limits can be sketched quickly.

By constitutional mandate, the President must be a native-born Mexican, son of Mexican parents (Art. 82), at least 35 years old, and resident in the country at least a year before his election. The Vice-Presidency established in 1904 was purposely omitted from the constitution of 1917, thereby removing a focus of intrigue, and enhancing the distance between the President and other national officials, most of whom he appoints.[2] Succession to the Presidency in case of death or disability is in the hands of Congress, under various circumstances outlined in the constitution (Arts. 84–85).

[1] Stephen S. Goodspeed, 'El papel del jefe del ejecutivo en México', *Problemas industriales e agricolas de México*, vii (Jan.-Mar. 1955), 13–208, discusses dominance of executive, and provides biographies of Revolutionary Presidents, with contemporary cartoons.

[2] Tucker, *Mexican Government*, pp. 102–10.

The President is given extensive, specific authority. Article 89 provides him wide latitude of appointments: ministers, attorney-general, governor of the Federal District and territorial governors, treasury officials, and all others whose appointment is not specified by law or the constitution. This embraces the military establishment, including ranks of colonel and above. He has unlimited power of removal of officials, but for appointments concurrence by the Senate is sometimes specified.

There is no merit system in the Mexican civil service, and bureaucrats have very little legal protection.[1] Himself a career civil servant, President Ruíz Cortines gave them a rise in salary, but also initiated the Law of Responsibilities, which requires senior officials to file financial statements, open to the public.

The President is the head of the military establishment, both in regard to internal order and external threat. Congress usually accedes to his request to mobilize state militia, especially at election times. With the consent of the Senate, the President has the power to declare war. This is usually followed by the suspension of certain constitutional guarantees and a special grant of power to the President to legislate by decree even in those fields nominally reserved to Congress. In this century, the only declaration of war was against the Axis powers in 1942, with limited suspension of individual constitutional safeguards.

The President normally conducts most foreign relations. He appoints and removes the Foreign Minister at will. Apart from required Senate ratification of treaties, he has complete control over the apparatus of diplomacy. Under Article 33, he can eject from the country any foreigner whose presence he deems detrimental to the welfare of Mexico.

Both on the positive and negative side, his control of legislation is substantial. Only the President can promulgate a law, by signing it and ordering its publication. He can veto legislation, *in toto* or by item. Hence in the unlikely event of Congress overriding a presidential veto, as it has done only twice since 1920, there is no constitutional way in which he can be forced to promulgate legislation still repugnant to him.

More important and quite apart from any extraordinary powers conferred on him by Congress, the President has positive authorization

[1] Antonio García Valencia, *Las Relaciones humanas en la administración pública Mexicana* (1958), pp. 107–13; this is an excellent history and analysis of the civil service; ch. 8 deals with contemporary problems of the civil servant. Tucker, *Mexican Government*, pp. 121–48, for description of public administration.

to meet crises. Draft legislation submitted to the Congress by the executive takes priority over other business and bills. Under implied powers, he and his ministers draw up the detailed regulations and codes to carry out constitutional mandates or to give administrative effect to general Congressional statutes. A valid regulation has the force of law. Until about 1938, it was customary for Congress to grant the President the power to govern by decree, often near the end of a Congressional session, nominally to be reviewed by the following session. In the past two decades, however, this delegation of its constitutional responsibility has ceased; President Cárdenas, in 1938, had the constitution amended and strengthened to prevent this action, on which much of the Díaz negation of the constitution had rested.

A powerful weapon which the President exercises is his budget-making prerogatives. Normally, after he and his ministers (with advice from interested groups in the 'official' party) have outlined the needs, requirements, and proposed financing of programmes, the budget is submitted to Congress about a fortnight before it terminates its session. There is little discussion, and no change in executive proposals on these fixed fiscal matters.[1]

In the office and person of the President, then, converge the extra-constitutional system represented by the evolving 'official party',[2] which he heads, and the formal organs of Government stipulated in the constitution. The role which he plays in party matters has been changing, and in turn, the function of the President as constitutional head of the state has altered. With the growing complexity of social, economic, and even political life in recent times, fusion of party and formal organs goes on apace. Both have begun to stabilize on an institutional rather than personalistic basis.

THE LEGISLATIVE BRANCH

Congress is the legislative branch, nominally a second and co-ordinate power equal to the executive. This theoretical equality has been generally breached in practice, partly because the members of Congress, drawn from the same 'official party' as the President and his Cabinet, defer to the executive more as head of the party than as head of state.

Congress consists of a lower house, the Chamber of Deputies, and a Senate. Each Deputy in 1958 represented 170,000 inhabitants.

[1] R. E. Scott, 'Budget Making in Mexico', *Inter-American Economic Affairs*, ix (Autumn 1955), 3–20.
[2] See below, Ch. XV.

Deputy and an Alternate are directly elected by popular vote every three years; neither can be immediately re-elected, although an Alternate can become a Deputy and a Deputy his Alternate. Each state has a minimum of two Deputies, each territory one. There are at present 162 Deputies, of whom the PRI elected 153 in July 1958; the remaining nine were scattered among minor parties.

The Senate, composed of two Senators for each state and the Federal District, at present has sixty members. They are popularly elected at the same time as the President and serve the same six-year term. Since its inception, the 'official party' has monopolized the Senate; all Senators elected in July 1958 with President López Mateos are PRI members.

Annually Congress convenes for one regular session, 1 September, to 31 December. At its opening, the President is required to present a 'State of the Nation' report, a summary message with suggestions for legislation. Radio and television now carry this as an important public event of great solemnity, and the discourse is widely circulated in the press. Between regular Congressional sessions a Permanent Committee (15 Deputies, 14 Senators) remains in the capital to transact routine business: the preparation of reports on pending legislation, and formulation of agenda for the forthcoming session. In an emergency, the Committee has the power, almost never invoked, to summon Congress for an 'extraordinary' session.

We have noted the emphasis on executive rather than legislative functions in the constitution of 1917, as compared with the 1857 constitution. However, the 1917 constitution does confer duties on Congress. Its function is to legislate. In this field its actions fall into three general categories of law: ordinary, organic, and regulatory. The ordinary law carries out an activity already authorized by the constitution. Organic laws are general codes that define and regulate an organ of Government, specifying its jurisdiction and broad mandates; a Ministry or a semi-autonomous body like Petróleos Mexicanos (Pemex) must function within the Organic Law constituting it. Regulatory laws are detailed administrative and legal codes on various subjects. Congress, over a twenty-year period, has concerned itself almost exclusively with the latter type law, ten times as much legislation falling into that class than for the other two combined.[1]

Bills which become law derive from various sources. Drafts introduced by the President must take priority, with bills submitted

[1] Tucker, *Mexican Government*, pp. 95–97; the legislation of 'ordinary' and 'organic' laws was quantitatively about equal.

by state legislatures in second place. Congressional bills drawn by members are third. Most Congressional actions emerge from the labours in each chamber of standing committees, of which that on Legislative Studies is central. Bills must be passed by both houses, signed by the President, and published in the official gazette before becoming effective as laws three days after such publication.

Each chamber has some exclusive prerogatives, which tend to be nominal in view of the strong executive system. The Chamber of Deputies approves the annual budget, discusses taxes, and verifies election returns. It considers accusations made against public officials, and can bring impeachment proceedings before the Senate. The latter has the exclusive power to ratify treaties as well as high presidential appointments. It also can declare that the constitutional powers of a state have 'disappeared', or that a 'conflict of arms' disturbing to constitutional order has arisen, permitting Federal intervention to designate a provisional state administration.

Congress, because of presidential pressures, one student declares, 'is not really fulfilling its constitutional duties and it is not likely to in the foreseeable future'. He adds, 'On the whole, it serves as little more than a convenient training ground for ambitious young politicians . . . as a kind of convenient patronage for certain political and functional leaders, or as a quiet tapering-off appointment for older politicians who no longer are as efficient as they once were. . . .'[1]

THE JUDICIARY AND LAW

The third branch of Government is the judiciary. There is a Federal judiciary, and a system of state courts. The President appoints (with Senatorial approval) the twenty-one members of the Supreme Court, highest in the Federal system, and these judges in turn appoint justices for the circuit and district courts. The President, with majority support in both houses of Congress, may remove judges for misbehaviour. As the press of judicial business has grown, the size of the Supreme Court has been successively enlarged and the court system expanded.

In 1917 the Supreme Court was a single, eleven-man bench which in 1928 was subdivided into three chambers (*salas*): civil, criminal, and administrative. In 1934, in a vain attempt to cope with an increasing backlog of unheard cases, a labour *sala* was added, and a fifth general chamber was temporarily authorized in 1951. The circuit court system is relatively new, again a device to improve the

[1] Scott, *Mexican Government*, p. 265.

administration of justice by providing a layer of courts between the district courts and the Supreme Court. To relieve the latter's load, five circuit courts were established in 1951 and in 1954 a sixth was formed especially for the Federal District.

Administrative changes left undisturbed the tradition, dating from the native period, that law and justice is a main concern of Government. The heritage of civil law, adapted first in Spain and then to conditions in New Spain and Mexico, forms the context in which the judiciary discharges its responsibilities.

The Rule of Law

Mexico falls into the great class of countries which follow the civil law, as distinct from the common law tradition. Hence its judicial practices are more comparable with those of France, Italy, and Spain than they are with the traditions developed in Great Britain, the United States, and a number of the members of the British Commonwealth. In common law, precedent and custom form a growing corpus of legal tissue; the law is always being sought; it is evolutionary, flexible, often uncertain. Civil law, on the other hand, derives from absolute principles, compiled primarily in the Roman *Corpus Juris Civilis* of Justinian, and after Roman times, modified and adapted to national ends and needs. The Code Napoléon(1804) exercised wide influence, and directly served as a model for many Mexican practices. Civil law aims at being scientific, systematic, clear, and codified to such a degree that precedent has little place. Changes and modifications in codes do not disturb the static, fixed general principles of civil law, but merely alter and extend their application.

Civil Law Tradition

Therefore, in Mexico, law is tantamount to codes, numerous compilations of extremely detailed prescriptions. 'The expression, "rule of law" is not employed in my country', a distinguished Mexican jurist recently told a North American audience. 'We speak instead of the "Estado de Derecho" [state of law], as the Germans and the French, and of the "principio de legalidad" [principles of legality] as they do.' The 'principle of legality', he explained, 'means that all action on the part of the courts and the administrative authorities must conform to a law, that is, to a general, pre-existing rule.'[1]

[1] Gustavo R. Velasco, 'The Rule of Law in Mexico', in David S. Stern, ed., *Mexico: a Symposium on Law and Government* (1958), pp. 9–12; see also in the same volume, Lucio Cabrera A., 'History of the Mexican Judiciary', pp. 22–31.

These 'pre-existing rules' are found in a hierarchy of codes. The first and paramount of these is the constitution. Its detailed specifics of procedure parallel similar documents in other Latin American lands and in European countries where the civil law tradition exists. They are in sharp contrast to the much more general, and sometimes vague, statements of the United States constitution, and obviously are at the opposite extreme from the 'unwritten' British constitution. Following the Justinian and Napoleonic models, the major Mexican codes are civil (with derivative procedural codes for various categories of crime); commercial; and from their own experiences, labour. Each code in its turn may give rise to bodies of procedural regulations.

In very general terms, the duty of the judiciary is to decide in each instance what sections of codes and then which of the contending interpretations of them apply to the dispute in view. Under the theory of government implicit in civil law countries, the function of the legislature is to fill in the details of a pre-existing general system whose principles have long been established, and the function of the executive is to administer the corpus of rules.

The judiciary decides only whether administrative actions conform to such rules. Neither in theory nor in practice do they affect the rules themselves. As implied above, both the substance and procedures of many, if not most, of these codified prescriptions are drafted by the executive as chief administrator, and then submitted to Congress for possible modifications. Once passed by the latter, and signed by the President, these become the 'pre-existing rules'. The judiciary merely settles disputes concerning the application of one or another to a specific case. In short, Mexico has no 'judge-made' law of real consequence such as may develop from judicial decisions based on common law. Furthermore, the Mexican Supreme Court has no powers, implied or direct, to declare laws 'unconstitutional'.

This foreshortened summary sketch does not do full justice to the complexities and ramifications of the Mexican legal system nor the protections it affords. With an almost opposite approach from that underlying the more familiar common-law tradition, civil law seems at first glance to lack the built-in Anglo-American guarantees deemed the corner-stone of liberty. However, these are present, in civil law, but in quite distinct form. It would carry us beyond the bounds of space to explain them in detail, but fortunately there is a great body of writings about Mexican civil law for those who wish to pursue the topic further.[1]

CIVIL LIBERTIES, CONSTITUTIONAL GUARANTEES, AND *AMPARO*

The first twenty-nine articles of the Mexican constitution are a 'Bill of Rights'. They guarantee freedom of expression, press; equality before the law; right to free petition and assembly; freedom of education (Art. 3), right to travel, to work; and numerous prohibitions: slavery, imprisonment for debt, retroactive laws, even monopolies. To restrain an executive action under one or more of these twenty-nine articles is a safeguard known as the writ of *amparo*. The use of the writ is specified in the constitution (Arts. 103, 107).

The writ of *amparo* is a bulwark of liberty, and one of Mexico's unique contributions to jurisprudence. It is obtainable under given circumstances to protect the citizen from damage to his interests or invasion of his constitutional guarantees. The word means 'protection', and to the layman appears to combine the characteristics of English injunctions, writs of *habeas corpus, mandamus,* and *certiorari.* Derived from the state constitution of Yucatán (1842), the writ can be issued only by a Federal Court, in non-political matters, and restrains the Federal bureaucracy from damaging actions.

The enormous backlogs in the courts arise from applications for *amparo*, almost routinely sought in a bewildering variety of contingencies. Each application is heard on its own merits; in the face of an adverse decision it is generally appealed to higher courts. Successful action on the part of the applicant does not repeal the law under which the proposed bureaucratic activity was initiated, but merely prevents it from occurring in that instance. Use of the writ became so much abused that in 1955 the Supreme Court tightened up in some degree the general rules governing its issuance. It still remains a silent and powerful guardian against tyranny of the national Government and its impingement on fundamental personal and individual liberties.

[1] See espec. S. A. Bayitch, *Guide to Inter-American Legal Studies* (1957); John T. Vance and Helen Clagett, *A Guide to the Law and Legal Literature of Mexico* (1945). General treatments include Helen L. Clagett, *Administration of Justice in Latin America* (1952), with a chapter on *amparo*, and her 'Law and Courts', in Harold E. Davis, ed., *Government and Politics in Latin America* (1958), pp. 333–67. Details on the Mexican system are summarized in Alberto Bremauntz, *Por una justicia al servicio del pueblo* (1955), and on individual liberties, Ignacio Burgoa, *Las Garantías individuales*, 2nd ed. (1954). Tucker, *Mexican Government*, pp. 111–20; Scott, *Mexican Government*, pp. 266–72.

Chapter XV

SINGLE-PARTY DEMOCRACY: THE EVOLUTION OF THE OFFICIAL PARTY

By aspiration and halting practice Mexico is a democratic nation. From independence its goals have been thus set. In these latter years of the Institutional Revolution the earlier gap between democratic theory and practice has been steadily closing. Yet, paradoxically, Mexico has virtually only one political party, usually known as the 'official party'. It is an important apparatus which enhances and reinforces the enormous reservoirs of power available to a centralized governmental system centred in the President.

Superficially this combination would seem conducive to despotism and tyranny, a total restriction of democratic impulses. In fact, the results have been the opposite: a gradual broadening of liberties and a widening of participation in national decisions. Part of the explanation for this lies in the nature, evolution, and workings of the dominant PRI (Institutional Revolutionary Party). Not the least of its virtues has been to bring to the Presidency able men, appropriate to the historic moment, as will be seen in Chapter XVI.[1]

DEVELOPMENT

To meet a specific historical situation, the 'official party' was created in 1929 as a cartel to control the localized political machines and interests. It has undergone several basic modifications, changing its name three times in accordance with its altered structure and emphasis. From 1929 through 1937 it was known as the National Revolutionary Party, PNR (*Partido Nacional Revolucionario*); in 1937 it became the PRM, Party of the Mexican Revolution (*Partido de la*

[1] The best, most extensive history and discussion of the 'official party' is Scott, *Mexican Government*, pp. 115–96; two unpublished recent theses also provide much data and insight: Frank R. Brandenburg, 'Mexico: an Experiment in One Party Democracy' (1956, Univ. of Pennsylvania), and Leon V. Padgett, 'Popular Participation in the Mexican "One Party" System' (1955, Northwestern Univ.); Tucker, *Mexican Government*, pp. 41–69, is descriptive; Philip B. Taylor, 'The Mexican Elections of 1958' (1959), is provocative and clashes with views expressed in Padgett's 'Mexico's One Party System', *Amer.Pol.Sci.R.*, li (Dec. 1957) 995–1008. Many details of the early days of the 'official' party are given in Emilio Portes Gil, *La Crisis política de la Revolución y la próxima elección presidencial* (1957). See also Cline, 'Mexico: a Maturing Democracy', *Current History* (Mar. 1953), 136–42.

Revolución Mexicana). From 1945 onwards it has been the PRI, Institutional Revolutionary Party (*Partido Revolucionario Institucional*).

These minor changes in name in fact mark real and significant internal developments. The historian can see four, possibly five, clear stages in the evolution of the party. First the pre-constitutional (1910–17) and early post-constitutional years (1917–28). Next the formation of the PNR and its activities until the accession of Cárdenas to the Presidency in 1934 mark a distinct epoch. Thirdly, the consolidation and rearrangement of party elements on a functional rather than a geographical basis during his presidential years (1934–40), under the name of PMR. Lastly, an increasing institutionalization, democratization and complexity of party structure and operations under Presidents Avila Camacho, Ruíz Cortines, and López Mateos (1940–60).

Some observers would add a fifth stage, possibly now beginning to emerge. Interest groups within the PRI, restless for various reasons, threaten to withdraw from the cartel and dissolve the PRI into three main national political parties. One would be agrarian based, another labour based, and the third would embrace middle-class and bureaucratic groups as well as numerous fringe and splinter interests now in the heterogeneous section (Popular) of the PRI.

Pre-Party Years

The matrix from which the party sprang in the years from 1910 through 1928 is the chaos created by the breakdown of organized political life during the militant years of the Revolution, and the attempt following the constitution of 1917 to stop continued bloodshed by unstable armistice arrangements among regional military leaders. From these complicated times a coalition of forces represented by Adolfo de la Huerta, Alvaro Obregón, and Plutarco Elías Calles managed by 1920 to impose some order on Mexico and to bring about an uneasy peace. Agrarian and labour forces had tentatively entered the realm of politics, though as considerably junior partners to the military chiefs on whom they perforce leaned for political success.

Of the triumvirate, de la Huerta was eliminated by his unsuccessful efforts to revolt against Obregón, who was President from 1920 to 1924, when he was succeeded by Calles. It appeared that a system alternating these two strong men, each with powerful military and civilian backing, would mark the new order of Mexican politics, instead of the one-man rule of Díaz. The constitution was amended: 'no re-election' was to mean 'no successive re-election', thus permitting Obregón to step back into the Presidency at the close of the Calles term in 1928. Presumably Calles would have similarly resumed this post in 1932, but before Obregón had been officially inaugurated as President, he was assassinated by a religious fanatic unconnected with any real political movement. Apart from removing from the scene one of the major figures of the Revolution, his death posed serious political problems for the followers of Obregón and Calles. The latter could not succeed himself, for this would have rekindled the original sparks of the Revolution ignited by Madero's stirring cry of 'no re-election'.

Birth of the Party, 1929

To solve this dilemma, Calles, his followers, and the allied groups supporting Obregón, created in 1929 a cartel, the PNR, National Revolutionary Party. Thus the one-party political system was an invention forced by circumstance. The party was a coalition of military chiefs, each with considerable autonomy in his locality, and locally supported by small groups of peasants and labour unions. Through his prestige and power, Calles became 'Highest Chief'. As the power behind three civilians who followed one another as part-term Presidents (1928–34), he also spent a good deal of time whittling aways the strength of individual regional chieftains, while building up the strength of the single dominant party. It was still operating in an atmosphere of internal family quarrels among chiefs of the Revolution and possible successful counter-revolution by vested interests outside the family circle.

As a political machine the PNR was able to mobilize nearly all the political power of Mexico through its informal and loose machinery. It regularly defeated opposition candidates of short-lived dissident groups at the polls. In the Calles period the party obtained an unshakable hold on political life that has never subsequently been successfully challenged.

Calles, the dominant political boss but also the successful businessman, miscalculated the situation as he grew more and more remote from newer trends. Under the double impact of world depression and the growing conservatism of Revolutionary generals who had translated political power into personal wealth, the Revolution seemed to have come to a standstill by 1933: agrarian reform had stopped, labour gains wilted, talk of democracy ceased. Calles erred by assuming that Lázaro Cárdenas, a popular and successful general, would be another docile puppet President. In the elections of 1934, as the official presidential candidate of the PNR Cárdenas could hardly lose; nor did he.

THE FUNCTIONAL PARTY: 1934 AND AFTER

Despite the expectation that he would be elected without campaigning, Cárdenas made pre-election visits to every part of the Republic, building up local support and, more important, reviving hopes that the Revolution would now again begin to fulfil its earlier promises. Elected with mass support, he then proceeded to reorganize the official party in such a way as to block and upset its working, as contrived originally by Calles. When the inevitable test of strength came, Cárdenas won; Calles went into exile, never to exercise significant power again.[1]

Cárdenas replaced the regional chieftain base of the party with 'functional' non-regional units: military, labour, agrarian, and 'popular'—unorganized proletarian. Each of these social and economic interests formed a national 'sector' of the party, co-ordinated at the national, state, and local levels by committees on which each was represented. Each sector's line of force reached from the centre through regions, states, and small localities, to provide candidates, ideas, power, and votes for the single, presidentially dominated party.

The essential feature of the new system, as distinct from the earlier version, was that through caucus or presidential order, all offices were allotted by sectors, and the sole candidate was supported by the other three sectors, i.e. seats in Congress were apportioned in advance, with so many to the military, so many to the agrarian, so many to labour, and the remainder to the popular sector. In a state where the official PRM candidate for the Senate represented labour, the popular, agrarian, and military sectors of that state voted for him, in return for reciprocal party support elsewhere. This system extended down to municipal elections.

The designation of candidates rested almost completely with the President. He might consult with the National Executive Committee, who in turn had solicited advice and suggestions from lower and local echelons. But the final decision was the President's, as national political boss. One result of the Cárdenas reorganization of the party was to nationalize and centralize politics. Direct control over local elements was removed from regional chieftains, who had previously manipulated them.

[1] For a Communist-slanted, but essentially correct view of these years, see Nathaniel and Sylvia Weyl, *The Reconquest of Mexico: the Years of Lázaro Cárdenas* (1939), esp. Ch. 13, 'The Functional Party'. See also, W. Cameron Townsend, *Lázaro Cárdenas* (1952).

Other results were equally important. To provide a counterpoise to military domination of politics, Cárdenas brought into being two potential military forces and prevented their merger. A national labour movement, the CTM (*Confederación de Trabajadores Mexicanos*), was organized on a mass basis and led by a brilliant intellectual, Vicente Lombardo Toledano, who drilled his minions as a paramilitary organization. In parallel fashion the CNC (*Confederación Nacional de Campesinos*) was organized as a rural reserve; collective agrarian communities, ejidos, were grouped into leagues, and the leagues into the central confederation which acted as a voice of the peasants in political circles. Through membership in unions, or ejidos, popular class Mexicans automatically became members of the official party. Bureaucrats and teachers, each with organizations like unions but not classified as labour, similarly formed the backbone of the popular sector.

Natural and irreconcilable conflicts of basic interests among the sectors were resolved by the party leader, the President. In a given decision he could and did act arbitrarily against any given sector's interests. But so great was the advantage of the system in general, and so sure and effective the sanctions against those who failed to conform, that revolts against presidential ukase were few and ineffectual. As Scott has noted, 'At this stage, the President of the Republic became the single most powerful leader in the party and the country'.[1] He ruled, as well as reigned.

This power base, whose lines of command emanated from and terminated in the Presidency, permitted Cárdenas to carry forward vigorously the Revived Revolution. This is also the stage in the party's evolution when it was most nearly monolithic. Earlier it had been a rather loose alliance of local machines and later new elements and changed forms reduced its monolithic character. It has always retained most of its monopolistic political features.

Although the official party did not take the name of PRI (Institutional Revolutionary Party) until 1945, the trends which resulted in the new name were ushered in by President Avila Camacho and his national policies of unity, adjustment, and moderation during the years of the Second World War.[2] The basic framework provided by President Cárdenas was preserved, but one important change was made. The military sector, as such, was dropped. There had been considerable dissatisfaction expressed both by civilian critics and by the military themselves, at their overt identification with

[1] Scott, *Mexican Government*, p. 116.
[2] Cline, *U.S. and Mexico*, pp. 261–305, gives details.

The Organization of the PRI

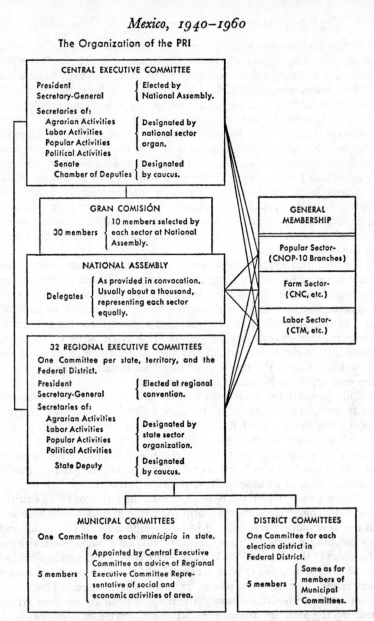

direct political action. Hence after December 1940 the official party had a triangular base: the farm, labour, and popular sectors.

Military men who wished to combine politics with their professional careers could and did affiliate themselves with civilian organizations grouped within the popular sector. That tendency, however, is decreasing as years pass. The military has relinquished the active political role it played during earlier periods. We shall touch on this development again below (Ch. XVIII).

The main features that distinguish the present PRI from its predecessors are the increased number of interest groups which have entered the 'official' fold, the decentralization of power to state units of the PRI, the growing responsiveness to public opinion, and the transfer of many of its earlier extra-legal functions to regular constitutional organs of Government. Noteworthy too is its broadened base and internal reforms, designed to encourage more active participation by the people. The cumulative weight of alterations brought about by industrialization, urbanization, education, shifting of class structures, increased transportation and communications, and the other developments which have been or will be noted, has changed the structure of the party, and especially the role of the President as party leader.

Descriptions of ten or twenty years ago labelling the PRM as an authoritarian, monolithic, almost irresponsible arm of Cárdenas are now anachronistic.[1] The President is still constitutional head of the state and party leader, but for numerous reasons he can no longer rule absolutely.

ORGANIZATION: THE SECTORS

In its previous phase, under Cárdenas, the PRM had a definite, clearly collectivist, proletarian orientation which in the past twenty years has been modified. The modifications have come about largely through affiliating unlike organizations, representing various class levels, within a given sector. For instance, now within the farm sector are not only the members of collectivist ejidos, the original CNC, but also organizations representing wage-earners on private lands, and the technicians, the Mexican Society of Agronomists. Within the labour sector, still largely dominated by the CTM (purged of its Communist leadership) are two fairly sizable blocs with diametrically opposed views on most matters. The popular sector has now become even more heterogeneous than it was at the outset, and is the main beneficiary of recent social and economic

[1] J. Lloyd Mecham, 'Mexican Federalism: Fact or Fiction?' *A.Amer.Acad.Polit.*, ccviii (March 1940), 34–35; Frank Tannenbaum, *Mexico: the Struggle for Peace and Bread* (1950), p. 94.

changes. To the old core of bureaucrats and teachers have been added organized groups of intellectuals, small merchants and industrialists, artisans, yeoman farmers, women's organizations, street vendors, and military personnel. (See Appendix Table XII.)

Looking at these sectors a little more closely, one immediately finds that evidence about party membership and that of the sectors is contradictory, incomplete, and generally unreliable. Professor Robert Scott has presented a documented general picture for about 1958. He notes that the situation includes sub-alliances and co-operative efforts between like groups of different sectors in the give and take of day-to-day politics, overlapping memberships, and other factors. Appendix Table XII illustrates sector memberships. It shows that the farm sector, with 2·6 millions (40·5 per cent.), is largest; labour, with 2·1 millions (31·8 per cent.), comes second; the popular sector is smallest, with 1·8 millions (27·7 per cent.) of the total 6·6 millions. 'Efforts to measure the relative political influence of each sector', Professor Scott warns, 'are not likely to be very fruitful.'

At present there remain outside the fold of the official party only a very few groups who do not have a direct voice in the formulation of sector and thus PRI programmes. Perhaps the most important of these are the members of the Catholic Church, large industrialists and bankers, and the few remnants of the large landholding class. Their views are made known in other ways, often through ephemeral opposition parties.

By absorbing new interests as they have appeared in significant numbers, the PRI has diversified its membership. With each sector now embracing greater numbers and types of component organizations, the President and party officials who strive to maintain intra-party balances and party harmony now have greater room for manoeuvre and compromise. In contrast to the personal, detailed scrutiny that Cárdenas gave proposals, and the limitless power he wielded, the President now takes a different line of action, which has been summarized by Professor Scott:

The President's function as party chief and political master of the country now consists of balancing interests, of adjusting conflicts so as to avoid disruption of economic and social development, and of encouraging participation in the national political system by as many Mexicans as possible, in order to reduce still further the possibility of interruptions in the peaceful operation of the political system.[1]

[1] *Mexican Government*, p. 117. Cf. Padgett, in *Amer.Pol.Sci.Rev.*, li, 998: 'the Mexican president no longer is able to govern in detail as he once could. Responsibility must be delegated to an increasing degree'.

Chapter XVI

RECENT PRESIDENTS, 1940–60

THE present generation of political leaders in Mexico were small children or yet unborn when Francisco I. Madero launched the Mexican Revolution in 1910. Many were still of university age when General Cárdenas revitalized the movement for radical reform and provided the main instruments to carry forward its objectives: a nationalized petroleum industry, a nationalized railway system, a functional monopolistic political machine, a communal farm programme, an organized and militant labour movement, and an assured place in the great coalition which in the Second World War defeated Fascist totalitarianism.

Presidents Manuel Avila Camacho, Miguel Alemán, and Adolfo Ruíz Cortines were his immediate successors. With party and popular support, they surmounted the main crises of their times. From their régimes Mexico emerged stronger in almost every respect. There is every reason to believe that fourth in this line of 'party Presidents', Adolfo López Mateos, whose term extends to 1964, will continue the main lines of policy of his predecessors.

This continuity is no accident. One important requisite for future presidential candidacy is proved ability to work smoothly in the current administrative team, and since 1940 the President's Cabinet has been the main preserve from which new presidential candidates have been selected. There are now numerous other requisites; after four nominations since Cárdenas, political scientists have been able to abstract the general pattern, and to indicate why some 'pre-candidates' fade so quickly from the scene after they have been launched.[1] One observer comments, 'What is amazing is the high level of competence and political ability the official candidates have demonstrated in the presidency',[2] and the record bears out that view.

MIGUEL ALEMÁN, 1946–52

The name of Miguel Alemán evokes few cheers in the Mexico of 1960. He is, as Mexicans say, 'a shot cartridge', because in the

[1] Philip B. Taylor, 'The Mexican Elections of 1958', *Western Pol. Science Quarterly*, xiii (Sept. 1960), 722–44; Scott, *Mexican Government*, pp. 211–16. See above, Ch. XV, concerning the workings of the party.
[2] Scott, *Mexican Government*, p. 216.

closing months of his régime and as ex-President he and his cronies used political influence for economic gain and enriched themselves at public expense. His following in government circles is still powerful. They link Big Business and the formulators of policy, but countervailing pressures keep both him and his followers from the excesses that cost him the genuine support he had enjoyed before and during early presidential years.

Born at Sayula, Veracruz, in 1902, Alemán inherited the prestige of his father, a famous local hero of the Revolution. Educated locally, with a law degree from the National University, the young man served his political apprenticeship under President Portes Gil. Helpful in the fierce intra-party struggles by which Cárdenas ousted Calles,[1] Alemán as a reward became governor of Veracruz at the age of 34. Winning a good reputation in state politics, he was elevated to the national arena in 1940 as campaign manager— which means the party's and the candidate's key man—for Manuel Avila Camacho. In that capacity he became acquainted with every important local, state, and national politician.

These relationships were strengthened from 1940 through 1946 when, as Minister of Government (*Gobernación*), he was made responsible for internal security, the conduct of elections, and the supervision of the innumerable details of a sprawling executive bureaucracy. He deserves much of the credit for the deft handling of troublesome matters such as Axis espionage and Sinarquista threats to order, and the development of unity, harmony, and domestic stability in the Avila Camacho régime.

In May 1945 a secret conclave of leading men in the party agreed that he should be the next 'official' presidential candidate. Both his major rivals, General Miguel Henríquez Guzmán and Javier Rojo Gómez, seemed likely to return to the more extreme policies of the Cárdenas régime,[2] just at a time when Mexico was partially committed to a policy of industrialization begun during the war. Following the earlier precedent set by Cárdenas and Avila Camacho, Alemán campaigned in all parts of the Republic, on the moderate platform which the newly organized PRI had concocted. Unlike them, Alemán presented no Six-Year Plan full of 'class struggle' slogans; he sketched broad lines of advance, and on his campaign visits held round-tables and forums to allow the expression of local opinion. Alemán was elected in 1946 with approximately

[1] See above, pp. 151–2.
[2] See above, p. 32

three-quarters of the votes, much of the remainder going to General Henríquez Guzmán.

As President, Alemán pushed industrialization forward with all the numerous resources available. He negotiated international loans to put the transportation system on a solid basis, and transformed the national oil monopoly, Petróleos Mexicanos (Pemex) from an economic shambles into an efficient and productive part of the developing economy. He established the Ministry of Hydraulic Resources to bring more land into agricultural production, and sketched out an elaborate plan of irrigation Commissions.[1] Broad powers were given to Nacional Financiera, the government development corporation, to fill in the gaps of the economic system. All these efforts resulted in mounting agricultural production, industrial growth, per capita income, gross national product, and increased school facilities.

But by 1952 there was a general feeling in Mexico that Alemán had gone too far and too fast, and that a slackening of tempo was needed. The forced pace of economic change had resulted in corruption and scandals. Moreover, to keep the new policies moving in the direction he believed important and necessary, Alemán had used a heavy political hand; there were several notorious cases of the forced imposition of state governors. Widespread labour unrest had resulted from his curb on wages in an effort to keep down production costs and his use of troops at an early stage to prevent strikes in the oil industry. Similarly, his apparent lack of interest in the ejido programme of communal farms[2] had generated discontent in agricultural circles.

The present disrepute into which the Alemán administration has fallen may well prove ephemeral in the long term. Alemán's personal greed seems inexcusable, but the corruption prevalent during his term of office may well have been a local manifestation of 'normal' laxities that seem always to plague a post-war world, and also the regular price that is paid in the earliest phase of rapid industrialization. Such considerations may redirect attention to the real contributions Alemán made during his term as President. He took a few of the partially sketched social and economic projects evolved during Avila Camacho's term, developed their framework, started their implementation, and left to his successors an improved Mexico moving in the direction he had clearly outlined.

[1] See above, Ch. VII.
[2] See below, Ch. XVII.

ADOLFO RUÍZ CORTINES, 1952–8

Alemán's successor was Adolfo Ruíz Cortines, a quiet, able bureaucrat who prevented Mexico from exploding into renewed violence. Again, he was the PRI's alternative to a renewed enthusiasm for General Guzmán. This was no time to toss a match into the powder keg.

A native of Veracruz like Alemán, Adolfo Ruíz Cortines was born in 1890 of a relatively poor family. Left fatherless when only three months old, he was educated in local schools. He has a Revolutionary pedigree in his own right; in 1912 he left Veracruz for Mexico City where he became a public supporter of Madero, not long before Madero was murdered; later he supported Carranza, and worked in his secret police. While acting in minor posts— paymaster, staff—he also became secretary to General Jacinto B. Treviño. During President Obregón's régime, Ruíz Cortines served in the army as an administrative officer, leaving that post in 1926 to become Director of Social Statistics. He filled various bureaucratic posts, including one term as Deputy, until 1940, when he came into Alemán's orbit. As Camacho's campaign manager, Alemán appointed Ruíz Cortines treasurer, because of his irreproachable reputation in money matters. While Alemán was Minister of Government, Ruíz Cortines assisted him as his chief executive officer for nearly four years.[1] As a reward for efficiency and party loyalty, Ruíz Cortines was given official support and won the governorship of Veracruz in 1944. He resigned that position in 1946 to become campaign manager for Alemán. History repeated itself when Alemán appointed him Minister of Government, a useful stepping stone to the Presidency.

Despite many assertions in the press that the President of Mexico can virtually name his successor, this is not wholly true. At the time it was widely, and probably correctly, rumoured that Alemán expected to nominate a member of his so-called 'gang', but that both ex-Presidents Avila Camacho and Cárdenas firmly vetoed the idea. All three 'great electors', the President and the two ex-Presidents, were able to agree on Ruíz Cortines, who was also acceptable to the army and to other party leaders. Thus nominated by the PRI, Ruíz Cortines campaigned in the usual fashion on a platform largely consisting of promises to 'continue President Alemán's work' when he replaced the chief whom he had followed up the ladder for twelve years.

[1] Salvador Pineda, *El Presidente Ruíz Cortines* (1952).

As President, Ruíz Cortines more than carried out his campaign pledges. He continued the constructive work, but purged the Government of some of the more reprehensible practices inherited from the prevous administration. He sacked a number of grafters, and by manipulating elements of the Left without unduly committing himself, he managed to reverse or hold in abeyance proposals advocated by *alemanistas*. At the same time, he accelerated the detailed planning and consultative activities that now occupy so much executive time, to bring into some harmony the agricultural and industrial development of Mexico. There were few innovations made from 1952 through 1958, but the complex machinery of government and administration seemed to run more smoothly than before. Above all, morality in the public service probably reached a level seldom achieved in Mexico.

In his final State of the Nation message to Congress (1 September 1958), President Ruíz Cortines told them that as the responsible leader of the nation he had tried to set new standards of harmony, unity, and hard work. He also stated that while a great part of his term had been dedicated to implementing policies initiated by his predecessors, he was leaving to his successors an enriched legacy, as well as a duty to keep Mexico on its upward path.[1]

ADOLFO LÓPEZ MATEOS, 1958–[64]

Ruíz Cortines was followed by Adolfo López Mateos, the present President of Mexico. He took up Ruíz Cortines's theme in his own first Message on 1 September 1959, when he said:

Our basic effort is maintaining peace and the necessary freedom to assure the full development of man and society. Our domestic policy is inspired in this principle, the realization of which requires complete harmony among all branches of public authority.

The greatness of the nation, he proclaimed in closing, can be achieved only through a combination of ideals and work, on the part of both Government and people, especially at this time of 'impetuous growth and transformation'.[2]

Adolfo López Mateos is as old as the Revolution. He was born in a small town in the state of Mexico on 26 May 1910. His father was a dentist and his mother a grand-daughter of a hero who had

[1] Adolfo Ruíz Cortines, 'El último informe', *El Universal*, 2 Sept. 1958.

[2] Adolfo López Mateos, 'First State of the Union Address: Full Text', *The News: Mexico's English-Language Newspaper*, 2 Sept. 1959; 'Texto íntegro del informe', *El Universal*, 2 Sept. 1959.

fought against the Emperor Maximilian in 1865. Like Ruíz Cortines, López Mateos lost his father before he knew him. His mother moved the family to Mexico City, where she supported five children on a small income. López Mateos won scholarships and prizes in oratory, shone in athletics, and supported himself by working in a library. After leaving his secondary school (Toluca) he taught history and literature at the Normal Institute in Toluca by day and took classes in law at night. As a student-politician, he was a leading light in the Socialist-Labour Party. When Carlos Riva Palacio, then head of the PNR (predecessor of the PRI) came to Toluca in 1929, López Mateos made the speech of welcome. Persuaded by Riva Palacio to change his party allegiance, he became secretary of the PNR's Regional Committee, a position which gave him the opportunity to complete his law degree at the National University in Mexico City.

The friendship between Alemán and López Mateos started before either had risen to political prominence. The eye of General Cárdenas was drawn to López Mateos by his social reform activities. In the ferment of the years following 1934, he worked for various government agencies, notably the Treasury, and then was sent to Toluca Institute as rector to put its muddled affairs in order, a task requiring three years. In 1946 he was elected Senator from the State of Mexico as a reward for his campaign speeches in favour of Alemán. The latter sent him on a number of international missions, and promoted him Ambassador to Costa Rica. A member of the presidential circle, López Mateos was appointed by Ruíz Cortines to be his campaign manager in 1952.

As Minister of Labour in the Ruíz Cortines administration, López Mateos built up an impressive reputation as an able, fair, but tough official. In 1954 he increased his reputation when he averted a general strike for cost-of-living increases without losing the PRI support from organized labour. During his period of office the Ministry dealt with 62,191 disputes, only thirteen of which developed into strikes. His office also handled with finesse the explosive political issue of Mexican migrant contract labour to the United States, getting agreements that protected the *braceros* and controlled their flow.

When the time came for the selection of the next President by the 'great electors', to which President Ruíz Cortines was now added, a number of elements coincided to single out López Mateos from a field of five or six. The younger PRI members felt strongly that power had lain too long in the hands of the old-line Revolutionaries, who were now aging and out of tune with the times, and even the real needs of Mexico. Most important, López Mateos was unique in having the tacit approval of three major party figures: ex-Presidents Alemán and Cárdenas, and the head of the PRI, President Ruíz Cortines. Business interests, now again a factor in politics, also supported him, as did labour, although nominally he belonged to the popular sector of the PRI.

A political scientist who made a special study of the 1958 campaign and elections summed up his findings by saying 'The consensus is that López is reasonably honest and efficient, personally attractive, intellectually superior to most . . . and ideologically moderate. He is clearly devoted to Cárdenas, and the regard is reciprocated. No better combination of qualities could be imagined.'[1]

The PRI in due course ratified the decisions of the higher powers, and López Mateos conformed to tribal *mores* by stumping the country, expounding his views and intentions.[2] As any candidate now must, López Mateos had something to offer to every group: continued agrarian reform, the right to strike, and free enterprise; improved living standards through industrialization; maintenance of nationalized petroleum and railway enterprises; a harmonious balance between rural and urban interests. He also stressed the new and unusual need for Mexico to take a larger, more positive role in international affairs. His extensive campaign tour especially included smaller cities and towns, where he held conferences with local figures. Special teams were sent to remote places with tape-recorders to obtain opinions and personal messages to be relayed to the President-elect. In speeches aimed at these elements, López Mateos emphasized his concern that more benefits of the Revolution should be channelled to rural Mexico. This at least brought from Lázaro Cárdenas the cachet of overt approval which he had withheld from Ruíz Cortines.

One really new note was struck in López Mateos's assertion that closer, reciprocal relationships should be established between the Government and the Roman Catholic Church. In response to a reporter's question, he said, 'I was raised in a Roman Catholic

[1] Taylor, 'Elections of 1958', p. 727. For other sketches of López and his career, see Scott, *Mexican Government*, pp. 218–36, which details his campaign and platform; 'The Paycheck Revolution', *Time* (8 Dec. 1958), pp. 30–44.

[2] *La campaña electoral de 1957–1958* (1958); Juan Espinosa, *Presente y futuro de México* (1958) (results of local round-tables); José Barrales V., ed., *El Pensamiento político de Adolfo López Mateos* (1958) (major campaign and early presidential speeches).

background, but I practice no religion'.[1] Professor Scott indicates that the recent rapprochement between the Church and the PRI fits in with a new Vatican policy for Latin America. The Church seeks to identify itself with liberal social and political doctrines. This coincides with the PRI's recent relaxation of its traditional dogma, including anti-clericalism.[2]

After sporadic labour riots in the interim between election and inauguration, most of the major problems were under firm control. As President, López Mateos could expect to devote a great deal of his term to keeping growth alive, balanced, in Mexican hands, and expanding, sentiments which were marked by cheers during his inaugural address on 1 December 1958.

A SUMMARY

Despite thunder from the Left and some mutterings from the Right, it can be shown that all interest groups have benefited since 1940, some merely more than others. In the Cárdenas decade middle- and upper-class interests were sacrificed for agrarian and labour ones; during the Alemán régime the balances swung violently in the opposite direction, but the pendulum now seems to be making much shorter sweeps, nearer the centre. In most countries this would be hailed as stability and a desirable state of affairs, as it is by most Mexicans. Ritual chants of 'betrayal of the Revolution', however keep complacency from setting in, and furnish ammunition for critics, foreign and domestic, with a nostalgia for the more exciting days of the Revolution.[3]

---

[1] *Time* (8 Dec. 1958), p. 141.

[2] Scott, *Mexican Government*, pp. 231–3. See below, Ch. XVIII.

[3] Simpson, *Many Mexicos*, pp. 293–5; George I. Blanksten, 'Foreign Policy of Mexico', in Roy Macridis, ed., *Foreign Policy in World Politics* (1958), pp. 323–50; Hanke, *Modern Latin America*, vol. 1: *Mexico and the Caribbean*, pp. 68–95, esp. pp. 80–82.

Chapter XVII

BROADENING THE DEMOCRATIC STREAM: ELECTIONS AND PARTIES

PARTLY stemming from its origins, but now thoroughly embedded, is the official party's (PRI's) main function of providing political stability and continuity in constitutional government through the election of 'party Presidents'. With the complex forces and mechanisms that now keep the wheels turning, most observers doubt that any one caudillo or demagogue could capture the whole apparatus and irresponsibly impose his will from the President's chair. Just as the Government has matured in the past two decades, the political system has now 'outstripped the ability of any individual to manipulate it for his own purposes'.[1] Before the invention of the official party, every presidential election touched off a rebellion. Since that time, elections have been peaceful. The unsuccessful revolt of General Saturino Cedillo in 1938 was seemingly the last of the old-style attempts to resist the Government by regional armed uprisings.

With a tradition of full-term civilian Presidents since 1946, the official party is now more prone to search among the Cabinet members for viable successors. The feeling among outside observers is that ex-Presidents have a stronger hand in vetoing particular names on the roster than they have in imposing a particular personal favourite. With the widened scope of government action, in all fields, there is a somewhat similar option by high party functionaries on candidates for state governorships.

Closely connected with stability and peaceful succession, the official party has a general function of preserving continuity of major programmes such as irrigation, transportation, communications, social security, and education. In his first Annual Message in September 1959, President López Mateos took note of the fact that it was unwise and impossible to judge national progress by particular presidential periods—the programmes form part of a more comprehensive party approach that will be implemented, irrespective of the personality or personal inclinations of the particular incumbent.

---

[1] Scott, *Mexican Government*, p. 106.

Argument may occur over emphasis or means, but the major goals remain the same.

The education of the electorate for political action is one such goal. Mexico's official party has oriented its activities toward making more and more Mexicans politically aware and active though it has not fully exploited these possibilities. One of the chief drawbacks to its functioning has been a really small rank and file. Most of its business is carried on by arrangements through leaders representing larger or smaller organized interest groups. Even when party membership has been opened directly to individuals, rather than indirectly via their affiliation with some recognized component of a sector, individual responses have been lukewarm. Despite much ignorance and lack of interest among the electorate, the party performs an important duty in patterning the policies, presenting the issues, educating the masses and getting the people to vote.

The chief business of a political machine is to win elections. This the PRI does by the normal and expected process of providing services to its membership, not only in the form of patronage offices to hard-working politicians, but through directing government attention and policies to those tasks which its sectors and their components believe essential for continuance of their political support. It has an elaborate apparatus to carry out this function. Various other groups have, from time to time, attempted to create workable national parties, which withered chiefly because they could not possibly deliver the goods. The PRI does.

RECENT ELECTIONS, 1940–58

For many years the official party has swept the presidential elections as well as by-elections for Congressional and state posts. The following table summarizes presidential polling.

TABLE 31

Results of Presidential Elections, 1940–58

('000 of votes)

Winner	Official Party vote		Party of National Action		Other		Total votes
	No.	Per cent.	No.	Per cent.	No.	Per cent.	(100·0%)
Avila Camacho	2,176·6	93·1	151·1	6·5	9·8	0·4	2,337·5
Alemán ...	1,786·9	80·1	443·4	18·7	29·6	1·2	2,359·9
Ruíz Cortines	2,713·4	76·4	285·6	8·1	552·2	15·5	3,551·2
López Mateos	6,769·8	90·4	705·3	9·5	10·3	0·1	7,485·4

This table, among other things, shows that more and more Mexicans go to the polls. The increase in figures between 1952 and 1958 represents the enfranchisement of women during the Ruíz Cortines term. Contrary to predictions by opponents of the move, the women did not flock to reactionary, or Church-oriented parties, but in the main voted as did the men, supporting the official party, which had expanded its organizations to include their particular interests and had even, in some instances, nominated some women for lesser government posts.

In general, the votes for the non-official parties and candidates represent a protest vote against the PRI or its candidate. Since Cárdenas was elected in 1934 by 100 to 1 majority there have been these four presidential elections and three additional by-elections for Congressional seats. In each, the official party has garnered a minimum of 75 per cent. of the cast ballots. In view of its history and organization, this is not a particularly noteworthy fact. More relevant here is the size and nature of the opposition.

The PRI is now so secure that it can afford to relax and does not need many of the repressive measures it earlier took in dealing with the opposition. This in large part accounts for the peaceful nature of political campaigns and elections. In sharp contrast with earlier days, armed clashes between partisans simply do not now occur. Under the most extreme provocations in 1958, PRI followers and leaders used restraint; obvious efforts by the Party of National Action (PAN) to harvest a useful crop of martyrs were frustrated. One of their members was unfortunately killed, the sole fatality to mar the record. In the more relaxed atmosphere, the opposition parties go on campaigning, certain of defeat long before the ballots are counted.

THE NOMINAL OPPOSITION

Critics of one-party democracy in Mexico face one major disconcerting fact: at the moment there is no alternative to it. However much the evolution of a system of multi-party politics might be desirable in theory or in fact, the base on which to build successful rivals to the monopolistic official party does not at present exist.

Its very success cuts the ground from under those who most disapprove of its methods. Not only does the PRI win all elections, but it takes note of the votes against it and incorporates into its programme any really popular issues that seem to attract votes to minority parties. In short, with no real hope of gaining political power, the few and small opposition parties have as their main function that of criticism rather than constructive action.

This narrow limit within which opposition parties can act has had disruptive effects on their internal working and development. In nearly every case, an opposition party must choose either to co-operate with the PRI, or to oppose it. If it decides to remain within the main stream of political life, and co-operates with the Government, and even on occasion with the PRI, it finds its best ideas and leaders siphoned off into the official party, where rewards are larger and certain .On the other hand, if it decides to strike an independent stance, withholding co-operation and attempting to woo the mass electorate away from the PRI, it is forced into extremist promises that generally run counter to the temper of the times and the inclinations of most voters. It soon becomes demagogic, or in the Mexican view, anti-Revolutionary, or both, and thereby loses any real mass political appeal.

Thus the opposition parties with ideas and programmes always face a fundamental dilemma which none of them has solved. Nor have splinter groups who have become irritated with PRI policy and separated from the official fold had any greater success. Again their efforts merely give the official party some measure of the real discontent with PRI policy and practice, which can be taken into account. In nearly every case, the dissidents return quietly to the PRI ranks, without prejudice or reprisals.

Party of National Action (PAN)

Of the numerous splinter groups which oppose the PRI, only the Party of National Action (PAN) has anything approaching a continuous party history. It came into being in 1939 around a nucleus of conservative business and professional men, and gathered in other moderate elements genuinely disturbed by what they believed to be the proletarian excesses of the Cárdenas régime. It has always tended to be a regional party, in the sense that whatever strength it can muster generally comes from urban centres in the West and North, especially Guadalajara and Monterrey. While never visibly linked to interests of the Catholic Church, it was reputed to be pro-clerical.

Within its leadership there have been two main factions, vying for control, each with distinct opinions on political tactics. The founding group, headed by Efraín González Luna, urged that PAN remain aloof in permanent opposition to the Revolution.[1] Other elements have advised co-operation and participation in national activities as a 'loyal opposition'. Through this approach, it hoped to gain concessions and modifications of PRI and governmental policies most repugnant to PAN.

In 1940 it had no presidential candidate of its own, but supported General Juan Andreu Almazán in a tense election in which issues were not fully clear. Again in 1946 it merged its small strength with the supporters of the main opposition candidate, Ezequiel Padilla. But in 1952 and also in 1958 it nominated its own men. Results of those elections seem to indicate that on their own PAN candidates can obtain only between 8 and 10 per cent. of the ballots. One reason for this poor showing has been PAN's small membership, limited to the middle- and upper-classes outside the Metropolis and the Core. In 1952 it tried to broaden its base by bringing into its files the leaderless peasant remnants of the Sinarquistas, a Fascist-like movement which through its own excesses had fallen into disrepute and been outlawed.[2] In that same year, in imitation of PRI, PAN attempted to functionalize its structure, and include a few unions, both of workers and of white-collar employees. All these efforts brought small returns at the polls, and split the party anew.

The alliance with Sinarquistas was dissolved, and PAN's other small lower-class support faded. In 1958 it nominated as a 'loyal opposition' presidential candidate Luis H. Alvárez, an irresponsible and quite mediocre figure. Alvárez waged a vigorous, demagogic campaign, charging the PRI with all the ills that ever befell Mexico, including drought; he even claimed that PAN would carry out the aims of the Revolution more effectively! His statements became so pro-clerical that the Church disavowed its connections with PAN, and especially its efforts to capture the newly enfranchised female vote. Again electoral results were negligible, and disruptive. When PRI members of Congress counted the votes, they announced that PAN had won six Deputy posts. The intransigent wing of PAN leadership immediately issued a statement that these Deputies would boycott the Government and not take their seats. Not long thereafter, the 'loyal opposition' contradicted this statement by

---

[1] Efraín González Luna, *Humanismo político* (1955), is a selection of speeches and writings giving PAN (or the González Luna faction of it) positions on many issues.

[2] For the rise and fall of Sinarquismo, see Cline, *U.S. and Mexico*, pp. 318–20; Whetten, *Rural Mexico*, pp. 484–522; Tucker, *Mexican Government*, pp. 61–62; Scott, *Mexican Government*, pp. 182–76.

saying that they would participate in the Government. In fact, four of the six did assume their duties.

These several developments underline not only PAN's weakness at the polls, but also its basic irresponsibility, divided and poor leadership, and lack of any constructive contribution to a real multi-party political system. And it is the most potent, long-lived, and significant of the minority parties!

THE FUTURE

Part of the official party's record of invincibility at the polls arises from another of its important functions: interpreter of the Revolution. At the outset the official party was a league of Revolutionary chieftains bent not only on remaining in power, but protecting the ideals and gains of the movement to date. Part and parcel of this self-appointed apostleship of the party is its continuing task of determining who and what was and is 'Revolutionary'.

No Mexican Marx, Engels, or Trotsky had formulated an embracing ideology in advance. But once the party as a whole has agreed on a particular doctrine, that view is 'official', until replaced by subsequent party pronouncement. Fortunately it does not pretend to infallibility, much less omniscience. Hence it can respond without undue embarrassment to pressures that cause reversals, shifts in emphasis, or expansion of goals. It thus has a built-in mechanism for accommodation. The very length of time that the party has been performing the task of enunciating the ideology of the 'true' (at the moment) Revolution has tended to identify the party with the Revolution in the great mass of Mexican minds. To be for one is to be for the other, with deviations from either likely to arouse suspicion. This pragmatic approach works.

Notwithstanding criticism and pressures, the party has performed and is performing the almost impossible task of keeping some sort of dynamic balance between two sets of Revolutionary goals, essentially incompatible with each other. The social and economic goals which have developed, on the one hand, are radical, with stress on upheaval, rapid and observable removal of any barriers to immediate benefits, and suspicion of the formation of any élites; unchecked, these goals would, as they did in earlier years, hopelessly divide class from class, region from region, generation from generation. On the other hand, the *political* goals of the Revolution were formulated chiefly to stem the excesses of Díaz; on the positive side, they emphasize national unity, moderation, stability, accommodation rather than extirpation in clashes of interest.

Through the PRI there is a link of sorts between what is now popularly called the 'revolution of rising expectations'—demands by the masses for more of the good things they never had—and a steady progress toward a sane political nationalism based on Western democratic norms. Elsewhere I have called the blend 'an American "Middle-Way",' pragmatically developed in Mexico, for Mexicans, by Mexicans.[1]

A few political scientists profess to see on the horizon another step in the evolution of the official party. They contend that sufficient unrest exists among the politically active elements and their leadership to warrant re-examination of the system, which seems to be providing rewards to sectors disproportionate to their political weight. As imbalances increase with the growing labour force and political consciousness stirs the transitional class groups and the masses, they think that fundamental strains will become too great to be settled by the quiet intramural consultations that have been the key feature of the PRI's success in forestalling potential public clashes. Each sector would thus become the nucleus of a separate, national party. Much of this view is based on restlessness within ranks of labour, preceding and following the 1958 elections.

In our view, the dissolution of the PRI into its components is not imminent. There are several factors supporting the *status quo*. Among them is the party tradition to bend always to the breeze and seek internal adjustments to changing situations. Labour problems have apparently been stabilized under López Mateos, possibly selected as candidate because of his outstanding record as Ruíz Cortines's Minister of Labour. Agrarian discontent received the same prompt handling; in his first nine months in office, López Mateos's régime distributed 1·8 million hectares to ejidos, a record. More important, on the positive side, there are no indications that a small, single-interest group as a party in open and fair fight would appreciably improve the position it can now gain by intra-PRI bargaining. Hence the incentive for remaining within the fold is strong.

On the negative side, as has been seen, the record of parties which have attempted to go it alone is not reassuring. At present, then, the probabilities are great that in both the by-elections scheduled for 1961 and in the presidential election in 1964 the PRI or its equivalent will maintain its hegemony. On the basis of the evidence available in 1960 one can concur in the recent statement made by Professor Silvert: 'Labour difficulties offer some hint that the PRI may eventually break into its component interest parts, but it would

[1] Cline, *U.S. and Mexico*, p. 406.

be a rash man indeed who would presume to predict when this split will occur.'[1]

For some time to come, opposition to the PRI is likely to take the main form and general directions it has since 1940. The PAN will probably continue to exist, in its unrewarding role as gadfly and safety-valve for those who wish to make a safe protest vote. Similarly, small splinters within the PRI are likely to break off to promote, for one election only, some cherished approach already turned down in full party councils. But to mobilize effective opposition, any new party will have to demonstrate a number of facts, each difficult to substantiate: that it is more Revolutionary, more democratic, more pragmatic, more tolerant of internal criticism, more capable of leadership and responsibility, more nationally-minded, and more likely to win elections than the PRI.

The statements attributed to Betty Kirk, London *Times* correspondent in Mexico, provide a useful summary of views widely shared both by Mexicans and outside observers. Fully familiar with recent Mexican evolution, she said 'a multiplicity of *effective* parties might mean total chaos'. She added,

The PRI enforces order, but at the same time, in a sense, it's a three party system . . . . Effective balance of conflicting interests within one party is the secret of Mexico's stability and progress over the past two decades. Sooner or later the worst abuses are corrected—else Right or Left would dominate![2]

HOW DEMOCRATIC IS MEXICO?

Perhaps democracy is too valuable a commodity to leave in hands of experts, but one able political scientist has for some years been attempting to measure how 'democratic' various Latin American Governments are. The continuing study by Professor Russell H. Fitzgibbon uses an elaborate questionnaire on several major and minor traits, circulated among forty leading U.S. Latin Americanists —business men, editors, scholars, government officials. Freedom of speech, press, assembly, the responsibility of Government to citizens, are among many aspects each of which receives a graded score. Professor Fitzgibbon, using specialized techniques and IBM

[1] K. H. Silvert, 'Political Change in Latin America', in the American Assembly of Colombia University, *The United States and Latin America* (mimeo, N.Y., 1960), ii. 14.
[2] Selden Rodman, *Mexican Journal* (1958), pp. 155–6, quoting interview material.

computers, finally provides a ranking on the basis of weighted, composite scores.[1]

In the total community of twenty nations, Mexico rose from seventh place in 1945 and 1950 to fourth in 1955. It was first among countries with appreciable population of Indian background.[2] The recent rebound of Argentina from Peronismo edged Mexico into fifth place in 1960. Like Brazil and Chile of the larger states, Mexico has shown a steady climb since 1945. The small 'model' states, Uruguay and Costa Rica, with little populations and few problems, have been at the top over the period.

We shall take some liberties with Professor Fitzgibbon's recent unpublished summary, a provisional statement of raw (unweighted or unadjusted) scores since 1945, to illustrate Mexico's place and the favourable changes to 1960. Even these tentative findings (Table 32) are interesting.

TABLE 32

Democracy in Latin America: Selected Principal Countries, 1945–60
(Raw Score Data compiled by Russell H. Fitzgibbon)

MAJOR NATIONS*	1945	1950	1955	1960	AVER-AGE*	RANK AVER-AGE	1960
Argentina	628	536	499	705	592	5/6	4
Brazil	482	605	633	648	592	5/6	7
Chile	713	733	713	741	725	3	3
Colombia	684	598	507	652	610	4	6
Mexico	546	570	640	663	579	7	5
SMALLER NATIONS							
Costa Rica	730	703	746	768	739	2	2
Uruguay	772	789	820	786	792	1	1

* Responsibility of author for categories of 'Major' and 'Smaller' nations, averages 1945–60, and rank based on averaged raw score. Raw scores from general communication to panel by Professor Fitzgibbon, 16 May 1960. Countries with raw scores below 650 in 1960 omitted.

[1] Results for 1945, 1950, 1955 are published in Russell H. Fitzgibbon, 'Measurement of Latin American Political Phenomena: a Statistical Experiment', *Amer. Pol.Sc.R.*, xlv (June 1951), 517–23, and his 'A Statistical Evaluation of Latin-American Democracy', *Western Pol. Quarterly*, ix (Sept. 1956), 607–19. Results for 1960 appear in a hectograph preliminary note sent panel members (including the author), and stress that considerable additional analysis of raw scores will be made, but rankings will not change.

[2] Scott, *Mexican Government*, p. 302.

Chapter XVIII

POLITICAL CONSTANTS: MILITARISM, THE CHURCH, COMMUNISM

MANY traditional, general elements influence Mexican politics. Some of these historic forces have undergone marked change during the past two decades. Among them, militarism, a dominant feature in the first half of the nineteenth century and of the Revolution through 1940, has been virtually eliminated as an active and overt political force. The Catholic Church and its activities evoked a virulent anti-clericalism throughout much of Mexico's national history, culminating in the great period of the nineteenth-century Reforma, and again in the inter-war years of the twentieth century. This, too, has declined. A more recent constant influence on Mexican political and social developments stems from international Communism, exemplified and promoted by the Soviet Union after 1917. While Communist influence in Mexico is not large at present, it would be unwise and incorrect to underestimate the potential force that these three elements might bring to bear in Mexico if the current prosperous and stable economic and political situation changed substantially. However, at present each is quiescent and latent.

MILITARISM

One of the most remarkable trends in Mexico, dating from its entrance into the Second World War, is the professionalization of its army and the removal of militarism as an open element in domestic politics. Its decline was an aftermath of the Cárdenas reform of the official party, in which he essentially removed the power base of local, political generals whose appeal often dated from the militant days of the Revolution; thereafter political generals became anachronistic. These aging heroes were put on the retired list. They did not fit conveniently into the modern, streamlined, and mechanized forces which emerged from the training programmes co-sponsored by Mexico and the United States as part of a general hemispheric defence effort. In the decade following 1942, the Mexican army became a professional, non-political corps, a model of its kind. It will be recalled that as a sign of the shift in this direction the military sector of the official party was dropped in 1940 by President Avila Camacho.[1] Professionalization of the armed forces implied their withdrawal, individually and as a group, from the open arena of politics. A recent study by Professor Lieuwen of political activities of the armed forces in Latin America as a whole emphasizes the major shift in Mexico from its earlier militaristic tradition in a chapter significantly entitled 'Curbing Militarism in Mexico: a Case Study'.[2] He places Mexico with Colombia, Chile, Costa Rica, Uruguay, and other 'non-political army' countries.

Other students of the Mexican scene similarly have noted the fading of militarism under the Institutional Revolution. Professor Stanley Ross in 1956 took special note of it, and more recently wrote concerning Mexico, 'Not only has political life been quite peaceful, but the election of three successive civilians as president presents, perhaps, the subordination of the military to civilian control.'[3] Posing important research problems for fellow Mexicanists in 1960, yet another historian asks, 'Why after all has the Mexican Army become the most non-political of any major Latin American country?'[4] Thus Professor Lieuwen has not only his own excellent data but the weight of expert opinion to back his important assertion that 'Militarism has been dead for over a generation. . . . Mexico has unquestionably solved its problems of militarism.'[5]

Yet experience and example should signal caution. In the quotation above we would substitute 'latent' for 'dead'. In Argentina, for example, the army was until 1946 one of the most 'non-political' in Latin America; circumstances brought it directly into political action, where it remains. In the case of Mexico, every President is careful in each Annual Message to indicate the benefits his administration is bestowing on the armed forces, fully cognisant that widespread dissatisfactions in the ranks and grades could herald political storms. In short what has happened is that the military have become one of several interest groups in the complicated political equations rather than, as formerly, the almost single dominant one. So long as its legitimate claims are heard and given

[1] See above, p. 155.

[2] Edwin Lieuwen, *Arms and Politics in Latin America* (1960), pp. 101–21, 168–70.

[3] Stanley R. Ross, 'Some Observations on Military Coups in the Caribbean,' in A. Curtis Wilgus, ed., *The Caribbean* (1956), pp. 110–28; also his 'Mexico: Golden Anniversary of the Revolution', *Current History*, Mar. 1960, 150–4, 180.

[4] Potash, 'Historiography of Mexico', p. 382.

[5] *Arms and Politics*, p. 121.

just due, it is unlikely to revert to direct political, much less military action, to gain its objectives.

As a national and nationalizing element, the disciplined Mexican army is now an influence for stability, a far cry from its earlier role as a chief force in political instability. This achievement alone would mark the Institutional Revolution as a success.

THE CHURCH AND ANTI-CLERICALISM

From first days of the Conquest, the Roman Catholic Church and its universal doctrines have been a part of the Mexican heritage. Relations with the Vatican form a large and special chapter of colonial history, and an almost equally bulky portion of the national history.[1] A main motif in nineteenth-century Mexico was the Liberal Reform efforts to assert supremacy of state over Church. The anti-clerical bent of leaders of the Revolution, especially during the régime of President Lázaro Cárdenas, has similarly been evident. A moderate Catholic author, Father J. J. Considine, reporting recently on the present situation, sums up this long interaction by saying 'In no other country is there a history of such bitter strife between the state and the Church as in Mexico.'[2] He reports that the election of Manuel Avila Camacho in 1940 eased many of the historic strains, especially notable under the advanced anti-clericalism of the 1920's and 1930's in Mexico. He records that 'In a most extraordinary fashion', a Mexican gentleman explained to him, 'the Church-state conflict melted away when Avila Camacho uttered three words, "Yo soy creyente" (I am a believer).'[3] On the other hand he indicates that Avila Camacho and his successor, President Alemán, while not pushing earlier anti-clerical programmes, were equally friendly and helpful to Protestant efforts in Mexico, and ˋadds 'Protestant activity in Mexico today is at an all-time high.'

The swing away from anti-clericalism seems now to be a fixed policy of the Institutional Revolution. Professor Scott, a political scientist, has traced changes in attitudes on the part of the Vatican and of the political leaders that in the past decade have converged to permit a *modus vivendi*. He states that it in part 'reflects the effects of a new Vatican policy for Latin countries, under which the Church seeks to identify itself with more liberal social and political doctrines than it has supported heretofore'. He adds that 'neither in Mexico

---

[1] J. Lloyd Mecham, *Church and State in Latin America* (1934) devotes three chapters to Mexican affairs from 1821 to 1933, pp. 395–450.

[2] John J. Considine, *New Horizons in Latin America* (1958), p. 267.

[3] Ibid. p. 268.

nor elsewhere do all members of the Church, lay or clerical, identify with this new approach'.[1] A sign of the times was that López Mateos as presidential candidate appeared and spoke from the same platform as a Catholic priest. The tenor of both addresses was that in place of Mexican factions there were now 'only Mexicans anxious for social justice'.

The Church is still a vital institution, despite the long travail under the Revolution, and the restrictive legislation which can still be enforced against it. For 1957 Catholic writers compiled statistics indicating that the country had 9 archbishops, 34 bishops, 6,020 priests, 1,990 seminarists, and 18,560 religious sisters, a total probably greater than at any time in the colonial period.[2] According to Father Considine, 97 per cent. of the Mexicans are nominally Catholic; less than a million Protestants (3 per cent. of the 1958 population) are claimed by several active sects.

It could probably be said that at the moment the Church and Church-state relationships in Mexico are not a major preoccupation either of people or of their Government. The Revolution could not extirpate four centuries of Mexican Catholic heritage, nor could the Church reverse the Revolution. For the moment at least there seems to be a stable, informal agreement on the part of each to co-operate in areas of common concern rather than to agitate about possibly insoluble issues that through world history have plagued the explosive relationships of State to Church.

COMMUNISM

During recent Mexican history there has been a varied response to appeals of the U.S.S.R. and to international Communism. Similarities of doctrine about the Revolution—Mexican or Russian—and aims of revolution-born Government often obscure the fact that the Mexican one is indigenous and owes little or nothing to any Comintern. Mexico was the second Western Hemisphere nation to recognize the Soviet Union (1924), but enthusiasm for its policies and actions cooled to the point that in 1927 diplomatic relations were broken off, not to be resumed until the Second World War (1942).

At the beginning of the Cold War, Mexico officially and unofficially purged many Communists from posts they had obtained under

---

[1] *Mexican Government* (pp. 232–3).

[2] 'Catholic Statistics for Latin America, 1957, compiled by William J. Gibbons, S.J., from official figures as published in the Annuario Pontifico, Vatican City, 1958', table 2, in Considine, *Latin America*, p. 332.

Lázaro Cárdenas, himself non-Communist but militant Left. At present (1960) Mexico maintains diplomatic relations with the U.S.S.R. and satellites, but is a Western-style democratic republic, and thus a staunch defender of the Free World.[1]

International Communism's doctrines and promises have failed to capture a significant majority of Mexicans, or to have developed into any significant domestic political force. Among intellectuals and students there has for many years been an open sympathy and even support for Communism, but despite persistent efforts it has failed to make any real inroads or establish serious apparatus in government, labour, or military circles. A recent official report notes, 'In Mexico, where Communists have been free to operate over a long period of time, communism occupies a peculiar position. . . . The Mexican Revolution was of the home-grown variety, and there was no place in it for Communist influence.'[2]

The main cause for the indifferent success by Communists in Mexico lies in a basic lack of doctrinal appeal. Mexicans pride themselves on the fact that *their* Revolution ante-dated the Russian one by a number of years, rejecting as incorrect the 'official' Soviet views of Mexican history.[3] There is little in Communist ideology that cannot be paralleled, and at an earlier date, from Mexican Revolutionary slogans and documents. Hence they look on Moscow less as a font of knowledge about revolutionary activities and tactics than as a place that can learn much from Mexican experience, not a wholly acceptable view to the Soviets. In the same vein, the very 'foreign-ness' of Communist dogma runs counter to the deep-seated distrust that the Revolution inspired concerning outside manipulation of Mexican affairs. Combined with a latent xenophobia that runs through the marrow of Mexican nationalism, Communism is suspect for having no real Mexican roots. As a late and foreign

[1] Robert J. Alexander, *Communism in Latin America* (1957) is a standard general account. Uruguay recognized the U.S.S.R. in 1922.

[2] Corp. for Econ. and Indust. Research, *United States–Latin American Relations: Soviet Bloc Latin American Activities and their Implications for United States Foreign Policy* (1960), p. 32. S. Walter Washington, 'Mexican Resistance to Communism', *Foreign Affairs*, xxxvi (Apr. 1958), 504–15.

[3] Karl Helbig, 'Mexiko in Andere Sicht', *Übersee Rundschau*, Feb. 1959, pp. 24–6, summarizes Mexican history as it appears in the *Soviet Encyclopedia*. According to this account, the Revolution in Mexico took the 1917 Russian October Revolution as its guide, with the Mexican Communist Party founded in 1919 to 'lead the battle for the Mexican proletariat'. This view attributes the break in relations with the U.S.S.R. to 'bourgeois Presidents', including Cárdenas, whose main crime was to give asylum to the 'arch-traitor, Trotsky'. Resumption of relations in 1942 is attributed to 'pressures from agrarian and workers' groups'. For a different account, see Cline, *U.S. and Mexico*, pp. 294–9.

doctrine, offering few really novel ideas not already worked out in Mexican vernacular, its visible impact is slight.

Nor is the hidden influence much more effective. The normal Communist tactic in Latin America of allying with a strongly nationalist group or party for its own ends runs directly into the situation we have sketched where there is but one real party in Mexico, the PRI, run by Mexicans for Mexicans. Major figures do not need or even want Communist political support. Since the Institutional Revolution took shape about 1940, PRI leaders in fact have taken special pains to 'de-Communize' key posts. In a sane and mature way, Mexicans have kept the reins of their own fate in their own hands, without hysteria and witch-hunts.

Yet there is no question but that there are real Communists in Mexico. Published reports would indicate that hard-core, card-carrying Communists do not exceed 10,000 persons, and probably may be only half that number.[1] There is an overswollen staff at the Soviet Embassy, known to be active in numerous shadowy enterprises. On a more open plane it carries on various cultural and propaganda programmes that often penetrate into hinterlands a considerable distance from Mexico City.[2]

There is also a substantial, if quantitatively indeterminate transient body of exiles in Mexico who have fled their own lands, especially the United States, when unmasked as secret adherents of Communism. When they even seem to break bounds, as some apparently did in the Labour-student riots of 1958, they are under Article 33 unceremoniously packed out of the country; so long as they live quietly, talking as they do endlessly and monotonously about art and life, Mexicans tolerate their presence. It is thus difficult to evaluate the total extent of the Communist apparatus in Mexico, or its present or potential value to its masters in the Kremlin.

We do have some testimony about Communist ineffectiveness on the political and even cultural scene in Mexico. No recognized Communist political party exists. Mexican reaction to the spectacular and eye-catching Soviet trade fair and exhibit that moved from New York to Mexico City, and to the visit paid by high Soviet officials at that time is interesting. More than 900,000 Mexicans viewed the 2,400 exhibits, listened to Dmitri Shostakovich conducting concerts, and gazed politely on Deputy Premier Anastas

---

[1] 'Soviet Bloc . . . Activities', table 1, p. 25, estimates 5,000. Perhaps another 25,000 could be labelled 'strong fellow-travellers'.

[2] Helbig, 'Mexiko', p. 25; the purpose of this interesting article is to alert the German public that their own writers are often taking this Soviet line.

Mikoyan. They were asked to note their opinions of what they had seen. There were a number of parrot-like eulogies of the achievements of the Soviet comrades, but striking a note all foreigners are accustomed to hearing in Mexico was a more typical statement: 'A marvellous display of scientific, industrial, and artistic achievement—but we produce better consumer goods right here in Mexico.' More probably reflecting deep-seated feelings of a great body of Mexicans, one wrote, 'Very impressive, very formidable. Now I would like to hear a few words from the Hungarians.'[1]

[1] Thayer Waldo, 'How the Reds Woo Mexico', *Parade* (14 Feb. 1960), p. 10.

Chapter XIX

DEMOCRATIC VISTAS: THE PRESS AND LITERACY

BASIC to the democratic credo and doctrines of the Mexican Revolution is that sound politics and good government rest on an informed and literate electorate. The press in Mexico is free to discuss issues, its effectiveness being limited by the proportion of literacy.

THE PRESS

Mexico had newspapers and magazines as early as the eighteenth century. Most of that ephemeral press was short-lived, but it looms large in the nation's literary traditions, and is a valuable source to historians of early Mexican history. Here we shall briefly scan the recent scene, which has been helpfully summarized in English by Lic. Daniel Cosío Villegas.[1] Writing in 1954, Cosío Villegas reported that 1,213 periodicals appeared with some regularity, but six states lacked any cultural publications.[2] Of the whole group, many were of recent origin: 52 per cent. were under five years old, about a third twenty years old, and less than 10 per cent. had been running for more than twenty-five years. Thus great growth came after 1945.

The current press as a whole is the child of the Revolution. The lifespan of any given title is unpredictable, but still likely to be short. So far as types and periodicity are concerned, the largest portion is monthly journals (about half), followed by weeklies (one-quarter), and dailies with barely 10 per cent. There were some 130 of the latter, scattered through 54 cities, half of which maintain more than one. Cosío emphasized the fact that the greater proportion of places have no daily papers.

Since 1954 there has been substantial growth. Our figures for 1954 differ slightly from those of Cosío Villegas, but can be compared with information for 1958, drawn from official sources. Table 33 presents the picture of growth and draws attention to the lessened

[1] 'The Press and Responsible Freedom in Mexico', in Angel del Río, ed., *Responsible Freedom in the Americas* (1955), pp. 272–90.
[2] Campeche, Colima, Durango, Morelos, Tabasco, Tlaxcala.

concentration of publishing activities in the Metropolis in 1958 as
compared to 1954.

TABLE 33

Mexican Periodicals, 1954 and 1958

	Totals		1958 Federal District		Total increase 1954 cpd. with 1958	
	1954	*1958*	No.	Per cent.	New	Per cent.
Dailies ...	184	241	76	31·5	57	31·0
Weeklies ...	458	851	467	55·0	393	84·9
Fortnightly ...	183	274	114	41·5	91	49·6
Monthly ...	796	1,233	871	70·0	437	55·0
Others ...	274	816	637	78·0	512	187·0
TOTALS ...	1,895	3,415	2,220	62·2	1,490	79·5

Sources: DGE, *Compendio estadístico, 1955*, table 99 (pp. 174–5); *1958*, table 102
(pp. 180–2); rearranged and percentages by author.

From this it can be seen that there is a basic division between
periodicals published outside and inside the capital respectively.
For illustrative purposes, we can briefly compare newspapers in
provincial areas with those of the Federal District.

The Provincial Press

The provincial press plays an important role by speaking for its
local areas. With some remarkable exceptions, however, local papers
generally fall rather far below metropolitan standards in technical
skills, but one recent student avers that their spirit makes up for
this lack.[1] Outside the metropolitan area, Puebla, only eighty-five
miles from Mexico City, supports five dailies. Guadalajara, second
largest city and capital of the West has three. Some twenty-nine
other cities in 1960 had at least two papers; twenty-two smaller
places were served by a single daily.

One unusual feature of the Mexican provincial press is the chain
of thirty-six newspapers owned by Colonel José García Valseca. It
is the largest in Latin America. Built up over the past fifteen years
its newspapers are beginning to set a fairly high standard for local
journalism. They publish some world news, national news, but
emphasize local happenings reported in objective fashion. Colonel

[1] Marvin Alisky, 'Growth of Newspapers in Mexico's Provinces', *Journalism
Quarterly* xxxvii (Winter 1960), unpaged.

García Valseca sends his key editors and reporters to the Mexico City headquarters of the enterprise for rigorous training. Here they often form the core of candidates at UNAM for advanced degrees in journalism, not regularly offered at provincial universities. The chain has evolved a wire service, which augments news with feature items to be utilized at the discretion of local editors.

Other provincial newspapers subscribe to one or more of the several national news services in Mexico City.[1] Some even buy international wire service offerings, but it is more usual for papers to share a Mexico City correspondent.

Papers in the larger cities not served by the García Valseca publications are likely to be independent dailies. They enjoy a certain measure of freedom, often not exercised in the national capital, to criticize local politics and politicians. They can be a real force by drawing national attention to local events. Opposition of the local press is credited with the downfall of the PRI boss of San Luis Potosí in 1958. A number of such recent incidents to show the rising importance of the provincial press have been gathered by Professor Alisky, who also notes the slightly erratic but lively crusades of very small local weeklies. Often their wild charges are the result of poor journalism, or even paid propaganda, but every now and then they do hit a live mark. They lack the cogent headlines, attractive page make-up, and striking graphic materials that are now beginning to characterize the best of the local newspapers. But the provincial press fills a real demand, which is summarized by Professor Alisky: 'The more complicated the environment of the Mexican hinterlands, the greater his need for current information becomes. . . . The emerging middle class of Mexicans, living far removed from the national capital, can get details of the region about them only through a regional newspaper.'[2]

The Metropolitan Press

To some degree gaps in local coverage are made up by six newspapers issued in Mexico City, four of which are general. Cosío Villegas estimated in 1954 that their total daily circulation, local and national, was about 360,000 (670,000 on Sunday), about equal to

[1] API, Asociación de Periódicos Independientes (Independent Newspapers Association); AAE, Asociación de Editores de los Estados (Association of State Editors); AMI, Agencia Mexicana de Información (Mexican News Agency), and one which is Mexican and transmits in Spanish, Mexico Press Service, are the principal ones.

[2] Alisky, 'Newspapers'.

the combined circulation of all dailies outside the metropolis, which he placed at approximately 350,000. Despite the apparent dominance of the metropolitan press, Cosío Villegas avers that 'no newspaper . . . enjoys nationwide acceptance for the veracity of its news or the authority of its opinions', comparable, for instance, to *El Sol* of Madrid in its time, the London *Times* or *Manchester Guardian*, the *Christian Science Monitor* or the *New York Times*.

Despite their limitations, the metropolitan dailies are flourishing businesses. As information media they compare in technical matters, in circulation-building devices, and in coverage with great metropolitan newspapers elsewhere in the world. In some departments they may even excel them, especially in Sunday supplements devoted to arts and letters, where the great names of the Mexican intellectual community may be seen. Daily editions regularly use nearly all international wire services, augmented by efforts of a growing corps of professional journalists. These specialists are now numerous enough to form several special associations which attempt to maintain standards and improve ethics of the Fourth Estate in Mexico.[1]

Contents

Cosío Villegas attempted an analysis of the content of periodicals for 1954. He found that the press as a whole had rather a wide scope. Despite official anti-clericalism, religious propaganda journals outnumbered cultural; of the 97 religious journals in the Federal District, 55 were Catholic, 35 Protestant. Among the 79 cultural journals, half can be classed as 'artistic-literary', with the remainder quite varied: 13 devoted to cinema, 6 to radio and TV, and 3 miscellaneous.

A major group of 149 technical periodicals is worthy of special notice. Of these the medical journals are outstanding (36); also covered are other fields: economic-commercial (65), labour union (20), engineering (11), farming (3), legal (7), military (2). Besides these organs of special groups and interests, the District supports 90 of generally informative character, for various age levels, and still another 200 for such highly specialized small clientele that they cannot readily be classified.

The most recent official data are not quite as detailed, but they provide a summary for 1958. The information is grouped in Table

[1] Alisky lists *Sindicato Nacional de Redactores de la Prensa* (National Newspaper Editors' Union), *Asociación Mexicana de Periodistas* (Mexican Journalists' Association), *Asociación Mexicana de Fotógrafos* (Mexican News Photographers' Association).

34 both for the nation as a whole and for the Federal District, making it comparable with the statements of Cosío Villegas for the earlier date.

TABLE 34

Types of Mexican Periodicals, 1958

Class or Object	National		Federal District		Per cent. in Federal District
	No.	*Per cent.*	*No.*	*Per cent.*	
Informative	1,063	31·3	276	17·2	25·8
Literary	218	7·2	111	7·4	51·0
General	669	19·5	305	18·9	45·5
Religious	321	9·4	159	9·9	49·5
Others	1,144	32·6	751	46·6	65·6
TOTALS	3,415	100·0	1,602	100·0	47·0

Source: DGE, *Compendio estadístico, 1958,* table 102 (pp. 182–6). Rearranged, percentages by author.

A Mexican Critique

Cosío Villegas emphasized certain salient matters of general interest. First is the over-concentration of the press in the Metropolis. In 1954, the Federal District contained a disproportionate share of all periodicals: 52 per cent. of the newspapers; 71 per cent. of the cultural publications; 42 per cent. of the religious; and 74 per cent. of the technical. Secondly, for its total population, and especially that outside the immediate metropolitan orbit, Mexico is under-supplied with periodical publications. He attributed this in large part to the geographical dispersion of communities, and the relatively large body of non-literate or sub-literate members within the general population. Thirdly, the lives of the journals are precarious. Finally, there is an ingrained scepticism among Mexicans concerning the information conveyed by these publications, with the possible exception of the highly respected technical periodicals. 'The Mexican reader', states Cosío Villegas, 'does not believe that the national press is sufficiently independent of the government, the Catholic hierarchy, or powerful economic and political interests, national or even foreign.'

In short, the Mexican press attracts its share of local and world-wide criticism. The commercial press is said to be timid, over-sensational, over-influenced by official optimism, and possibly more concerned over profits than honest and objective presentation of news. The same charges are levelled at the comparable press in the United States, Great Britain, France—in short, wherever it exists. However, it is worth remarking that as compared with perhaps twenty years ago, the Mexican press has visibly matured. Scandals occasionally expose venality, but journalistic standards exist and are rising. As Cosío Villegas also asserts, 'it is a free press which does not make use of its freedom'.

Freedom of the Press

Mexicans can and do point with pride to such freedom.[1] In the last thirty years there has not been a single instance of a paper being suppressed by decree. At the same time they deplore that, among the many benefits which industrialization has brought to the emerging nation, the press as an industry has prospered, possibly at the cost of the personal journalism that keeps men free. 'In Mexico, at any rate, the business world has produced very few heroes willing to fight and die for a worthy cause', is the way in which Cosío Villegas puts the case.[2]

Yet despite these strictures, it can be seen that rising literacy, improved transportation, the appearance of new periodical organs in increasing numbers, improvement in typography and technical presentation all denote a healthy, vigorous growth of clientele and of the press itself. Its obviously growing specializations equally argue the emergence of national complexities and widespread interests unknown or submerged in earlier days when the locality or region formed the exclusive bounds of most Mexicans' emotional and intellectual universe.

LITERACY

Newspaper circulation, like democracy, is limited by illiteracy. The formal and informal educational organs of Mexico have faced that problem for many years.

Literacy figures are always suspect; no agreed definitions are universal, and most Governments seek those which show their population in the best light. The most recent (1958) Mexican Statistical Compendium, issued annually, takes refuge in what amounts to silence on this matter. It merely reprints findings of the Census data of 1930, 1940, and 1950, rather than estimates, as in

---

[1] Luis Castaño, *El régimen de la prensa en México* (1958) discusses legal and other guarantees.
[2] 'The Press', p. 230.

other tables, for 1958. It shows that in 1950 the total population over 6 years old numbered 21·0 million; of these 11·8 million (56·2 per cent.) were literate, 8·9 million (41·8 per cent.) illiterate, with the remainder unknown.

There is a regional aspect to the 1950 problem of illiteracy. In Table 35 we have rearranged the Census information to show the variations by regions. The high illiteracy rates in the Indian-centred South and the newly urbanizing Core are not surprising. In these two regions, which account for 40 per cent. of the national area and 53 per cent. of total population, were concentrated nearly three-quarters (72·2 per cent.) of the illiterate 1950 population over 6 years old.

TABLE 35

Illiteracy, by Regions, 1950

('000 persons over 6 years of age)

Region	Total population	Total illiterates	Region's illiteracy per cent.	Per cent. of nation's illiterates
Metropolis	2,540·0	461·9	18·3	5·1
Core	8,570·1	4,460·2	52·0	50·0
West	2,286·8	877·2	38·4	9·9
North	4,156·7	1,147·7	27·8	12·8
South	3,474·6	1,991·8	57·4	22·2
Republic of Mexico ...	21,028·2	8,938·8	40·0	100·0

Source: SDE, *Compendio estadístico, 1958,* table 23 (pp. 52–57), rearranged, calculations, percentages by author.

Later data show that under the impact of various special efforts there had been a drop in illiteracy from 50 to 39 per cent. in the population aged 6–40 years, from 1950–4.[1] After praising the fact that literacy in Mexico had risen from 30 per cent. in 1917 to 65 per cent. in 1954, Professor Alisky estimates that recent population growth has eroded some of the gains, and that currently 'the percentage of the population able to read and write totals perhaps no more than 55'.[2] A general statement on literacy might be that in 1960 not less than 55 per cent. and probably not more than 60 per cent. of Mexicans over 6 years of age were literate. Thus there is a considerable way to go.

[1] Oscar Lewis, 'México desde 1940', pp. 185–256.
[2] Alisky, 'Newspapers'.

THE REVOLUTION, 1940-60

Chapter XX

EDUCATION:
THE HOPE OF THE REVOLUTION

THE feeling that education is a panacea and the hope of fulfilling the Revolution has become so fixed a dogma in today's Mexico that no one really questions it. Much has been done to provide the Revolution's other social objectives: social security, public health, and similar needs. But educational advances under Article 3 of the constitution place all these in the shadow. The numbers of teachers, pupils, schools, and budgeted pesos for education take on national significance as concrete manifestations of how the Revolution at any moment is faring in the social field.

As a national concern, education has political and economic as well as social implications. Not so very long ago it was possible to predict with some degree of accuracy the ideological hue of a new presidential régime by the political leanings of the Minister of Education, and changes proposed by the administration in Article 3 of the constitution, which regulates and defines education in terms of the Revolution. Few can or do oppose the basic concept of public, free, compulsory education; the cry is for more, and better.

All social classes find they can support this cause. In enlightened self-interest business approves of education, and through taxes and other means provides much of the economic support for expanding educational programmes. It is widely felt that education will gradually enlarge the much-needed domestic economic market, improve productivity in industrial enterprises, and increasingly furnish the semi-skilled and skilled hands now in short supply. The traditional middle classes have long nearly worshipped education; it is a continuing class trait, now shared by many new recruits to the class. Transitional and lower classes find education a magic passport for social mobility and greater opportunities. Even doctrinaire reformers agree that agrarian reform will not be complete without an enlightened peasantry.

Small wonder, then, that education always outranks national defence in recent Federal budgets, and that there are more teachers than soldiers in Mexico. The urge to be educated, to educate, takes on the aura of a national crusade. 'To educate is to redeem' is a slogan of the early Revolution. But education has a long, honourable history, to which the Revolution only adds important later chapters. There are excellent general treatments which discuss many general and special aspects here reluctantly omitted.[1]

BACKGROUND

As early as 1523 Fr. Pedro de Gante created in Texcoco one of the first American schools to instruct Indians. By teaching them Spanish as well as religion, he started Mexico on the long road toward a unified language. By 1551 the direct ancestor of the present great National Autonomous University of Mexico had been founded under viceregal sponsorship, to provide the trained people needed in New Spain; by 1775 the University of Mexico had conferred 25,882 bachelors' degrees and 1,162 doctoral degrees; eighty of the doctors became Mexican bishops. From its beginnings as a colony to the present, Governments in Mexico have supported education as an important means to meet the pressing needs of each epoch.

A main task of the Spanish conquerors was to transplant and root European culture in New Spain. This meant establishing institutions for Indians, mestizos, and the Spanish minority. Need for teachers led to the early founding of the Academy of San Juan de Letrán, said to be the first normal school in America. From about 1572 until their expulsion in 1767, the Jesuit Order had a major influence on colonial education. In the late eighteenth and early nineteenth centuries part of Mexico was world famed for the excellence of its technical schools, especially the Mining School. Opened for instruction in 1792, it trained a number of the leaders of independence. Although individual institutions were excellent, one of the widespread discontents on the eve of independence arose from limited educational opportunities offered to all but a privileged few of the highest classes.

The early difficulties of organizing the Republic inhibited real educational advance. A spate of writings, a profusion of planning, did, however, attest to an urge to endow the new nation with an adequate system. Disputes between Church and state, each claiming exclusive responsibility for education, lay near the heart of the

[1] Marjorie C. Johnston, *Education in Mexico* (1956) is a sound, recent summary with bibliography. See also George F. Kneller, *The Education of the Mexican Nation* (1951). On earlier phases, George I. Sánchez, *Mexico: a Revolution by Education* (1936), and his *Development of Higher Education in Mexico* (1944); George C. Booth, *Mexico's School-Made Society* (1941).

Reforma, culminating in victory for secular elements. The foundation of the National Preparatory School in 1867 was its chief symbol. In the Restored Republic and in Mexico under Díaz, this school became a citadel of Positivism, tailored to Mexico, justifying the social and economic policies of the day.[1]

In 1893 came the first national legislation requiring compulsory free education. A small beginning, it was part of a late Díaz centralizing programme to foster primary education. By the end of the Díaz régime, only an estimated one-fifth (slightly under 1 million pupils) of Mexico's eligible school population was receiving any instruction in the 12,419 schools supported by the states and municipalities, and the 671 in the Federal District. But the National University, which had been closed since 1865, was refounded.[2]

The Revolution from 1910 to about 1923 had inadvertently but thoroughly wrecked the pre-existing educational network, never more than a skeleton, that had slowly developed under Díaz. Starting from scratch, leaders of the Revolution had to rebuild. Thus the present educational system is completely the creation of the Revolution. 'Mexico's struggle for democracy is symbolized by the public school', recently wrote a distinguished North American educational specialist.[3]

Advances, 1923–60

The achievement since 1923 has been substantial. It has been duly reported by professional observers at several points along the way. Their consensus is that while laudable urges often outstrip resources, and further expansion is needed to include more of the school-age population, the results attained in less than four decades are little short of spectacular. Professional educators and laymen alike praise the Mexicans for their steady determination to build a workable and comprehensive system giving constant attention to a functional education related to their own needs and traditions, rather than borrowing unsuitable foreign models. 'The obstacles, seeming at times insuperable, still loom large', writes Dr. Marjorie C. Johnston, 'but the movement has kept to its course, and can be credited with tangible achievements.'[4] The Ministry of Public

[1] Irma Wilson, *Mexico: a Century of Educational Thought* (N.Y. Hispanic Society, 1941); Leopoldo Zea, *El Positivismo en México* (Colegio de México, 1943–4); Cosío Villegas, ed., *Historia moderna de México*, iii; *Vida Social*, pp. 633–743.

[2] Cosío Villegas, *Historia moderna*, iv; *Vida social* (1957), pp. 529–690, for Porfirian period to 1910.

[3] Johnston, *Education*, p. 26.

[4] ibid.

Education usually ranks near or at the top of annual government budgetary figures. Its share seldom falls below 10 per cent. of national public expenditures, as is shown in the following table, which indicates that the Institutional Revolution has maintained and surpassed the fiscal pace set earlier. The 1960 quota exceeds even the best efforts of previous Mexican Governments long famed for their attention to education; in his 1960 Annual Message President López Mateos emphasized that his Government was expending 5·5 million pesos daily on education.

TABLE 36

Ministry of Education, Budgets, 1921–60

Year			Million pesos	Per cent. total national budget
1921	...	...	12·3	4·9
1923	...	...	52·3	15·0
1925	...	...	21·7	7·1
1930	...	...	33·2	11·3
1935	...	...	44·5	16·2
1940	...	...	75·3	11·9
1945	...	...	170·0	10·8
1950	...	...	314·0	9·1
1955	...	...	711·8	12·5
1960	...	...	1,900·0	18·6

Sources: Kneller, *Education*, table 1 (p. 81) [1921, 1923, 1925, 1940] ; Booth *Mexico's School-made Society*, p. 40 [1930, 1935]; DGE, *Anuario estadístico ... 1943–1945*, table 364 (p. 763) [1945]; table 34, above [1960].

Yet, impressive as these figures are as clear evidence of continued, sincere, and magnificent efforts, no responsible Mexican official feels complacent. From the President down, all are aware of the serious gaps, especially in primary education where limited opportunities annually keep many hundreds of eligible children without schools and teachers. We shall specify some of these gaps in more detail after observing some undoubted successes.

ARTICLE 3: REVOLUTION AND EDUCATION

The organization and administration of the school system stems from Article 3 of the constitution. That revolutionary mandate changes from time to time, varying with the political and intellectual climates of the day. After spirited debates in the 1917 Constitutional Convention of Querétaro, Article 3 originally stressed that education was to be free, secular, and primarily guided by the national government. It was then pointedly anti-clerical.

Under able leadership, the concept of national responsibility soon enlarged. Responsibility included other specific obligations: the extension of elementary education to all parts of the Republic and to the adult population; the elimination of illiteracy; the formation and training of professional teaching staffs imbued with Mexican ideals (rather than foreign); co-operation with families of pupils to improve the whole group; and co-ordination of Federal systems with those of states and municipalities.[1]

The revived Revolution, under Cárdenas, restated the objectives of Mexican education in radical socialistic terms, based on Marxian scientific materialism. New goals embraced coeducation, sex instruction, and other advanced and extreme doctrines derived from the doctrinaire Left's image of what the ideal new 'socio-economic' Mexican should be. Article 3, amended to include these directives in 1934, formed the Cárdenas Six-Year educational programme. Though many excesses were trimmed from the Article and its application in 1940, the Cárdenas surge left indelible marks on Mexican education. Perhaps the most important of these was to arouse widespread hope and expectation among the disinherited masses that their redemption could be achieved through education, that it was definitely for the masses as well as the comfortable classes.

The Institutional Revolution

The Institutional Revolution's programme appeared in yet another—the last—revision of Article 3. Influenced to a great degree by the statesmanship of Jaime Torres Bodet, this version reflected stress on unity, moderation, conciliation, and a new broadened international outlook. Article 3 now prescribes that education, whether in national, state, or municipal institutions, must develop harmoniously all the faculties of the human being, encourage patriotism and a consciousness of international solidarity. It must be free of religious doctrine, be based on proved results of science, and provide a bulwark against ignorance and its consequences: slavery, fanaticism, prejudice. Further, it is to be democratic, to be

[1] Kneller, *Education*, p. 62. Systematic coverage of changing concepts appears in Alberto Bremauntz, *La Educación socialista en México* (1943), Chs. 1–8.

connected with national developments, to encourage personal dignity, family integrity, social good, and fraternity, and to stress the equality of citizens before the law. Class strife and other controversial aspects of the previous version are pointedly omitted.

Particular Ministers of Education have placed a strong personal impress on the development of education. José Vasconcelos, above all, is the great figure; his ideas and actions in 1923 elevated the Ministry to its present high status in government circles, and established its basic purposes and much of the apparatus. Jaime Torres Bodet, Minister under President Camacho, recalled to the same post by President López Mateos, has nearly the same stature. In common they, and intervening Ministers, have stressed the need for Mexican education and its goals to be adjusted to Mexican ends. Education is based on concrete social activities as well as theoretical abstractions. All agree that it must extend as widely and as deeply as possible. The Ministers have all emphasized the school as a unifying factor to forge a nation from its disparate parts, although each leader has had a different vision of the nation that would so emerge.

THE STRUCTURE OF EDUCATION

The basic structure of education now leads a child, under ideal conditions, from nursery schools for those under 4 years of age through post-graduate work, with numerous possible ramifications for special purposes. Generally after kindergarten training, a pupil goes on to 6 years of primary, 3 years of secondary, and 2 years of preparatory school, followed by a 3- to 7-year university course.

Another pattern is to follow primary education with 5 years of preparatory, then a 6-year curriculum in normal school, or school of commerce, music, plastic arts, or pre-vocational studies. Yet a third route leads from secondary school directly to normal school, school of nursing, vocational or military school, or higher school of agricultural sciences. Vocational schools at the preparatory level can lead to technical fields of specialization such as those offered at the National Polytechnic Institute. The diagram on p. 197 provides a schematic view of the educational maze that has evolved in response to the recent constant and varied national necessities, opening many opportunities for Mexican youth.

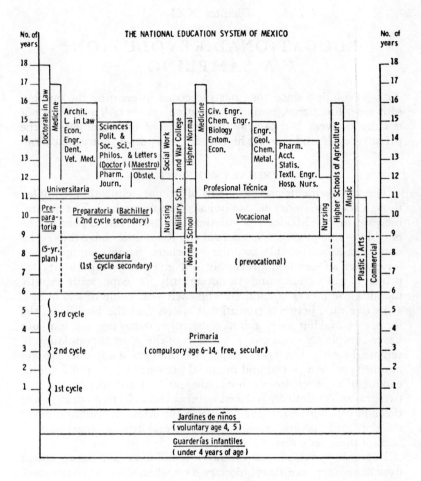

THE NATIONAL EDUCATION SYSTEM OF MEXICO

Chapter XXI

EDUCATIONAL REVOLUTION:
A SAMPLING

THE Revolution since 1923 has succeeded in creating the outlines of a new, functional, national education system. All parts are not equally evolved. We can only note some of the highlights of the primary levels, and then the higher ranges of post-primary education.

PRIMARY EDUCATION

The achievements and problems of primary education, complex though they are in detail, can quickly be summarized. The general increase in the Mexican population inevitably has expanded the eligible 6–14 age-group. Leaders of the Revolution have thus had a double task: to provide facilities—teachers, schools, equipment— for masses of children previously not given any opportunity for primary instruction, and simultaneously to cope with rapidly mounting numbers of children who each year come of school age.

In this race between educational efforts and the birth-rate, the former is making slow gains, constantly narrowing the gap but never completely closing it. Dispersion of the general population in remote hamlets has also complicated matters. Drop-outs are yet another problem; social and financial pressures have caused a mass exodus of children from schools after at best completing the first two grades. A relatively reduced number thenceforth moves upward through other primary levels. Thus many Mexican children never see the inside of any schoolroom. The majority of those who do remain there only about a year.

Depressing as this picture seems, it is still a marked improvement over the earlier, pre-Revolutionary days when scarcely 10 per cent. of the eligible children outside the capital had any hope of primary instruction. More important, if the rates of gain evident in recent years can be continued, facilities to include primary instruction for all but a negligible minority can be developed within another decade. The focus will then shift to improvement of programmes for the early years and further development of the succeeding grades for the augmented number who will not be forced to drop out. Table 37 synthesizes main facts about the Mexican efforts and their achievements in providing facilities during recent years. The figures include the public schools (24,915 in 1957) as well as private (1,873), and 'mixed' (2,402).

TABLE 37

Primary Education in Mexico, 1950–60

(*All types of schools*)

Year	Primary schools ('000)	Teachers ('000)	Pupils (million)	Total eligible	Per cent. in school
1950... ...	24·1	72·2	3·0	6·2	48·5
1951... ...	24·7	75·5	3·2	6·4	50·0
1952... ...	25·6	80·1	3·3	6·3	52·0
1953... ...	26·6	84·8	3·5	6·5	53·9
1954... ...	27·3	89·1	3·7	6·7	55·2
1955... ...	27·8	93·9	3·9	6·8	57·4
1956... ...	28·4	98·0	4·1	7·0	59·5
1957... ...	29·2	103·4	4·4	7·2	61·0
1958... ...			4·6	7·4	59·5
1959... ...			4·9	7·6	64·5
1960... ...			5·1	7·8	65·5

Sources: DGE, *Compendio estadístico, 1953,* pp. 11, 129; *1955,* pp. 141, 174, 177

Elementary education is divided into three cycles of two years each, under a plan of study uniform throughout the Republic. All children study the same material at the same time, at the same rate. The teacher is encouraged, however, to use methods best adapted to the group and school, so long as the main aim is retained: 'harmonious development of each child's physical, intellectual, ethical, esthetic, civic, social, and vocational needs and interests', to quote a recent summary.[1]

There is a considerable difference between urban and rural areas in opportunities for primary education. Most rural schools now provide at least two grades, and increasingly, the third. They seldom offer instruction beyond the fourth; less than 10 per cent. have the fifth and sixth grades, completion of which is requisite for further progress in the educational system. Under 10 per cent. of the total rural pupils are in these final two grades. Cities, on the other hand, offer the full primary cycle through the sixth grade. Thus

[1] Johnston, *Education,* p. 31; Kneller, *Education,* ch. 1.

Mexico, 1940–1960

proportionately rural areas have less schools for their eligible children, and the rural schools offer fewer opportunities. Statistics readily reveal the differential (Table 38).

TABLE 38

Primary Education: Urban-Rural, 1955–7

Highest Grade	SCHOOLS (*1957*)				PUPILS (*1955*)			
	Number		Per cent.		Thousands		Per cent.	
	Urban	Rural	Urban	Rural	Urban	Rural	Urban	Rural
First ...	84	1,576	1·3	7·0	715·5	942·7	31·0	57·5
Second	236	7,994	3·5	35·4	463·3	390·3	20·1	23·8
Third...	305	8,508	4·6	37·6	384·0	194·7	16·6	11·9
1–3...	625	18,078	9·4	80·0	1,562·8	1,527·7	67·7	93·2
Fourth	507	2,805	7·7	12·4	302·8	68·8	13·1	4·2
Fifth ...	348	527	5·1	2·4	248·4	27·0	10·8	1·6
Sixth ...	5,124	1,176	77·8	5·2	193·5	16·9	8·4	1·0
4–6...	5,979	4,508	90·6	20·0	744·7	112·7	32·3	6·8
Totals	6,604	22,586	100·0	100·0	2,307·5	1,640·4	100·0	100·0

Sources: Schools, DGE, *Compendio estadístico, 1958,* table 93 (p. 164); pupils, I. M. de Navarrete, 'Educación pública . . .' *Investigación económica,* xviii (1958), 21, 55, table 5. Percentages by author.

As the number of schools and teachers mount, attention is already beginning to shift from providing basic first-grade facilities for each eligible child to the problem of providing more grades, and diminishing drop-outs between first and second grades. A recent study, for instance, looks specifically into the matter of what facilities exist and are needed for the age group 7–12, from second through sixth grade.[1] The statistical outline of that problem shows heartening progress, as well as much distance yet to go. The figures of Table 39 can be read to mean that as existing schools offer more grades fewer

[1] Ifigenia M. de Navarrete, 'El Financiamiento de la educación pública en México', reprinted in UNAM, Seminario de Problemas Científicos y Filosóficos, *Suplementos,* 2nd ser., no. 15 (1959), pp. S15–243–279, version used and cited.

students now drop out of school after grade one, but that drop-outs above second grade (7 years) are still serious.

TABLE 39

School Population, 7–12 Years of Age, 1950–60

(*millions*)

	1950	Per cent.	1955	Per cent.	1956	Per cent.
Total group, age 7–12 ...	4·07		4·63		5·27	
Total pupils in school ...	3·03		3·94		5·11	
Group 7–12 not in school ...	1·04	25·5	0·69	14·7	0·16	3·4
Total group, 6–14 years ...	6·01		6·83		7·78	
Total 6–14 not in school ...	2·09	35·0	1·91	28·0	1·74	22·4
Drop-outs, 6–14 group ...	1·05	17·5	1·22	17·8	1·58	20·3

Source: de Navarrete, 'Educación pública', table 1; percentages by author.

The implications of these sad facts are several and important. One is that the Mexican educational system, failing to move more than half the population beyond the second grade, must later supply education through extension courses and other means to those who never got to school at all, or had only the rudiments of education. Closely related is another important one: that even with first- and second-grade education in childhood, many Mexicans reach maturity as functionally illiterate. Another is that only a small reservoir of persons qualified for entrance to regular university training exists, because the feeder systems progressively narrow their streams as pupils move upwards.

A GENERAL VIEW

In 1950 Census officials ascertained the total years of education completed by persons over 25 years of age. Such figures reveal results of the educational efforts over two decades since 1930. Table 40 gives a general profile of the nation's educational levels, and highlights the urgent need for adult educational plans. About 90 per cent. of the adults in 1950 had no schooling at all or never advanced beyond the primary cycle.

TABLE 40

Levels of Educational Experience, 1950

('*000 persons over 25 years old*)

Level	Years/grades completed	Persons	Per cent.
Primary	Grades 1–6	4,588·0	45·6
Secondary	Grades 7–9	275·2	2·6
Preparatory	Years 10–12	154·6	1·4
University	Over 12 years	106·3	1·0
Not indicated	... ...	617·3	6·0
No schooling	... ...	4,363·6	43·4
Totals	... ...	10,105·0	100·0

Source: DGE, *Compendio estadístico, 1958*, table 24 (pp. 57–58), rearranged percentages by author.

In the decade from 1950 through 1960, as has been seen, the highest priority has been given to providing schools and teachers for those turning 6 years of age. Mexican investigators stress that these efforts must continue, in order to accommodate the increased number of eligible children who seek admission each year. There is general agreement that with quite feasible increased public investments, both by the national Government and by state governments, the problem can be solved over the next decade.[1] The findings and projections by one group are summarized in Table 41.

TABLE 41

Estimated Needs for Schoolrooms, Primary Education, 1957–65

Year	Annual increment Primary school population ('000)	Rooms needed (at 20,000 pesos each)	Annual needed outlay, construction ('000 pesos, 1955 value)
1957		72,693*	1,453,860
1960	171·2	3,424	68,480
1965	226·9	4,538	90,760

* Current deficit.
Source: SDE, *Diagnóstico*, table, p. 44.

UNIVERSITY SYSTEMS

In numerous addresses President López Mateos has underlined the key role which higher education must play in Mexican development. To provide the leadership and skills required by the present

[1] de Navarrete, 'Educación pública', pp. 274–6.

stage of the Revolution, he urges further expansion of the university system. Familiar from long personal experience in the educational field, he has had special interest in professional training. He is the first President in many years who has won whole-hearted support from the growing intellectual community, themselves products of the institutes and universities which have evolved in the changing atmosphere of the Revolution.[1]

It has been shown that a relatively reduced number of students, having completed their primary education, move on to advanced levels. A picture of post-primary education where a total enrolment of a little over 332,000 was officially recorded in 1958 is given in Table 42. This school population probably represents about 6 per cent. of the total 14–29 age-group potentially eligible for such training.

TABLE 42

Post-Primary Education, 1958

(*'ooo enrolled students*)

PRE-PROFESSIONAL/PRE-VOCATIONAL	*Thousands*	*Per cent.*
Secondary	151·4	45·6
Pre-vocational	5·8	1·8
Preparatory	17·8	5·2
Sub-total	175·0	52·6
SUB-PROFESSIONAL, TECHNICAL, VOCATIONAL		
Vocational	13·7	3·9
Commercial	43·9	13·6
Teacher training (Normal)	30·1	9·0
Various special curricula	42·3	12·7
Sub-total	130·0	39·2
PROFESSIONAL (UNIVERSITY LEVEL)	27·4	8·2
TOTALS	332·4	100·0

Source: DGE, *Compendio estadístico, 1958*, table 96 (pp. 170–71); main categories, percentages by author.

[1] Adolfo López Mateos, *El Señor Presidente . . . en la Universidad Michoacana: Palabras pronunciadas . . . el día 8 de Mayo de 1960* (Celaya, Gto., Centro de Estudios Históricos, 1960).

While there is still a relatively small reserve of leaders and specialists, the number of the latter is increasing steadily. One measure of this is the number of persons who have been added to the various official rosters indicating they have passed specified requirements and been given 'titles' attesting to their special qualifications. Possibly as important as the increasing number of specialists is the changing pattern in advanced education. The more traditional 'professions'—law and medicine—have steadily been reduced in proportion since 1950, giving way to 'newer' fields in commerce, industry, and its allied development. Even air pilots are Mexican trained.

Degrees ('titles') in commerce outrank any other group. They include auditors, private and public accountants, commercial experts, bookkeepers, graduates of secretarial schools, and others who staff the business and government bureaucracies. The group here labelled 'Others' is an astonishingly heterogeneous one, comprising engineers, architects, agronomists, dentists, nurses, midwives, pharmacists, scientists, veterinarians, cartographers, teachers, Ph.D's in social sciences, marine pilots, and even others. The annual number of degrees and titles from all post-primary training has more than doubled over the decade, as is shown in the following table.

TABLE 43

Professional and Vocational Degrees and Titles, 1948–57

Year	Total conferred ('000)	Medicine	Law	Combined Per cent.	No. ('000)	Per cent.	Others (Per cent.)
		(actual degrees)			*Commerce*		
1948	6·1	674	255	15·1	3·0	48·5	36·4
1950	5·8	777	238	17·4	3·0	51·4	31·2
1955	14·2	1,088	381	10·4	7·0	49·3	40·0
1957	16·7	880	488	8·4	8·3	49·5	42·1

Sources: DGE, *Compendio estadístico, 1953*, p. 195; *1955*, p. 173; *1958*, pp. 177–78; data regrouped, tabulated, percentages by author.

It is not possible to give even brief summaries of the many and excellent specialized schools, institutes, and programmes that produce the vocationally trained, the technicians, and the sub-professionals, but useful recent descriptions, with suggestions for further reading, are accessible.[1] The same sources give many details of the university systems. Here we are able to suggest only some of the principal features.

As throughout the total educational system, there is a sharp distinction drawn between national institutions, supported and directed by the Ministry of Education, and state institutions, supported by state funds and only very generally supervised from the national capital. Apart from these, there is a very small number of private institutions, not supported by public funds, and free, within quite broad limits, to develop their own curricula.

Important among the first are the National Autonomous University of Mexico, nearly universally abbreviated UNAM (Universidad Nacional Autónoma de México), and its more recently established companion, the National Polytechnic Institute. Fourteen Mexican states maintain at least one university, varying widely in size and quality, and Jalisco has two. Notable private efforts include the famous Institute of Technology and Advanced Studies in Monterrey and Mexico City College. As might be expected, two-thirds of the professional facilities and activities are centred in Mexico City.

State Universities

Courses offered by state universities are quite limited in comparison with those of national and private institutions. They have fewer faculties. These principally teach those skills locally most needed: pharmacy, nursing, obstetrics, commerce, social work. The newest state university is the one in Chihuahua, formed by consolidating a number of local institutions and inaugurated in 1955. Some state universities have a colonial tradition. Michoacán likes to trace its ancestry from an Indian school founded in 1540, while Puebla claims to have been founded in 1578. San Luis Potosí (1624) and Guanajuato (1732) also boast early beginnings and long histories. Strong state institutions are credited to Chihuahua, Jalisco, Mexico, Nuevo León, Puebla, and Veracruz.[2] A recent movement to strengthen these state universities now links them together through a national association.

National Universities

Capping the Mexican educational system, and directly responsible for maintaining advanced teaching and research facilities, are the

[1] Johnston, *Education*, pp. 54–81; Kneller, *Education*, pp. 112–63.
[2] Johnston, *Education*, pp. 87–90.

venerable National University, UNAM, and its friendly rival, the National Polytechnic Institute. Their aims are to impart higher education for professional careers, training the qualified research workers, university professors, and technicians to organize and carry on research, principally related to national conditions and problems, and to extend as widely as possible the benefits of culture, national and universal.

UNAM

In 1929 the University was granted 'autonomy', or the privilege of running its own internal affairs, and in 1945 again was reorganized as a public corporation, juridically separate from the state. The Polytechnic Institute does not have 'autonomy' but is a direct dependency of the Ministry of Education. As such it is responsible for a variety of pre-vocational, vocational, and sub-professional technical programmes.

The National Autonomous University is divided into 17 teaching faculties and 15 research institutes, including supervision of the National Library. On its 400th anniversary in 1953, UNAM began moving its facilities from the crowded centre in the national capital to University City, a spacious but distant site designed especially to house its students and faculties. The total plan is daringly functional, the decorations recalling Mexico's various heritages, and it includes a stadium seating 100,000 spectators. Despite protests and problems, the move has been completed.

To match the special attention given to reorganization and the new site, UNAM, from which a majority of government officials have graduated, has been granted increasingly large budgets in recent years. Its faculty and student body have thus grown rapidly in the past two decades. In 1940 it enrolled a little over 17,000 students, including the Summer School and the various preparatory schools connected with it; by 1954 this number had doubled. Over the same period, its teaching staff increased from about 2,300 to 5,400, more and more of them on a full-time basis.

An interesting analysis was made of the student body in 1949, which may still be valid in outline though certainly changed in many details a decade later. At that time, of the 23,000 students enrolled, 29 per cent., were offspring of business men; another 20·6 per cent. came from government employees' families, with about 10·6 per cent. from homes of professional men. The remainder were drawn from unidentifiable sources.[1]

[1] Lewis, 'México desde 1940', citing a study by L. Mendieta y Núñez.

Educational Revolution: a Sampling

The Polytechnic Institute

The National Polytechnic Institute, founded by Cárdenas in 1936, also has its own City, less ample than University City and less striking in design. It is a spacious, well-planned area with modern buildings, laboratories, shops, library, stadium, and other facilities normally found on North American campuses, but equally as often lacking on their Latin American counterparts. Counting the enrolment in the Institute itself and in technical schools near-by under its direction, the student body in 1954 was about 24,000 students. In some 46 Federal and state institutes also supervised by the Institute were yet another 21,200 students. Much of the instruction and many of the curricula for professional degrees parallel those of UNAM, with a greater tendency at the Institute to combine fields such as engineering and architecture and to emphasize more strongly practical fieldwork. Several men serve simultaneously on both faculties.

The Institute of Technology (Monterrey)

Although students of UNAM and the Institute view them as chief rivals because of their proximity, in fact an able competitor in the field of education is the Institute of Technology and Advanced Studies, an unusual and excellent institution, in distant Monterrey. It is unusual because it is the product of private initiative, and depends to a large degree on support by its local patrons. Founded in 1942 by a group of Monterrey industrialists to provide personnel for local enterprises, it was modelled on the Massachusetts Institute of Technology, from which many of them had graduated. The Institute in Monterrey offers vocational training and professional degrees in engineering, architecture, and the business fields. To the new and beautiful campus come not only youth from the area, but from all over Latin America, many of them on scholarships. Its standards are high, and the Institute is accredited in the United States by the Southern Association of Colleges and Secondary Schools.

Impressive as are statistics and descriptions of increasing efforts in higher education, a central fact remains that gaps between needs and supply are wide. The number of well-trained young men and women must be enlarged to staff and lead the developments of modern Mexico. The numbers who enjoy opportunities for advanced training and university work are still too restricted. Yet, as in most things related to Mexico, it is wise to measure the distance come, not that still to go. There is unquestionably a growing cadre, augmented constantly. The evident rewards from education are magnetizing attention to the problems. Not only the Federal and state governments, but new industries, even foreign enterprises, are taking a real, enlightened self-interest in providing greater opportunities for Mexican youth. All these signs point to renewed and continued developments in Mexican education and culture.

Chapter XXII

AGRARIANISM:
A BASIC REVOLUTIONARY GOAL

A CENTRAL objective from the outset of the Mexican Revolution, now embedded in Article 27, has been radical revision of the unbalanced land-tenure system. The 1910 cry of 'Land and Liberty' rallied Revolutionary bands, especially in those parts of the Republic where deep-seated resentments against the oppression and injustices connected with land had long smouldered. Although the Revolution was neither fought nor wholly won for agrarian goals, agrarianism is a powerful force, still vital half a century after Madero.

The dominant position that land and its many aspects retain on the Mexican scene has given rise to an extensive and ever-expanding number of books on the subject. Several basic early treatments tend to emphasize agrarianism, and give a history up to about the time of President Cárdenas.[1] A lesser handful of books and articles, generally employing data from the 1950 Census, carry developments to about that date.[2] In Chapter XXVIII we discuss agriculture since about 1950.

HISTORIC AGRARIANISM, 1915–34

On 6 January, 1915 Venustiano Carranza as First Chief of the Revolution issued a broad land law, usually taken as the point of departure for present agrarian movements. With added materials, it formed the base of Article 27 of the 1917 constitution of Querétaro, which outlined several alternatives for the redistribution of land, to correct the imbalances of the Porfirian and earlier periods.

Article 27 had as a premiss that at some earlier point in history, all land had belonged to the nation, and the latter still retained its

[1] George M. McBride, *The Land Systems of Mexico* (1923); F. Tannenbaum, *The Mexican Agrarian Revolution* (1929), and his *Mexico*; Eyler N. Simpson, *The Ejido* (1937); Lucio Mendieta y Núñez, *El Problema agrario de México*, 5th ed. (1946); Whetten, *Rural Mexico*, are major summaries, based on information to and before 1940, each with considerable bibliography.

[2] González Santos, *La Agricultura* gives an excellent synthesis; H. Flores de la Peña, 'Crecimiento demográfico, desarrollo agrícola, y desarrollo económico', *Investigación económica*, xiv (1954), 519–36; Clarence Senior, *Land Reform and Democracy* (1958); E. Flores, *Tratado de economía agrícola* (1961).

original power. Governments—Spanish and earlier national—had permitted land to become private property, but had failed to exercise proper controls. Hence, monopolies and other defects had developed which the Revolution must correct for the general social and economic welfare of the nation. Article 27 therefore empowered Governments to restore the presumed pristine equilibrium at the expense of private holdings. The national Government was enjoined to give lands to towns and villages which had need of them. Further, it was to aid them in the recovery of their own ancient lands which illegally or unjustly had passed to private hands, including mortmain, dead hand of the Church. The state was to break up large properties, where necessary. Among the collateral mandates was that of fostering development of small- and medium-size private holdings.

These, then, were the basic goals of agrarianism. A compromise at the time, Article 27 embraced at least three mutually exclusive approaches. Which the Revolution shall choose to fulfil aspirations for land reform still arouses controversy. Each course tends to have a regional background in its Revolutionary cachet.

One group, stemming chiefly from the views voiced by Emiliano Zapata, stressed the return of 'lost' communal holdings to rural Indian villages. Generalizing from purported Aztec practices they took the concept of the ejido, prevalent in central Mexico at Conquest and modified by Spanish practice, as the basis of their proposals: title to lands, and regulations about their uses were to be vested in the landholding village. This doctrine had little meaning for the great mass of Mexicans from non-Indian Mexico, especially the North. For them 'land and liberty' summarized a different claim: the right of each family to own a private fee-simple plot of adequate land and exploit it as yeoman farmers.

A third programme, partially developed by nationally-minded urban thinkers, viewed the future of Mexican land tenure and use as a mixture. Large estates, haciendas, would continue to produce the food and export crops essential to national economy. But to relieve the rural wage worker of the political and economic pressures inherent in the hacienda system, he would be given small subsistence plots to supplement his earnings. Therefore the peón who for generations had been a paid plantation hand, would work part of the year on an hacienda and under its discipline, but for the remainder he would, as a small agriculturalist, have some leisure to work his own small plot for his own purposes.

The Revolution, early and late, has never fully reconciled these divergent points of view, swinging from one to another, often to extremes.[1] Agrarian reform has thus been confused, uncertain, difficult to assess. At all times the three main strands have been the bases for action.

The earliest and still a continuing approach is known as 'Restitution'. Peasants seize land forcibly, and then argue that they are 'restoring' lands stolen from them or their presumed ancestors. Earlier the Government had little option but to validate the action. As matters settled down in the 1920's and early 1930's, the state was increasingly able to require villages to petition for such restitution before taking direct action. But the problem of unauthorized land seizures has by no means disappeared. Attempting to force the hand of the new administration, agrarians before the inauguration of President Adolfo López Mateos resorted to such tactics.[2] By action and statement he made it clear that his administration was not inclined to view illegal possession by such 'parachutists' as a *fait accompli*, and that agrarian reform would continue to go forward through established legal modes.

More widely used by Revolutionary Governments has been the concept of grant or donation, the *dotación*. Under this doctrine, an agrarian group—village or other nucleus—petitions for land on the basis of need. They must show that their group can and should work the area in question rather than its private owners. If the Government agrees, the land is expropriated and the owner is recompensed with government bonds. Title to the land then is transferred from the private owner to the communal group. The fact that various such communal groups, not the national state, legally own their lands marks the Mexican system off from other comparable ones, such as the Russian, where the state (national Government) itself holds title to all land within national boundaries.

THE CÁRDENAS REFORMS

Up to the time of President Cárdenas, agrarian reformers had hesitated to tackle the basic problem of expropriating haciendas. These were large integrated holdings dedicated mainly to production of big money crops like sugar, cotton, sisal fibres. Current economic considerations did not alter Cárdenas's view that land should be made available to peasants.

He expropriated these large units, and turned them into co-operatives—the communal ejido. Thus he added co-operative

[1] Senior, *Land Reform*, pp. 13–31.
[2] *Paracaidistas* is the common Mexican label used for persons, dropping unannounced as 'parachutists'.

production to communal ownership. Before the Cárdenas era, about 7·1 million hectares (about 17 million acres) of land had been redistributed. During his six-year term as President, this total was more than doubled, to 16·8 million hectares (about 41 million acres). The core of the Cárdenas concept was that small and large-scale communal units, ejidos, would provide training in democracy for the peasant and foster social justice. At the same time the ejidos would feed the nation, and the larger communal units would produce exportable surpluses. None of these things happened.

The economic and technical phases of the Cárdenas programme were spectacular failures. In the new areas, topographical details were lacking or disregarded. Legal and bureaucratic tangles were inevitable, with almost insoluble disputes over such difficulties as boundaries, placement of drainage and irrigation works, and crop allocations. Elements not subject to presidential fiat, like the conjunction of favourable temperatures, sufficient moisture at proper times, slopes, soil fertility, and suitability for proposed crops were flouted by novices in the fields. They lacked knowledge of management, distribution, and other specialized skills, and talents necessary to successful agricultural enterprises, precarious under the best of circumstances. As a consequence, too many people flocked to the few good plots, pulverizing them into small units, creating a problem of 'minifundia' even more serious than latifundia. Clarence Senior compares this error to a 'captain who allows a lifeboat to be loaded far beyond capacity'.[1]

In such a confused situation, venality of leaders on ejidos contributed yet another negative factor, with agrarian issues and forces always a political football on the local, state, and national levels. Politicians lacked the technical knowledge essential to successful agrarian reform; technicians lacked political acumen and power. The peasantry was unprepared by background, education, possibly even motivation, suddenly to take on major responsibility for planning and executing a viable national agricultural policy.

The political and psychological success of the Cárdenas land reform became a permanent legacy. Land monopoly seemed to have been broken. The peasants idolized Cárdenas, with good reason, as 'their' President. The economic failure of the Cárdenas policy, however, led to an important reassessment of Mexico's agricultural potential and policies.

[1] Senior, *Land Reform*, p. 209.

Agrarianism: a Basic Revolutionary Goal

'Land for the landless' was an unbeatable election slogan, which President Cárdenas did much to provide with meaning. But economic and sociological facts soon began to emerge which clearly showed that an election slogan is no substitute for a workable long-term programme. Unexpected, even disastrous implications, appeared when the slogan was applied widely and indiscriminately to the Mexican case. After 1940 there seemed to be no alternative to a review and reorientation of the Revolutionary agrarian programme. The agricultural sector was not producing enough even to feed itself. Lines of policy change were foreshadowed when it became clear that Manuel Avila Camacho would succeed Cárdenas as President.

The revised programme of the Institutional Revolution may be said to have five prongs or fingers. First, as is politically essential, considerable land has been redistributed to the landless, on a reduced and somewhat more rational basis. Secondly, to create new resources, irrigation and related hydraulic projects have been planned and mounted; thirdly, areas suitable for agriculture but unexploited have been opened to colonization, notably 'the March to the Sea' along the Gulf's tropical lowlands; fourthly, modernization of agriculture has encompassed many endeavours, from upgrading extant lands and techniques to providing basic and auxiliary services—education, transportation, credit, technical assistance, and the like. Finally, to reintegrate the agricultural section for needed increases in production, policies were initiated which provided small and medium-size private owners with benefits equal to those enjoyed only by peasants on ejidos. To the basic programme, remarkable for its continuity and success since 1940, each President has added personal variations and smaller or larger contributions.

Land Distribution

In this 'team' approach, care has been taken to preserve earlier reforms, and to pursue a modified version of the Cárdenas ejido programme. Up to 1958, Revolutionary Governments since 1915 had restored or granted a total of 43·5 million hectares (about 107 million acres) of land to peasants.

On a lesser scale, President Cárdenas's successors have continued land distribution. In millions of hectares their contributions are not unimpressive: Avila Camacho, 6·6; Alemán, 5·4; Ruíz Cortines, 3·5, together about a third of the total distribution. President Ruíz

Cortines in his final message to Congress (1958) noted that there was simply not much more land to be redistributed. President López Mateos won much support as candidate by promises to revive agrarianism. In his annual report to Congress on 1 September 1960 he summarized the policies his administration was following by saying that it was redistributing all lands legally disposable, developing ejidos based on cattle-raising and on forest products, and aiding productivity to bring greater economic returns to ejidatarios. He pointed out that in twenty-one months his régime had granted ejidos at the rate of 150,000 hectares monthly, or a total of 3·2 million hectares (nearly 8 million acres). He pointed out that he had cancelled a number of private rental contracts made by venal agrarian leaders with private interests, and in other ways had kept the Revolution moving toward its goals of agrarian reform.[1]

Expropriation of private holdings, especially large estates and even more specifically those held by foreigners, has slowed down under the Institutional Revolution. Before other programmes could be carried out it was necessary to disentangle the debts represented by agrarian bonds and straighten out other serious defects in agrarianism. Yet to keep the spirit of the Revolution visible, at the close of the Ruíz Cortines régime, his Government did negotiate settlements and expropriate large foreign-owned holdings at Cananea, Cloete, and Bavicora, on Mexico's northern boundary. However, both land distribution and continued reduction of latifundia reiterate the Institutional Revolution's intention of pursuing older agrarian reform paths, while simultaneously striking out in newer and more productive directions.

The Land Law of 1949

On the basis of experiment and experience during the Avila Camacho years, President Alemán had Article 27 of the constitution revised on 12 February 1947, early in his tenure of office. In due time (30 December 1949) the Agrarian Code was altered to suit the recommendations of Mexican technicians and others who had been alarmed at the pulverization of Mexico's few resources. It also provided protection and incentives for private owners.

For the ejido programme the Code set the minimum ejido grant at 10 hectares (24·7 acres) of irrigated land or 20 of seasonal land. This was designed to reverse trends towards minifundia. It also provided norms for distribution of public lands in colonization areas

[1] López Mateos, *2° Informe* (1 Sept. 1960).

being opened up. Ensuring the coexistence of private holdings, the Code guaranteed them legal protection but under several stipulations. Certificates of 'inaffectibility' were authorized, exempting them from future expropriation, for holdings of up to 100 hectares of irrigated land or 200 of seasonal land or pasture. As further protection against loss of property by 'parachutist' tactics, lands were made subject to *amparo* proceedings, which had previously not covered agrarian matters. Special assurances were given to certain larger landholdings used to produce badly needed crops or products: cotton up to 150 hectares; and up to 300 hectares of bananas, coconuts, grapes, coffee, sugarcane, and some other lesser crops. To stimulate cattle-raising, lands suitable to graze up to 500 head or their equivalent in other livestock also became eligible for certificates of inaffectibility, without regard for needs of neighbouring villages for land. In individual cases, after such needs have been canvased, as many as 50,000 acres of pasturage can be made exempt for twenty-five years under private control. These prescriptions apply equally to Mexicans and foreigners. As for many years past, foreigners are prohibited from owning real estate within 100 kilometres of land boundaries or 50 from sea coasts.

Other Aspects

The several programmes already noted—the development of hydraulic resources, combating disease in sea-coast areas, multiplication of communications, credit, and the like—have pushed forward the general policy of colonization. Under the Agrarian Code, persons who cannot obtain land in their own areas become eligible for grants in these new territories. Statistics for 1958 indicated that there were 924 such colonies, occupying 6·2 million hectares of land. As a new variation, López Mateos announced in his inaugural address and in his first State of the Union Message (1959) that ejidos and grants were being created for exploitation of forest resources. Thus the policies of the Institutional Revolution have been to create new resources and utilize unexploited ones, rather than subdivide into uneconomic units the small and poor land resources inherited by the Revolution.

The doctrines were summed up by President Ruíz Cortines in his synthesis to Congress toward the end of his term in 1958. The ejido and the smallholding, he affirmed, were the two pillars of Mexican agriculture, bound together in a general plan to raise the social and economic levels of rural Mexico. To fortify both, he and predecessors had multiplied road construction, credit institutions, and conservation programmes, amplified hydraulic works, generalized the use of fertilizers, provided price guarantees for crops, developed new high-yield seeds, created new industrial markets for rural products, developed rural education, especially vocational schools, and had been placing rural workers under social security protection. Above all, efforts had been constantly made 'to create a new mentality' among the previously oppressed peasantry.

MAJOR RESULTS, 1915–59

No one doubts that in the long view agrarian reforms have been needed, and generally successful. The Revolution, whatever its shortcomings in detail, destroyed a simple agricultural system unsuited to the healthy growth of the nation. Before the outbreak of the Revolution about 1 per cent. of the population owned most of the land.

This hacienda complex was characterized by absentee ownership, unmerciful exploitation, and a rapacious land hunger that stripped surrounding villages of any source of agricultural livelihood. The system supported and was in turn aided by a Government which maintained discipline over landless peons, little better than serfs. The tide of Revolution swept this system away. There are no responsible voices raised to recommend the unwise and impossible task of restoring it.

It is rather difficult to obtain reliable statistical data on many aspects of the agrarian system of present-day Mexico. While there is necessarily no conspiracy of silence, at the same time figures about land and land tenure are politically radioactive, both in domestic and foreign circles. They are published gingerly, and in small quantities. The most complete series derives from the 1950 Census. Comparison of its findings with those of the Census of 1910 show that over forty years the number of farms rose from about 48,000 to 1·4 millions. The latter figure includes ejidos with several shareholders, with a result that the number of farms is less than the number of landholders in 1950, around 3·3 million.[1]

The same 1950 Census figures state that there were engaged in agriculture about 4·7 million people, then 57 per cent. of the total labour force, cultivating around 16 million hectares. This would

[1] Senior, *Land Reform*, pp. 27–28.

provide an average of about 4·2 hectares per person. With three different systems in effect such an average is misleading. The ejidatarios under communal systems enjoyed about 6·4 hectares apiece, small private holdings averaged 1·3 hectares, and owners of plots over 5 hectares, considered 'larger' holdings, averaged 38·3, with wide regional variations.[1]

Comparable, more detailed, figures have been developed by Luis Yáñez Pérez. His technical studies provide a substantial block of data, drawn in part from unpublished sources. One of his summaries indicates differences between ejido and private plots. The number of families in each system is about the same.

TABLE 44

Cultivated Areas, 1950, Ejido and Private Plots

	EJIDOS		PRIVATE		NATIONAL TOTAL	
	No.	*Per cent.*	*No.*	*Per cent.*	*No.*	*Per cent.*
Heads of families ('000)	1,378·3	50·0	1,365·6	50·0	2,743·9	100·0
Cultivated land ('000 *ha.*) ...	8,790·9	44·1	11,137·4	55·9	19,928·3	100·0
Average plot (ha.)	6·38		8·16		7·2	

Source: Yáñez Pérez, *Mecanización*, table 23 (p. 83), adapted. Percentages by author.

Other investigations published by Sr. Yáñez Pérez pursue further the matter of comparative size of landholdings, fundamental to an assessment of land reforms and to plans for improving production. He found that the great body of holdings, whether worked by private or ejido systems, fell below 10 hectares (24·7 acres). Here, although the two systems are not absolutely congruent, we can juxtapose his data.

---

[1] Ríos Díaz, 'Agricultura', pp. 53–76.

TABLE 45

General Structure, Land Tenure, by Size of Holdings, 1950

('000)

	EJIDOS		PRIVATE HOLDINGS	
	Ejidatarios	*Per cent.*	*Plots*	*Per cent.*
Without lands ...	11·07	0·80		
Less than 1 ha. ...	101·85	7·39		
From 1–4 ha. ...	467·87	33·95		
Minifundia ...	580·79	42·14	To 5 ha. 1,020·75	82·54
From 4–10 ha. ...	580·89	42·14	5–10 ha. 88·02	7·12
Small plots ...	1,161·68	84·28	.... 1,108·77	89·66
Over 10 ha. ...	216·64	15·72	.... 127·95	10·34
TOTALS... ...	1,378·32	100·00	.... 1,236·72	100·0

Source: Yáñez Pérez, *Mecanización*, tables 24, 26 (pp. 85, 91), adapted.

It would seem from this that land reform had accomplished one major objective: placing land in the hands of many. At first glance it would appear that the latifundia of pre-Revolutionary days had disappeared.

Private Landholdings

Let us look for a moment at the alleged disappearance of latifundia. The same source gives detailed information on private holdings of over 10 hectares. It tells us that although the holdings below 10 hectares predominate in number, their total area is far outstripped by the few above that size. In 1950 some 708 very large [over 800 hectares] owners still controlled 32 per cent. of the cultivated private area; about half the total such land was in medium and large plots owned by 10 per cent. of the proprietors; the remaining fifth was divided, as we have seen, among more than a million smallholders. Table 46 provides specific information.

TABLE 46

Privately Owned Rural Lands, 1950

(*'ooo of proprietors*; *'ooo hectares*)

Size of holding (hectares)	Proprietors		Total Area	
	No.	*Per cent.*	*Amount*	*Per cent.*
0 – 5	1,020·7	82·54	1,504·4	13·51
5 – 10...	88·0	7·12	686·3	6·16
Small holdings ...	1,108·7	89·66	2,190·7	19·67
10 – 25	72·1	5·83	1,208·5	10·85
25 – 50	30·5	2·47	1,131·6	10·16
50 – 100	15·9	1·28	1,192·6	10·71
Medium holdings ...	118·5	9·58	3,532·7	31·72
100 – 200	6·0	0·48	864·0	7·76
200 – 400	1·9	0·15	527·2	4·73
400 – 800	0·8	0·07	474·0	4·26
Large holdings ...	8·7	0·70	1,865·2	16·75
Over 800 Very large holdings	0·7	0·06	3,548·8	31·86
TOTALS	1,236·6	100·0	11,137·4	100·0

Source: Yáñez Pérez, *Mecanización*, table 26 (p. 91), adapted.

Information presented by Sr. Yáñez, again based on 1950 data, about returns to agriculturalists exploiting plots of these various sizes is quite revealing. The total number of private proprietors included in his study differs slightly from the figures given in the table above, but seems representative enough of the half of the Mexican agricultural system still in private hands to warrant the following summary (Table 47, p. 220).

This indicates that small plots of up to 10 hectares produce very low-value crops, and correspondingly meagre incomes for the proprietors, whose combined contribution to national income is pitifully small. At the other extreme, remaining very large holdings (average 2,063 hectares) in the hands of 708 proprietors in 1950 provided each with more than a million pesos income, and accounted for 35 per cent. of total agricultural incomes. Prosperity and mechanization seem possible only on plots of such magnitude.

TABLE 47

Incomes of Private Agriculturalists, by Size of Holdings, 1950

Size of plot (hectares)	No. of proprietors ('ooo)	Per cent.	Average size plot (worked) hectares	Average annual income (pesos)	Total group income Amount (million pesos)	Per cent.
Without land ...	71·5	19·82				
0·1 – 5·0	73·3	20·32	1·05	626	45·9	1·85
5·1 – 10·0	88·0	24·40	3·16	1,884	165·8	6·68
Small holdings ...	232·8	64·54			211·7	8·53
10·1 – 25·0	72·1	20·00	7·39	4,406	317·8	12·81
25·1 – 50·0	30·5	8·46	15·83	9,438	288·0	11·61
50·0 – 100·0 ...	15·9	4·42	31·67	18,881	300·8	12·12
Medium holdings	118·5	32·88			906·6	36·54
100·1 – 200·0 ...	6·0	1·65	63·33	37,756	225·4	9·08
200·1 – 400·0 ...	1·9	0·51	126·66	75,512	140·2	5·65
400·1 – 800·0 ...	0·8	0·23	253·32	151,025	126·6	5·10
Large holdings ...	8·7	2·39			492·2	19·83
Over 800·1 Very large holdings	0·7	0·19	871·04	1,229,983	870·8	35·10
Totals	360·7	100·00			2,481·3	100·0

Source: Yáñez Pérez, *Mecanización*, table 31 (p. 108), adapted.

But the large political and economic question, without obvious answer, is how to permit the 71,504 landless non-ejidatarios to obtain land? How to raise the incomes of those with extant uneconomical plots smaller than 10 hectares? To subdivide the remaining large holdings could mean merely to ruin a going system without appreciably raising incomes of the landless or those on minifundias.

At the moment then these small private holders tend to be the problem children. Although we have seen how misleading averages can be, the following table showing average annual incomes from ejidal and private systems suggests the nature of the problems.

TABLE 48

Average Annual Incomes, Agrarian Systems, 1950

	Annual income (pesos/year)	Persons ('000)
EJIDO	1,004·79	1,222·9
PRIVATE HOLDINGS		1,236·7
Plots under 5 hectares	352·04	1,020·7
Plots over 5 hectares	6,877·24	128·0
NATIONAL AVERAGE	1,537·91	

Source: Yáñez Pérez, *Mecanización*, table 32 (p. 110).

SUMMARY

The least that can be said about Mexican agrarian reforms since 1915 is that there has been a manifest redistribution of land as a result of the Revolution. A lack of clear doctrine, or rather the interaction of at least three different major approaches, makes final assessment of 'success' difficult. It is clear that emphasis has shifted from radical agrarianism to planned agricultural improvement, for the best utilization of Mexico's restricted land resources.

Successive grants of small, uneconomical bits of land since 1915 and especially between 1934 and 1940 have neither automatically brought democracy nor marked economic improvement. There are few reliable data on changes in psychological state. The major upsurge of agrarianism in the time of Cárdenas has left in its trail the pressing need for further renovation of the system to meet the economic as well as the political needs of the nation and has exposed some major fallacies in ideological and doctrinaire approaches to land reform.

A jolting lesson, brought home clearly, is a basic consideration, 'Mexico has poor land, and little of it. The fundamental problem of poverty could therefore not be solved by the "right distribution of land", which was the main slogan in 1910.'[1]

[1] Pedro C. M. Teichert, *Economic Policy Revolution and Industrialization in Latin America* (1959), p. 13.

Chapter XXIII

LABOUR: A REVOLUTIONARY POLITICAL MOVEMENT

As a fundamental basis of the Revolution, Article 123, the 'Magna Carta of Mexican Labour', ranks with Article 27, embodying doctrines of agrarianism and nationalized sub-soil resources. By it the Mexican labour movement gained in a stroke one of labour's most coveted objectives: recognition. In many other, more mature economies, the achievement of this goal alone has required years of constant struggle.

As a favourite child of the Revolution, Mexican labour has had a somewhat unique experience. It has never faced some of the other issues that inevitably trouble organized labour seeking to establish a partnership in an economy: survival and permanence, ideology, appropriate structure, discipline, and programmes. These are all provided by the Revolution, i.e. Article 123.

Two outstanding facts colour the Mexican development. First, the modern labour movement formed part of the militant Revolution; therefore, from the outset it has had an honoured place in social and economic circles, assured by Article 123. Secondly, the movement has been more political than economic in outlook, tactics, and goals. There has never been an anti-labour Government in Mexico since 1917; conversely, there has never been an anti-Government labour party or programme of consequence.

Issues and goals of Mexican labour have been posed in political terms. The normal economic objectives are generally settled, with consultation, by the Government. Labour supports and has a major place in the official party; in turn, it receives rewards and even penalties, in accordance with Government's total needs and policies.

Concerning labour's evolution in Mexico, a major fact must be kept in mind: a political labour movement existed before there was actually a modern industrial economy. The latter has blossomed in the past two decades within bounds set by the Revolution, and these most assuredly embrace the classic prescriptions of Article 123. Neither wholly captive of Government, nor able to make major gains wholly free from reliance on it, the Mexican labour movement remains one of the most important in Latin America, where it is widely respected and sometimes copied.[1]

LABOUR AND THE REVOLUTION

The Mexican labour movement lacks a historian. We have only partial histories; economists view labour without time perspective.[2] In brief space we cannot remedy that defect, but can only touch on the later history since labour's modern appearance on the Mexican scene was initiated by the *Casa de Obrero* (House of Labour) in 1912.

Early labour won a place in the Revolutionary family by forming 'Red Battalions' and participating in the military struggle from 1915 through 1917. Rewarded by the Constitutionalists with Article 123, labour soon became part of the normal political elements, vying with agrarians, militarists, and other special interests in the political arena.

In the period around 1929, when the official party was being born to resolve the serious crisis caused by Obregón's assassination, the then small but vocal movement made a nearly fatal decision. After enjoying a brief honeymoon with Government during Calles's presidency, when the Ministry of Labour was firmly established with Cabinet rank, the major labour confederation (CROM) failed in 1928 to support either Calles or Obregón, and overestimating its own power, refused to join the subsequent cartel, or official party, through which Calles ruled after 1929. Seeking to 'go it alone' as an independent labour movement, the group found no real success, and nearly disintegrated. It has not made that error again, nor is it likely to.

Lázaro Cárdenas revitalized organized labour by making it part of the new 'functional' party, in return for support in carrying forward his reform programmes. From disconsolate fragments in 1936 he brought into being the main labour confederation, CTM (*Confederación de Trabajadores Mexicanos*). Then led by Vicente

---

[1] For the preparation of this chapter I am greatly indebted to Dr. Ben F. Stephansky, former Labour Attaché, U.S. Embassy in Mexico, and an unpublished summary he prepared, 'The Mexican Labor Movement: an Interpretation of a Political Labor Movement', cleared for public use 12 July 1957.

[2] Up to 1933 the story is well told in Marjorie Clark, *Organized Labor in Mexico* (1934); comprehensive on very recent trends, with full data, is Guadalupe Rivera Marín, *El Mercado de trabajo* (1955). To some degree between these are useful but incomplete volumes by Rosendo Salazar, *Líderes y sindicatos* (1953), and his *Historia de la CTM* (1956). There is a large polemical pamphlet literature, poorly explored.

Lombardo Toledano, it organized many new unions. Its incorporation into the official party, along with confederations of bureaucrats, gave permanence and continuity to the labour movement, and accounts largely for the present political cast of labour activities.

The Institutional Revolution, while preserving a central concern for labour, has cut back its militant activities, purged it of Communism, and imposed discipline. In turn, labour has developed an ideology, based on its duty to help other sectors build a new and prosperous Mexico. It has become more preoccupied with social and economic questions than political ones.

ORGANIZED LABOUR: STRUCTURE AND NUMBERS

There are six confederations of industrial and commercial unions, which embrace all but about 20,000 workers in very small independent unions.

The CTM (Confederation of Workers of Mexico) dominates and overshadows its five small rivals.[1] Estimates of its membership range from 500,000 to 1·3 millions, mainly from unions in fields of electric power, railways, mining, petroleum, telephone, with representation from nearly all branches of the industrial economy. The CTM includes 20 national unions, 31 state federations, and more than 100 local and regional federations. It is the 'official' representative of organized labour within the PRI.

In addition to the industrial and commercial federations are those of the bureaucrats and the agrarian groups. Second in size to CTM is the Federation of Government Workers (FSTSE), with twenty-eight unions and a membership of more than quarter of a million. It is the backbone of the popular sector of the PRI. Rival farm federations similarly represent agrarian interests in the party: CNC (National Farm Federation), and UFCM (Union of Farmers Federations of Mexico), organized in 1950 as a counterweight to the more radical CNC.

In turn, all these federations, except UGOC (General Union of Workers and Farmers of Mexico) are affiliated with the democratic hemispheric international labour body, the ORIT: Interamerican Regional Organization of Workers. Major United States bodies— A.F. of L.-C.I.O., United Mine Workers—as well as the larger more responsible unions and confederations of Latin America join

---

[1] CROC (Revolutionary Confederation of Workers and Farmers), *c.* 40,000–70,000; CROM (Regional Mexican Labour Federation), *c.* 40,000 members; these compete with each other and CTM. UGOCM (General Union of Workers and Farmers of Mexico), about 20,000, chiefly Communist-dominated unions.

their Mexican colleagues in ORIT. The CTAL, Workers' Federation of Latin America, also with its headquarters in Mexico City, is Communist-dominated. The UGOC, which has 20,000 members or so, is the only Mexican federation affiliated with it.[1]

Official figures tend to show fewer organized wage-earners than do registers of political units representing labour interests. With rapid industrialization, there has also been a rise in number of unions, and in total membership. During the four most recent years for which figures are readily accessible, the growth in each appears in the following table.

TABLE 49

Growth of Organized Labour, 1954–7

	No. of Unions	*No. of members ('000)*
1954	8,623	967·7
1955	8,920	980·0
1956	9,361	1,000·5
1957	9,114	1,013·4

Source: DGE, *Compendio estadístico, 1958,* table 124, p. 212.

LABOUR AND THE GOVERNMENT

The powers which permit the Federal Government, through the Minister of Labour (and the President), to set limits within which organized labour can develop and act derive from Article 73 of the constitution, giving Congress the responsibility for enacting laws to carry out Article 123. The present labour code, enacted in 1942, sets forth detailed prescriptions concerning the numerous general provisions of Article 123 to be administered by the Minister of Labour. Collective contracts, hours and wages, employment limitations, holidays and vacations, severance liabilities, social insurance, strikes and lockouts, required housing and educational privileges, are among principal topics thus specified.[2]

In return for recognition—a place at the council tables of party and Government—labour has tacitly accepted certain limitations, as full co-partners in the Revolution. It cannot engage in all-out warfare against industry, nor exert full economic pressure against

---

[1] USBFC, *Investment in Mexico*, pp. 80–81. Detail is also found in Chicago Univ., Research Center in Econ. Dev. and Cult. Change, *U.S.-Latin American Relations: U.S. Business and Labor in Latin America* (1960), pp. 72–100.

[2] Summaries of each in USBFC, *Investment in Mexico*, pp. 82–85.

the Government to obtain more desirable wages and conditions. In the total system, the claims of labour for more wages, for example, must be weighed by the Government against such national considerations as trade balances, export prices, the level of domestic prices, the preservation of an attractive climate for domestic and foreign investment, and other elements producing general economic development, now a major goal of the Revolution.

Backed by the President, the key figure in adjusting these various elements is the Minister of Labour. He, in consultation with labour itself, other Cabinet colleagues, and party members, essentially opens and shuts the valves of labour militancy. He largely determines whether the publicly demanded changes will be made in wages or conditions. The wage policy he imposes must be accepted by labour; any changes must come through peaceful means.

Mexican labour is free to strike. But it is the Minister who determines the Government's range of tolerance, as to extent and duration. When strikes persist beyond acceptable limits, the Minister can and will invoke all necessary party and government apparatus to bring the situation back into line. Since about 1946 strikes have almost always been settled by arbitration or conciliation, more frequently by the latter.

The political background and context in which labour operates has attenuated the development of trade union techniques of settling minor grievances. Lacking the research and statistical studies made by comparable labour movements elsewhere in the world, Mexican labour has no real basis for pressing wage demands, beyond the traditional cry of 'More!'

Official statistics tend to bear out these broad generalizations. In 1957, when the present President was Minister of Labour, for example, there were reported some 13,364 conflicts, of which 193 developed into strikes. More than half (6,765) the conflicts arose over variations in renewal of labour contracts. Conflicting claims over sick pay accounted for the second largest number of cases that came before the Ministry of Labour. Charges of violation of contract numbered only 1,413. Wages problems were the cause of 1,023 (7·7 per cent.) of the total conflicts. But of the 193 strikes, 161 related to the wages of only 7,137 workers, a tiny minority in the estimated million or more membership of organized labour. This number is in sharp contrast to earlier years of the Institutional Revolution, such as 1944, when there were 887 strikes, involving 166,000 workers.[1]

[1] DGE, *Compendio estadístico, 1958*, tables 127, 128 (pp. 216–17); USBFC, *Investment in Mexico*, p. 81.

Labour: a Revolutionary Political Movement

López Mateos promised in his first State of the Union address that he would stimulate legitimate labour organizations. However, he gave warning in veiled fashion that they must act in the interest of the workers—an oblique thrust at corrupt leadership—and be prepared to make sacrifices to 'the superior interest of the nation'. Wildcat strikes, and especially some of the irresponsible attempts to put pressure on the new administration in pre-inauguration days, have quietly been resolved.

The two-year record under 'Labour's President' is interesting. It differs little from earlier Institutional Revolution administrations. President López Mateos reported on 1 September 1960 that of the total 1,437 threatened strikes during 1959–60, only fourteen actually took place. The remainder were called off or resolved by conciliation before they occurred. The same conciliatory apparatus arranged contract revisions in 847 cases where no strike threats were even present, including major unions like those of miners, electricians, and textile workers. Wage increases averaged 15 per cent. Labour laws were amended to allow aircraft crews to form unions and sign collective contracts.[1]

The present administration is carrying out an attitude announced by López Mateos as candidate. 'Mexican laws uphold the workers' right to strike, and the men who govern Mexico respect, and will demand that others respect this right, when it is legitimately invoked.' But, he said, the

Constitution provides for a legal manner through which the desires of the [working] people may be realized. To act outside the law, which amply recognizes the rights of workers, is to betray the working class. Whosoever goads the workers into an unnecessary strike, outside the law, knowing full well that existing economic conditions do not permit of excessive demands, is an enemy of the workers.[2]

LABOUR AND THE ECONOMY

Enterprises find that the availability and efficiency of Mexican labour vary widely by region, with the most numerous and best hands in large urban centres. The most serious shortage is in the middle supervisory range: capable and dependable foremen, small unit supervisors, and subordinate managers. There is therefore a sharp wage differential between the unskilled and semi-skilled workers and those relatively few persons with supervisory talents.[3]

[1] López Mateos, 2° *Informe* (1 Sept. 1960).

[2] PRI, 'The Labor Policy of the López Mateos Administration, in the Government of Mexico, a brief speech . . . July 29, 1959' (Mexico, 1959).

[3] USBFC, *Investment in Mexico*, p. 79. See important study of manpower in manufacturing, Banco de México, *El Empleo de personal técnico en la industria de transformación* (1959).

227

Both foreign and Mexican economists are preoccupied with the problem of productivity. Productivity is merely the output of a worker in an hour; this can be measured in monetary terms. The level of efficiency has important implications for social and political, as well as economic policies. For example, if productivity rises, the same labour force will obviously produce more in the same work week. One able Mexican, Dr. Alfredo Navarrete, has recently summarized the developments in Mexico since 1940, indicating the steady rise in productivity. On the basis of trends from 1940 through 1955, he predicts that from 1955 through 1965, productivity should increase about 3·5 per cent. per year, or a total of 35·46 per cent. for the decade. He expects a rise in the labour force of about 32·31 per cent. and a very slight reduction in the number of hours each man must annually devote to his work.

TABLE 50

Employment and Productivity, 1940–65

	1940	*1950*	*Predicted 1965*
Average hours worked per week	44	44	44
Man-hours worked per year (millions) ...	12,859	18,926	30,748
Productivity, pesos/man-hour (1955 prices and value)	2·63	3·56	4·89
Per capita product: labour force (pesos) ...	6,029	8,152	11,194
Per capita man-hours per year	2,265	2,268	2,270
Unemployment: per cent. of labour force	1·01	0·88	0·77

Source: Alfredo Navarrete R., 'Productividad, ocupación, y desocipación en México, 1940–1965', *Trimestre económico,* xxiii (Oct.–Dec. 1956), table 1, p. 418.

The total output, or product, of the enlarged labour force will thus increase about 35·36 per cent. by 1965. To reach these attainable goals, Dr. Navarrete observes that the economy will have to provide 264,000 new jobs yearly, with an average annual investment of 5 per cent. of the gross national product, and continue the processes of up-grading Mexican labour.[1]

The Revolution, and more especially the Institutional Revolution, retains its respect and concern for labour, as a way of life as well as an economic commodity. Workers have a tremendous responsibility to keep the current boom going.[2]

[1] Navarrete R., 'Productividad', pp. 415–23.

[2] Abram J. Jaffe, *People, Jobs and Economic Development* (1959), p. 270, concludes that the Mexican economy, cannot grow fast enough to 'provide jobs for the growing working force'. The author disagrees.

THE STATE AND THE ECONOMY

Chapter XXIV

THE STATE AND THE ECONOMY: PARTNERS

THE Institutional Revolution differs significantly from earlier periods since 1910. One of the clearest and most important of these distinctions lies in its economic policies.

Although the earlier phases of the Revolution pioneered in political and social realms, they seldom strayed in the economic field far from the orthodox lines of the day. The years from 1910 through the middle 1920's were primarily concerned with political problems: the creation of political stability was a paramount goal. Their economic programmes were not successful. With a Mexican record of default on bonds and other obligations as a result of the Militant Revolution, and with xenophobia at a high pitch, there was small incentive to domestic or foreign investment. Few local sources had creative capital. World-wide depression snuffed out the very small beginnings of economic development, initiated after political tranquillity had been precariously achieved, chiefly through the single-party mechanism invented in 1929.

The years of Lázaro Cárdenas were concerned essentially with social rather than economic matters. But many actions in his times had important economic implications. For example, nationalization policies in railways, agricultural holdings, and above all, petroleum, were socially and politically, not economically, motivated. These actions, all probably necessary and psychologically sound, gave Mexicans a new sense of national identity and freedom to determine their own fate, a spirit nearly unique in the Latin American community. Foreign control of the basic elements of economic life were thus erased, clearing the ground for the next phase. That was to build a national economic system which should provide for the heirs of the Revolution the long-promised material benefits, within the Revolutionary framework of institutions constructed since 1910.

The Second World War provided a suitable transition period. The time was ripe, and opportunity was at hand. International credit and prestige had been re-established, when Mexico placed important material and human contributions behind the Allied war effort.[1] Emphasis shifted from re-dividing the small resources to increasing the productive capacity of Mexico.

Pressures of war clearly revealed the inability of this rudimentary, semi-colonial economic system to support its people. Pulverized into small and uneconomical land plots, agriculture showed its painful inadequacies. The shutting off of manufactured exports by Mexico's traditional suppliers similarly highlighted the small and poorly organized national industrial plant. Creaking and inefficient communications were temporarily patched with outside aid to carry goods, especially critical minerals, for the arsenals of democracy, but their real weakness was fully exposed. These and other considerations made a policy shift imperative.

NEW DIRECTIONS: CO-PARTNERSHIPS

The new directions, begun under President Manuel Avila Camacho, preserved but modified many older programmes; emphasis changed as major new departures were fostered. Economic rather than social criteria measured agrarian recommendations: enlarged land units were distributed within the ejido or communal systems, and new stress was placed on increasing the amount of productive land. The policy also encouraged the coexistence of small- and medium-size private holdings by giving them equal financial and technical assistance, not long before restricted only to the communal system.

A main keynote of the new departure was industrialization. Widely debated as to desirability, weight of circumstances brought a definite decision: Mexico must industrialize to progress. The birthday of the Institutional Revolution is 21 April 1941, when the first Law of Manufacturing Industries became effective. It provided tax exemptions to Mexican industries, especially new ones and those thought necessary for further stimulation of Mexican manufactures.

A new generation of businesslike Mexicans, whom the late Sanford Mosk has labelled the 'New Group', worked out a coherent and attractive broad plan for an industrialized Mexico, to be coupled with a renovated agricultural Mexico. Their social and industrial programme became the base of new government economic thinking. The larger part of their plan appears in modified form in the charter of modern Mexican industrialism, the 'Law for the Development

---

[1] Mexican contributions of materials, war-labour, even token troops are described in Cline, *U.S. and Mexico*, pp. 271–8.

of New and Necessary Industries' (Feb. 1946), still in force.[1] The New Group programme thus fully adopted in 1946 and subsequently elaborated by the Institutional Revolution, aims to raise the standards of living of all Mexicans. For these benefits they were and are expected to accept certain burdens: inflation; disciplined and peaceful labour; the premiss that rural and urban industrialization will outrank agrarian reform as the main focus of the Revolution until the two phases are balanced.

GOALS

The balanced approach, to which Mexico owes so much of its recent stability and spectacular prosperity, can be quickly sketched. In it agriculture has a full partnership with industry.

Since most of Mexico is rural, the agricultural sector must become prosperous to provide the needed domestic market for manufactured goods. It must also provide high-quality raw materials (some previously imported) for the developing industrial machine. Above all, it must now as never before feed the whole nation, to prevent recourse to costly and embarrassing imports of grains. It should also produce export crops to increase its own and national prosperity.

For its part, industry is expected to help to enrich agricultural areas. The industrial sector is to purchase its products, in raw or semi-processed state at fair prices. It must make finished manufactured goods widely available and competitive in quality and price in the world market. Among these are fertilizers, insecticides, tractors, pumps, and other needed items for the modernization of agriculture. By expanding, industry must also provide employment for emigrating rural workers, many of whom are being displaced by rural mechanization and advanced farming techniques.

Fields, as well as factories, form part of the industrializing process, as Mexican policy-makers see it. Together they are to provide for national needs and produce a diversity of exportable commodities. This is a modified version of economic nationalism, 'autarky', one of the major modes of thought in underdeveloped and emerging states the world over. The Mexican version works.

A foreign developmental economist sings the praises of the balanced system which he observes has come about since 1940. 'Partly as a result of these social, political, and economic changes',

[1] Sanford Mosk, *Industrial Revolution in Mexico* (1950), chs. 1–6, 'Attitudes and Points of View', summarizes early discussions preceding and encompassing first main decisions; 'Law for the Development of New and Necessary Industries' (1946), translated, app. A to USBFC, *Investment in Mexico*, pp. 139–43.

he says, 'Mexico has shown an enviable rate of growth. . . . In this respect it has been outstanding among the Latin American nations and the underdeveloped areas of the world in general.' He added, 'Mexico's policy of balanced growth made it possible to raise considerably the per capita level of living. The Mexican Revolution, through its impact on the economic development of the country, has made Mexico an independent and self-reliant partner in the world trading community.'[1]

GOVERNMENT AND THE ECONOMY

Like the co-partnerships between sectors of the economy, another exists between Government and business. Some matters can be left to the Government, as its field of prime responsibility. But equally strong is the conviction that private enterprise must supplement the Government's activities and take social and economic responsibilities, as well as profits. Government does not plan industrialization, but makes it possible by other developmental functions: communications, irrigation, electrification, priorities of tax exemptions for needed industries (to attract private investment), flexible and sympathetic tariff policies. Government and business are partners, sharing the common goal of increased production and productivity. In joint planning, business can and should provide data and opinions on major government economic decisions.

Government, in this view, does not compete with private industry in fields which the latter can handle. Government does have a prominent, even leading, role, but this is not state intervention in the usual sense of the term. Setting the main lines of the Institutional Revolution, the early programmes, says Mosk, proposed 'business intervention in government rather than government intervention in business'.[2]

From 1917 the constitution (Arts. 27, 28, 123, 131) prescribed that the state should intervene in the economy for general public welfare. To this end the new programmes and policies developed between 1940 and 1950 were summarized and in the latter year given force in the 'Law of Attributes of the Executive Branch in Economic Matters'. Here the Ministry of Economy was assigned a

---

[1] Teichert, *Policy Revolution*, p. 161. His ch. 12, 'The Mexican Experience of Balanced Growth' (pp. 153–61) is a relatively up-to-date summary, carrying the story to about 1957, as does Werner Lichey, *Mexiko: ein Weg zur wirtschaftlichen Entwicklung* (1958).

[2] Mosk, *Industrial Revolution*, p. 29.

broad mandate in fields of production, distribution, and consumption of goods; price controls were to be handled by a special Commission. The chapter of the law on general executive guidance stipulates that the President should foster at all times full co-operation of private initiative, and plan co-ordinated and balanced—'sane' says the law—growth of the total economy. And, the law repeats, the executive is to intervene only in cases where the general welfare and public interest are clearly involved.[1]

The allocation of Federal funds outlines the implementation of new ideas and policies in the early years of the Institutional Revolution. Public funds, from 1939 through the penultimate year of President Alemán, were spent as follows, according to a study by a Mexican economist (Table 51):

TABLE 51

Expenditure of Federal Funds, 1939–51

(*Million pesos*)

	Amount	Per cent.
Agriculture	3,004·2	19·45
Transportation, communications... ...	6,894·1	44·63
Electrification, petroleum...	2,712·1	17·56
Social: schools, &c	1,953·3	12·65
Other	882·5	5·71
	15,446·2	100·0

Source: Diego G. López Rosado, 'Las Obras públicas de la Revolución', *Investigación económica*, xvi, pp. 59–74, table, pp. 66–67.

Shorn of earlier excesses, the modified current mixed Mexican system is nearly unique. A group of German economists recently analysed in detail its workability. They stress its lack of easy categorization. After careful analysis that revealed past weaknesses as well as the strength of the Mexican system they concluded, 'All in all, it appears that Mexico is on the right track; it consequently can in a few years bring Mexico into the ranks of the "developed" countries (Entwicklungsländer).'[2] Mexicans obviously hope to remain on that path.

[1] Fernando Zamora, 'Fundamentos constitucionales de la intervención estatal en materia económica', in UNAM, Escuela Nacional de Economía, *La Constitución de 1917 y la economía Mexicana* (1958), pp. 199–218.

[2] Lichey, *Mexiko*, p. 127. Basis for this optimistic forecast appears in the chapter entitled 'Mexikos Weg in die Zukunft', pp. 124–7. George N. Sarames, 'Third System in Latin America: Mexico', *International Economic Affairs*, v (Spring 1952), 59–72, describes it as a functional system that is neither capitalistic nor socialistic.

Such a passage is devoutly desired by most Mexicans, but it is not necessarily inevitable. Continuance of the upward spiral of development and expanding prosperity depends on contingent elements, over some of which the Mexicans have no direct control. On the domestic scene the boom rests primarily on the willingness of various sectors to continue co-operation for the good of the collectivity, ranging from reinvestment of entrepreneurial profits in the Mexican economy (rather than their flight abroad) to labour's acceptance of wage limitations. As the Mexican economy becomes more complex and integrated on a national basis, so it becomes more responsive to world trends and conditions. A major depression or recession, or a war, would quickly alter many of the delicate balances which keep the dynamic and expanding system functioning satisfactorily. But from 1941 to 1960, the Mexicans showed that such success is possible, partly through the unusual relationships between government and the economy.

'In practice, there is no possible conflict between private initiative and the state', repeated President López Mateos in July 1959. 'The latter is not prepared to assume the task of business promotion, and the former is not interested in sectors where profits are low or absent.' The limited resources available to Mexico, he added, make it essential to use them wisely. 'It is not enough to plan carefully and assign priorities to public investment; it is necessary for private investors to co-ordinate their actions, in order to avoid over-production in some fields and shortages in others.'[1]

[1] NF, *The Economic Development of Mexico* (1959), speech by Adolfo López Mateos, p. 10. The pamphlet summarizes activities of Nacional Financiera over twenty-five years.

Chapter XXV

FINANCING A REVOLUTION

IN the present partnership between Government and business, each plays a role, and in some instances there is joint participation and shared responsibilities. Here we shall look at these matters in the field of finance. To the public sector fall the important decisions about budgets and taxes.

NATIONAL BUDGETS

Often less moving than many rhetorical statements on 'advancing the Revolution' or 'balancing the economy' are the cool facts of national budgets. They also give a closer measure of intent and policy. But by necessity a régime's scope of action is limited by the amounts of public revenue which can reasonably be expected to flow into the national treasury, to be allotted among the various expenditures recommended or authorized by the President, his ministers, and his party colleagues in Congress.

Many considerations, both fiscal and political, enter the budget's composition. Mexican history makes it clear that service on the public debt is a prime requirement, to prevent the tragic interventions of the nineteenth century and to reduce international friction. The army, the bureaucrats, judges, and Congress must be paid. Gradually a set of priorities builds up, but there is always some latitude for discretion once essential expenses have been covered.

An examination of the budgets from the end of the Alemán to the opening of the López Mateos régimes helps to chart the course which the Institutional Revolution has taken. By observing the theoretical per capita shares and allotments, the benefits to the individual Mexican may be obtained. None of the several measures employed is infallible, but together they do suggest certain directions of public policy.

To provide a basis for discussion, details of federal budgets are presented in Appendix Table XIII. They show that the Governments have been covering their basic needs, and simultaneously have been allotting considerable sums for economic development, and for broadening social and cultural programmes that spell political stability and increased opportunities. An important trend immediately apparent from this table is that budgets as a whole have increased steadily. Over the decade from 1950, the peso has changed its value and population has grown. Disregarding the former for the moment, the following table indicates a nearly fourfold budget increase. The per capita figures show a rise from about 100 to 300 pesos.

From Table 53, and additional information for 1959 and 1960, we can get a quick view of how Presidents Alemán, Ruíz Cortines, and López Mateos used their budgetary discretion. To simplify matters, the final year (1952) of the first, the middle and last years of the second, and the two budgets submitted by President López Mateos have been selected, showing separately the sums devoted to economic development, and to social and cultural programmes, the remainder being shown as other governmental expenses. To adjust for growing populations, the per capita shares for each of the selected years is shown. This table synthesizes Appendix Table XIII.

TABLE 52

National Budgets, 1950–60

(*Million pesos*)

Year		Budget	Pesos per capita	Total budget increase over 1950 (per cent.)	President
1950	...	2,745·2	105·8	—	Alemán
1951	...	3,025·7	115·0	9·8	
1952	...	3,999·2	146·5	46·0	
1953	...	4,160·4	148·0	51·6	Ruíz Cortines
1954	...	4,827·7	162·0	75·7	
1955	...	5,681·4	189·8	106·2	Ruíz Cortines
1956	...	6,696·4	218·5	143·5	
1957	...	7,577·9	241·0	175·1	
1958	...	8,402·5	260·0	208·0	
1959	...	9,386·0	281·0	250·8	López Mateos
1960	...	10,386·0	300·0	272·1	López Mateos

Sources: 1950–1, Cline, *U.S. and Mexico*, table 18 (p. 241); 1952–5, Appendix Table xii; 1959–60, 'The Federal Budget for 1960', BNCE, *Comercio exterior*, vi (Jan. 1960), 2–3. Percentages and per capita figures by author.

TABLE 53

Budget Categories, Selected Years, 1952–60

(*Budgets in 'ooo pesos; per capita in pesos*)

Year	Economic Development			Socio-Cultural			Other		Totals (100·0%)	
	Budget	Per cent.	Per capita	Budget	Per cent.	Per capita	Budget	Per cent.	Budget	Per capita
1952...	1,550·8	38·8	57·0	605·4	15·0	22·1	1,843·2	46·2	3999·4	146·5
1955...	2,499·3	44·5	84·0	986·1	17·0	33·0	2,196·0	38·5	5681·4	189·8
1958...	3,713·0	44·5	115·0	1,595·5	18·8	40·1	3,094·0	36·7	8402·5	260·0
1959...	3,956·0	42·3	118·3	2,572·0	27·4	77·1	2,858·0	30·3	9386·0	281·0
1960...	4,369·0	42·6	127·6	3,126·0	30·6	91·6	2,756·0	26·8	10,251·0	300·0

Sources: Appendix Table XII; table 52.

It is evident that there have been continuing increases, absolute and on a per capita basis, in sums for economic development and for social and cultural programmes, with varied and slower growth of expenditures for other government responsibilities. Proportionately, Alemán spent least for economic development and educational-welfare agencies, most on other matters. Promises made by López Mateos to make the Government more efficient (less costly) and to step up efforts in welfare, education, and other social and cultural fields seem borne out by the table. For the first time during the Institutional Revolution their budgetary shares in 1960 each exceed that of other bureaucratic concerns. But together economic development by direct government effort and its programmes for the social Revolution have never fallen below one-half, and now are approaching three-quarters of the annual budgets.

Attention to principal items—those amounting to 5 per cent. or more of annual budgets—gives us an additional reading. Table 54 selects these for typical years of the Institutional Revolution. The figures show that as Mexico pays off its foreign and domestic debts, more money becomes available for its internal programmes. They also show that defence falls below education as a budget item. Education has risen from about 11 per cent. to nearly a fifth of the annual budget. One-half its budgetary increase from 1959 to 1960 was applied to pay rises for teachers.[1] About a quarter of the funds since 1952 have gone for the development of communications,

[1] BNCE, 'The Federal Budget for 1960', *Comercio exterior* (int. airmail ed.), vi (Jan. 1960), 3.

major public works, and the hydraulic projects discussed in Chapter VII. A certain flexibility in day-to-day operations appears in a contingency fund, usually used to provide food subsidies; the Government purchases from producers at a fair market price and sells the necessities to mass consumers at a loss.

In summary, the budgets shown in Table 54 confirm conclusions derived from other sources. Prosperity has made it possible for national Governments to pour needed sums into economic and social development. Expenditures for these programmes have levelled national budgets to the point that they now represent about three-quarters of federal spending. Thus there is relative congruence between political pronouncements of the PRI, campaign promises of presidential candidates, and the actual policy as measured by budgets. The Revolution is being advanced as promised, under-written by a booming economy.

TABLE 54

Principal National Budget Items, 1945–60 (Selected Years)

(Million pesos)

	1945		1952		1958		1960	
	Amt.	Per cent.	Amt.	Per cent.	Amt.	Per cent.	Amt.	Per cent.
GENERAL								
Contingencies... ...			263	6·5	1,052	12·5	976	9·6
Public Debt	286	18·1	981	24·4	901	10·7	861	8·5
BASIC FUNCTIONS								
Defence	158	10·0	329	8·2	591	7·0	1,082	10·6
ECONOMIC PROGRAMMES								
Communications ...	159	10·1	697	17·4	1,639	19·5	2,764	26·8
Hydraulic Resources ...			419	10·5	777	9·3	a	a
Investments	78	4·9	243	6·1	645	7·7	1,222	12·0
SOCIO-CULTURAL								
Public Education ...	170	10·8	428	10·7	1,153	13·7	1,900	18·6
TOTAL*	1,573	100·0	4,000	100·0	8,403	100·0	10,251	100·0

* Includes minor items not tabulated.　　　　　　　　a. Not separated in source.

Sources: DGE, *Anuario estadístico, 1943–5*, table 364 (p. 763), actual expenditures, 1945; Appendix Table XII (1952, 1958); 'Federal Budget for 1960', BNCE, *Comercio exterior*, vi, 2–3.

Who pays for all this? The answer falls into two parts. One is that some of the expenditures are self-amortizing: costs of much of the economic development, financed directly from Federal budgets, comes back directly in increased tax revenues, or through the creation of capital which is mobilized by using other government means to keep the prosperity alive and spreading. Thus an auxiliary to government budgets is the activity of Nacional Financiera, the semi-autonomous development corporation charged with keeping the private sector of the economy flourishing, even if it must borrow abroad to do so. We shall note its role below (pp. 244 ff.).

TAXES

Tax policy can be social policy as well as fiscal necessity. There is some tinge of discrimination in Mexican taxes, especially in the case of confiscatory income taxes. But the tax system as such has not been customarily wielded as an important instrument of Revolution. For much of its history, Mexico has been too hard-pressed to obtain moneys for its essential needs, and now for its development of society and economy, to afford the luxury of attempting to alter social classes through tax legislation.

Mexico has for many years differed from many other Latin American countries and from its own earlier practice by having a varied tax base. In the nineteenth century public revenues were drawn primarily from import and export levies; hence the objective of any revolutionary move was the customs house at Veracruz. Fiscal reforms in the late nineteenth century radically altered that pattern. Apart from an income tax, the Revolution has added nothing new to the system inherited from Díaz; rather, it has tried to improve the workings and apply the revenues to different purposes. The Institutional Revolution has tinkered very little with this orthodox system.[1] As has been stated, its chief contribution was to provide tax exemptions and concessions for industry, especially in the decade 1940–50 when the present economic boom was getting under way.[2]

In recent years tax returns have been geared more directly to domestic activities than to world trade conditions, although these are by no means a negligible consideration. Mounting gross national product rather than the sale of Mexican goods abroad is the dynamic element which permits current administrations to plan expanded

[1] Walter F. McCaleb, *Present and Past Banking in Mexico* (1920); the definitive treatment of modern taxation is Harvard Univ., Int. Program in Taxation, *Taxation in Mexico* (1957), with much historical data. See also G. F. Aguilar, *Los Presupuestos mexicanos desde los tiempos coloniales hasta nuestros días* (1947).

[2] See above, p. 232.

economic and social programmes with the expectation that tax mechanisms will feed the needed sums into federal coffers.

A broad view of the sources of income supporting the record budgets for 1959 and 1960 has been given by the Banco Nacional de Comercio Exterior in the Newsletter it prepares in English for the many persons interested in Mexico's economic development. This is shown in the following table.

TABLE 55

Federal Revenues, 1959–60

(*Million pesos*)

Taxes and sources	AMOUNTS		PER CENT.	
	1959	*1960* (*Est.*)	*1959*	*1960*
TAX REVENUES				
Income	2,800	3,100	29·7	30·1
Industry and Trade ...	2,080	2,467	22·2	25·0
Import	1,400	1,420	14·9	13·6
Export	950	890	10·1	8·6
Public Services	400	498	4·2	4·8
Natural Resources Use ...	235	230	2·6	2·2
Miscellaneous	313	320	3·3	3·1
Sub-total	8,178	8,925	87·0	87·4
OTHER				
National Property Rents ...	232	177	2·5	1·6
Profits from capital	380	550	4·1	5·3
Internal loans	600	600	6·4	5·7
Sub-total	1,212	1,327	13·0	12·6
TOTAL FEDERAL REVENUES	9,390	10,252	100·0	100·0

Source: 'Federal Budget for 1960', BNCE, *Comercio exterior*, vi, 2.

The figures show that federal revenues derive from three or four main sources. Half come from combined income taxes, personal and corporate. Import and export levies on foreign trade add another fifth or quarter. The remainder is made up by various taxes and diverse minor revenues, including about 6 per cent. from internal bond issues.

Equally revealing is the changing pattern of principal revenue sources since both the industrial and Institutional Revolution emerged clearly. Some of the burden formerly carried by foreign trade and a substantial weight supported by other means have, in the past five years (1955–60), been transferred to the industrial system and the higher incomes it furnishes for so many. As earlier tax exemptions run out, and industrial production and values soar, that 'modernized' sector of society is shouldering more and more financial responsibility for the advancement of economic and social programmes. The shift is clearly manifest in Table 56.

TABLE 56
Principal Sources of Federal Revenues, 1945–60

Sources	AMOUNT				PER CENT.			
	1945	*1950*	*1955*	*1960*	*1945*	*1950*	*1955*	*1960*
Income taxes	296	766	1,985	3,100	21·0	21·0	22·0	30·1
Industry and commerce	274	543	1,066	2,467	19·5	14·8	11·8	25·0
Foreign trade	383	991	2,558	1,388	27·2	27·0	28·4	22·2
Other	451	1,441	3,414	3,297	32·3	37·2	37·8	22·7
Total annual revenue ...	1,404	3,741	9,023	10,252	100·0	100·0	100·0	100·0

Sources: DGE, *Anuario estadístico, 1943–1945*, table 363 (p. 762); DGE, *Compendio estadístico, 1955*, table 319 (p. 392); Table 55 above. Rearranged, percentages by author.

To sum up, it may be said that there is a sound relation between public revenues and expenditures. The latter emphasize the main social and economic goals long posited by the Revolution.

Chapter XXVI

INVESTMENT STAKES

UNDER the partnership arrangements between the Mexican Government and the domestic economy, many of the social and cultural obligations of the Revolution are shouldered by the state, which also has the responsibility of seeing that free enterprise does not become anti-social. To link the economy to the Government a number of semi-autonomous bodies have developed in Mexico, authorized and underwritten fiscally by the state but given a rather free hand to co-operate and aid private interests in the economic development of the nation. In 1959 these semi-autonomous economic institutions were placed under a special Secretariat of the Presidency to assure that their individual planning and programming did not overlap and were in the best interests of the country as a whole. Nacional Financiera is the most important of these bodies.

Apart from the official and semi-official organs, private enterprises form the major sector of the economy. We shall note later the contributions of their efforts to Mexico's current economic boom. Here it is interesting and important to touch briefly on the flow of foreign capital into Mexico, where in general it is put to productive use by Mexicans. An impressive item in Mexico's economic upsurge is that foreign investment trebled from 1940 to 1950; it has again doubled from then to 1958. The world investor obviously seems to share Mexico's own confidence in its future.

NACIONAL FINANCIERA

Nacional Financiera, now the chief development arm of the Government, was created by President Cárdenas on 30 August 1933, as a very minor semi-private finance company to sell rural real estate. Soon, on 24 April 1934, he added the tasks of creating a Mexican stock market and acting as the fiscal agent for the Government. NF was authorized to organize, administer, and change any type of enterprise in which the Mexican state had an economic interest. Until 30 December 1940 NF operated primarily in the field of agricultural land credit. It now is the main guide of total economic development.

A revised charter coinciding with the policy shift of 1940 noted above, opened a new epoch in NF's life. The 1940 Charter directed NF to regulate the securities market, to promote the investment of capital in industrial enterprises, to be trustee for the Government in issuing public securities, and to furnish credits and funds for those sectors of the national economy in which commercial credit was lacking or inadequate. NF, especially encharged to provide long-term credits, was to be content with modest monetary yields rather than the large immediate profits normally expected by the Mexican investor, individual or institutional.

One of NF's early prime aims has been accomplished. It has developed a national securities market, through Mexico's two stock exchanges. These date from 1941 when NF's own first securities were offered. That year a total of 727·5 million pesos worth of its fixed-income securities were put into national circulation. In 1958 the total value was 12,161·1 million pesos, of which only about 15 per cent. were NF securities. NF invests both in public and private securities. In 1959 about 10 per cent. of its funds was invested in public securities—government bonds for roads, irrigation, &c.— 90 per cent. in those issued by private Mexican enterprises. It also guarantees other private domestic loans.

Foreign Development Loans

In 1947 its mandate was again broadened. NF became the sole agency authorized to negotiate foreign loans. For these the Government set the condition that foreign credits must be utilized in one or more of the following ways: to exploit Mexico's natural resources; to improve technology; to increase production in important sectors of the national economy; to decrease the number of items the nation must import; and to develop exportable articles.

NF has been quite successful in obtaining from international sources the necessary long-term credits strategically needed to improve and expand the Mexican economic system. Large capital investments mainly for communications, irrigation, and electric power, have required such negotiations. The Export-Import Bank, International Bank for Reconstruction and Development, Bank of America, Chase Manhattan, and other institutions, impressed with NF's prudence and record, have made substantial loans. From 1942 through 30 May 1959 the authorized extent of such loans totalled $992 million. Of this sum, NF had in 1958 received $755 million. It has already (1959) repaid $329 million, leaving an unpaid

balance of $426·5 million. In reserve NF has the additional author-
ized foreign credits to draw against when needed.

Investment Pattern

Since NF's establishment, net profits on its operations have been
506·6 million pesos, of which 345·8 million were made since 1952.
Its chief purpose, however, is not to make profits but to finance the
Mexican economy wisely. It opens up new areas to attract private
capital into them. By 31 December 1958 it had channelled into
national enterprises nearly 9,000 million pesos. These came from its
own funds, foreign loans, and several other sources of credit. The
total investment in Mexico's future was summarized by NF's
General Director on its 25th anniversary as follows (Table 57):

TABLE 57

Financing Provided by Nacional Financiera, 1940–58
(*Million pesos, to 31 Dec. 1958*)

	AMOUNT	PER CENT.
BRANCHES OF INFRASTRUCTURE		
Transportation and communications ...　...	2,364·4	26·2
Electric energy　...　...　...　...	1,698·1	19·0
Irrigation and other public works　...　...	286·3	3·3
Sub-total　...　...　...　...　...	4,348·8	48·5
BASIC INDUSTRIES		
Petroleum and coal　...　...　...　...	548·4	6·1
Iron and steel　...　...　...　...	653·8	7·2
Cement and other construction materials　...	49·3	0·6
Sub-total　...　...　...　...　...	1,251·5	13·9
OTHER MANUFACTURING INDUSTRIES		
Cellulose and paper　...　...　...　...	325·2	3·6
Vehicle assembly and fabrication　...　...	641·4	7·2
Food and related products　...　...	430·3	4·8
Textiles and clothing　...　...　...	178·5	2·0
Fertilizers, insecticides, chemicals　...　...	323·9	3·6
Others　...　...　...　...　...	415·9	4·6
Sub-total　...　...　...　...　...	2,315·2	25·8
OTHER ACTIVITIES　...　...　...　...	1,033·2	11·8
TOTAL　...　...　...　...　...	8,948·7	100·0

Source: José Hernández Delgado, 'Nacional Financiera, S.A., Symbolizes
Mexico's Industrialization', NF, *Economic Development*, p. 21. Sub-totals
and percentages by author.

Investment Stakes

In his 1960 State of the Union Message, President Adolfo López Mateos brought these figures even more up to date, supplying the following data which, with added percentages, are given in Table 58.

TABLE 58

Total Financing, Nacional Financiera, to 1 June 1960

(Million pesos)

	Amount	Per cent.
Electric power, transport communications ...	5,823	52·0
Basic industries: oil, iron, steel, cement	2,014	18·0
Manufacturing industries	2,287	20·3
Other	1,053	9·7
Total	11,177	100·0

Source: López Mateos, 2° Informe (1 Sept. 1960). Tabulated by author.

Policies and Programme

A personal view by one of its present senior officials perhaps reflects NF's current institutional thinking. He ticked off the possible sources of development investment: Mexican family savings; various industrial reserves against depreciation, &c.; domestic loans; net capital from favourable international balances of payments. Then he stated that Mexico cannot afford to lower its rate of investment in the total economy without various difficulties and general regression. On the contrary, he considered that the rhythm must speed up, to provide rising standards of living for the masses. He added that the main source of investment funds should be taxes, especially those on higher income groups, and from the increased working force. Fuller employment means a larger market, a wider tax base, and increased small family savings for investment. Foreign investment, he stated, should remain a 'useful but complementary part of the large task of developing Mexico'.[1]

President López Mateos speaking at a ceremony on 2 July 1959, celebrating the twenty-fifth birthday of NF, indicated that it would be expected during his term to increase its present operations. He noted that Mexico's imperatives are to increase employment and to raise incomes of the rural population. These goals will require greater expenditure on agricultural improvements and in new,

[1] Navarrete R., 'Financiamiento del desarrollo económico de México', in UNAM, Problemas de desarrollo económico mexicano (1958), pp. 135–9.

primarily smaller, industries needing only modest capital investment. Added to the industrial scheme would be craft industries, workshops and plants to transform raw materials, and yet others to integrate the total system. He called on NF to build its resources and double its activities in these lines.

Specifically he stated that new legislation would permit NF to raise its working capital from 200 million to 500 million pesos. New shares were to be offered for sale to small and medium-scale investors, to mobilize more domestic savings for industrial promotion. He said that 'History in Mexico has determined that the State many times assumes the role of a pioneer. Nacional Financiera has been the prime instrument in the execution of this policy, with the object of accelerating economic development . . . in coordinating efforts directed at breaking the circle of our traditional limitations.'[1]

Thus to public moneys which the administrations of the Institutional Revolution have had at their disposal, have been added the sums borrowed and developed by NF from scattered hoards at home and abroad. There has been some criticism of NF's policies and methods, but on a balanced appraisal, Nacional Financiera seems to have done an important and remarkable job over its twenty-five-year life.[2]

THE FOREIGN INVESTMENT STAKE

Foreign investment represents a sizable, strategic, though not a dominant, stake in the Mexican future, but it is a growing one. Of direct foreign investments in 1957, the Bank of Mexico estimated that 78·4 per cent. came from the United States, 13·5 per cent. was Canadian, 4·3 per cent. from the United Kingdom, 1·0 per cent. Swedish; Germany, Argentina, Cuba, France, Italy, Holland, Brazil, Denmark, and Belgium had a combined total of 2·8 per cent.[3] The rise, as well as the fields into which capital has flowed, can be seen in Table 59. It indicates clearly that the 1957 total of $1,200 million was mainly invested in manufacturing, but also spread unevenly through other segments of the Mexican economy. The 1958 figures given in pesos do not differ significantly from the 1957 dollar figures reproduced in this table.[4]

[1] NF, *Economic Development*, p. 12.

[2] Mosk, *Industrial Revolution*, pp. 236–41; Cline, *U.S. and Mexico*, pp. 337–8, 343–6, 363–4.

[3] Rice, 'Basic Data', p. 14.

[4] 'Inversiones extranjeras directas en México', table 296, SDE, *Compendio estadístico, 1958*, p. 441, showing a 1958 total of 14·62 pesos v. 14·56 million for 1957.

TABLE 59

All Direct Foreign Investment in Mexico, 1940–58

($'000)

	AMOUNTS			PER CENT.		
	1940	*1950*	*1957–8*	*1940*	*1950*	*1957-8*
Agriculture, livestock ...	383	527	20,175	2·3	0·9	1·7
Mining	8,020	24,692	211,191	48·3	42·7	17·6
Petroleum	—	75	18,402	—	0·1	1·5
Manufacturing	4,691	20,296	413,274	28·2	35·5	34·6
Construction	n.d.	331	16,157	—	0·4	1·3
Electricity, gas, water ...	678	1,765	230,755	4·1	3·0	19·1
Commerce	1,984	7,186	218,290	12·0	12·4	18·2
Transport, communications	758	2,582	63,532	4·6	4·5	5·3
Other (hotels, &c.) ...	58	427	8,294	0·5	0·6	0·7
Total	16,572	57,881	1,200,070	100·0	100·0	100·0

Source: Rice, 'Basic Data', table 10, p. 14; percentages by author.

Private direct investments from the United States far outstrip government loans and grants. From 1946 through 1958 the latter totalled about \$41 million (30·5 loans, 10·6 grants), including grants to aid Mexico in eradicating foot and mouth disease.[1] With

TABLE 60

Direct United States Private Investment in Mexico, 1950 and 1958

($ *million*)

Activity	1950		1958	
	Amount	Per cent.	Amount	Per cent.
Agriculture	3	0·7	*	—
Mining, smelting	121	29·1	195	25·0
Petroleum (expl.)	13	3·1	19	2·4
Manufacturing	133	32·0	364	46·5
Public utilities	107	25·8	85	10·9
Commerce	30	7·2	93	11·7
Miscellaneous	9	2·1	*[756]	3·5
Totals	416	100·0	781	100·0

* Included in totals, but not specified in source.

Source: Chicago Univ., *U.S. Business and Labor in Latin America*, iv, table 7 (p. 8). Percentages by author.

[1] National Planning Assoc., *U.S.-Latin American Relations: U.S. and Latin American Policies affecting their Economic Relations* (1960), table I-c(14), p. 92.

stabilization and growth in Mexico since 1950, United States private capital has entered in rapidly increasing quantities. It has notably shunned agricultural enterprises, and predominantly has gravitated toward manufacturing and commerce, where it is, under Mexican laws, mixed with local funds and subject to national supervision. Since the following figures appeared in January 1960 outlining the direct investments from United States sources, the Mexican Government has purchased foreign holdings in public utilities, as we shall note below. Table 60, above, gives the picture at the time when President López Mateos took office in 1958.

THE DOMESTIC STAKE

Perhaps the most significant fiscal feature of Mexico's economic boom is that it was largely self-generated. At present domestic sources of capital far outweigh foreign ones in keeping it going. Up to about 1950 foreign investments were slow to underwrite Mexican enterprise, hence the burden fell on Mexican governmental, semi-official, and private local shoulders. Through the official banking system and a phenomenal growth of private credit institutions, supplemented by NF, insurance companies, and other domestic agencies, perhaps as much as 80 per cent. of the necessary funds have come from national sources.[1]

Reporting to the nation in September 1960, President López Mateos stated that during 1959 private Mexican institutions issued 900 million pesos worth of credit, duplicating the amounts for 1958, without inflationary effects. The Government, while balancing its budget for 1959, had increased its investment stake, again without undue inflation. In 1959 the total value of Mexican stocks and bonds held largely by private investors amounted to 14,300 million pesos, a rise of 1,000 million over 1958. Both NF and the Bank of Mexico had been divesting themselves of such holdings during 1959. He assured the Mexican public that the peso would remain firm, noting a marked rise in the dollar reserves from 1958 and favourable balances of trade to support his promise.[2] Thus in 1960, due primarily to efforts of Mexicans themselves, the harmonious growth continued in the now well-established pattern of partnership between Government and private interests.

[1] Lichey, *Mexiko*, pp. 96–123 is the most extensive analysis; USBFC, *Investment in Mexico*, pp. 10–22.

[2] López Mateos, *2° Informe* (1 Sept. 1960).

THE CURRENT ECONOMIC BOOM

Chapter XXVII

BALANCED BOOM, 1940–60

FOREIGN observers who professionally analyse the growth and development of national economies of the world are astonished by two phenomena in Mexico: the magnitude of recent Mexican growth, and its generally balanced nature. One recently wrote, 'Had Mexico in its economic development kept up with population growth only, this would have been an achievement in itself, since the population increase of three per cent. per year is one of the largest in the world.' Professor Teichert added that the Mexican rate of economic growth was proportionately larger than that of other Latin American economies. However, the Mexican increase does not depend on a single, readily exploitable resource as do other notable cases: petroleum in Venezuela, copper in Chile, cattle and wheat in Argentina.[1]

On the balanced nature of growth, the same author notes that

Mexico is one of the few republics that has achieved a considerable degree of industrial development without neglecting its agricultural sector. Its economic development has advanced on all fronts simultaneously and at the same rate. Mexico has not followed the Argentine example of undue stress on the industrial sector to the detriment of agriculture.

This outsider's view is shared by recent German analysts.[2]

'Since 1940', writes yet another observer, 'Mexico has recorded remarkable progress. Today she boasts of a diversified industrial complex producing a wide range of consumer and production items. Since 1952 there has been a conscientious effort to introduce order and balance in the economy.'[3] Professor Ross remarks that from 1952 through 1958 the gross investment in agriculture increased more rapidly than investment in the economy as a whole, and states that 'By 1958, 40 per cent. of Mexico's agricultural production was providing raw materials for industry, and agricultural exports were bringing in significant amounts of foreign exchange.' He concludes, 'The economic progress of Mexico has been impressive. However,

[1] Teichert, *Economic Policy Revolution*, ch. 12: 'The Mexican Experience of Balanced Growth', pp. 153–61. Cf. Lichey, *Mexiko*; Jaffe, *People, Jobs, and Economic Development*, ch. 13: 'The Model Applied: Mexico', pp. 247–69, dealing with the Mexican period 1940–55.

[2] Teichert, *Economic Policy*, pp. 153–61; Lichey, *Mexiko*, pp. 124–7.

[3] Ross, 'Mexico: Golden Anniversary of the Revolution', p. 151.

much remains to be done if the standard of living of the rapidly expanding Mexican population is to continue to rise.'

Preoccupation with the social as well as the economic aspects of Mexico's new prosperity is one characteristic of the enormous literature on Mexico's recent, startling growth. No responsible voice within or outside the country has been raised to defend the nineteenth-century 'trickle theory' of letting the rich, undisturbed, get even richer, with the expectation that benefits will eventually trickle down to the masses. Rather, current Mexican discussions revolve around how to keep their dynamic economy balanced in the growth of productive sectors and the returns more equitably distributed.[1]

CHANGING PATTERNS AND TRENDS, 1930–59

To understand what 'balanced development' implies, and to note what effect the efforts since 1940 have had in reshaping the Mexican economy, we must dip briefly into economic history. A quick profile of the economy is provided by the elements which constitute its annual output, and the relationships they bear to each other.

There are two general measures: national income, and Gross National Product (GNP). Earlier economists were content to add up the incomes received in each sector, the total constituting national income. More recent and sophisticated approaches to the same matter use Gross National Product.

Gross National Product can trap those who are not familiar with reading economic jargon. It is expressed in monetary terms, which are distinct from what economists call 'real' terms. The difference arises from the fact that price levels, hence the value of the Mexican peso, do not remain constant; as inflation advances a peso buys less goods or services. To obtain 'real' figures for GNP, allowances must be made for the degree to which purchasing power has diminished; the present official calculations take the 1950 price levels as the basic measure. Thus we have one figure for 'monetary' GNP, representing the valuation of goods and services for that year; in addition, we have a 'real' figure, which, allowing for inflation, reduces the pesos of that year to the same value as 1950 prices and

---

[1] Alfredo Navarrete, jr., 'Los Programas revolucionarios y el futuro progreso económico de México', PRI, *Cuadernos de Orientación Política*, i (Mar. 1956), 17–25. The Office of Economic Investigations of NF annually prepares a select bibliography on Mexican economics for the standard *Handbook of Latin American Studies*. See also René Espinosa Olvera, 'Los Recursos humanos en el desarrollo económico de México', *Investigación económica*, xvi (1956), 335–49.

pesos. The accompanying diagram quickly shows that after 1950, 'real' GNP and 'monetary' GNP differ, the latter being considerably higher.

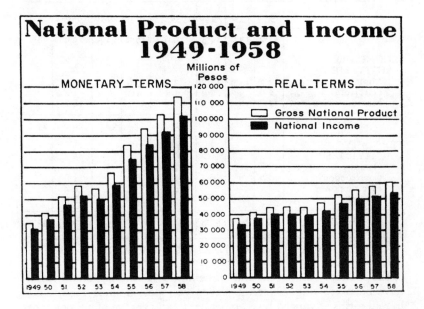

National Product and Income 1949-1958

Although not originally prepared for the sort of comparative presentation we shall make, there are several useful, technical compilations and calculations of national incomes and national product, extending from 1930 through the more recent years, to 1959. As these figures are numerous and complex, they are relegated to Appendix Table XIV. The sub-tables in this table, carrying us from 1930 through 1957, can be interpreted to mean that various sectors—agriculture, mining, petroleum, manufacturing, commerce, and construction—show clear trends. Mining has consistently declined, relatively speaking; petroleum, never a really major activity, has tended also to shrink in comparison with other sectors. Manufacturing and commerce have risen. Agriculture, after a marked decline, has once again regained its major place in the whole. These findings are illustrated in the following summary table.

In the same Appendix Table XIV, Sub-table D illustrates a different trend. It shows the growth, actual and relative, in output

TABLE 61

Sectors of the Mexican Economy, 1930–57

(*Per cent. of national income or national product (100·0 per cent.)*)

	1930	1935	1940	1939–45	1945	1950	1951–4	1957
AGRICULTURE ...	21·6	17·6	14·5	19·9	17·2	21·5	19·8	24·2
SECONDARY ACTIVITIES								
Mining	13·2	14·9	12·7	3·0	7·8		2·5	
Petroleum... ...	2·6	3·2	2·3	1·4	1·1		1·4	
Manufacturing ...	12·8	16·3	24·2	17·6	25·2		16·1	
Sub-total ...	28·6	34·4	39·2	22·0	34·1	28·8	20·0	27·1
TERTIARY ACTIVITIES								
Commerce ...	18·6	21·2	20·7	28·0	24·8		29·1	
Construction ...	6·7	6·2	6·4	1·9	6·2		1·8	
Electric power ...				0·5			0·5	
Others	24·5	20·6	19·2	27·7	17·7		28·8	
Sub-total ...	49·8	48·0	46·3	58·1	48·7	49·7	60·2	48·7

Source: Appendix Table XIV, Sub-tables A–C.

of the economy. Both real and monetary GNP and national income have been growing. Over the eleven-year period since 1948, GNP in real terms advanced by 43·0 per cent., an average of 3·6 per cent. annually. The rate of change has not been steady; an actual decline appeared in 1953. Marked spurts occurred in 1950, 1954, and 1955, and above-average increases appeared in 1951 and 1956. The figures also suggest that the gap between 'monetary' and 'real' terms has grown to the point where in 1959 the nominal or monetary values are some 47·6 per cent. above the real ones. This is the degree to which purchasing power of the peso has fallen since 1950, or conversely, that prices have risen.

INDIVIDUAL SHARES

The Mexican population has been increasing at about the rate of 3 per cent. a year. It would seem that GNP, in real terms, has been slightly ahead, with its annual average rise of nearly 4 per cent. We can further calculate what share each Mexican and each employed one would have if GNP and national income were equitably distributed. This operation tells us whether the output of the economic system is really increasing faster than the burgeoning Mexican population, and how much gain each worker seems to be making. Table 62 gives information about these per capita shares. In human terms, these figures mean that more and more Mexican workers are better off. The average monetary share has risen from 4,550 pesos a year in 1950 to 9,900 in 1959. But costs of shoes for the children, food, rents, and other expenses have also risen. In 1959 with an average income of about 820 pesos a month, the household was maintained on just a little better (13 per cent.) basis than was possible on only about 380 pesos a month in 1950.

TABLE 62

Per Capita Shares, GNP and National Income, 1950–9

(Pesos per person annually)

	1950	1955		1959	
		Amount	Per cent. gain over 1950	Amount	Per cent. gain over 1950
GROSS NATIONAL PRODUCT					
Monetary					
Total Population ...	1,610	2,830	75·6	3,680	128·0
Economically active ...	5,000	8,750	75·0	11,100	122·8
Real (1950 base)					
Total Population ...	1,610	1,720	6·7	1,900	18·0
Economically active ...	5,000	5,470	9·4	5,750	15·0
NATIONAL INCOME					
Monetary					
Total Population ...	1,450	2,510	72·1	3,270	125·8
Economically active ...	4,550	7,760	70·0	9,900	117·2
Real (1950 base)					
Total population ...	1,450	1,570	8·2	1,700	17·2
Economically active ...	4,550	4,860	6·8	5,150	13·0

Source: Appendix Tables IV and XIV (D).

Slightly different but comparable conclusions were reached by Fernando Zamora Millán, in a comprehensive study recently published in Mexico for the orderly planning of national and regional development.[1] He converted 1957 prices and values to 1950 levels. For adjusted 1957 national income, he employed a slightly different figure than was used in Table 62. Sr. Zamora's results,

[1] Fernando Zamora Millán, 'Análisis del ingreso', SDE, *Diagnóstico*, pp. 343–50.

adapted for use here, appear in Table 63. Using the same bases for other matters, Sr. Zamora concluded that from 1950 through 1957 agricultural production had improved 100 per cent., petroleum production 160 per cent., production of electrical energy 150 per cent., industrial manufacturing 75 per cent., mining 40 per cent., while the national population had grown only about 21 per cent. Hence real progress can be documented.

TABLE 63

Per Capita Shares, Real National Income, 1950 and 1957

(after Zamora M.)

	1950	1957
National income (million pesos)	55,266	80,094
Per capita, total population (pesos per person) ...	2,140	2,520
Per capita, economically active (pesos per person) ...	6,650	7,750
Per cent. increase, total population share		17·7
Per cent. increase, economically active population share		16·6

Source: SDE, *Diagnóstico*, p. 350; per capita shares, increases calculated by author.

THE DISTRIBUTION OF NATIONAL INCOME

Serious but almost inevitable has been the unbalanced distribution of such benefits. The fruits of progress, Mexican economists note with some conern, have tended to be gathered by a rather small group, with the result that proportionately the large and growing body of salaried workers and wage-earners receive smaller returns from the new prosperity than do those who provide initial and continuing investments.[1] Various studies establish the imbalance, and the Government since about 1947 has recognized the problem, calling for more equitable redistribution. A study made in about 1954 concluded that more than half of the national income returned to less than a quarter of the economically active population; agriculturalists and labourers, the most numerous of the economically active, shared a relatively small portion of it.[2]

[1] Jorge Espinosa de los Reyes, 'La Distribución del ingreso nacional', UNAM, *Problemas del desarrollo económico mexicano*, pp. 161–224.

[2] Emilio Mújica Montoya, 'Los Salarios en la economía nacional', *Investigación económica*, xvi (1956), 565–81.

World experience in newly industrializing countries suggests that such concentration is the first of three general evolutionary phases of national income distribution. Following an initial burst of high returns to entrepreneurs, the second stage generally sees the rate of increase level off, with a stable, usually fairly high return to them. In highly developed areas, the third phase is a general equalization, narrowing the wide differences between the incomes of the rich, middle class, and poor, as the latter two groups improve their social, political, and bargaining positions. Income-taxes, which cut excesses at the top, and redistribute wealth and income, could be an important factor. Already in Mexico that device, while not developed extensively, is being used more than in most Latin American countries as social policy both for theoretical and practical reasons.[1]

Mexican economists feel that their country is not necessarily condemned by immutable economic laws to a long span of inequality of income distribution, that redistributive trends can be strengthened without removing all incentives for investment. This can be accomplished by continued government efforts in aiding responsible labour movements, conceding moderate agrarian reforms, enlarging the social fields, notably education, and up-grading the working force through better technical training, apart from any other direct fiscal measures that may also prove feasible.[2]

PROFILE, 1959

Finally, by courtesy of Nacional Financiera, which furnished unpublished figures for this study, we can sketch the profile of the economy in 1959, and note relations among the sectors. Here we are dealing with Gross National Product, in monetary terms; fortunately we can also derive the average per capita contribution (related to incomes) of the labour force that produced it. The results are nearly self-explanatory.

[1] Víctor L. Urquidi, 'El Impuesto sobre la renta en el desarrollo económico de México', *El Trimestre económico*, xxiii (Oct.–Dec. 1956), 424–37.

[2] Espinosa de los Reyes, 'Ingreso nacional', p. 181. See also Emilio Alanís Patiño, 'Los Problemas de desarrollo industrial de México', BNCE, *Comercio exterior*, vi (Aug. 1956), 347–51; ix (Sept. 1956), 418–21, re per capita shares. Jaffe, *Economic Development*, p. 270, seems uninformed when he states that Mexico has neglected education in failing 'to attack the problem of economic development on as wide a front as possible'; see above, ch. XX, and Manuel Bravo J., 'Los problemas de la enseñanza y el desarrollo económico', BNCE, *Comercio exterior*, ix (Feb. 1959), 75–77.

TABLE 64

Labour Force, GNP, and Per Capita Contributions, 1959

(*Labour force in '000; GNP in million pesos*)

		AMOUNTS		PER CENT.		PER CAPITA CONTRI- BUTION Pesos/Worker
		Labour Force	GNP	Labour Force	GNP	
AGRICULTURE	...	6,140	27,938	55·7	22·9	4,550
SECONDARY						
Mining	... ...		2,928		2·4	
Petroleum	... ...	130*	4,514	1·2	3·7	57,000*
Manufacturing	...	1,460	28,548	13·3	23·4	19,500
Sub-total	... ...	1,590	35,990	14·5	29·5	22,600
TERTIARY						
Construction	... ...	353	6,100	3·3	5·0	19,000
Commerce	... ...	1,033	24,766	9·5	20·3	24,500
Transportation	...	401	5,978	3·7	4·9	14,820
Services	... ...	1,463	21,228	13·3	17·4	14,400
Sub-total	... ...	3,250	58,072	29·8	47·6	17,800
TOTALS	... ...	10,980†	122,000	100·0	100·0	11,100

* Includes all extractive. † Omits 448 not specified, 90 unemployed.
Source: NF, Letter to author, 2 June 1960; percentages of GNP in source; others by author.

This table shows that previous trends continue. Agriculture and manufacturing now are nearly balanced, in value of goods and services. Commerce is almost equal with them. Services (including government services) are not far behind. Petroleum has made some recovery since 1945, but mining, a mainstay of the colonial and semi-colonial economy, continues to lose relative importance. We can also note variable productivity: agriculture lags far behind the other segments in per capita contribution, suggesting that it remains rather primitive.

Another important sign of change in Mexican economy is the fall in proportion of agricultural workers. As that sector increases in efficiency, and other opportunities open, there is a shift from primary activities to others. As late as 1930 some 70·2 per cent. of employed Mexicans were in agriculture or related activities. The figures dropped to 58·3 per cent. in 1950, which was, however, above the present 55·7 per cent. The fall is expected to continue.[1]

The various figures and data given above indicate that since 1940 the Mexican economy has been divided into four parts: agriculture, manufacturing, commerce, and a mixed group of various secondary and tertiary activities. With the exception of mining, all have been developing and expanding, at slightly different rates. Their relative contributions to the total economy show a fair balance, despite large disparities in productivity and efficiency, where agriculture records very low marks.

A semi-official report of February 1960 suggests that the various established policies and programmes are operating successfully. For 1959 it announced good crops, especially in basic foods and export items, and the continued growth of heavy industry. New oil strikes, the development of petro-chemical industries, a rise in electric power output, and improvement in the standard of living were further indications of a healthy, balanced, and dynamic economy.[2] These salutary developments were reaffirmed in the Presidential 'State of the Union' Message of September 1960.

Perhaps more important, so far as the individual Mexican family was concerned, are the other facts recorded for 1959. The cost of food had dropped by 2·5 per cent. from October 1958 to October 1959, and the wholesale price index had crept up only 0·5 per cent. over that period. This arresting of inflation, together with increases in productivity and wages, had meant 'quite a considerable improvement of their real income'. This is one reason why labour discontent died so rapidly after President López Mateos's inauguration in December 1958.

Many of the uncertainties and minor setbacks of 1957–8 disappeared during 1959, and the boom trends were still vital in late 1960. The agricultural system was producing bumper crops of all sorts; the industrial plant's larger output was helping hold inflation in check; tourism and exports were bringing in foreign exchange; and there prevailed political tranquillity, intellectual activity, and hope.

In his First Message, President López Mateos in 1959 had emphasized that Mexico was in the midst of 'impetuous growth and transformation' that required hard work to maintain and control. A year later, on 1 September 1960, he used less exhortatory tones, confining himself to summarizing continued gains. Among them

[1] Yáñez Pérez, *Mecanización*, pp. 371–88.
[2] BNCE, 'The Mexican Economy in 1959', *Comercio exterior*, vi (Feb. 1960), 3–4, 12.

was a rise in salaries of approximately 15 per cent. during 1959–60, while price indices had remained nearly stable: a 1 per cent. over-all rise, with the cost of food up only 2·6 per cent. Basic food costs had remained the same: tortillas, wheat flour, eggs, sugar, milk. The halting of inflation that rapidly eroded gains during recent years is an important victory for Mexico's people and Government.

Chapter XXVIII

AGRICULTURE: A PRIME ACTIVITY

As in other segments of Mexican life, one of the major questions which any national Government must quickly settle is whether to place its emphasis on political agrarianism, thus fulfilling the political and social aspirations of the Revolutionary dogma—or to stress economics—agricultural improvement, a slower, less dramatic and politically less appealing path to the same ends.

Leaders of the Institutional Revolution have been developing a compromise position, the chief result of which has been slowly rising standards of living for the agricultural population, although their gains have not been as spectacular as those of the more urbanized portions of the economy and society. Old-line doctrinaire reformers consider that this compromise policy represents an unwise betrayal of the Revolution. It has the merit of economic success.[1]

With a new emphasis on technical problems and the best planned utilization of their land, including tenure systems, numerous Mexicans in the past decade have carefully considered present and future developments in a torrent of articles and some excellent professional and technical books.[2]

THE NEO-MALTHUSIAN MYTH

Not long ago it was common for foreign analysts to forecast with alarming certainty that Mexico would be unable to feed the projected population of the 1950's, 1960's, and later. Fortunately these gloomy assertions of the neo-Malthusians were wrong.[3] The changes

[1] Jesús Silva Herzog, *El Agrarismo mexicano y la reforma agraria* (1959), is a long, brilliant polemic against present policies, by one of President Cárdenas's 'brain trust'.

[2] Magisterial is Yáñez Pérez, *Mecanización*; summary in Ríos Díaz and others, 'Actividades Primarias', SDE, *Diagnóstico*, pp. 55–138, with numerous tables, maps, diagrams. See also Edmundo Flores, *Tratado de economía agrícola* (Mexico, 1961).

[3] William Vogt, *The Road to Survival* (NY, Sloan Associates, 1948), pp. 169–77; Gill, *Land Hunger*; Tannenbaum, *Mexico*, pp. 182–92; Simpson, *Many Mexicos*, pp. 320–1, are illustrative accounts of neo-Malthusian writings. Cline, *U.S. and Mexico*, pp. 69–72, 371–86, takes a more optimistic view, based on early policies of the Institutional Revolution.

in output, policies, and knowledge about land and its uses since 1940 have currently provided a moderately optimistic view, which is the basis for present plans.

In the race between rising population and increased food supply, victory for the latter can be demonstrated. If for a moment we assume that basic foodstuffs were equitably distributed among the population, we can note the rising per capita shares of a combined total of the four principal crops. Table 65 provides this information. Detailed data beyond 1957 are not available.

TABLE 65

Per Capita Shares, Principal Food Crops, 1945–57

Year	PRODUCTION ('000 metric tons)					PER CAPITA kg./person	Per cent. increase over 1945
	Maize	Beans	Wheat	Rice	Combined		
1945 ...	2,186·2	150·0	346·7	121·1	2,804·0	128	—
1950 ...	3,122·0	250·3	587·3	186·6	4,146·2	161	25·8
1955 ...	4,490·1	448·9	850·0	209·7	5,998·7	194	51·5
1957 ...	4,500·0	410·4	1376·5	239·9	6,526·8	208	62·4

Sources: DGE, *Anuario estadístico . . . 1943–1945*, table 210 (pp. 533); DGE, *Compendio estadístico, 1955*, table 123 (pp. 201–4); 1958, table 135 (pp. 223–5).

The Mexican diet, while based on the above foods, is also supplemented by a wide range of other items. No very recent reliable information is at hand to show increases over the figures published in 1956 on data gathered by the United States Embassy in 1950–2. The average per capita caloric intake was then about 2,285 daily, of which maize and wheat made up 58·4 per cent.; animal products such as meats, eggs, fish, and milk, another 11·9 per cent.; and the remainder came from fruits, vegetables, beans, sugars, and fats. At the time when this study was made it was thought that 9,117,000 metric tons of foodstuffs were consumed annually. There seems to be no doubt that while more food than ever before is now currently available in Mexico, shortages and malnutrition still prevail among some segments of the population.[1]

AGRICULTURE IN A CHANGING ECONOMY

In the shift of emphasis from radical agrarianism to planned land use, the role of agriculture in the economy has necessarily been

[1] USDC, *Investment in Mexico*, p. 32.

redefined. We have already seen that it has been assigned primary activities: to feed the nation, to furnish raw materials to the growing industrial plant, and to develop a variety of exportable crops. It is now fulfilling these mandates.

Perhaps more important here, agriculture retains a predominant position in the economy. One of every two employed Mexicans draws a livelihood from it and related primary activities: cattle-raising, exploitation of forest resources, and fishing. In 1959 we note that its contribution to the gross national product was nearly ten times that of mining, and outstripped all other activities except manufacturing, which it approximately equalled (Table 64).

Analysts divide Mexican crops into two general classes: food, and export/industrial. Five crops—maize, beans, wheat, coffee, and cotton—use 84·3 per cent. of the cultivated land and account for 72·1 per cent. of the total value of production (Appendix Table XV). All crops have increased in output, and generally in value. Since 1939 Mexico's cultivated area has increased by more than 40 per cent., production has doubled, and productivity has risen. New lands, new crops, improved techniques have all contributed. Data to support these assertions on the twenty-one leading Mexican crops in 1957 (the most recent available figures) appear in Appendix Table XV.

FOOD CROPS

Since very earliest times, maize has been Mexico's major food crop, and it remains so to this day. Wheat, rice, beans, some potatoes, and a wide variety of fruit and lesser vegetables also diversify the Mexican food supply.

In a sense, Mexican society is bifurcated into those who cling to the pre-Conquest, basic maize-beans-squash diet, and those who favour wheat, bread, rice, and other non-indigenous staples. In fact, there is a startling correlation between those who adhere to ancient food habits, and those who form the poverty-ridden 'Remote Mexico', wearing sandals or going barefoot by custom or circumstance.[1] Of the population over 1 year old in 1950, 13·6 million ate bread and wore shoes; of the 11·4 millions who ate maize, 6·6 millions used *huaraches* (sandals), and another 4·8 millions went barefoot.[2]

[1] See above, pp. 111–12.
[2] Daniel Moreno, *Los Factores demográficos en la planeación económica* (1958), pp. 164–5.

In hectares, value, and production maize predominates among food crops. It also accounts for from half to two-thirds of the harvest area. In many parts of the Republic maize is grown solely for subsistence. Areas which produce surplus crops are the fertile plateaus in the Bajío between Mexico City and Guadalajara, and in Veracruz and Michoacán. In 1957 maize was harvested from 5·4 million hectares of land, yielding about 4,500 million kilograms, valued at 3,148 million pesos. The 1959–60 season brought forth 5·5 million tons from 6·0 million hectares, providing again an exportable surplus.[1] Here it may be recalled that in his first State of the Union Message President López Mateos proudly reported that not only had Mexico ceased imports of this crop but had adequate reserve supplies. In 1959 the nation was actually exporting maize to South America; a total of 43,000 tons was sold abroad.[2]

Next to maize, wheat is Mexico's major cereal. Introduced by a Negro servitor of the Spaniards at the Conquest, it had long been imported. Now Mexico is not only meeting its growing internal requirements, but produces enough surplus wheat to warrant signing the International Wheat Agreement in 1959. Wheat is grown primarily in the North, on irrigated lands; smaller amounts come from the West and the Core. With urbanization has come increased demands which have been more than met through improved technology and larger plantings; production, yield per hectare, and value have all risen markedly. Table 66 gives some idea of this over a recent four-year period.

TABLE 66

Wheat Production, 1954–7

			Area ('ooo ha.)	Production ('ooo kg.)	Value ('ooo pesos)	Yield (kg./hectare)
1954	...	...	764·9	839·4	655·5	1,122
1955	...	...	800·0	850·0	676·4	1,063
1956	...	...	937·0	1,242·5	1,025·5	1,329
1957	...	...	958·0	1,376·5	1,166·7	1,437

Source: 'Cultivos principales', *Revista de estadística*, xxii (Nov.–Dec. 1959), 699.

[1] *Revista de estadística*, xxii (Nov.–Dec. 1959), 699. See Appendix Table XIV.

[2] 'Mexico Exports Corn', BNCE, *Comercio exterior*, vi (2 Feb. 1960), 9. The first shipment was 5,000 tons, worth $5 million. López Mateos, *2° Informe* (1 Sept. 1960); he emphasizes Mexico's role as an exporter rather than an importer of maize.

Agriculture: a Prime Activity

Beans and rice form part of nearly every Mexican meal. In these, Mexican production also covers domestic needs. Rice has a certain local fame; it is the main crop of two large co-operative ejidos— Lombardía and Nueva Italia in Michoacán. But the centre of commercial production is Sonora, with lesser harvests in Veracruz and Tabasco. Bananas, because of disease, have declined as an export crop. For national needs they are being supplemented by larger plantings of pineapples, oranges, and other fruit. Traditionally there has been limited interest in raising much beyond the staple foods except tomatoes, but cantaloupes, Persian melons, and numerous vegetables are increasingly grown as cash crops, especially for the United States market. However, the most important consideration is that Mexico is feeding itself. It is also beginning to develop exportable surpluses in the staples which not long ago it imported.[1]

EXPORT AND INDUSTRIAL CROPS

Cacao and henequen (sisal) are crops that have had earlier export and industrial importance. To these in recent years have been added cotton and coffee.

Cacao, used by pre-Conquest Indians for money, has had its ups and downs since the Spaniards introduced it to Europe. After long neglect a revival of interest began in the 1940's. Production is localized to the Grijalva–Usumacinta basin area, with a small patch in central Veracruz. Special programmes to improve the trees since 1946 have begun to show results. Production has advanced from an average of about 1,000 metric tons per year in the 1930's to 1·5 million in 1957. In the years 1953–7 the crop has more than doubled in value from 36·6 to 76·3 million pesos.[2]

Before the First World War, Mexico had a world monopoly of henequen, a hard fibre which is used extensively for binder-twine. World competition reduced the markets, and expropriation of the chief plantations in Yucatán the quality of the product, but henequen is still a sizeable commodity; acreage and value have risen steadily since 1950, to 118,000 metric tons in 1957, valued at 209 million pesos.

Coffee and cotton are Cinderella crops in Mexico. Both had ancient, somewhat undistinguished histories before the last two

[1] Excellent detailed studies of individual principal crops appear in Yáñez Pérez, *Mecanización*, pp. 129–75, discussing yields, possibilities of mechanization, and related comment.
[2] USBFC, *Investment in Mexico*, p. 35; DGE, *Compendio estadístico 1958*, table 135 (p. 225).

decades. Both have risen spectacularly as money crops as a result of the irrigation and agricultural programmes of the Institutional Revolution. Average cotton production in 1945–9 was 532,000 bales; by 1952 it had leaped to 1,239,000, grown primarily on the irrigated zones bordering on the United States. Production in 1957 amounted to about 2,080,000 bales (of 230 kg. each). Its value was 3,035 million pesos, as compared to the 1953 crop value of 1,424 million. Mexico exports part of its harvest and utilizes part of it for national textile industries.[1]

Mexicans became coffee drinkers in the eighteenth century, but not until recent times has much area been devoted to the crop. A slow rise in the 1930's was temporarily stemmed a decade later when many Germans as enemy aliens left managerial positions on coffee plantations; but Mexicans who replaced them rapidly acquired the necessary skills, and under the spur of high prices during the Second World War greatly augmented the output. In 1946 national production was about 55,400 metric tons. By 1957 it had risen to 123,800, about three-quarters of which was exported. To stimulate production and crop improvement, President Alemán in 1949 created a National Coffee Commission, that concentrates its efforts on the major centres in Veracruz and Chiapas. Following Brazil and Colombia, Mexico now is one of the main coffee-producing areas of the world.[2]

Sugar-cane and tobacco, both requiring further processing before use, are also a pair of colonial money crops which currently feed Mexico's industries. Much of the cane is grown on ejidos. Improvements of various sorts—technical, marketing, new varieties—have turned Mexico from an importer to a potential and occasional exporter of cane products, usually sugar. Tobacco, an indigenous crop, is mostly consumed locally; some very minor export of leaf tobacco, usually to Europe, is offset by imports of nearly an equal amount of specialized leaves. The producing area, mainly in Nayarit and Jalisco, now has a stabilized output of about 35,000 metric tons a year, an increase over the 20,000 before the Second World War.

CURRENT POLICIES

The continuing policies of encouraging expansion and diversification of crops, pursued since about 1940, have been successful. They have had a double effect: the renovated and improved agricultural

---

[1] USBFC, *Investment in Mexico*, p. 36; DGE, *Compendio estadístico 1958*, p. 224.
[2] USBFC, *Investment in Mexico*, p. 35; DGE, *Compendio estadístico 1958*, p. 225.

system has covered domestic needs and released surpluses for export; the same process has cut down, and in many cases eliminated, imports of foodstuffs. Representing 44 per cent. of Mexico's total exports in 1957, agricultural exports were more than double in value its imports, 3·8 million compared with 1·7 million pesos.[1]

Long-range programmes embrace many policies already discussed: greater distribution of arable land; construction of more dams and irrigation works; increased use of farm machinery, fertilizer, and pest controls; agricultural and related research, and extension services; further farm credits, price supports, and controls on distribution of basic foods; a system of crop insurance; tariff and trade controls to assure domestic consumption needs and also to foster export of surpluses; and promotion of domestic processing. In communications, interest is growing in tertiary market roads now that the primary network is complete and the secondary ones well-developed.

President López Mateos in his first State of the Union Message indicated that these now rather well-established lines would be followed during his term of office. Specifically he announced some slight changes in the objectives of official agricultural policy. Now that the nation was producing its basic foodstuffs and even exporting some, and inasmuch as these were abundant crops previously singled out for promotion as export items—cotton, coffee, for example— official efforts would now concentrate on the elimination of other imported items, the raw materials utilized in Mexican industry. Of these, wool and rubber would head the list. He also stressed that since the nation was now among the agriculturally exporting nations, Mexico was participating and would continue to participate in world efforts to stabilize international prices and aid the development of orderly marketing practices for crops, such as wheat, cotton, and coffee.[2]

[1] Rice, 'Basic Data', p. 6.

[2] Adolfo López Mateos, 'First State of the Union Message', p. 8A. Facts and figures in his second such message (1 September 1960) indicated that the policies were being carried out.

Chapter XXIX

THE RETREAT FROM COLONIALISM: EXTRACTIVE INDUSTRIES

To many older economic activities in Mexico, recent years have seen a multitude of new ones added and expanded. The Institutional Revolution and industrialism have become almost synonymous since 1940. While earlier phases of the Revolution sought to reform the political and agrarian structures developed to 1910, this latest phase aims to renovate and modernize Mexico's economy, to lift it from the 'semi-colonial' or 'semi-feudal' state common to most Latin American nations during the nineteenth and early twentieth centuries. The process is by no means complete. It is, however, more than a mere dream. Resulting from cumulative efforts and plans over many years, Mexico is beginning to lose the appearance of a 'semi-colonial' area.

For much of its recent history the Republic was primarily a supplier of raw materials to industrialized areas of the world. Its fibres, minerals, and petroleum, developed by a small group of local and foreign capitalists, went abroad, and in return it received manufactured articles, even foodstuffs. For local consumption, its own industrial plant provided a few products: beer, glass, soap, and other homely items not worth the shipping costs to foreign exporters. A few merchants and agencies sufficed to handle the trade, and often the small amounts of capital required for commercial and industrial transactions. As security against loss and inflation, local capital normally went abroad or poured into real estate, either urban holdings or plantation enterprises. Most of these elements have now been transformed. Since 1940 Mexico has been in the throes of an industrial revolution.

EXTRACTIVE INDUSTRIES: SEMI-COLONIAL ACTIVITIES

After independence the extractive industries in Mexico lay mostly in foreign hands. Mining, with a pre-Conquest history of sorts, amounted to little until Spaniards developed it towards the mid-sixteenth century. Oil is relatively new, developed first by and for outsiders.

The Retreat from Colonialism: Extractive Industries

For many decades Mexico was one of the world's great producers of bullion—gold and silver—after the conquerors found that the small Indian hoards extracted by placer mining were only a token of what could be extracted through organized efforts, with which Cortés and his successors were thoroughly familiar. From 1522 to 1550 1·5 million pesos worth of bullion was forwarded to the homeland; by 1803 Baron Alexander von Humboldt calculated that the Mexican mines had yielded some 2,000 million pesos worth of specie, two-fifths of the total New World production since 1492.[1]

At the end of the nineteenth century attention was turned to other Mexican deposits. Industrial metals became more important than specie; the discovery of petroleum, and the world-wide growth of its market, focused international attention on these riches. Both were industrialized by foreign capital. Mining tends still to remain in the hands of such owners, but after a fairly long and acrimonious history, foreign petroleum holdings in Mexico together with refining and processing apparatus were almost totally expropriated in 1938. As the story of oil expropriation and its settlement is a complicated but familiar one, we do not propose to repeat it here.[2]

MINERALS AND MINING

Even after 400 years of unremitting effort, men have not exhausted Mexico's mineral deposits. It remains one of the richest countries in the world in minerals of all sorts, many unexploited or undiscovered. Those which have been known since 1519 have sufficed to give Mexico a long and distinguished place in mining history. The lure of minerals brought the first settlers, after early Spanish reports that gold was to be had for the asking. Gold, more prosaic silver, and later the industrial metals, have kept part of the Mexican economy going since mid-sixteenth century.[3] Now Mexicans expect and hope that a portion of their resources of industrial minerals will be diverted to their own extensive industrialization. These views are not wholly idle.

[1] Clarence H. Haring, *The Spanish Empire in America* (1947), pp. 261–8; Bailey W. Diffie, *Latin American Civilization: Colonial Period* (Harrisburg, Penn., 1945), pp. 104–19, 366–85.

[2] Cline, *U.S. and Mexico*, pp. 239–60; important new information appears in E. David Cronon, *Josephus Daniels in Mexico* (1960), pp. 154–271, based on MS. sources.

[3] A summary history of colonial Mexican mining appears in ch. 1 of Walter Howe, *The Mining Guild of New Spain and its Tribunal General* (1949), with subsequent detailed treatment to independence; see also, Robert C. West, *The Mining Community in Northern New Spain: the Parral Mining District* (Berkeley and Los Angeles, Univ. of Calif. Press, 1949), with excellent bibliography.

Iron and Coal

Ultimately national power, both economic and political, rests on steel, and indirectly on the elements—chiefly iron and coal—which produce it. Mexico has both. It has an abundance of iron, averaging 60 per cent. iron content. Deposits are located in several areas, the single largest being Cerro del Mercado in northern Durango, alone

MINING

LEAD
COPPER
MANGANESE
ZINC
ANTIMONY
MERCURY
TIN
IRON
COAL
GOLD
SILVER
SULPHUR

estimated at a minimum of 75 million metric tons. In 1956, total Mexican iron deposits were conservatively estimated at 230 million metric tons. Further explorations have added 60 million more, reported President López Mateos in September 1960.[1]

Mexican coal resources are nearly as impressive in quantity, though less so in quality. Estimates of known coal deposits range

[1] USBFC, *Investment in Mexico*, p. 47; López Mateos, *2° Informe* (1 Sept. 1960), noting a 20 per cent. increase in reserves.

from 2·0 to 3·3 thousand million tons, the largest single body of coking grade coal being at Sabinas in Coahuila. Its thousand million tons is the only known coal in Latin America that can be coked without blending, despite the formation of considerable ash-residue. Remaining Mexican fields contain large amounts of coal but it is not suitable for efficient coking. As yet these reserves remain untapped. Annually about 1·4 million metric tons of coal are mined. Nearly all is converted to coke and used almost exclusively by industries. Gas or charcoal, petroleum products and hydraulically-produced electricity are employed for normal domestic fuel and power.[1]

Industrial Metals

Besides iron and coal, gold and silver, Mexico has a wide range of industrial metals. Many of these are shown in the map on p. 272. About half of its mineral exports consist of lead, zinc, and copper. Minerals as a whole comprise about 28 per cent. of the total exports.

Mexican mining prosperity and production depend directly on world market prices, especially those of the United States, to which Mexico ships nearly all its mineral exports. Since 1942, for instance, the production of antimony, arsenic, gold, and silver has decreased, and that of cadmium, copper, tin, mercury, lead, and tungsten has remained stationary. Upward trends are recorded for graphite, manganese, zinc, iron ore, and sulphur. The production of principal metals for 1950–8 is given in Appendix Table XVI.

Mining in the Economy

In relative and absolute terms mining has been declining for some years, plagued by both technical and financial problems. To rehabilitate the industry, a basic supplier for the nation's industrial plant, the Mexican Government has established subsidies for small and medium sized operations, has lifted taxes for producers who will agree to increase output in given lines, and has prohibited states and territories from taxing the production and export of minerals. Despite these efforts, however, it was reported in 1960 that mining did not participate in the general upward recovery of the economy during 1959, but remained static.[2]

The exhaustion of some historic veins, as well as the discouraging

[1] U.S. Congress, House, *Fuel investigation: Mexican Petroleum* (80th Cong., 2nd Sess., House Report 2470, 1949), pp. 35–38; USBFC, *Investment in Mexico*, p. 56.

[2] Rice, 'Basic Data', pp. 10–11; BNCE, 'Mexican Economy in 1959', p. 4.

effects of taxation, contributed to the decline. Transportation difficulties and power shortages have also been factors. It is believed that more intensive exploration programmes can remedy the first, while present government programmes seem well on the way to correcting the other drawbacks. While not as spectacular as other segments, mining still has a future in Mexico, as well as a long past.

PETROLEUM AND PEMEX

Before 18 March 1938 petroleum was a bad word in the lexicon of the Revolution. On that day President Lázaro Cárdenas expropriated the foreign-developed and foreign-owned oil industry. Mexicans hail this event as the beginning of their real economic independence.

Much of the furor on both sides has died away, now that Mexico has punctually paid the claims pressed by the United States and British companies. It has also made clear its determination to retain the nationalized industry at any cost. Petroleum problems can again be discussed without the polemic overtones which bedevilled them until about 1950.

Unfortunately many of the published treatments of the Mexican oil industry still faithfully review events only up to and through expropriation. Others rehearse the many and complex problems which were still unsolved by the end of President Alemán's term in 1952. Up to that year inexperienced Mexican workers, hostile boycotts, overdoses of politics, unruly labour, and a number of other negative elements seemingly combined to prove the expropriated oilmen's claims that Mexicans could never make a go of the industry, and would have to call them back.[1] This did not happen; nor now can it.

Nationalized petroleum is a heritage of the Revolution with which no administration would dare to meddle. The current view is adequately expressed by President López Mateos, addressing Congress in 1959. 'In a world where the international oil industry faces surplus production problems', he said, 'the irrevocable position of Mexico is and will be not one step backward in oil nationalization.' This was a prelude to the announcement of a new Regulation added to Article 27 (covering sub-soil rights).

The reform appeared on 24 August 1959. It redefines the role

[1] There is an enormous polemic and scholarly literature, covering the situation to around 1950. See esp. Merrill Rippy, 'The Mexican Oil Industry', *Essays in Mexican History: The Charles Wilson Hackett Memorial Volume* (Austin, 1958), pp. 248–67; J. Richard Powell, *The Mexican Petroleum Industry, 1938–50* (1956).

that private enterprise can play in developing Mexican oil and mineral resources. It especially authorizes Pemex to enter the field of petrochemicals. The Regulation, stressed the President, 'offers time and time again an expression of our purpose that nationalized oil, a conquest of the Revolution directed toward our economic independence, and as part of our national patrimony, cannot be touched except in benefit of Mexico'.[1]

After 1952

The rise of the industry, especially since 1952, is another Mexican success story in the economic field. The management of the ex-propriated holdings was turned over to Petroleos Mexicanos (Pemex), a semi-official national corporation; 1938 national legislation gives it monopolistic privileges. In 1946 President Alemán put a hard-driving and capable businessman, Antonio J. Bermúdez, in charge of Pemex, who remained until 1958. Backed by two administrations, which counted heavily on the dynamic flow of oil to supply power for the industrial system, Bermúdez rather quickly put Pemex back on its feet. By 1952 the nationalized industry was producing about 80 million barrels of oil annually, the largest output since the halcyon days of 1921 when Mexico had led the world in output.

Pemex, under Bermúdez and sympathetic Governments, made a number of important changes, often criticized in the Mexican press. One was to contract with foreign companies to explore and seek new fields. It can no longer be stated, as it was earlier, that Pemex utilized only wells proved by private industry between 1901 and 1930. Although most of the exploration and new strikes, either by Pemex itself or through contracts, have still been made along the Gulf coast, they have established the reserves of a number of fields, both petroleum and gas. In 1960, Pemex drilled 591 new wells of which 106 were in new fields. The new Director, Pascual Gutiérrez Roldán, is continuing Pemex's successful policies.

One of the most spectacular new fields is near Macuspana in eastern Tabasco and south-western Campeche, adjacent to the Grijalva–Usumacinta Commission area. Conservatively rated among the great fields in North America, it has huge gas deposits and light crude. At Pemex City (Ciudad Pemex) a gas absorption plant was inaugurated on 3 March 1958, to handle 500 MCF of gas per day; shortly after opening, it was recovering daily 16,000 barrels of hydrocarbon liquids, collected from forty-eight wells. Dry gas, for

---

[1] López Mateos, 'First . . . Address'.

industrial and other purposes, will go to the Mexico City area, furnishing Coatzcoalcos, Minatitlán, Veracruz, Córdoba, Orizaba, and Puebla en route.

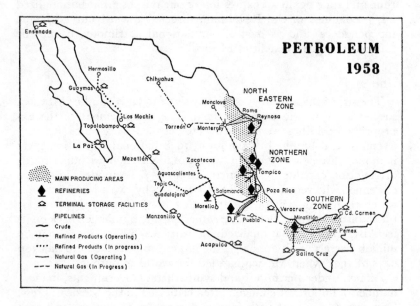

Proved Reserves

In the oil industry, exploring activity can be measured by growth of proved reserves. In 1952, President Alemán reported these at 1,395 million barrels, twice the 1937 (pre-expropriation) figure. In turn Ruíz Cortines said that the 1953 proved reserves of 2,300 million barrels had risen to 3,500 million in September 1958. A year later, President López Mateos indicated a rise of 582 million barrels, making the 1959 total more than 4,000 million barrels. His most recent report (September 1960) gives 776·5 million cubic metres, an increase of 133 million over 1959. Details of such explorations and proved reserves appear in a professional journal.[1]

Through its vigorous exploration programme, Pemex has increased proved reserves to the point that Mexico has no immediate worries for the near future. At the same time the amounts of crude pouring

[1] Eduardo J. Guzmán, '1958 Developments in Foreign Petroleum Fields: Mexico', Am. Ass. of Petrol. Geologists, *Bulletin*, xliii (July 1959), 1505–17, with maps, graphs.

from more than 2,600 operating wells amounted to 300,000 barrels daily in 1960, a new record.

The petroleum industry which the Mexican Government took over in 1938 was designed chiefly for foreign export. The refineries built before expropriation were all in the Gulf coast area, far from centres of national consumption. To make Mexico self-sufficient, the object of national policy, Mexicans have had to construct nearly 7,000 kilometres of new pipelines to bring oil from the fields to central and regional refineries and storage tanks, facilities that the Institutional Revolution has had to build. In 1938 the existing ones had already deteriorated and their refining capacity was only about 100,000 barrels a day.

By the end of the Ruíz Cortines administration, Mexican refining capacity had grown to about 330,000 barrels a day, with cracking capacity at another 70,000. López Mateos reported in 1960 a refinery at Ciudad Madero as completed, at a total cost of 175 million pesos; it adds 100,000 barrels a day capacity. In addition, Pemex has had to build or acquire a tanker fleet and various kinds of plants for kerosene production, sulphur recovery, specialized lubricants, gas absorption, and others. The principal refineries in operation in 1958, with annual capacity in millions of barrels, were Ciudad Madero (17·6), Atzcapotzalco (29·1), Minatitlán (15·6), Salamanca (12·9), Arbol Grande (2·4), Reynosa (2·6), and Poza Rica (2·4).[1]

The major tasks of erecting refineries, the necessary auxiliary plants, and the storage and distribution network for domestic consumption took place under a six-year plan (1952–8). It is nearly completed. Pemex has now moved into the next phase: the production of highly specialized products formerly imported. By 1959 it had reduced the necessity of importing some of these.

Petrochemicals

Even more recently Pemex has ventured into petrochemicals: plastics, synthetic rubber, and basic industrial items such as anhydrous ammonia, aromatics, raw materials for detergents, and industrial alcohols. A five-year plan of development has been approved; it is estimated that products worth about 1,300 million pesos annually can be manufactured to replace similar imported items on

[1] Rice, 'Basic Data', pp. 7–8; USBFC, *Investment in Mexico*, pp. 51–6; Rice, 'Economic Developments in Mexico, 1958', WTIS, pt. 1, *Economic Reports*, no. 59–36 (1959), pp. 7–8; Ruíz Cortines, 'Ultimo informe'; López Mateos, 'First State of Union Address'.

the domestic market. In February 1960 the first plant at Atzcapotzalco was producing daily 40–50 tons of basic raw materials for
detergents. This alone, during 1960, would cut imports by 500
million pesos.[1]

Problems

Pemex has unusual problems as a semi-public monopoly. It must
market its refined and special products at fixed, rather low prices. It
cannot, in general, finance its operations by selling stock, but must
pay for development from surplus. From this, Pemex has to pay the
indemnity to expropriated owners, and also normal production taxes
to the Federal treasury. At a fixed 12 per cent. rate, these amounted
to 2 million pesos a day in 1960. For expansion and development
Pemex has had recourse, through NF and other government
agencies, to occasional loans from abroad, but about 87 per cent. of
its growth since 1946 has been self-financed. However, to give the
petrochemical field a start, the López Mateos administration made
a direct government investment of about 4·2 million pesos in 1960.

In marketing its products the national monopoly has usually had
to tread a narrow path between satisfying a thirsty and growing
national market, and exporting enough petroleum abroad to earn
foreign exchange for needed equipment.

President Ruíz Cortines in 1958 stressed the rise in domestic
consumption of Pemex products; during his six years of office,
petroleum consumption rose 57 per cent., diesel oil 12 per cent., and
kerosene 80 per cent. Official statistics indicate domestic sales of
1,620 million pesos in 1952 and 3,654·0 million in 1958; for 1959
we have already noted that petroleum contributed 4,514 million
pesos to gross national product (3·7 per cent.).[2] Pemex's Director
estimated Mexican daily consumption at more than 400,000 barrels
of oil and gas; the annual demand grows by about 8–9 per cent.[3]

'The oil industry nears its total integration', reported President
Lópex Mateos in 1959. A year later on 1 September he announced
two outstanding developments: the establishment of the petro-
chemical industry, and the solution to most of Pemex's fiscal
problems, which include an investment for new works in progress
of some 2,062 million pesos.

[1] BNCE, 'Mexican Economy in 1959', p. 4; 'Good Year for Pemex', *Comercio
exterior*, vi, 10.
[2] See above, p. 260.
[3] 'Good Year for Pemex', p. 10.

The Retreat from Colonialism: Extractive Industries

Table 67 indicates the increases in production and other aspects of the petroleum industry after it recovered from the shock of expropriation. It reveals operating efficiencies and other reforms largely attributable to Bermúdez. Nationalized oil is one of the dynamic elements in the Mexican industrial revolution.

TABLE 67

Pemex, 1952 compared with 1958

	1952	1958	Per cent. increase
Exploited oilfields	58	70	20·7
Operating wells	1,324	2,653	100·1
Productive wells drilled	185	286	54·6
Unproductive wells drilled	117	93	—
Personnel ('000)	35·8	45·5	27·0
Salaries and wages (million pesos)	464·7	1,097·7	136·3
Volume of crude produced (million cubic metres)	12·5	16·0	28·0
Value of crude (millions of pesos)	290·0	455·4	57·0
Domestic sales, refined products (million pesos)	2,082·0	3,653·9	75·6
Natural gas (million cubic metres)	2,649·3	7,437·7	180·0

Sources: DGE, *Compendio estadístico, 1955*, tables 159–63 (pp. 241–6); 1958, tables 168–74 (pp. 269–80). Percentages by author.

Chapter XXX

INDUSTRIAL REVOLUTION: MANUFACTURES

IF we did not know from other sources that all segments of the economy, except perhaps mining, were almost equally booming, the statistics on manufacturing would suggest that nearly all Mexicans were building factories or working in them.

There has always been some industry in Mexico, even in pre-Conquest times, with minor manufacturing activities during the colonial years and the nineteenth century. In common with other Latin American countries, a slow and small expansion took place in the first quarter of the present century, but the real Mexican outbursts post-date 1939.[1] Between 1939 and 1951 Mexican industrial volume doubled, much of the increase coming in the expansion of established facilities: iron, steel, sugar, cement, paper, chemicals, glass, cordage. With favourable laws and an attractive climate for investment, many new industries were created in the late 1940's and early 1950's to produce rayon and acetate, alkalies, plywood, fertilizers, electrical equipment, aluminum, tin, and many minor products.[2]

TRENDS AND PROBLEMS

Growth trends, marked by increases in quantity, quality, and kinds of manufacturing, continue. But Mexico is possibly not fully self-sufficient in any one field of industry—demand seems still to outstrip supply. On the other hand there are now very few products which are not produced or assembled in Mexico, by nationals for a Mexican market. The Government maintains the concept of 'saturation' of industrial fields; when it believes that production threatens to outstrip demand, it withdraws support. To date almost no industrial fields have thus been declared 'saturated'.[3]

[1] Standard coverage of this interesting topic is George Wythe, *Industry in Latin America* (1945); a comprehensive summary view, as of about 1952, IBRD, *The Economic Development of Mexico* (1953).

[2] USBFC, *Investment in Mexico*, p. 61.

[3] Rice, 'Basic Data', p. 13.

Industrial Revolution: Manufactures

Despite growing pains, Mexican manufacturing has recently developed into one of the most important sectors of the economy. In 1959, for instance, some 1·4 million Mexicans drew their livelihood from it, outstripping all sectors but agriculture; manufacturing contributed 28,548 million pesos to monetary gross national product, and accounted for 23·4 per cent. of the total, making it the single largest sector.[1] To increase markets, production, productivity, and investment, private and public efforts seem permanently combined.

For planning purposes Mexican statisticians have divided manufacturing into twenty-three broad categories, within each of which are numerous subdivisions. According to the 1954 value of products, textiles were in first place; beer products second; iron and steel third; flour mills fourth; and rubber manufactures fifth.[2] Some idea of the present panorama may be gleaned from the reports for 1958 and the second and third quarters of 1959, the most recent data available, which are tabulated and ranked by value in Appendix Table XVII. It shows that iron and steel now outstrip all other activities by a wide margin; beer still comes second, with rubber manufactures, soaps and detergents, and products from flour mills following in that order.

Appendix Table XVII does not fully reflect the manufacture of certain important production and consumer goods whose components are partially made abroad and imported to Mexico for assembly. Electric motors, motor cars, and trucks are included among the former, with radios, television sets, refrigerators, electric stoves, and a multitude of minor products chiefly for the growing consumer market.[3] Sears, Roebuck is among the many firms which have not only pioneered in catering for these new buyers, but have aided in developing locally manufactured products as well.[4]

Estimates of the physical volume of various enterprises now take 1945 as the base year. The continuous rise is indicated in Table 68.

Naturally, the value of output has also risen. The Under-Secretary of Industry and Trade, recently addressing the National Chamber of Manufacturing Industry, reminded them that manufactured products had increased in net value by 69·3 per cent. from 1950 through 1957, and that 40 per cent. of new productive investment

---

[1] Data kindly furnished directly by NF.

[2] USBFC, *Investment in Mexico*, table 43, p. 61.

[3] Rice, 'Basic Data', table 9.

[4] Daniel James, 'Sears, Roebuck's Mexican Revolution', *Harper's Magazine* (June 1959), 1–6. Part of the 'revolution' was fixed prices; Sears deals with 2,000 local suppliers.

TABLE 68

Index of Physical Volume of Industrial Production, 1946–58

(1945 = 100·0)

			1946	1950	1955	1958
General (all sectors)	...	...	100·1	122·7	155·8	192·1
Mining ...	...	...	73·8	92·4	90·6	97·3
Petroleum	...	...	110·0	153·5	234·7	326·1
Electrical energy	...	...	108·1	144·2	228·2	296·5
Construction	...	...	113·2	154·2	205·9	255·4
Manufacturing ...	...	...	102·0	121·4	152·9	187·1

Sources: DGE, *Compendio estadístico, 1955*, table 172 (p. 254); *1958*, table 175 (p. 285).

was going into manufacturing enterprises.[1] He observed the lack of continuity in integrating the manufacturing industry; some products only pass through first stages of processing before exportation while too many companies depend on foreign-made components even though domestic suppliers are available. Moreover, he pointed out some remaining characteristics and problems which show where the Mexican industrial system is incomplete or immature. Other mistakes that he recorded are too little or too much production for actual needs. Many plants are inadequate in size; others are planned over-optimistically with excessive capacity for present and even immediate future markets.[2]

Recent Trends

Earlier growth continues. In 1959 more than 1,900 new enterprises were launched in Mexico with an initial capital of 1,400 million pesos. More than half (580 million pesos) went into consumer goods. Some equilibrium having been reached between production goods and consumer goods, capital goods and heavy industries now seem to be expanding.[3] Another manifest trend is the deflection of investment and growth to secondary industrial centres. Favourable climate, transport, power, labour supply, and a ready market had long attracted nearly every type of manufacturing to the Federal District. Many of the same factors have made Monterrey, Guadalajara, and Puebla secondary clusters. While

[1] 'Industrialization Problems', BNCE, *Comercio exterior*, vi, 10.
[2] Ibid.
[3] BNCE, 'Mexican Economy in 1959', p. 4; Rice, 'Economic Developments in Mexico, 1957', WTIS, pt. 1, *E.R.* no. 58–36 (1958).

there is no apparent slackening in the flow of capital to the metropolitan area, rates of growth and proportionate amounts of new money pouring into the secondary centres seem slightly ahead of that going into the District.

Yet another interesting and significant trend is the 'joint venture' approach. Foreign capital is increasingly being invested in established Mexican firms, to mutual advantage. Earlier the general pattern was for Mexican capital to participate in a foreign-directed subsidiary. In recent months United States industrial enterprises such as Philco International have become minority stockholders in Mexican establishments, increasing their operational capital and bringing to them important patents and technical knowledge. For instance, Sylvania Company has arranged with Focos, a Monterrey light bulb manufacturer, to produce mercury vapour lighting apparatus for the first time in Mexico. Subsidiaries, of course, also appear in profusion.[1]

ELECTRIC POWER: A NEWLY NATIONALIZED INDUSTRY

Electricity has supplemented the use of petroleum and coal for industrial power. Drawing on various modes of generation—steam, hydro-, diesel-, and internal combustion plants—power output rose from 2,462 million kwh in 1939 to 5,702·8 million kwh in 1953, with installed capacity over the same period growing from 680,500 to 1·7 million kw.[2] By 1956 the latter had risen to 2,069,000 kw installed capacity. By 1960, President López Mateos reported to Congress on 1 September, capacity had reached 2,348,899 kw.

His Annual Message of that year contained a real surprise when he touched on the topic of electric power. He first noted that a goal of his administration is to add 2·5 million kw to Mexico's potential capacity by the end of his six-year term. His advisers believe that production of power is perhaps the single most important element in stimulating economic and social growth. He reviewed the fact that in 1959, when he had last reported, about half Mexico's electric power was produced by private enterprises, the other half by the state through its Federal Electricity Commission. Study of the concessions under which the private companies operated, notably

---

[1] Unclassified Foreign Service Despatch 906, U.S. Embassy, Mexico, *Monthly Economic Summary*, Jan. 1960, App. 1.

[2] USBFC, *Investment in Mexico*, p. 56. Innumerable details on the history and outlook of electric power are found in Cristóbal Lara Beautell, *La Industria de energía eléctrica* (1953).

American and Foreign Power Company (U.S.) and Mexican Light (Canadian), showed that it would be about forty-five years before their holdings reverted to the nation. The same studies made clear the imperative necessity of doubling Mexico's electric output as soon as possible, in a rhythm too accelerated for these privately-owned enterprises. Further, the Government felt that like oil, electric power should be in national hands, as a key element in economic development.

Rather than resorting to expropriation, however, the Government of López Mateos approached these problems in a more orthodox manner, the results of which were to transfer control of the privately-owned and operated foreign electric companies to Government hands. In April 1960 the Government purchased outright the holdings of the American and Foreign Power Company, with a capacity of 309,000 kw. Then, without paying premium prices, the Mexican Government purchased 90 per cent. of the common and preferred stock of the Canadian company, which then agreed to turn over control on 27 September 1960. The President stated that a book value of the two companies, totalling 3,375 million pesos, was acquired by the state for 650 million pesos, and opened the way for national intregration and expansion of the now nationalized electrical power industry.[1] Thus power shortage, a serious obstacle to further industrialization, seems on the way to resolution.

In 1958 the electric power industry had relied on hydro-electric power to furnish 45 per cent. of electrical output, the remainder from steam, diesel, and internal combustion plants. Then the national production of 8,918 million kwh had required the purchase of an additional 479 million kwh for industry.[2] Presumably the new efforts and developments in 1959–60 will permit Mexico to become self-sufficient in this important field.

IRON AND STEEL

Among Latin American nations, all struggling with somewhat similar problems, Mexico ranks second behind Brazil as a producer of iron and steel. The common needs for co-operation, exchange of information, and other joint activities brought into being at Santiago, Chile, in October 1959 a Latin American Iron and Steel Institute, constituted by the sixty-one major firms, including Mexican, which

---

[1] López Mateos, *2° Informe* (1 Sept. 1960), in special chapter on 'Acquisition of Electric Resources'.

[2] DGE, *Compendio estadístico, 1958*, tables 178–85 (pp. 286–95).

produce and fabricate iron and steel in the area. The group expects
to keep up the rapid advance which has marked the major countries
of Latin America except Chile in recent years. This progress, as well
as Mexico's position among its Latin American colleagues, is shown
in the following table.

TABLE 69

Latin American Production of Iron and Steel, 1956 and 1958

('000 metric tons)

	Pig-iron Ingots		Steel Ingots		Finished Steel	
	1956	*1958*	*1956*	*1958*	*1956*	*1958*
Argentina	35	34	203	230	631	850
Brazil	1,152	1,300	1,375	1,600	1,142	1,300
Chile...	367	303	381	349	276	232
Colombia	116	147	100	143	81	119
MEXICO	408	501	888	1,103	710	930
Others	—	60	48	78	75	95
Latin America ...	2,078	2,345	2,995	3,503	2,915	3,526

Source: 'Panorama y perspectivas de la industria siderúrgica en América Latina',
BNCE, *Comercio exterior*, x (Feb. 1960), 20–23.

Mexico was the first Latin American country to install a modern
integrated iron and steel plant, the Monterrey Iron and Steel Works,
which began producing in 1903. Until 1945 it was the only producer
of pig-iron in the country. In 1951 Altos Hornos, at Monclova,
began large-scale production. Later other smaller plants were added,
of which La Consolidada was the third largest.

Early in 1960 the Director of Altos Hornos announced that it had
absorbed La Consolidada; the new company has increased its
capital from 175 million to 300 million pesos, with reinvestment
reserves of 75 million pesos. In 1958 Altos Hornos had produced
358,000 metric tons of steel, and La Consolidada 151,000; comparable 1959 figures were 415,000 and 180,000 respectively. The new
company is expected to produce 600,000 metric tons in 1960, and a
million by 1963. From the Mexican point of view, equally important
was the added note: 'The principal steel companies of the country
are now Mexican property'.[1]

[1] 'Altos Hornos Takes Over La Consolidada', BNCE, *Comercio exterior*, vi, 11.
La Consolidada was foreign-owned, in part.

Mexico, 1940–1960

For many years Mexico's imports of basic steel outstripped national production. From 1925–9, for instance, local production hovered around 67,000 metric tons, with imports of 107,000 tons. Since the Second World War, production has risen sharply; imports have risen too, but the latter has precipitously fallen in relation to national output. In 1951, for example, Mexico consumed 737,000 tons of steel, of which 364,000 were imported.[1] In 1958 the production by Mexican plants was 988,378 tons of steel; an importation of an additional 107,445 tons brought the total Mexican consumption to about 1·1 million tons. By 1963 the industry expects to produce annually 2·0 million tons.[2] The expanded output of the iron and steel industry for selected years is shown in the following table.

TABLE 70

Mexican Production of Pig-Iron, Steel, and Fabricated Steel, 1939–58

| | ('000 metric tons) | | Per cent. of 1950 | |
	Pig-iron	Steel	Pig-iron	Steel
1939 ...	99·2	142·2	42·5	36·5
1946 ...	240·3	257·9	105·4	65·0
1950 ...	227·4	390·1	100·0	100·0
1954 ...	261·4	525·0	115·0	148·0
1958 ...	459·1	988·4	218·2	252·1

Sources: USBFC, *Investment in Mexico*, p. 168; *Revista de estadística*, xxiii, 191 [1958]; percentages by author.

The principal mills make a wide variety of products, with smaller plants tending towards specialization. La Consolidada, for instance, makes more than 35,000 sizes and shapes of items, upward from nuts and bolts to structural steel. Nearly all make tubes and pipes, and a great number of other humble but essential objects like wire, nails, and tinplate, taken for granted in a modern economy but long imported by Mexicans. In certain specialities, such as tubular materials, domestic needs are now covered by national production, but as manufacturing as a whole expands, new needs and markets appear.

[1] USDC, *Investment in Mexico*, p. 168.

[2] 'Producción industrial: Siderúrgia, 1958', *Revista de estadística*, xxiii (Mar.–Apr. 1959), 191; DGE, *Compendio estadístico, 19:8*, table 256 (p. 389, imports, 'Hierro o acero en lingotes etc.'); 'Panorama y perspectivas de la industria siderúrgica en América Latina', p. 22. Tons are metric.

A number of manufacturing enterprises use steel, whether nationally or foreign-produced. Metal furniture, razor blades, and household gadgets are examples. The development of a canning industry in turn has increased the need for containers, usually produced by speciality plants. Closely allied are numerous assembly plants for motor cars, refrigerators, motors, and the like, which utilize prefabricated parts, supplemented by others of domestic manufacture. This mixture appears in the production of railway freight cars at a factory at Irolo, Hidalgo, originally subsidized by NF; highly specialized parts are imported, but plate and structural work come from Mexican producers.

We can observe some major features of the iron and steel industry, reflected in the summary statistics reported in the most recent compendium issued by the Ministry of Industry and Economy. It indicates that this expanding industry not only supplies a highly important set of products but is a vital element to the economy through its own purchase of raw materials, payment of wages and salaries, and its other transactions.

TABLE 71

Principal Characteristics of the Iron and Steel Industry, 1955 and 1958

(*Values in '000 pesos*)

	1955	*1958*
Number of establishments	24	27
Number of employees	2,221	2,924
Number of labourers	13,572	16,893
Salaries paid	44,063	71,336
Wages paid	121,481	178,029
VALUE OF PRIME MATERIALS USED		
Prime process: pig-iron	113,205	199,780
Second process: steel...	355,447	695,715
Third process: fabrication	564,943	1,101,159
Other	211,777	377,034
VALUE OF PRODUCTION		
Prime process: pig-iron	165,690	230,974
Second process: steel	551,686	939,914
Third process: fabrication	932,909	1,634,897

Source: DGE, *Compendio estadístico, 1958*, table 177 (pp. 285–6).

However much they differ on other matters, economists and historians seem to agree that the differences between 'advanced' and 'less advanced' countries are complicated in detail, but that 'the core of mechanization and national power is a "coal-iron complex" which can produce large quantities of steel'. While it now seems that Mexico's manufacture of this essential resource is insufficient even to meet domestic needs, the increased output is in itself a major and significant index of Mexico's climb from its earlier 'semi-colonial' economic status.[1]

POLICIES, 1959

In his oft-quoted State of the Nation Address of 1 September 1959, President López Mateos had some important comments to make on Mexico's industrialization: 'It is not the purpose to industrialize at all costs, but in the measure benefiting our general economy. . . . Special efforts are being made to avoid implication of an onerous burden for the Mexican people through the process of industrialization.'

Translated into fact, this meant that Mexican manufacturers could no longer look to the Government for preferential tariff treatment for products priced far above world prices; he reported that his Government had already vetoed several such proposals, as throwing too great a burden on national consumers. President López Mateos indicated that, like his predecessors of the Institutional Revolution, his actions would be

directed to the support of private enterprise tending to fortify the development of national industry, to stimulate creation of new industrial enterprises, to attain better use of financial resources, technicians and materials used in industry, and to expand the internal and external market of industrial goods of national production.[2]

[1] Marvin D. Bernstein, 'Foreign Investments and Mineral Resources; a Few Observations', *Inter American Economic Affairs*, xiii (Winter 1959), 42.
[2] López Mateos, 'First State of Union Address'.

MEXICO ON THE WORLD SCENE

Chapter XXXI

MEXICO:
INTERNATIONAL ECONOMIC PARTNER

THE economic boom which is transforming Mexico has also augmented its international economic transactions. Foreign trade has risen, and with it has come an impressive increase in balance-of-payment activities. Long significant in international economics, Mexico has recently strengthened a position it has held since the early sixteenth century.

FOREIGN TRADE

Mexico has a brisk foreign trade as an exporter of items useful to the world economy and as an importer of others which it has not or cannot produce nationally. Table 72 surveys the growth of foreign trade, both in volume and value.

TABLE 72

Foreign Trade: Imports and Exports, 1940–58
(Values in million pesos; volume in '000 metric tons)

	IMPORTS		EXPORTS		TOTAL TRADE	
	Volume	Value	Volume	Value	Volume	Value
1940 ...	844·6	699·0	4,083·4	960·0	4,928·0	1,629·0
1945 ...	1,973·6	1,604·4	2,983·1	1,271·9	4,956·7	2,876·3
1950 ...	2,319·0	4,403·4	5,291·0	4,339·4	7,610·0	8,742·8
1958 ...	5,398·6	14,107·5	7,953·1	8,846·1	13,351·7	22,953·6

Source: DGE, *Compendio estadístico, 1958,* tables 247, 264 (pp. 370–404), combined by author for total trade.

Figures for January–October 1959 indicate a volume and value comparable with 1958. Underlying factors seem to assure a continuation of the Mexican role as an international trader of some consequence.

Composition of Trade

Import patterns have been changing as the economy has developed. Capital goods have risen to prime importance, amounting

Mexico, 1940-1960

annually to more than 40 per cent. of the total. Raw and semipro-cessed materials come next, running at about 30 per cent. Consumer goods of all sorts run a poor third, about 18 per cent., emphasizing the relatively small proportion of finished manufactures imported. The list of commodities, ranging from hay to books, nails to pianos, antibiotics to aeroplanes, fills seven finely printed pages in the annual statistical summary for 1958, counting only those whose value ran above a million pesos.[1] As we have seen, it is national economic policy to eliminate, so far as possible, imports of food which can be produced in Mexico, and to develop manufacturing towards self-sufficiency, where feasible. Thus Mexican planners and investors scan these import figures with a constant eye for those items which the Mexican economy should make itself.

Exports are as diversified as imports, and like them, the relative importance of different groups has changed greatly. In Díaz's time, for instance, minerals comprised 62 per cent. of exports, with vegetable, animal, and forest products providing the remainder. By

TABLE 73

Exports, by Tariff Classifications, 1958

(*Value in million pesos*)

Tariff Section Categories	*Value*	*Per cent. by tariff sections*	*Per cent. of spec.*
Raw materials	3,314·9	37·47	46·8
Comestibles	2,408·4	27·23	34·1
Manufactured items, by materials	474·7	5·37	6·8
Combustibles, mineral lubricants	376·0	4·25	5·4
Chemical products	221·4	2·50	3·2
Machinery and steel products	138·6	1·57	1·9
Miscellaneous manufactured items ...	91·4	1·03	1·3
Vegetable oils	28·2	0·32	0·3
Arms, munitions, other	11·2	0·13	0·1
Tobacco and beverages	8·3	0·09	..
Specified, by tariff categories	7,073·1	79·96	100·0
Value added by customs valuation... ...	1,773·0	20·04	
Total export value	8,846·1	100·00	

Source: DGE, *Compendio estadístico, 1958,* table 269, p. 409; per cent. of specified calculated by author. Other percentages in source.

[1] DGE, *Compendio estadístico, 1958,* table 256, pp. 386–92.

1950 agricultural products amounted to 55·4 per cent., minerals to 35 per cent., and manufactures to 10·2 per cent.[1] While not wholly satisfactory, a summary of the comparative values of various categories of exports, arranged by new tariff classifications of 1 January 1958, provide some view of the recent composition of items which Mexico sold abroad. Rearranged slightly in Table 73, this table indicates that about half of Mexico's exports (by value) are raw materials, with perhaps a third special agricultural products, and the remainder semi-processed and manufactured items.[2]

Direction of Trade

Mexican foreign trade is largely, though not exclusively, with the United States. They have been principal trading partners for nearly a century, and more especially after they were linked by rail in 1888. For a considerable period, the United States has been the market for about three-quarters of Mexican exports, and in return, has furnished Mexico with around three-quarters to four-fifths of its imports. The remainder of the trade is subdivided among ninety-two other countries and dependencies. Appendix Table XVIII lists Mexico's principal trading partners. The direction of trade is immediately obvious. More than 90 per cent. of exports go to North America and Europe, which in turn supply nearly 97 per cent. of Mexican import needs.

The bulk of Mexico's North American trade is actually with the United States; trade with Canada is small. From Mexico go metals, raw cotton, coffee, cattle, vegetables, henequen, and some sugar. From the United States comes nearly the whole range of manufactured items, but more especially non-ferrous raw materials, specialized machinery, railway equipment, motor vehicle parts. Canada furnishes newsprint, among several other minor items.[3]

Before the Second World War, Europe had a larger market in Mexico than at present; slowly these countries seem to be regaining lost ground. The composition of trade is much like that with the United States, on a reduced scale. Notable perhaps is the obviously small success which the Soviet Union and Iron Curtain countries have had in attempting to woo Mexican trade.[4] Such small interchange as exists between the Soviet bloc and Latin America is

[1] USBFC, *Investment in Mexico*, pp. 101–2.
[2] Int. Economic Consultants, Inc., *U.S.-Latin American Relations: Commodity Problems in Latin America* (1959), pp. 86–87.
[3] USBFC, *Investment in Mexico*, p. 104.
[4] Robert L. Allen, *Soviet influence in Latin America* (1959).

confined to four countries, most in South America. Mexicans have noted some of the difficulties of trading with the satellites and Moscow.[1]

Mexican trade with its Latin American neighbours is slight, as it is with the Orient. The long visit which President López Mateos made to six countries of South America in January–February 1960, to discuss closer bilateral economic relations and problems of the Latin American common market, was undoubtedly a political triumph, but, given the present profile of relationships, not likely to have very much real impact in the near future. Mexican intentions of participating actively in the reciprocal regional trade arrangements being developed among South American nations was signalized on that trip when President López Mateos signed a treaty in Buenos Aires joining Mexico to the Free Zone (common market) already formed among them.[2]

Japan has recovered since the Second World War to re-enter the Mexican trade picture in a small way. Imports from Oceania are largely rubber, which the government now hopes to grow in Mexico.

Trends and Balances

Up to 1941 Mexico had a long history of favourable balance of trade, going back seventy-five years. It is now a net importer of goods, balancing its books by 'invisible' exports (see facing page). As its own economy begins to produce capital goods, its present reliance on such imports will undoubtedly decrease. There is some expectancy that its manufactured goods will continue to mount as export items along with the minerals and agricultural crops noted earlier: cotton, wheat, coffee, henequen, even a small amount of maize.

Mexico remains the second largest customer in Latin America for United States exports, eighth in the world. It is usually second or third among Latin American sources of United States imports, and about fifth or sixth on a world basis. Recent figures indicate that this established general trend is fairly constant.[3]

Increases in trade, its diversification, and global extension all

[1] 'Latin American Trade with Communist Countries', BNCE, *Comercio exterior*, vi (Jan. 1960), 5–7.

[2] 'La Gira presidencial y el ingreso de México en la Zona de Libre Comercio', ibid., x (Jan. 1960), 2–3.

[3] 'Trade of the United States with Latin America: Years 1956–58 and Half-Years January 1958–June 1959', USBFC, WTIS, *Statistical Reports*, pt. 3, no. 59–35 (1959); see also statistics, back covers, BNCE, *Comercio exterior*, vi (Feb. 1960), Jan.–Oct. 1959 data.

point to the continued and increasing importance of Mexico in the world of international trade. Recent changes in composition are further evidence that the country is moving from its earlier 'semi-colonial' economic status.

BALANCES OF PAYMENT

At a glance it would seem that Mexico should be in debt to a great part of the world, for seemingly it buys more than it sells. Fortunately it has invisible or non-trade items which help it to balance the international books. Included in them are tourist expenditures, long-term capital movements (direct private investment, reinvestment earnings, public loans), and remittances from Mexican workers in the United States. For Mexico these non-trade items are relatively more important in balances of payment than in most other Latin American countries.[1] Normally they offset the excess of imports over exports.

In 1957 and 1958, for the first time in some years, deficits occurred. These were paid from reserves in the Bank of Mexico, derived from internal sources, as distinct from international ones. Figures for 1959 indicated that once again Mexico was in the black. As balance-of-payment statements are somewhat lengthy statistical tables, we are summarizing selected ones in Appendix Table XIX. Table 74 gives the net balances for recent years showing how much Mexico has gained or lost in total international economic transactions during that year.

TABLE 74

Summary, Net Annual Balances-of-Payments, 1953–9

(*$ million*)

	Positive Balance	*Deficit*
1953	27·58	
1954	41·70	
1955	116·25	
1956	8·39	
1957		27·77
1958		85·13
1959 (Jan.-Sept.)	20·86	

Sources: DGE, *Compendio estadístico, 1955,* table 302 (p. 373); *1958,* table 289 (p. 438); BNCE, *Comercio exterior,* vi (Jan. 1960), 'Statistical Reports'.

[1] USBFC, *Investment in Mexico,* p. 106.

In general, then, it can be said that the growing Mexican economy, reflected in a sharp rise of international trade, has increased the number, amount, and kinds of balances of payments (Appendix Table XIX). Invisible, or non-trade, items normally offset the unfavourable commodity balance. Peculiar to Mexico among Latin American nations are dollars obtained from border and tourist transactions, and remittances from Mexican contract labour.

TOURISM

Most travellers find Mexico enchanting, but until recent years the converse was not necessarily true. The Institutional Revolution, among its many other changes in outlook, has purposely attempted to provide attractions and accommodations making travel to and in Mexico simple and delightful. It is good business. Investments in hotels, as well as schools to improve tourist services, and the many related activities all pay national dividends, in goodwill and money.

The importance of the tourist dollar may be measured by the fact that in 1958 it outranked mining, petroleum, construction, or transport, so far as revenue and contribution to gross national product: its 6,994 million pesos ranked fourth as an economic activity, after agriculture, manufacturing, commerce, and services.

Most tourists come from the United States, in waves of more than half a million annually. Their numbers become more impressive each year. The following table summarizes them.

TABLE 75

Tourism, 1936–58

(*'ooo persons*)

				Total foreigners entering Mexico	Total tourists from U.S.A.
1936	...	...	...	134·4	107·2
1940	...	...	...	182·7	139·6
1945	...	...	...	207·8	165·9
1953	...	...	...	504·1	424·1
1955	...	...	...	636·9	532·8
1958	...	...	...	795·8	657·6

Sources: DBE, *Anuario estadístico, 1943–45*, tables 63, 64 (p. 141); DGE, *Compendio estadístico, 1955*, tables 48, 52 (pp. 70–74); *1958*, tables 45, 53 (pp. 88, 99–100).

Daily traffic is constant across the northern border, where many towns and cities are situated, part in Mexico, part in the United States. Statistically these frontier transactions are included with tourist expenditures. Their joint contribution to balance of payments is herewith summarized.

TABLE 76

Tourism, Frontier Transactions, and Bracero Remittances, 1953–8

($ *million*)

	Tourism/Frontier		Bracero remittances	
	Amount	Per cent. total Income	Amount	Per cent. total Income
1953	313·6	31·0	33·7	3·3
1954	342·6	32·3	27·9	2·6
1955	349·9	27·5	25·0	1·9
1956	508·2	36·2	37·8	2·7
1957	591·5	42·1	33·2	2·4
1958	559·6	40·3	35·7	2·5
1959 (9 mos.) ...	480·6	45·0	22·2	2·0

Sources: DGE, *Compendio estadístico, 1955*, table 302 (p. 373); *1956–7*, table 325 (p. 461); *1958*, table 289 (p. 437); BNCE, *Comercio exterior*, vi (Jan. 1960), Statistical Reports.

In view of the importance of tourism, it is not surprising to find President López Mateos indicating continued government encouragement of the industry. One of his early moves raised the Bureau of Tourism to sub-Cabinet status, with a mandate to improve the 'promotion of this activity of cultural and economic benefit to the country'. In his 1959 State of the Union Address he stated that

In the field of tourism it is the intention of the Government to increase by modern methods the number of Mexican nationals and foreigners who, by visiting the various regions of the country, can better appraise the country, further the bonds of human understanding, improve individual and collective culture, and intensify the nation's economic movement.

A year later he reported that 536,644 foreign tourists had visited Mexico during that time; these, plus frontier transactions, had added 8,312 million pesos to national income, a 60 per cent. increase over 1958.

CONTRACT LABOUR: *BRACEROS*

A group of Mexicans known as *braceros* who contract to perform labour, usually agricultural, in the United States are an economic asset to each country. We have seen above that their remittances, in dollars, are a minor but constant element in Mexican balances of international payments. Even more significant is their symbolic status as a special group under protection of international agreements which guard their working conditions, welfare, and civil rights. On each side of the international border are groups who oppose continuance of the programme: organized labour in the United States, and nationalistic Mexicans who feel that their own economy can absorb these hands rather than having them go abroad as a sign that they cannot earn a living in Mexico.[1]

The present programme is an outgrowth of measures taken during the Second World War, when from 1942 Mexican hands contributed to the manpower shortage in the United States. They now work in the United States under supervision of the United States Department of Labor, authorized by Public Law 78 to maintain standards set in accord with international agreements.[2] This orderly programme, useful to both nations, should not be confused with the illegal migration of Mexicans to the United States, the 'wetbacks' whose plight has given rise to sympathetic treatment in novels.[3]

[1] Fred Eldridge, 'Helping Hands from Mexico', *Saturday Evening Post*, 10 Aug. 1957, pp. 28–29, 63–64; Paul K. Reed, 'Statement of the U.S. Section, Joint U.S.-Mexico Trade Union Committee . . . before the House Agriculture Sub-Committee, June 11, 1958' (mimeo., Washington, 1958).

[2] Cline, *U.S. and Mexico*, pp. 391–4. Ernesto Galarza, 'Trabajadores mexicanos en tierra extraña', *Problemas agrícolas e industriales de México*, x (Jan.–June 1958), 1–84, summarizes current working arrangements and bilateral accords.

[3] Luis Spota, *Murieron a mitad del río: novela* (Mexico, 1948); Carey McWilliams, *Ill Fares the Land* (1942), ch. 13, deals with a problem that now almost has disappeared.

Chapter XXXII

MEXICO AND ITS NEIGHBOURS

MEXICAN officials are well aware of Mexico's status as a small power in the arena of international affairs, and base their policies on that appreciation. Like other nations in the same category, Mexico must rely on moral rather than physical force to carry its points when these conflict with the views of other countries. Within these important limitations, however, Mexico plays a significant role in hemisphere, and to a much lesser extent, in world affairs.

President López Mateos in his campaign promised that under his direction, Mexico would take a more active interest and participate more widely in international affairs. In the first months of his régime, it has done so, led by the President himself. His extended visit to South America to discuss problems of a common Latin American market, and his general goodwill journeys to Canada as well as the United States are examples of his Government's broadening of Mexican foreign relations.

As part of this programme López Mateos, to dramatize the basic Mexican belief in the juridical equality of national states, in 1960 raised to the rank of embassies all Mexican diplomatic posts abroad, noting in his Second Annual Message that 'Mexico is probably the first country to adopt this policy'. Within his executive offices, he also established a new Bureau of Cultural Affairs to carry out the numerous obligations incurred by Mexico in signing various cultural and educational pacts. In September 1960 he reported that his Government had increased the number of countries with which Mexico maintains diplomatic relations and had striven to strengthen friendly relations throughout the world.

PRINCIPLES OF MEXICAN FOREIGN POLICY

The present general aims of Mexican foreign policy were also summarized by President López Mateos in his Second Message: to adhere strictly to a respect for the principles of international law, 'to promote moderation, cordiality, and tolerance and mutual understanding', as well as to foster beneficial collaboration, to uphold the dignity of man, and of freedom, independence, and equality of countries and 'the inalienable right of these to enjoy the benefits of peace in a world that must urgently reorganize itself to make justice and right a reality'. These are not new goals; with little variation they have been stated and reaffirmed by each succeeding President since Lázaro Cárdenas.[1] Even in techniques, the present administration so far has added little; the only difference has been in the increased emphasis López Mateos has placed on face-to-face meetings with other heads of states.[2] In general, then, the current Government is carrying forward with additional vigour principles and policies long accepted, without significant innovations or departures.

Paramount among cardinal principles which guide Mexican conduct in its relations with other countries, both directly on a bilateral basis, and collectively within multilateral international organizations, are non-intervention and self-determination of peoples. Unlike some of its fellow members in the inter-American community, Mexico construes non-intervention not only to include prohibition of a single outside state's meddling in the internal affairs of another country, but also collective action by a group of states. Mexico's own background during the nineteenth century and more especially during the militant phases of its own Revolution go far to explain its deep-seated tenacity to these dogma. Mexicans have a special sensitivity to their own and others' international actions which could be labelled intervention or the blocking of the legitimate aspirations of a people to modify their political, social, and economic conditions, by revolution if necessary. López Mateos called attention to this feeling when in his First Annual Message he stated, 'The principles of our foreign policy emanate from our historical experience. We were forced to defend our territory, our sovereignty, and our integrity.'

Mexico's geography, history, and size combine to align it with its Latin American neighbours, all of whom rank as small nations in the traditional classifications of international politics. Mexico has to

[1] SRE, *Las Relaciones internacionales de México, 1935–56, a través de los mensajes presidenciales* (1957) and *La Política internacional de México, 1952–6* (1957). There is no standard diplomatic history of Mexico, nor balanced coverage of recent policies. But see Blanksten, 'Foreign Policy of Mexico', in Macridis, ed., *Foreign Policy in World Politics*, pp. 323–50; Cline, 'Current Mexican Foreign Policy and U.S. Relations', *Orbis* (1961, in press).

[2] Second Message (1 Sept. 1960), citing his conferences with Presidents Eisenhower (U.S.), Betancourt (Venezuela), Kubitscheck (Brazil), Frondizi (Argentina), Alessandri (Chile), Prado (Peru), and Prime Minister Diefenbaker (Canada). On an otherwise clear desk, López Mateos has framed photographs of Presidents Eisenhower and Gamal Abdel Nasser (U.A.R.).

defend no strategic or economic stakes outside its own borders. With much of the world, it lacks the means as well as the urge to develop atomic weapons. During most of its national life, Mexico has been on the defensive, seeking to preserve its political and economic independence against external influences and forces that Mexican leaders felt would limit national self-determination. As Mexico has gained strength and stature through successes of its Revolution, many of the over-exaggerated fears that were a legacy of the past have waned, and with them xenophobia has abated. But the non-aggressive tendencies that accompanied this defensive outlook remain as an important heritage behind Mexican views of international affairs.

The convergence of national with regional traditions, joined by attitudes common to smaller nations, accounts in large part for the Mexican emphasis on juridical rather than political solutions to conflicts. Within the general hope for world peace that is essential to all countries, but particularly so to smaller ones which can do but little to decide the issues over which great Powers clash, the Mexicans urge an international programme in which law alone would be used to solve international disputes. Mexico also shares with its Latin American colleagues of the Western Hemisphere and with newly emerging nations of Asia and Africa a firm conviction that non-political, international means must be found to increase domestic rates of economic and social advance.[1]

Until very recently the concern of Mexicans over their own domestic problems far outweighed any widespread interest in external affairs. Budgets for the Ministry of Foreign Relations reflect that attitude. Seldom do they exceed 2 per cent. of the total (Appendix Table XIII). Newspapers generally carry scant amounts of foreign news, perhaps with the exception of happenings in Washington. Outside of official circles there has been little public discussion or debate on issues of foreign policy, nor do they generally form principal themes of political campaigns. The persistence of strongly nationalistic sentiments even in routine matters of foreign relations was strikingly attested by President López Mateos's remarks on his return from the United States and Canada in October 1959.

Alighting from the plane, his first duty was to reassure the welcoming crowd that he had not sold Mexico out. He reviewed briefly the principles he had maintained during his visit; these he termed the fixed and rigid positions of the Revolution, which every President must now defend: 'No relations with Franco. No label of Communism for peoples seeking their own internal recovery. Only

[1] Jorge Castañeda, *Mexico and the United Nations* (1958), pp. 2–11.

Mexico can fix the direction and import of any foreign investment. As to oil, which belongs to the nation, only the people of Mexico, solely the people of Mexico, can exploit it.'[1]

But in 1960 the President voiced a view that is widely held by a younger generation of Mexican intellectuals and politicians. In commenting upon the first fifty years of the Mexican Revolution, he pointed out that quite properly the country had previously been primarily concerned with reconstruction of its own life and society, but having succeeded, should now widen its horizons. He indicated that Mexico must be prepared to share more fully in plans for mutual aid and development, especially of nations recently emerged from colonialism and the lesser developed ones within the American community. He gave his own opinion that such programmes should give first priority to the improvement of rural populations, but that in nearly all social and economic matters 'We have something to give and something to receive: experience, techniques, finances.'

BILATERAL RELATIONS

With no investments abroad to guard and with no hegemony outside its own boundaries to defend, Mexico's direct dealings with other countries tend to be of a routine deplomatic nature. Its Foreign Office sends as Ambassadors to many world capitals distinguished Mexican intellectuals, or career foreign service officers of high calibre. The Minister of Foreign Relations is often selected from the latter, as was the case with Manuel Tello, who assumed that post under President López Mateos.

For practical purposes, Mexico's most important and extensive relations are with countries near it: Guatemala, the United States, and Cuba. After Washington the intensity and number drop off almost in direct ratio to the distance of the other capitals from Mexico City. Spain, with which a number of Latin American nations maintain a warm though often politically meaningless connexion, is one of the few European countries with which Mexico has no formal diplomatic ties; from the time of President Cárdenas, Mexico has recognized only the Republic of Spain, the seat of whose Government in exile is Mexico City.

From time to time the Mexican Government dispatches special trade or cultural missions to supplement its normal representation in a given country or area. In return, the Mexican capital is increasingly the locale of various international meetings of economic,

---

[1] PRI, *The Voice of Mexico in the United States and Canada: Speeches by Adolfo López Mateos* (Mexico, 1959), pp. 77–78 [19 Oct. 1959].

scientific, and cultural bodies, both official and non-governmental. But, broadly speaking, professionals in the Ministry of Foreign Relations devote a considerable amount of their time and energy to scanning developments in neighbouring countries.

Guatemala

Although Mexico's relations with its northern neighbour, the United States, are vastly more important and complex, those with Guatemala perhaps give clearer insight into Mexican foreign policy in action. The most serious diplomatic crisis of President López Mateos's short tenure has involved Mexico's southern boundary partner. To Guatemala, Mexico is not a 'small power', but a very large one; Mexico's preponderant area, population, advanced economy, and military potential loom large when viewed through Guatemalan eyes. Relations between the countries have a long, varied, often colourful history; many Guatemalans still believe that part of the present Republic of Mexico historically and unjustly was taken from them.[1]

On 28 December 1958, less than a month after President López Mateos was inaugurated (1 December 1958), Guatemalan air force planes attacked five Mexican fishing vessels as 'pirates' illegally within Guatemalan territorial waters, a claim denied by the Mexicans. The Guatemalan planes killed 3 Mexicans, wounded 16 others, and destroyed 2 of the vessels. After quick outbursts of anger in the Mexican press, the new régime calmed popular feelings and suggested to Guatemala that the matter be adjudicated by the International Court, each side to agree in advance to abide by its decisions. When Guatemala refused this solution, Mexico broke off diplomatic relations on 23 January 1959, turning its affairs there over to Brazil.

On 1 September 1959 President López Mateos reported the episode at length in his Message to Congress. He stated that the position of his administration was to uphold Mexican honour, but to seek a solution that would not humiliate Guatemala, a resolution compatible with the dignity of both Governments. A year later to the same Congress he could relate a success.

Probably because it would put Mexico in a poor light for him to visit the United States and Canada in October 1959 with his southern fences unmended, President López Mateos early in September 1959 accepted offers by Chile and Brazil to use their good offices in

[1] There is no adequate account of Guatemalan diplomatic history, much less studies of Mexican-Guatemalan relations.

re-establishing relations with Guatemala. An accord was rather quickly worked out and simultaneously published in each country on 15 September, renewing without prejudice their diplomatic intercourse. 'Victory for peace between peoples and harmony among nations!' announced López Mateos at the time and again in his Message of 1 September 1960.

The United States

A key feature in the foreign policies of both Mexico and the United States is their maintenance of close, cordial, and friendly bilateral relations. This 'Era of Good Feeling' dates from 1938 when the firm but sympathetic handling by the administration of Franklin D. Roosevelt of the issues caused by President Cárdenas's expropriation of the foreign-owned petroleum industry in that year made clear to Mexicans that many of the shibboleths that had been obstacles to real mutual understanding no longer had any real basis. Accord between the Presidents laid the foundation for a series of formal agreements in early 1941 which settled nearly all outstanding diplomatic problems between the neighbouring countries.[1] In the ensuing two decades, through the administrations of Presidents Truman and Eisenhower and of Presidents Avila Camacho, Alemán, Ruíz Cortines, and López Mateos, this original rapprochement has been cumulatively strengthened; in the twenty-year period, despite natural differences of view on particular matters, there has not been a serious ripple to mar the general placidity, no tension-building episodes to inflame public opinion.

The ebb of anxiety in Mexico since 1941 concerning the designs of the United States on its territory or independence—political and economic—is a fact. Gilberto Loyo summarized the views of a majority of responsible Mexican officials and intellectuals when he said recently that because of earlier history, 'Mexico has distrusted all foreign interests or powers that could be a threat in this respect.' He adds, 'But after World War II we lost this fear. We no longer worry about there being any serious possibility of being politically conquered by any outside power.'[2] Nor is the threat of economic conquest any greater, so long as the present vigilance is maintained over the flow of foreign capital into national enterprises under conditions set by the Mexican Government. Thus it was more than polite rhetoric when President López Mateos on the occasion of his

[1] Cline, *U.S. and Mexico*, pp. 234–51; much new detail in Cronon, *Josephus Daniels*, ch. 10.

[2] Gilberto Loyo, 'Profile of Mexico Today', *Mexico This Month*, iv (Sept. 1960), 23.

visit to the White House reaffirmed the current view of his régime and countrymen by stating that 'the Mexican people have forged a mentality that welcomes cultivation of peaceful relations with other peoples of the world, particularly with respect to the United States'. He was echoing sentiments expressed in the final Message of President Ruíz Cortines (1958), who had taken special note that Mexican-U.S. relations were especially friendly, thanks in large part to the efforts of the United States which took all occasions to 'demonstrate a spirit of cordial co-operation on all matters of common interest and reciprocal concern'.

López Mateos quite correctly noted that 'in this new era of mutual respect and growing reciprocal understanding' there existed a real friendship. For some time, he said, relations have been 'free of onerous distrust and bitterness of the past', without secret or limiting compromises at the present, and providing an atmosphere to plan mutually satisfying and beneficial arrangements for the future.[1]

A glance at the record substantiates these generalizations. From the occasion of the personal meeting of Presidents Roosevelt and Avila Camacho to discuss mutual co-operation for the Second World War, an institutionalized ritual has been established wherein the new President of either country, Mexico or the United States, is invited to the other, partly as a symbolic affirmation of continuing cordiality and willingness to let by-gones be by-gones, partly to clear up any potential difficulties before they become serious. The decisions and agreements reached at these 'little summits' cover a wide range, from plans for co-operative development of hydro-electric and irrigation projects along the Río Grande, to problems of credit, commodity prices, scientific co-operation in public health, malaria control, narcotics controls, migrant labour. From these visits have often come unexpected small gestures that reveal the sincere attempts by leaders of each country to remove barriers to understanding and bury the past: President Truman's spontaneous placing of a wreath on the monument to the Boy Heroes (Cadets in the war of 1848 who wrapped themselves in Mexican flags and leaped to their deaths rather than surrender Mexico City) evoked an almost hysterical wave of favourable public emotion in Mexico; mutual return of captured battle flags, and the Mexican Government's generous offer of fellowships to North American students have all come as by-products of the presidential conferences.

Possibly as important are the numerous non-official programmes

[1] PRI, *Voice of Mexico*, p. 12.

in almost every field fostering co-operation through mixed Mexican-North American bodies. Business men, librarians, scientists, school and university students, religious organizations, labour unions, lawyers, journalists, baseball players, in fact almost every interest, tends to have more or less elaborate and continuing projects aimed at increasing personal contacts between the peoples of each country and promoting mutual understanding and friendship. Much as the two Governments attempted to signalize the new era of good feeling by reciprocal restoration of war trophies, so recently Peabody Museum at Harvard University returned to Mexican custody the the ancient Maya jewels recovered from the Cenote at Chichen Itzá, a bone of contention since the Mexican Supreme Court in 1923 found in favour of the North American institution. 'No contemporary gesture of good will on the part of Americans has been more widely acclaimed in Mexico', wrote a reporter, 'except for the good will shown President Adolfo López Mateos when he toured the United Sates last fall as the guest of President Eisenhower.'[1]

It must also be noted that some Mexican critics, ranging from irresponsible doctrinaires to serious and patriotic intellectuals, still have reservations about the United States and its Mexican policies and the official Mexican responses to them. Among the professional Left, even the simplest actions (or lack of them) by the United States are automatically interpreted as 'imperialist' designs or tricks, to which vocal opposition is requisite. More significant, in intellectual circles there is a strong current which appears in writings and teachings that emphasizes the need for Mexicans to roll back the malign influence the United States is even inadvertently having on traditional Mexican and Latin American cultural values, substituting for them the trappings of a materialistic 'Coca Cola' civilization. In similar vein, many of the same writers seek a counterpoise to the economic hegemony of the United States by proposing various Latin American blocs, even reorganizing hemispheric bodies to omit 'Anglo America'.[2] And even today, after twenty years of the 'Era of Good Feeling', Mexican officials must be very circumspect in their praise of any action by the United States lest they be accused of 'Malinchismo'—delivering Mexico to the 'invader'.[3]

[1] Gerry Robichaud, 'Mexico to Get Back Priceless Maya Find', *Washington Post-Times Herald*, 1 Feb. 1960.

[2] Isidro Fabela, *Buena y mala vecindad* (1958); Jorge Castañeda, 'Pan Americanism and Regionalism: a Mexican View', *Int. Organization*, x (Aug. 1956), 373–89.

[3] From 'Malinche', the Indian woman who acted as Cortés's interpreter and whose counsel allegedly helped him conquer Indian Mexico.

But where foreign policy is made and carried out by responsible Governments, at the executive level, there is every reason to believe that the course of the past two decades will continue into the future. The arrangements are based on the premises that Mexico is a free and responsible nation, long past the need for tutelage, and that the United States neither seeks nor needs special advantages or privileges in Mexico. The basis for the entente also assumes that there is quite a wide range of affairs that can be worked out to mutual benefit on a quiet, bilateral approach without clash of interests or even principles, in an atmosphere where compromises between divergent national points of view are possible and desirable.

After some of the regrettable experiences each people and Government have undergone at the hands of the other in the past, this current equilibrium is remarkable, not only for its proved workability but for its endurance. Within it, Mexico is free to assume its own positions on international questions, often in contradiction to those of the United States, without impairing the basic bilateral connexions. For reasons of national interest or local political sentiments, Mexico does not always choose to enter into programmes which the United States sponsors. Over many years since their last trade treaty expired (1950), there has been no formal agreement between the United States and Mexico on that matter. Likewise, Mexico has felt unwilling to sign military assistance pacts with its northern neighbour, and hence has had a very minimum amount of grant aid: its $3·5 million over the decade 1950–9 forms a small proportion of the Latin American total of $423·8 millions, or the global sum of $26,079 millions which the United States taxpayers have made available for protection of the Free World in that period. Again, despite lack of formal agreements, United States and Mexican military co-operation is on a wholly satisfactory footing.

It is of the utmost importance to remember that when directly facing one another as neighbours over the diplomatic bargaining tables, Mexico and the United States are long-standing friends. Divergences between the policies of each, even public positions, on matters of multilateral concern do not affect this basic circumstance. The clash of views over handling Cuban problems, which emerged in the Seventh Meeting of Foreign Ministers of August 1960 (discussed below), was in a quite different context, that of the inter-American family of nations. Here larger principles, prestige, and other considerations came into play to complicate diplomatic calculations. On most non-controversial matters of international concern the United States and Mexico stand together. But neither is automatically committed in advance necessarily to support the other on a divided or emotional issue.

To summarize, geography has given Mexico and the United States a peculiar and enduring relationship, making them neighbouring republics. During their common national histories, their attitudes and policies toward each other have run through a whole wide gamut, even including armed conflict.[1] From long empirical experience have come the present pragmatic arrangements, characterized during the past two decades by official and private determination to be and remain friends, on a basis of mutual understanding and respect. This concurrence is on a solid enough footing to permit to each differences of views, even of votes in international meetings, without precipitating crises in their bilateral relations.

[1] See above, Chs. II and III.

Chapter XXXIII

MEXICO
IN WORLD AND REGIONAL ORDER

WITHIN the various international organizations dedicated to the development of world and regional order, Mexico takes an interested part. The general policies guiding its bilateral relations also underlie its conduct within multilateral organizations, but in some instances the tactics and public utterances differ from those employed in dealing directly with its immediate neighbours. Mexico shares the feeling of other Latin American states determined to preserve the freedom of action of the New World regional body, the Organization of American States, within the larger United Nations structure. Relationships between the two—OAS and U.N.—are sometimes ambiguous on particular points; their fundamental concepts which are also divergent present countries like Mexico, members of both, with some anomalies.

The U.N., more recently established, reflects a view that the OAS has historically rejected. It divides nations into various categories, and assigns large powers permanent seats on the Security Council, whose veto can override actions often desired by the more numerous smaller powers. The premiss of the OAS, on the other hand, is the juridical and voting equality of states, a majority (11 votes) being decisive. In the OAS, for instance, Mexico and the United States are equal in responsibilities and privileges, but in the U.N. the latter as a large power is a permanent member of the Security Council, and Mexico as a small one is not. There are other comparable differences that affect the status and role of Mexico in the one and the other multilateral organization, but perhaps the total importance of them diminishes in face of the main consideration that in each Mexico has a slightly wider scope of action than in its bilateral relations with the United States.[1]

THE UNITED NATIONS

As a faithful and valiant partner in the coalition which defeated Axis powers in the Second World War, Mexico was a Charter

[1] Manuel Canyes, *The Organization of American States and the United Nations,* 3rd ed. (1955).

Member of the United Nations. Mexican scholars and officials gave much study to the problems of organizing a global organization for peace in the preliminary discussions which preceded the adoption of the Charter in 1945. But, as an able group of national analysts recently noted in presenting suggestions for improving U.N. mechanisms and charter, the Mexican public in general has been relatively ignorant and seemingly uninterested in U.N. problems.[1] Officials are not.

In United Nations circles, certain topics have interested Mexico more than others. These include collective security, colonialism, international protection of human rights, preservation of national sovereignty in face of claimed jurisdictions by international organizations, and relations between the OAS and the U.N. As might well be expected, the activities of the Educational, Scientific, and Cultural Organization (UNESCO) attract special Mexican attention. Jaime Torres Bodet, Minister of Education, was its first Secretary-General.

Within the United Nations, Mexico takes a leading role in an informal 'Group' which the Latin American states formed during the first General Assembly in London to pool their individually small strength but substantial block of votes. Initially a lobbying committee to insure the election to key positions of as many Latin Americans as possible, it has evolved into a discussion group, helpful for clarification of issues to small delegations with limited staff. As a pressure body it has often co-operated with other groups of smaller states, notably the Arab world.[2]

Mexico and Mexicans have held responsible positions within the U.N., and discharged their duties with competence, sometimes brilliance. In the initial years of the U.N. when the Cold War began to bipolarize the world, Mexico was a non-permanent member of the Security Council. In 1952 Luis Padilla Nervo was President of the Sixth General Assembly.

Support of the United Nations and its allied and derivative specialized organizations forms part of official Mexican foreign policy. In an address to the General Assembly in 1959, President López Mateos reaffirmed Mexico's long interest and co-operation, as well as his Government's faith in the United Nations, expressing Mexico's 'conviction, based on the analysis of international conditions, that it [U.N.] represents our only hope of surmounting the

---

[1] Castañeda, *Mexico and the U.N.*

[2] John A. Houston, *Latin America in the United Nations* (1956), pp. 6–7. Félix Manuel Maúrtua, 'El Grupo latino-americano en las Naciones Unidas y algunos problemas jurídicos', *Revista peruana de derecho internacional*, xvi (Jan.–June 1956), 10–43.

world crisis'.[1] His own Annual Reports of 1959 and 1960 provide many details of particular Mexican activities within the organization on matters of traditional interest: disarmament, peaceful use of atomic energy, problems of radio-active contamination, maritime rights, among others. He repeated the basic Mexican approach, that the present Government is determined to maintain 'a doctrine of mutual respect, co-operation, peace with justice, and non-intervention'. He added that 'international organizations have found Mexico loyally and faithfully fulfilling its obligations'.

THE ORGANIZATION OF AMERICAN STATES

While Mexico is a faithful participant in United Nations matters, its main multilateral relations come within the context of inter-American affairs, specifically the Organization of American States. In the hemisphere, Mexico has high prestige as an independent spokesman for the Latin American point of view, based primarily on the fact that it has shaken off most of the ills that beset its colleagues from time to time—dictatorships, foreign control of economics, even national politics—and has clearly, through its own Revolution, set the nation on the road to social and economic betterment. Throughout its own history, and that of the Pan American movement, Mexicans have furnished leadership and needed support for the hemispheric organization, under quite diverse and changing conditions.

Mexico has played host to plenary meetings, signed innumerable accords and agreements, including the Charter of the Organization of American States, which rearranged its ancient structure and renamed it at Bogotá in 1948. Mexico sponsors several of its specialized organs, faithfully sends excellent delegations to OAS-sponsored international consultations and conferences, and otherwise comports itself as a responsible and valued member.

That it will continue to do so was publicly affirmed by President López Mateos. Addressing the Council of the OAS on 12 October 1959, he pledged his nation's full adherence to the regional body, and suggested certain lines of action it might usefully follow to become more effective. The political apparatus, he felt, had evolved in a satisfactory fashion, indicating that no new or radical changes should be made in the basic Charter. He mentioned that collective action in the economic field had not kept pace, and directed attention to it. His salutary recommendation was that rather than

---

[1] 'Address . . . October 14, 1959', PRI, *Voice of Mexico*, pp. 41–47.

fomenting high-sounding resolutions on all topics and acting on none, OAS agencies should select two or three basic problems for extended common study and solution.[1]

To bring OAS achievements in the economic and social fields to the levels of those in the political and juridical spheres means, President López Mateos said that a solution must be found for problems shared widely: pressures from great demographic growth, scarcity of resources, low standards of living. His own presidential messages have taken up many of these same themes, noting with satisfaction that the Inter-American Development Bank, a favourite Mexican international project for the promotion of social programmes, was now becoming a reality. The final passages of his 1960 Message reiterate that much of the world, and especially Latin America, is undergoing rapid and basic changes, all of which call for reassessment of what an 'international community really is'. Their importance requires that search must continue for the principles, procedures, and institutions 'that will harmonize facts with ideals'.

It is Mexico's view, as expressed in the same Second Message, that the OAS 'has an exemplary statute: the Bogotá Charter'. With the supplementary conventions signed by the American community, it is the basis for an international system which will survive and be of value, so long as these commitments are strictly observed by the member states. He further noted the congruence of Mexico's own principles of international politics with those underlying the American state system: respect for the self-determination of peoples, no interference by one country in the internal affairs of others, acceptance of the idea that the resolution of all conflicts should be by peaceful and legal means, proper punishment of a country or government which wrongs other countries or governments.[2] It may be noted how closely these sentiments parallel the collective views of the group of Mexican analysts who in 1956 attempted to summarize the national concepts of the main principles of inter-American relations.[3]

Against this background of attitudes concerning Mexico's proper

---

[1] 'Address', PRI, *Voice of Mexico*, pp. 17–24.

[2] 'Second Message', *The News*, p. 13A.

[3] Castañeda, *Mexico and the U.N.*, pp. 173–4, listing 'the pacific settlement of disputes; the non-recognition of the validity of territorial conquest; various principles relating to the status of foreigners . . . ; non-intervention; the common aspiration of the American republics for representative democracy; and finally, the principle of joint defense against outside forces'. See the slightly variant statements in Castañeda, 'Pan Americanism and Regionalism', pp. 373–89.

actions in the inter-American system, we can briefly review its posture at some of the more recent and important hemispheric conferences. These have been consistent. On the most important issues, Mexico has followed its own long-held convictions about 'non-intervention', which in a majority of cases has placed it in opposition to the principal efforts of the United States.

RECENT INTER-AMERICAN CONFERENCES

With a long history, the inter-American system has evolved an intricate schedule of meetings on many topics. Two types are of special significance. One is the plenary Inter-American Conference, generally held at about five-year intervals since the First in 1889; in 1948 the Ninth convened in Bogotá, and adopted the present Charter, while in March 1954 the Tenth met in Caracas. The Eleventh, several times postponed, is scheduled for 1961 at Quito.[1] At these meetings major policies of the OAS are decided. For emergencies, a series of Consultative Conferences of Foreign Ministers has developed in recent years. The first ones, held before, during, and immediately following the Second World War, were followed by the fourth of the series called in the face of the Korean crisis (1951). After a lapse the series has resumed, devoting main attention to tensions in the Caribbean.

Of the several principal topics debated in the plenary meeting by the American Republics at the Tenth Conference in Caracas— European colonialism in the Western hemisphere, fishing rights, for example—the most significant and even disrupting concerned Communism in the Americas, and specifically its apparent foothold in Guatemala.[2] Mexico took the lead in opposing, then in modifying, the very strong resolution presented by the United States condemning Guatemala; Mexico did not favour Communism but did feel that self-determination was being threatened, and that collective intervention, even verbal, was repugnant, possibly opening the doors to worse abuses. Somewhat reluctantly its delegation signed the recommendations condemning extension of Communism in the New World. The final version differed markedly from the one the

[1] H. F. Cline, 'The Inter-American System', *Current History*, xxviii (Mar. 1955), 177–84. In July 1961 the Quito meeting was again deferred.

[2] *Acta Final*, Secretaría de la Décima Conferencia Interamericana (Caracas, 1954). For details see Philip B. Taylor, 'The Guatemalan Affair: a Critique of United States Foreign Policy', *Amer. Pol. Sci. R.*, L (Sept. 1956), 787–806, esp. pp. 790–92.

United States delegation, headed by its then Secretary of State, John Foster Dulles, had hoped to obtain.[1]

Unrest in the Caribbean, partly as a result of the successful 26th of July Movement in Cuba and its apparent hopes of extending more widely its 'Peoples' Revolution', was a main cause for the Fifth Consultative Conference of Foreign Ministers, which convened in Santiago, Chile, in 1959. Indirectly aimed at both the Dominican Republic, whose dictatorship had given haven to Juan Perón, the deposed *caudillo* of Argentina, and to Fulgencio Batista of Cuba, and at the new régime in Cuba, the Conference witnessed no wide divergences in views. But again Mexico stood firmly on its traditional position that non-intervention, whether collective or by one state, remained a keystone of inter-Americanism. Mexico signed the final documents, which reaffirmed continental solidarity against extra-continental interference in hemispheric affairs, reiterated the need for respect of human rights and the exercise of representative democracy, as well as the strict observance of the non-intervention principle. The Mexican delegation was also willing to strengthen the powers of the Inter-American Peace Commission, which is empowered to investigate alleged breaches that threaten hemispheric peace, provided these special emergency powers be reviewed at the next scheduled general plenary meeting of the OAS.

Events and activities in the Caribbean also brought forth two subsequent recent meetings for consultation among the Foreign Ministers. The Sixth was called by Venezuela to discuss acts of aggression by the Dominican Republic, and the Seventh was convoked by Peru to discuss ways of maintaining peace and harmony, chiefly in face of threats to domestic tranquillity of various Latin American states posed by the Cuban revolutionaries. These meetings were held consecutively in San José, Costa Rica during August 1960.

The Sixth Consultation met to consider charges and proof that Rafael Leonidas Trujillo plotted and had nearly succeeded in having the liberal President Rómulo Betancourt of Venezuela assassinated on 24 June 1960. The background of the event need not detain us here, but involved Trujillo's attempts to aid his fellow 'strong men' in maintaining or returning to power; Venezuelans, after revolting against Pérez Jiménez, had elected the democratic group headed by Betancourt. The assembly at Costa Rica quickly

[1] U.S. Dept. of State, *Report of the Delegation of the United States of America with related documents.* Publ. 5692 (1955). SRE, *México en la X Conferencia Interamericana* (Mexico, 1958).

accepted the facts gathered by an OAS investigating team, and collectively convicted Trujillo and his Government. The question then arose what to do about the situation.

All delegations agreed that the immediate embargo of arms and other implements of war was requisite. This, in effect, had already been done. The Conference empowered the OAS Council to declare further economic sanctions by adding other items to the prohibited list. Urged on by Venezuela's delegation, the Conference also recommended that member states should break off diplomatic relations with the Dominican Republic, thus isolating it diplomatically until it ceased to be a threat to continental peace and security, i.e. until Trujillo's system was overthrown.

Mexico, long opposed to nearly everything for which Trujillo stands, supported these measures, but took the lead in opposing an ill-advised, impromptu suggestion made by the United States Secretary of State Mr Christian Herter to end the dictatorship: that a special committee of the OAS, made up of two-thirds of the member states, should hold and supervise free elections to establish democracy. This would have given unprecedented authority to collective intervention, permitting any fourteen nations to enter directly into the internal political affairs of a presumably erring American state who fell below 'democratic' standards. Although the move was ostensibly aimed at Trujillo, whose thirty year-old régime retained little or no popularity among the other Latin American nations, it could also be applied to Cuba—or to any régime, including the United States. The public compromise—sanctions first, supervised elections second—became in closed sessions 'sanctions only', dropping the United States' suggestion. This omission was at the insistence of Venezuela and Mexico, voicing the almost universal sentiment of the Latin American community.

In reporting actions of the Mexicans at the Sixth Conference, President López Mateos in his September 1960 Message tactfully stated that Mexico had 'opposed other measures which could have been construed as interference by the Organization of American States in the internal affairs of the Dominican Republic'. He went on to say that in accordance with resolutions signed there, Mexico had broken diplomatic relations with the Dominican Republic on 21 August 1960. He attempted to distinguish between the Dominican Government and its people. Between the Mexican and Dominican peoples there existed, he said, 'unalterable friendship'. He felt confident that it would be possible for Mexico in the future 'to manifest our solidarity and affection' for the Dominican people, a distinction he also drew between the Cuban Government and its people, the topic of the Seventh Consultation.

The Seventh Consultation, which after a day's recess from the Sixth re-convened in San José, brought into sharp focus many of the current issues facing Mexico, the United States, and other states in the OAS. Perhaps the kernel of the matter is the nature of the Cuban 26th of July Movement. United States officials, on the basis of considerable evidence, concluded that whatever its original nature may have been, by late summer 1960 it had been infiltrated to the point that it had become a beach-head for international Communism that threatened to spread more widely throughout the Western Hemisphere. The Latin American view, never wholly unanimous, generally opposes Communism, but is sceptical that the Cuban movement is much more than a radical, but nationally-supported, social upheaval to put an end to political and economic abuses that have plagued Cuba since its relatively late achievement of independence at the end of the nineteenth century.

Governments such as those of Mexico and Venezuela, where undercurrents of sympathy for the Castro régime are especially strong among the politically potent Left, and whose main policies also point toward social and economic reforms demanded by their own successful revolutions, must tread with special care a path that is full of political booby-traps. They, together with Governments such as those of Panama, Bolivia, Ecuador, and Nicaragua, among others, must not appear subservient to the United States lest they sacrifice domestic political support. Yet they cannot be too vocal in defence of Cuba, not only because of its possible Communist associations, but also because in many cases the exported version of the 26th of July Movement is at the moment a chief danger to their own régimes. Its inflammatory propaganda and clandestine activities have already made significant inroads among Latin American masses everywhere. Even more than usual, the Castro problem has interwoven touchy domestic and international issues into a single fabric. We shall note its effects in Mexico in the following chapter.

This background helps explain why even preliminaries to the Seventh Consultation were fraught with difficulties. In July 1960 the OAS Council debated holding the meeting, proposed by Peru, to deal with problems of continental solidarity, defence of the regional system, and maintenance of democratic principles against external threats. Partly the move was aimed to keep Cuba from carrying regional issues into the United Nations, where its anti-United States charges mobilized iron curtain country support, a weakening of the

OAS repugnant to most of its members. In the OAS Council vote, all countries but Cuba itself, Venezuela, and Mexico supported the Peruvian proposal to call the reunion to consider the threat of Communism via Cuba. It then turned out that no capital was willing to sponsor the meeting, all fearful of inciting anti-United States and other demonstrations that might lead to another 'Bogotazo'—raging mobs that swirled around the Ninth Inter-American Conference in Bogotá (1948). Costa Rica finally extended the invitation.

In the meantime the Cuban Government issued repeated statements that the OAS was little more than a tool of Yankee imperialism. In Moscow, Premier Nikita Khrushchev claimed Cuba as a protectorate, and stated that the Monroe Doctrine (originally a United States unilateral declaration that became multilateral by the OAS Charter and the Rio Treaty of 1947) was long dead and should be buried 'so that it should not poison the air by its decay'.

Thus even before the meeting, the major issues were outlined. Mr. Herter came prepared to make it unmistakably clear that Cuba was a point from which international Communism was invading the Western Hemisphere, and urged the Foreign Ministers to join him in issuing a warning to Cuba that it could not continue its present course without sanctions. The Cuban delegation, headed by Raúl Roa, was determined to rally the Latin American nations to its side and forestall and defeat any such strong resolutions. The meetings themselves were a gruelling test of stamina, sessions grinding on day and night to achieve some formulas to bridge the wide gap among positions.

Under the skilful and seasoned leadership of Dr. Julio César Turbay Araya (Colombia) elected as President, the tone of the initial debates was set. He said that if the Consultation had been called merely to discuss a conflict between the United States and Cuba, there would be much reason for popular support for the Cuban revolutionaries, but that the meeting was treating a different matter, a conflict between Russia and America, between democracy and Communism, and in such a basic struggle no American nation had the right to remain neutral. Somewhat unexpectedly President Betancourt of Venezuela sent a message stating that it was his Government's belief that only duly elected Governments should form part of the inter-American system, an obvious rebuff of the Cuban 26th of July Movement.

In the preliminary statements of attitudes, Manuel Tello set forth the Mexican thesis that all revolutions, including its own, pass through trying days for themselves and neighbours. But even their excesses do not warrant collective meddling in the internal affairs of that country. He was recalling the attempted 1914–15 inter-American efforts to settle the apparent internal chaos of Mexico.[1] It turned out, said Tello, that 'the apparent anarchy [in Mexico] was really an immovable decision of a people to find the road to real redemption'. Above all, he felt, it was incumbent to retain Cuba within the inter-American community, and leave exclusively to the Cuban people the task of working out their own destiny. He did not want the Conference to give way to temporary impatience.

The two main speeches came on successive days. On 24 August, Mr. Herter presented a well-documented statement outlining the Sino-Soviet intentions in America and linking them to developments in Cuba. His main point was that any Communist-controlled régime in the Americas constituted foreign intervention that menaced hemispheric security, and that Cuba was to be censured for welcoming, even inviting and abetting such extra-continental meddling. The next day Raúl Roa launched into a two-hour rambling rebuttal, in a rather hostile atmosphere caused in part by Premier Castro's remarks on the previous evening in defiance of the United States: 'We are friends of the Soviet Union and of the Chinese People's Republic.' Roa harangued the delegates, blaming all the ills of Cuba and Latin America on the United States, calling for the countries of the hemisphere to declare a 'second independence' from that country. He reaffirmed the fact that Cuba would accept aid from the Sino-Soviet bloc.

Once the oratory from the floor had ceased, the practical problems began. One group of countries initially proposed a rather mild resolution deploring extra-continental intervention.[2] The other came to the support of the United States' request for a resolution specifically denouncing Russian and Chinese Communist intervention and condemning of Cuba for fostering it.[3] As negotiations proceeded, one by one the 'soft-line' group shifted, usually on cabled orders from their capitals which were becoming convinced that OAS failure at Costa Rica would do irreparable damage to the inter-American mechanisms.

Brazil, Mexico, Uruguay, and Colombia submitted a series of resolutions that preserved the main contentions of the 'hard line'

---

[1] Cline, *U.S. and Mexico*, pp. 160–2, gives details.

[2] Bolivia, Venezuela, Mexico, Panama, Peru, Honduras, Ecuador.

[3] Argentina, Chile, Brazil, Nicaragua, Guatemala, Uruguay, Paraguay, El Salvador, Colombia.

but were couched in sophisticated language that did not name Cuba specifically. It followed the general approach that Manuel Tello had earlier suggested: 'We must demonstrate an Americanist comprehension of a young revolutionary movement that has not yet defined its [real] goals and at the same time make Cuba see that the inter-American system will not admit intervention in the sovereignty and independence of any people.' The pro-Castro delegate from Venezuela would not accept even these compromises, and was removed from his post by his own President. On hearing unanimous approval of the first point of the final 'Declaration of San José', as the document produced there was named, the Cuban delegation stalked out, obviously having failed in its mission.

The 'Declaration' energetically condemned intervention, or the 'menace of intervention' by extra-continental powers, as being hostile to continental unity and perilous to the peace and security of the hemisphere. It affirmed the right of any people to the 'free and spontaneous' development of its own national life, respecting civil rights and human liberties. It repeated that no American state had the right to interfere in the affairs of another, imposing its own ideology, or social, economic, and political principles. The 'Declaration' reasserted that the inter-American system is incompatible with any form of totalitarianism, and that member states should seek democracy. It asserted that all member states should 'submit to the discipline of the inter-American system' and that the firmest guarantees of their national sovereignty and political independence lies in their absolute obedience to prescriptions of the Charter of Bogotá.

The document ended with a statement that all bilateral controversies should be resolved peacefully through the mechanisms provided by the inter-American system, faith in which was reaffirmed. To carry out the latter prescription the Meeting created a Conciliation Committee to be composed of 'personages of the highest level' from Brazil, Colombia, Chile, Costa Rica, Mexico, and Venezuela to see if the differences between Cuba and the United States could be resolved.

Reactions to the 'Declaration' were varied. Fidel's answer was to call a 'People's Assembly' where before a crowd of 300,000 he told his followers he was going to establish diplomatic relations with Red China. He brought forth roars of approval when he tore up a copy of the 'Declaration of Costa Rica'. Mr. Herter felt that the 'Declaration' was 'a clear indictment of the Castro Government of Cuba, and particularly the role which it played in furthering the

Sino-Soviet efforts into this hemisphere'. 'Neither victors nor vanquished' was the quotation attributed to Colombia's Turbay. For his Government, Señor Tello of Mexico issued a supplementary statement that the resolution 'in no form constitutes a condemnation or a threat against Cuba, whose aspirations for economic improvement and social justice have the strongest sympathy of the Government and people of Mexico'.[1]

President López Mateos, summarizing in his Second Message the Mexican participation in the Seventh Consultation, was pleased to say that the national delegation had upheld the traditional principles of Mexican foreign policy: non-intervention and the self-determination of peoples. He affirmed that Mexico would always oppose interference by non-continental powers in American affairs, as it does the meddling by one state within the inter-American system in affairs of another. He reported that 'the "San José Declaration" represents the maximum common accord that could be reached at the Conference after difficult and prolonged negotiations'. As in the case of the Dominican Republic, he added some remarks about the sympathy and affection which the Mexican people held for the Cuban, currently inspired by 'legitimate aspirations of political, social and economic improvement'. For reasons which we shall adduce in the following chapter, he did not draw as sharp a contrast between the Cuban people and their Government as he had for the Dominican Republic.

As a final postscript, it can be said that the *ad hoc* Committee named in Costa Rica to mediate, on request of the two Governments, the problems outstanding between Cuba and the United States had been unable to act. The United States officially accepted its good offices, but up to January 1961 the Cuban Government had not. Mexico, however, remained optimistic that it can take the role of honest broker to restore unity and harmony to the inter-American community. Hopes of real success, never strong, dimmed even more when on 3 January 1961 the United States and Cuba broke official diplomatic relations.

[1] *Tiempo* (5 Sept. 1960), pp. 70–72; Milton MacKaye, 'Will Mexico go "Castro"?' *Saturday Evening Post*, v (29 Oct. 1960), 78. 'Fidel's Answer', *Time* (12 Sept. 1960), p. 43.

Chapter XXXIV

MEXICO AND CUBA:
REVOLUTIONS OLD AND NEW

WERE it not for the continental repercussions of the dramatic events that are linked to the Cuban 26th of July Movement and the group under Fidel Castro Ruz which overthrew the dictatorship of Fulgencio Batista, Cuba would not normally figure in a brief volume on Mexico. As it is, the only aspect of the Cuban revolution which will be discussed here is its effect on current affairs in Mexico.

The Cuban 26th of July Movement has had effects both on the domestic and foreign policies of Mexico, and one main result has been to intertwine the two aspects, internal and external, in a particularly important way.

'Baffling' is the adjective an American news weekly applied recently to the situation. 'In what it proclaims publicly, the Mexican government appears to be among Castro's firmest friends; in its own affairs, however, no one cracks down harder on communists and leftists. . . .'[1] This observation is correct, but does not reveal that very near the heart of the paradox is a power struggle within Mexican political ranks concerning the course which the Mexican Revolution itself should take.

From retirement, ex-President Lázaro Cárdenas emerged, to visit Havana at Castro's invitation, and on his return to heap praise on the Cuban agrarian reform programme; by implication he has indicated that Mexico should revive its own earlier radical agrarianism. The reappearance of the sixty-five-year-old hero did much to revitalize, at least vocally, more radical elements in Mexico, who directly or indirectly have connected López Mateos's attitudes toward Cuba with how 'Revolutionary' he and his Government really are.

The more moderate elements, still a majority among the people, in the PRI, and in the Government, have responded to these pressures by numerous statements, but with few acts. In an interview with a reporter dispatched by the *Saturday Evening Post* to ascertain if Mexico was likely to follow the Cuban example of turning overnight from a staunch friend of the United States and the Free World

---

[1] 'Mexico: Split Personality', *Time* (5 Dec. 1960), p. 32.

to an unscrupulous antagonist, a responsible Mexican Cabinet Minister anonymously but bluntly stated, 'Mexico will not commit suicide for Castro'.[1] This means that the President and his Government are unwilling to trade the dubious advantages of close ties with Castro's Government for continuing friendship and support from the United States, one form of suicide. Or, another, to allow pressure groups of the Mexican Left, abetted by Fidelistas (followers of Castro) and their international allies, to capture control of official Mexican policies. Such a surrender could quickly undo the major gains made over twenty years by the Institutional Revolution.

BACKGROUND

With these important issues unresolved at the time of writing (December 1960), it is yet possible to outline the background and note their rather clear evolution. One convenient point of departure is the fact that after his first and unsuccessful attempt to invade Cuba on 26 July 1953, a date that gives name to the movement, Fidel Castro and his brother Raúl were allowed to exile themselves in Mexico under an amnesty Batista granted them in 1955. In the Mexican capital they found help among Mexican sympathizers, who aided them in recruiting, and found veterans from the Spanish Civil War as instructors to teach the small revolutionary band guerrilla tactics. Many a Mexican recalls the idealism and dedication of the Cubans of those days. With good wishes from their Mexican hosts, the 26th of July Movement set forth on 26 November 1956—Fidel, Raúl, Ernesto ('Che') Guevera, and eighty others—in a small boat, the 62-foot *Granma*, that landed in eastern Cuba. Escaping Batista's army, twelve survivors and Fidel hid themselves in the rugged Sierra Maestra, where for more than two years they waged increasingly effective guerrilla war as their numbers multiplied, until on New Year's day 1959 they entered Havana as idolized heroes, Batista having fled to the Dominican Republic. Fidel assumed the somewhat unusual title of 'Premier'. In April 1960 he made it clear that democratic elections would be unlikely, telling a Brazilian newsman, 'Elections are a myth. The parliamentary system in Cuba reflected the old system which we are now destroying. Elections now would be a backward step. . . .'[2]

Here it is only necessary to note the increasingly international character of the Cuban 'People's Revolution'. Dedicated to re-shaping the Cuban economic and social structure along lines more

[1] MacKaye, 'Will Mexico go "Castro"?', p. 78.
[2] 'Elections are a Myth', *Time* (4 Apr. 1960), p. 35.

akin to those of the Sino-Soviet societies than the Mexican, leaders of the 26th of July Movement progressively became more anti-United States, and drew more heavily on Communist advisers, local and imported, who assumed major responsibilities for obliterating the older ways. Rather early Cuban propaganda organs labelled Mexico's President López Mateos 'the betrayer of the Mexican Revolution', and most of the other Latin American Presidents 'pro-imperialist' for dealing with the United States. As anti-Communism in Cuba became tantamount to national treason, political prisoners increased in numbers, with a steady exodus of Cubans into self-chosen exile. In July 1960 Nikita Khrushchev officially welcomed Cuba into the Soviet orbit by stating that if the United States intervened in Cuba, Soviet rockets would support the Cuban people, and by sending Sergei Kudriavtsev as Soviet Ambassador to Havana. A Canadian group had exposed him as the head of an espionage ring, and presumably he was expected to set up another in Latin America. In the United Nations the Soviet delegate warned the United States and the rest of the hemisphere: 'Do not touch Cuba. Do not threaten Cuba with your might because other countries also have much might. That is our policy toward the Latin American countries and toward Cuba.'[1] At the General Assembly of the United Nations, Castro in September 1960 placed himself and his régime in the Soviet bloc, almost completely ignoring the other Latin American delegations.

Two developments in Cuba have caused uneasiness in the whole hemisphere. One was the purposeful build-up of arms from Soviet sources.[2] It has been accompanied by several unsuccessful expeditions to overthrow Governments and to replace them by 'People's Revolutionary' groups. The other was an attempt to export the Cuban Revolution by subversion and agitation, to stir up peasant masses to escape their traditional poverty by direct seizure of lands or other properties. The chief intellectual architect of the present form of Fidelismo, the Argentine 'Che' Guevera, announced the policy as one of bringing Marxism 'through arming the people and

[1] In November 1960, pressed by a Cuban journalist to reiterate his pledge of Soviet rockets, Khrushchev dismayed Fidelistas by stating, 'I want that declaration to be, in effect, symbolic'.

[2] At the end of September 1960 it was estimated that Cuba had enough arms to equip with modern weapons from 9 to 100 full divisions; these include 100 tanks, up to 43 tons, 12 MIG jet fighters, unknown but large quantities of tactical Czech truck-mounted rockets, 100 self-propelled howitzers and cannons, 100 heavy (120 mm.) mortars, with about 3,000 Russian and Czechoslovakian weapons experts as instructors. All told, about $300 million worth of arms have been obtained in twenty-one months (*Time*, 14 Nov. 1960, pp. 36–38).

smashing the puppet dictatorial régimes'. Almost by definition the latter are those which do not accept Castro's bid for hemispheric leadership.[1]

Mexico, like most other countries, at first shared an admiration for the bravery of the Cuban overthrow of the dictatorship, and was slower than other democratic nations to cool towards the Cubans when they undertook a wave of summary executions of Batista supporters. Mexican feelings about those who had aided Huerta account in large part for that tolerance. Nor was much concern shown about Cuban confiscations of foreign properties. In fact, in the general atmosphere of euphoria, in which Mexicans felt somewhat flattered that the Cuban movement seemed to be paralleling their own, President López Mateos did not even mention Cuba in his First (1959) report to Congress. It seemingly posed no problems worthy of comment.

MERGING THE ISSUES

Beginnings of what Roscoe Drummond recently has called 'deep and treacherous crosscurrents in the politics of this most mature and stable of Latin American republics', however, had already begun to show.[2] In March 1959 Demetrio Vallejo, leader of the railway workers' union and a notorious Communist fellow-traveller, called an illegal wildcat strike, for which López Mateos jailed him and about 2,600 other strikers. Led by ex-President Cárdenas, the Left in Mexico began more frequently but in vain to demand 'justice and comprehension' for the strikers.

Exploiting the Mexican situation, Fidel Castro, who had announced 'I am the leader of an American revolution, not chief of a small country's government', brought Cárdenas to Havana, along with representatives of the more radical student and labour groups to witness the mammoth parades and celebrations commemorating the sixth (1960) anniversary of the 26th of July Movement.

In the meanwhile to prevent internal splits from widening, President López Mateos had warmly welcomed Osvaldo Dorticós, Cuba's President, who visited the Mexican capital. Statements at the time, chiefly for local consumption, pledged Mexican solidarity

---

[1] El Salvador, Haiti, Honduras, Nicaragua, Guatemala, Dominican Republic, Venezuela have expelled Cuban diplomatic representatives or broken off relations with Cuba; Argentina, Brazil, the United States have withdrawn their Ambassadors from Havana.

[2] Roscoe Drummond, 'A Size-Up of Mexico and Castro', *Washington Post Outlook*, 4 Dec. 1960, pp. 3–5.

with the people of Cuba, just at a point when the United States was in the midst of a seemingly endless series of crises with Cuba over curtailment of its sugar quota. When the United States Government requested some official explanation from Mexico, López Mateos formally indicated that the PRI's congressional leader, who had made the statements, was not speaking for the Mexican Government. This statement was one turning-point. Almost immediately the left-wing groups in Mexico began to organize demonstrations, marching past the United States Embassy chanting 'Cuba, yes! Yankees, no!'

Apparently not heeding the warnings of the earlier Vallejo fiasco, the head of the teachers' union, Othón Salazar, in August 1960 also led an illegal strike. He was unceremoniously removed from his post by the Government. Teachers and students staged demonstrations, demanding the reinstatement of Salazar, again with the same pro-Cuban slogans. In recurring battles between students and police two students were shot. They became martyrs, and to 'avenge' them, further disturbances erupted. To restore order and control, the Government began to round up and jail the most flagrant agitators.

This action brought matters to a climax. David Alfaro Siqueiros, the internationally known artist, for the past few months head of Mexico's Communist Party, promised in public the López Mateos régime 'no peace until all political prisoners are freed'. Without further ado, López Mateos jailed him, too, where he joined the other vocal Mexican supporters of Fidelismo:the Communist leader Dionisio Encinas, the journalist Filomeno Mata, and about 130 others.

Mexican politics and policies were even further polarized between the far Left and moderate groups by the Conference of Foreign Ministers in Costa Rica and its aftermath. In September 1960 a Senatorial Committee of the Mexican Congress approved statements made by the Mexican delegation there, and reiterated the 'sympathy and Mexican-Cuban friendship, and opinion that the Cuban revolution is an expression of the will of the Cuban people'.[1] Not long afterwards a PRI Deputy, Emilio Sánchez Piedras, made world headlines by accusing the United States of meddling in the internal affairs of Cuba and stating that justice was on the side of 'the noble people of Cuba'. Three United States Congressmen, invited to attend ceremonies on 16 September to mark the 150th anniversary of Mexico's independence, protested against the remarks and

[1] *Tiempo*, No. 958 (12 Sept. 1960), pp. 10–11. See above, pp. 317–18.

boycotted the ceremonial luncheon. To ease the situation, Mexican parliamentary leaders, headed by the President of the Senate, organized a champagne toast to the Americans, and hastily packed off Sánchez Piedras on a special mission. This did not quiet him; from southern Mexico he issued another anti-United States statement: its threats to Cuba he felt were 'as sinister as those of Nazism, Fascism and Francoism'.

The skirmishes between moderate and Left in Mexico continue. Towards the end of November 1960, the imprisoned Siqueiros went on a hunger strike vowing to persist 'until we get justice'—i.e. release to permit the organization of demonstrations in favour of Castro. He was joined in this protest by other political prisoners, but when in early December the Government freed nineteen minor figures, Siqueiros broke his fast, reportedly 'sipping consommé and apple sauce every three hours'. But as a sign of the régime's determination to preserve order he, Vallejo, and the ring-leaders were still behind bars at the end of the year.

CURRENT MEXICAN ATTITUDES

It seems obvious that the strategy of the Mexican Left is to ride Castro's popularity and influence to greater power within the PRI and the régime. What are their chances of success? No one can predict with certainty, but some trends are clear.

In the first place, apparently the majority of non-doctrinaire Mexicans have become disenchanted with the earlier image of Castro as the idealistic leader of liberation. Milton MacKaye reported on a wide range of interviews and other information which he gathered in October 1960: small shop owners, students, business men and others were almost uniformly favourable at the outset of the Castro régime, 'But Khrushchev's threat of hemispheric intervention and Castro's erratic behaviour have brought a marked disillusionment to the man in the street.' To this, one can add the statements of a large body of defecting ex-Castro officials—high army officers, judges, Ambassadors—and the Khrushchev–Castro acts in the September 1960 U.N. General Assembly. A young physics student at UNAM told MacKaye 'Cuba wanted reform and got Communism', adding 'We call ourselves leftists, but we do not think Marx and Engels have the answers to Mexican problems. . . .'[1] Drummond and others note that the Mexican press is uniformly critical of Castro's methods, although there seems to be general

[1] MacKaye, 'Will Mexico go "Castro"?', p. 77.

agreement that the long-term objectives of the 'People's Revolution' are probably desirable. There seems also to be a general consensus that the Cubans themselves will soon put an end to Castro's and Guevera's extremism. After that Mexicans expect that the Movement will lose some of its violence.

Within official circles, an early warmth toward Cuba has also visibly cooled, despite public statements—always carefully worded to distinguish between the people of Cuba and their present leadership. The Mexican Government grants few visas to Cubans, either to pro-Castro figures who are likely to stir up further domestic turmoil, or to anti-Castro exiles who would be a further embarrassment in a complex and explosive situation. Nor did the López Mateos régime accede to the urgent Cuban request to make available Pemex technicians to help run the expropriated refineries. Officials in Mexico keep a careful eye on the Cuban diplomats and their friends, the Russians and other iron curtain missions. When Vallejo, for instance, was clearly linked with Soviet plans, two Russian diplomats were expelled.

When asked directly by an American journalist to clarify what he meant by saying that his own Government was 'extreme left within the constitution' President López Mateos's reply seemed to most observers a warning against the tactics of Fidelismo: violence, unauthorized seizures, direct action by non-legal means. The President, after reiterating that the constitution of 1917 called for the betterment of the poorest sections of the population, emphasized that the constitution also meant, as he pointed out in his inaugural address, that 'we shall do nothing nor allow anything to be done beyond or against the law'. He emphasized that the individual rights—suffrage and other civil liberties outlined in the first chapter of the constitution—'are the foundation of the peace and order prevalent in the Republic and of Mexico's economic and social development'.[1]

Fixed in this determination to keep Mexico on the slower, evolutionary path marked out by the Institutional Revolution, but under the local and international pressures generated by the Left in politics, President López Mateos and his Government have an uncomfortable, but not really dangerous problem. 'The Mexican government is not the least bit afraid of exported Castroism', stated a recent report. 'It is too strong to be attacked, too alert to be subverted.'[2] The enigma of Cárdenas's ultimate aims and uncertainty

---

[1] Ibid., p. 77. [2] Ibid.

over how much strength he and his national and international supporters can eventually mobilize, however, make it evident that the López Mateos régime is unlikely to move very far toward joining any collective action against Castro. 'In Mexico we have a mature, stable friend of the United States', but the best that the latter Government can hope for from it is sympathetic neutralism on Cuban matters, the report ends.[1]

OFFICIAL VIEWS, SEPTEMBER 1960

Cuba and the problems Fidelismo raises figured prominently in the Second Annual Message which President López Mateos read to the Mexican Congress on 1 September 1960. In the long chapter on foreign relations he first reported that, with other countries, Mexico had offered its good offices to mediate in the conflicts between Cuba and the United States, but that preliminary conversations unfortunately 'Did not produce the desired effects'. However, he promised, Mexico would continue its efforts to promote friendship and harmony among the American republics.

He then summarized the positions taken by the Mexican delegations at the Sixth and Seventh Meetings of American Foreign Ministers. He ended that particular section of the Message by recalling that in June 1960 he had expressed in public 'the sympathy of the Mexican people for the legitimate aspirations of political, social, and economic improvement which inspire the people of Cuba', adding, 'I am happy to reiterate these sentiments now'. The following words have been variously interpreted as cautionary toward the United States to relax its pressures on Cuba, and on Cubans to work within the American community; he said that the fundamental unity of the American states goes beyond the formal political and juridical organizations that bind them together. The mission of the group 'is to remain united, in peace and harmony'. In 'this great family', President López Mateos asserted, 'Cuba, by right, occupies a special niche'.

Coming more directly to basic problems the President drew some sharp distinctions between the Mexican Revolution and the Cuban, without directly naming the latter. In the long epilogue to the regular message, in which he discussed the meaning of the Mexican Revolution on its fiftieth birthday, he took occasion to lecture Mexican youth: they had grown up in a Revolution which earlier generations had struggled to maintain, and did not always realize the sacrifices that already had been made in Mexico. Part of their restlessness was

[1] Drummond, 'Mexico and Castro'.

their desire 'to take their own part in the destiny of Mexico'. But part of it, too, was sheer adolescence, giving rise to 'efforts erroneously directed against the Revolutionary ideals or those promoted by the examples of struggles by distant and different peoples'. Again without mentioning Russia, China, or Cuba, López Mateos went on: 'Some countries are today fighting for objectives that our Revolution has already achieved, under the protection of a social movement that affirms and guarantees the dignity of the human being.'

Recalling that Mexicans had already achieved agrarian reform, based on human concepts and regard for rights, a Mexican labour movement which actually protects the worker, a system of 'quick justice', an educational system accessible to all, he stated that these gains had been unsurpassed in other revolutionary countries. Re-emphasizing the differences between the Mexican and the 'foreign' revolutions, the President emphatically said, 'I must say that it is precisely in other countries in a process of social, political, cultural and economic transformation where one can least find realizations such as ours'. The Mexican case differs in that its Revolution takes the individual 'as the objective of common effort, and the person maintains his dignity and liberty, as basic goals of a true revolution'. He pointed further to the circumstance that real gains do not come overnight; it took Mexico fifty years to create the rights and facilities presently enjoyed. Ostensibly still talking about youth, the message was plain for all to read when López Mateos concluded this section by saying, 'It is evident that the restlessness of new generations someti nes comes from an immature appreciation of the facts.'

Finally, he pledged that Mexico would continue, as in the past, to be 'independent, sovereign, free, prosperous, democratic, just, respectful and cordial with all other peoples'. One suspects that many of Mexico's troubles, and those of other countries too, would diminish if the Cuban Revolution came up to those high standards, products of the Mexican Revolution.

APPENDIX
FURTHER STATISTICAL TABLES

Appendix

TABLE I

Mexico, 1960. States and Capitals, Areas, Populations, and Densities

Con-stit'd.	State or Territory	Capital	Date Founded	Area: 'ooo sq. mi.	Est. Pop. ('ooo)	Density: persons/ sq. mi.
1846	Aguascalientes ...	Aguascalientes	1575	2·5	205·2	82·0
1953	Baja California ...	Ensenada ...	?	27·8	745·6	26·8
1859	*Baja California, S.	La Paz... ...	1535	27·8	75·2	2·7
1863	Campeche ...	Campeche ...	1540	19·7	160·7	8·1
1824	Chiapas	Tuxtla Gutiérrez	1564	28·7	1,203·9	42·0
1824	Chihuahua ...	Chihuahua ...	c. 1703	94·8	1,125·2	11·8
1836	Coahuila... ...	Saltillo... ...	1586	58·1	954·2	16·4
1857	Colima	Colima ...	1522	2·0	164·2	82·1
1826	Distrito Federal...	México ...	1521	0·6	5,407·1	9,012·0
1824	Durango ...	Durango ...	1563	47·7	837·9	17·5
1824	Guanajuato ...	Guanajuato ...	1554	11·8	1,600·6	136·0
1849	Guerrero... ...	Chilpancingo ...	?	24·9	1,108·1	44·4
1869	Hidalgo	Pachuca ...	1534	8·1	926·8	114·2
1824	Jalisco	Guadalajara ...	1531	31·1	2,103·4	67·8
1824	México	Toluca... ...	1533	8·3	1,675·8	201·1
1824	Michoacán ...	Morelia ...	1541	23·2	1,713·5	73·8
1869	Morelos	Cuernavaca ...	1530	1·9	400·1	201·2
1917	Nayarit	Tepic	1535	10·4	386·5	37·1
1824	Nuevo León ...	Monterrey ...	1596	25·1	985·0	39·2
1824	Oaxaca	Oaxaca ...	c. 1522	36·4	1,709·9	48·2
1824	Puebla	Puebla ...	1532	13·1	1,956·3	149·2
1824	Querétaro ...	Querétaro ...	1531	4·4	345·4	78·5
1902	*Quintana Roo ...	Chetumal ...	c. 1847	19·4	41·0	2·1
1824	San Luis Potosí ...	San Luis Potosí	1586	24·4	1,032·9	42·4
1830	Sinaloa	Culiacán ...	1531	22·6	844·8	38·4
1830	Sonora	Hermosillo ...	1742	70·5	677·2	9·5
1824	Tabasco	Villahermosa ...	c. 1596	9·8	437·8	44·7
1824	Tamaulipas ...	Cd. Victoria ...	1750	30·7	1,156·0	37·6
1851	Tlaxcala ...	Tlaxcala ...	c. 1535	1·6	342·0	213·0
1824	Veracruz... ...	Jalapa... ...	c. 1530	27·7	2,455·6	88·5
1824	Yucatán	Mérida ...	1542	14·9	622·5	41·0
1824	Zacatecas ...	Zacatecas ...	1546	28·1	800·3	28·4
1824	REPUBLIC ...	México ...	1521	760·1	34,200·5	45·0

*Territories; all others states, except Distrito Federal.

Sources: Constituted: O'Gorman, *Breve historia de las divisiones territoriales*; capitals founded: various sources; area: Cline, *U.S. and Mexico*, table 1 (pp. 409–10); est. 1960 population: DGE, *Diagnóstico económico regional*, table, p. 38; densities derived by author, to slide-rule accuracy.

Appendix

TABLE II

Regions and Growth, 1950–60

		POPULATION, 1960			GROWTH, 1950–60	
		'000	Per cent. national	Density 1950	Density 1960	Per cent. growth 1950–60
Federal District	...	METROPOLIS 5,407·1	15·6	5,240·0	9,012·0	83·0
		CORE				
Aguascalientes ...	...	205·2		71·4	82·0	9·7
Guanajuato ...	...	1,600·6		111·5	136·0	21·5
Hidalgo ...	...	926·8		104·1	114·2	10·2
México ...	...	1,675·8		157·5	201·1	21·0
Michoacán ...	...	1,713·5		61·4	73·8	21·2
Morelos ...	...	400·1		139·8	201·2	48·8
Puebla ...	...	1,956·3		122·1	149·2	22·5
Querétaro ...	...	345·4		63·7	78·5	22·5
San Luis Potosí	...	1,032·9		35·1	42·4	21·7
Tlaxcala ...	...	342·0		182·1	213·0	21·0
Veracruz ...	...	2,455·6		74·4	88·5	19·4
Regional sub-total	...	12,654·2	38·0	82·0	99·5	20·6
		THE WEST				
Colima ...	...	164·2		56·0	82·1	46·0
Jalisco ...	...	2,103·4		56·1	67·8	20·5
Nayarit ...	...	386·5		28·1	37·1	32·2
Zacatecas ...	...	800·3		23·6	28·4	20·5
Regional sub-total	...	3,454·4	10·0	38·4	48·0	22·8
		THE NORTH				
Baja California ...	...	745·6		7·7	26·8	232·0
Baja California, S.	...	75·2		1·9	2·7	28·2
Chihuahua ...	...	1,125·2		8·2	11·8	45·6
Coahuila ...	...	954·2		12·3	16·4	33·3
Durango ...	...	837·9		13·2	17·5	33·2
Nuevo León ...	...	985·0		28·6	39·2	32·5
Sinaloa ...	...	844·8		27·4	38·4	36·6
Tamaulipas ...	...	1,156·0		24·3	37·6	61·3
Regional sub-total	...	7,401·1	21·0	12·4	18·2	46·6

(*Continued opposite*)

(*Table II continued*)

Appendix

	POPULATION, 1960			GROWTH, 1950–60	
	'000	Per cent. national	Density 1950	Density 1960	Per cent. growth 1950–60
	THE SOUTH				
Campeche	160·7		6·2	8·1	32·2
Chiapas	1,203·9		31·7	42·0	34·4
Guerrero	1,108·1		36·8	44·4	20·7
Oaxaca	1,709·9		39·8	48·2	18·3
Quintana Roo	41·0		1·4	2·1	52·0
Tabasco	437·8		36·8	44·7	24·6
Yucatan	622·5		34·7	41·0	20·8
Regional Sub-totals ...	5,283·9	15·4	27·9	33·3	23·7
REPUBLIC of MEXICO	34,200·5	100·0	35·0	45·0	32·8

Sources: Population, 1950; Table I above; density, 1950: Cline, *U.S. and Mexico*, table 1, pp. 409–10.

TABLE III

Areas Irrigated, Reclaimed, Improved, 1926–58
*('000 hectares)**

TYPE OF OPERATION	PERIODS			TOTALS	
	1926–47	1947–52	1952–8	1926–58	Per cent.
LARGE-SCALE WORKS	774·1	377·2	388·7	1,540·0	59·0
SMALL-SCALE WORKS	52·1	146·4	175·7	374·2	14·3
OPERATIONAL IMPROVEMENT	—	—	17·0	17·0	0·4
COMMISSIONS					
Tepalcatepec		28·8	45·0	73·8	
Papaloapán		40·0	80·0	120·0	
Río Fuerte		70·0	130·0	200·0	
Grijalva-Usumacinta		—	267·1	267·1	
Valley of Mexico		3·1	13·5	16·6	
Yaqui Native Zone		—	11·0	11·0	
TOTALS		141·9	546·6	688·5	26·3
TOTAL AREAS	816·2	665·5	1,128·0	2,609·7	100·0
Per cent.	31·2	25·4	43·4	100·0	

* 1 hectare = 2·47 acres.

Source: Informe de la Secretaría de Recursos Hidráulicos del 10 de septiembre de 1957 al 31 de agosto de 1958 (1958), preliminary tables; data consolidated, retabulated, percentages by author.

Appendix

TABLE IV

Growth of Mexican Population, 1800–1960
(Millions)

Year	Population	Average annual increase (millions)	Census	Source of Data Official estimate	Source of Data Unofficial estimate
1800 ...	4·50	—			X
1810 ...	6·12	0·16			X
1820 ...	6·20	0·01		X	
1830 ...	6·38	0·02			X
1840 ...	7·02	0·06		X	
1850 ...	7·66	0·06			X
1860 ...	8·21	0·06			X
1870 ...	9·10	0·09		X	X
1880 ...	9·58	0·05			X
1890 ...	11·50	0·19			X
1895 ...	12·63	0·22	I		
1900 ...	13·61	0·19	II		
1910 ...	15·16	0·21	III		
1921 ...	14·33	− 0·08*	IV		
1930 ...	16·55	0·22	V		
1940 ...	19·65	0·31	VI		
1950 ...	25·78	0·61	VII		
1955 ...	29·68	0·78		X	
1956 ...	30·54	0·86			X
1957 ...	31·43	0·89			X
1958 ...	32·35	0·92			X
1959 ...	33·30	0·95			X
1960 ...	34·20	0·90			X

*Decrease

Sources: DGE, *Integración territorial de los Estados Unidos Mexicanos: Séptimo censo general de población 1950* (1952), p. 734, for 1800–1950; *Revista de estadística*, xxiii (Mar.–Apr. 1959), cover data, for 1955–9. Increase calculations by HFC.

TABLE V

Natural Increases of Mexican Population, 1900–58

Year			Live births per '000	Deaths per '000	Crude natural increase per '000
1900	...	...	...	36·4	33·6	2·8
1910	...	...	...	32·0	33·3	— 1·3
1922	...	...	...	31·4	25·4	6·1
1930	...	...	...	49·4	26·6	22·8
1940	...	...	...	44·3	23·2	25·4
1950	...	...	...	45·5	16·2	29·3
1951	...	...	...	44·6	17·3	27·3
1952	...	...	...	43·8	15·0	28·8
1953	...	...	...	45·0	15·9	29·1
1954	...	...	...	46·4	13·1	33·3
1955	...	...	...	46·2	13·3	32·9
1956	...	...	...	46·8	12·1	34·7
1957	...	...	...	47·3	13·3	34·0
1958	...	...	...	44·5	12·5	32·0

Sources: Julio Durán Ochoa, *Población* (Mexico, 1955), pp. 134–5, for 1900–50; *Compendio estadístico, 1955,* p. 60, for 1951–5; *Revista de estadística,* xxiii (Mar.–Apr. 1959), cover summary, for 1956–8.

TABLE VI

Indians in the Americas, 1940: Regions and Selected Countries
('000)

	No. of Indians	Per cent. of total population	Per cent. of total Indian population
CANADA, UNITED STATES ...	539·8	0·37	3·33
MEXICO, CENTRAL AMERICA, ANTILLES			
Mexico	5,427·4	27·91	33·48
Guatemala	1,820·9	55·44	11·23
Regional sub-total	8,105·2	19·03	50·00
SOUTH AMERICA			
Ecuador	1,000·0	40·00	6·17
Peru	3,247·2	46·23	20·03
Bolivia	1,650·0	50·00	10·18
Brazil	1,117·1	2·70	6·89
Regional sub-total	7,105·6	8·52	46·67
WESTERN HEMISPHERE	16,211·6	5·91	100·0

Source: Instituto Nacional Indigenista, *Densidad de la población de habla indígena* ...
after Angel Rosenblat, *La Población indígena de América desde 1492* ...
(Buenos Aires, Inst. Cultural Española, 1945), p. 19. Countries with
over 1 million Indians selected; percentages by Rosenblat.

TABLE VII

Indian Languages of Mexico: Monolinguals, 1950

	'000	Per cent.		'000	Per cent.
CENTRAL MEXICO			**WESTERN MEXICO**		
Nahuatl	212·8	26·8	Cora	0·2	
			Huichol	1·0	
			Tarasco	9·8	
Others			TOTAL	11·0	1·3
Huasteco	17·3				
Mazahua	16·3				
Otomí	57·6		**NORTHERN MEXICO**		
Totonac	54·3		Kikapoo	0·1	
Sub-total	145·5	18·3	Mayo...	2·5	
			Tarahumara ...	8·2	
TOTAL	358·3	45·1	Tepehuano	1·6	
			Yaqui	0·2	
SOUTHERN MEXICO			TOTAL	12·6	1·6
			W. & N. MEXICO		
Mixteco-Zapateco			TOTALS	23·6	2·9
Zapateco	60·7				
Mixteco	76·9		**GROUPS WITH LESS**		
Sub-total	137·6	17·3	**THAN 90 MONO-**		
			LINGUALS (NATIVE)	11·7	1·5
Mayance					
Maya	50·9				
Chol	18·9				
Chontal	1·5				
Tzendal	31·9				
Tzotzil	44·1				
Sub-total	147·3	18·5			
Others					
Amusgo	5·8				
Chatino	8·3				
Chinanteco ...	15·7				
Mazateco	47·2				
Mixe	21·0				
Populuca	1·6				
Tlapeneco ...	12·2				
Zoque	4·8				
Sub-total	116·6	14·6			
TOTAL	401·5	50·4			
CENTRAL &					
SOUTHERN ...	759·8	95·1			

Source: DGE, *Séptimo censo general de población . . . 1950: resúmen general* (1953), p. 231, table 30; adapted. Classifications by regions, percentages by author.

TABLE VIII

Indian Mexico: Monolinguals and Bilinguals (Native Languages), 1950
(*'000 persons over 5 years of age*)

State	Native speakers	Per cent. total Natives	Native per cent. in state population
Oaxaca	583·8	23·7	48·0
Puebla	297·5	12·1	21·6
Yucatán	279·4	11·9	63·8
Veracruz	252·7	10·3	14·7
Sub-total	1,413·4	58·0	
Chiapas	198·0	8·1	26·2
México	183·0	7·5	15·6
Hidalgo	179·6	7·3	25·2
Guerrero	124·7	5·1	16·0
Sub-total	685·3	28·0	
SUB-TOTAL ...	2,098·7	86·0	
San Luis Potosí ...	89·1	3·6	12·4
Michoacán	51·3	2·1	4·3
Campeche	32·9	1·3	31·8
Sub-total	173·3	7·0	
SUB-TOTAL ...	2,272·0	93·0	
Sonora	25·1	1·0	5·8
Tabasco	24·5	1·0	8·1
Chihuahua	22·4	0·9	3·1
Tlaxcala	22·2	0·9	9·2
Federal District ...	18·8	0·7	—
Querétaro	13·2	0·5	5·5
Morelos	11·7	0·5	5·1
Sub-total	137·9	5·5	
SUB-TOTAL ...	2,409·9	98·5	
Quintana Roo ...	9·6	0·4	43·7
Sinaloa	9·0	0·4	1·7
Jalisco	5·3	0·2	—
Guanajuato	4·7	0·2	—
Nayarit	3·8	0·1	1·6
Durango	2·6	—	—
Sub-total	35·0	1·3	
SUB-TOTAL ...	2,445·9	99·8	
Others*	1·7	0·2	
TOTALS	2,447·6	100·0	

* 7 states.
Source: DGE, *Compendio estadístico, 1953*, table 26, pp. 56–57; data rearranged, tabulated, percentages by author.

TABLE IX

Growth of Cities, 100,000 Population and Over, 1940–59
(Excluding Mexico City; populations in '000)

City	POPULATION			INCREASES				RANK	
				1940–59		1950–9			
	1940	1950	1959 (est.)	No.	Per cent.	No.	Per cent.	1950	1959 (est.)
Guadalajara ...	229·2	377·0	382·7	153·5	67·0	5·7	1·5	2	2
Monterrey ...	186·1	334·4	340·6	154·5	83·0	6·2	1·8	3	3
Puebla ...	138·5	211·3	252·8	114·3	82·5	41·5	19·7	4	4
Sub-total, 1940	553·8	922·7	976·1	422·3	76·4	83·4	9·0		
Mérida ...	98·9	142·9	159·4	60·5	61·4	16·5	11·5	5	6
Torreón ...	75·8	129·0	142·1	66·3	87·5	13·1	10·2	6	10
S. Luis Potosí	77·2	125·7	156·3	79·1	102·3	30·6	24·4	7	8
León	74·2	122·7	157·4	83·2	112·0	34·7	27·6	8	7
Cd. Juárez ...	48·9	122·6	220·0	171·0	351·0	97·4	78·1	9	5
Veracruz ...	71·7	101·2	123·4	52·7	72·5	22·2	20·9	10	12
Sub-total, 1950	446·7	744·1	958·6	512·8	118·2	214·5	28·9		
Culiacán ...	46·0	49·0	144·6	98·6	238·0	95·6	195·0		9
Mexicali ...	18·8	64·7	141·2	45·9	651·0	76·5	117·8		11
Matamoros ...	28·2	45·7	118·2	90·0	318·0	72·5	190·0		13
Aguascalientes	82·2	93·4	117·4	35·2	42·9	24·0	25·7		14
Toluca ...	43·4	53·0	115·4	72·0	166·0	62·4	52·6		15
Chihuahua ...	56·8	87·0	110·8	54·0	95·5	23·8	21·4		16
Morelia ...	44·3	63·2	103·5	59·2	133·2	40·3	63·7		17
Sub-total, 1959	319·7	456·0	851·1	454·9	149·0	395·1	86·5		
TOTALS* REPUBLIC	553·8	1,666·8	2,785·8						
Per cent. of national population ...	3·8	6·5	8·3						

*Cities over 100,000.

Sources: 1940 population: DGE, *Estados Unidos Mexicanos, 6° censo de población, 1940* (1941–6); 1950 population: DGE, *Integración territorial de los Estados Unidos Mexicanos* (1952), passim; 1959 population estimates: *World Almanac, 1959* (N.Y. 1959), p. 396, and *Encyclopaedia Britannica World Atlas, Unabridged* (Chicago, 1959), p. 63, table 3. All other calculations by author.

TABLE X

Mexican Localities, by Size, 1950

	Localities	Population
Over 500,000	1	2,234,795
250,000 − 499,000	2	710,438
100,000 − 249,000	7	955,335
75,000 − 99,000	3	274,703
50,000 − 74,999	11	653,303
40,000 − 49,999	11	507,855
30,000 − 39,999	10	323,138
20,000 − 2,999	22	545,806
URBANIZED : ...	67	6,205,373
10,000 − 19,999	92	1,259,484
5,000 − 9,999	215	1,472,397
2,500 − 4,999	609	2,063,467
SEMI-URBAN:	916	4,795,348
1,000 − 2,499	2,598	3,858,445
500 − 999	4,940	3,406,603
100 − 499	24,979	5,752,995
1 − 99	65,090	1,772,256
RURAL	97,607	14,970,299
UNKNOWN	438	
REPUBLIC	99,028	25,791,020

Source: DGE, *Séptimo Censo General de Población, 6 de junio de 1950. Resúmen general,* table 26A (p. 119). Verbal categories by author.

Appendix

TABLE XI

Income Levels, 1950–6: Economically Active Population
('000 families)

RANGES & INTERVALS				A	B	C	E	PER CENT.	
A/B	C	D	E	1950	1950	1950	1956	1950 (Av.)*	1956
		Pesos per month							
3,000+	3,000+		3,000+	20·4	—	20·4	79·5	0·5	1·5
2,999 1,500—			3,000 2,001—	64·3	22·0	—	97·5	1·0	1·9
1,499 1,000—			2,000 1,001—	92·5	28·8		478·2	1·3	9·6
2,999 1,000—	2,999 1,000—		3,000 1,001—	156·8	50·8	156·8	575·7	2·3	11·5
1,000+	1,000+	1,000+	1,001+	177·2	50·8	177·2	655·2	2·8	13·0
999 800—		1,000 700—	1,000 750—	88·1	29·7		434·8	1·5	8·8
799 600—		700 500—	750 501—	221·7	73·0		850·0	3·0	16·9
999 600—	999 600—	1,000 500	1,000 501	309·8	102·7	309·8	1,284·8	5·1	25·7
599 500—				118·6	66·7			2·0	
499 400—			500 401	277·7	142·4		515·6	3·7	10·4
399 300—			400 301—	428·3	363·1		589·1	9·5	11·9
599 300—	599 300—	500 300—	500 300—	824·6	572·2	824·6	1,104·7	15·1	22·3
999 300—	999 300—	1,000 300	1,000 300—	1,134·4	674·9	1,134·4	2,389·5	20·3	48·0
299 200—	299 150—	300 200—	300 201—	710·0	656·6	1,677·5	877·0	21·3	17·5

(Continued over)

RANGES & INTERVALS				A	B	C	E	PER CENT.	
A/B	C	D	E	1950	1950	1950	1956	1950 (Av.)*	1956
		Pesos per month							
199 150—		200 100—	200 101—	967·5	860·8		860·8	24·0	17·2
149 76—		100 50—	100 1—	1,320·0	1,119·5		219·6	28·9	4·3
75 1—		50 1—		190·6	460·5		4·2	10·2	
199 1—	149 1—	200 1—	200 1—	2,478·1	2,440·8	1,510·6	1,079·4	55·7	21·5
299 1—	299 1—	300 1—	300 1—	3,188·1	3,097·4	3,188·1	1,957·4	77·0	39·0 39·0
TOTAL				4,500·0	3,831·1	4,500·0	5,002·1	97·7	100·0
UNKNOWN				605·0	—	605·0	778·0	3·2	

* Averages. Sources A–D; sub-category averages do not total sum of parts.
Sources: A: DGE, *Séptimo censo general . . . 1950*; *parte especial* (1955), table 40.
    B: ibid. table 38–A.
    C: Lewis, 'Mexico desde 1940', table 18 (p. 229).
    D: Scott, *Mexican Government*, p. 90 n. 10, with percentages only.
    E: SDE, *Ingresos y egresos de la población, passim*, regional tables summed
      by author.
All percentages and averages by author.

Appendix

TABLE XII

Sector Organization, National Revolutionary Party, c. 1958
('000 of members)

Organization	Abbrev.	Probable class level	Memb.
I. THE FARM SECTOR			
1. National Peasant Confed. ...	CNC		
A. CNC Proper		Lower/Trans.	2,500
B. Peasant Union ...		Lower/Trans.	150
2. Mexican Agronomists' Society	SAM	Middle	10
Totals, FARM SECTOR ...			2,660
II. THE LABOUR SECTOR			
1. Workers' Unity Bloc (affiliates)	BUO		
Mexican Labour Confed. ...	CTM	Lower	1,500
Regional Confederation of Mexican Workers	CROM	Lower	35
General Confederation ...	CGT	Lower	25
Railway Workers' Union ...	STFRM	Lower/Trans.	102
Mining and Metal Workers' Union	STMMSRM	Lower/Trans.	90
Petroleum Workers' Union	STPRM	Lower/Trans./Middle	85
Telephone Workers' Union	STRM	Trans./Middle	10
Motion Picture Workers' Union	STPCRM	Trans./Upper	6
Various independent ...		Lower/Trans.	20
Bloc sub-total			1,873
2. Anti-Unity Bloc affiliates ...		Lower/Trans.	
Revolutionary Confederation of Workers and Peasants	CROC		150
Revolutionary Confederation	CRT		25
Electrical Workers' Union (3)			50
Various independent unions			15
Bloc sub-total			240
Totals, LABOUR SECTOR...			2,113
III. THE POPULAR SECTOR...	CNOP		
1. Civil Servants			
Bureaucrats' Unions ...	FSTSE	Middle/Upper	300
Teachers	SNTE	Middle	55
2. Co-operatives			
National Federation of Co-op.			275
National Co-operative League			3

(Continued over)

(Table XII continued)

Organization	Abbrev.	Probable class level	Memb.
III.—*continued*			
3. Small Farm Proprietors ...			
National Confed. of Small			
Owners		Trans./Middle	850
National Growers' Assoc.		Middle	15
4. Small Merchants/Industrsts.		Middle	40
5. Professional/Intellect. Grps.		Middle/Upper	55
6. Youth		All	75
7. Artisans/Service (non-sal'd.)		Trans.	70
8. Women's Groups			
Society of Technicians/Prof.		Middle	25
Other (auxiliaries, &c.) ...		Lower/Trans.	10
9. 'Diverse Persons' (not other-			
wise specified)		All	75
TOTALS, POPULAR SECTOR			
NATIONAL REVOLUTIONARY			
PARTY, ALL SECTORS ...			6,621

Source: Scott, *Mexican Government*, pp. 166–7. Adapted, and class levels placed by author.

Appendix

TABLE XIII

Selected National Budgets, 1950–8

(million pesos)

	1950	1952	1955	1958
GENERAL				
Legislature	31·9	23·5	30·5	38·1
Presidency	2·7	3·2	7·7	8·8
Judiciary	10·0	19·2	29·3	35·4
Attorney-General	4·6	5·6	8·6	12·3
Contingencies	598·9	263·3	488·6	1,051·7
Public Debt	554·0	980·7	799·5	900·8
Sub-total	1,202·1	1,295·4	1,364·2	2,047·1
BASIC FUNCTIONS				
Government	20·0	29·1	41·5	50·9
Foreign Relations	37·7	51·3	82·7	92·0
Treasury	137·6	110·4	216·9	263·8
Defence	257·1	328·6	451·7	591·3
Mil. industries	20·7	28·2	39·0	48·9
Sub-total	473·1	547·6	831·8	1,046·9
ECONOMIC				
Agriculture	42·9	60·9	115·9	220·3
Transportation	459·2	696·6	948·6	1,638·5
Economy	24·9	28·1	37·7	52·0
Merchant Marine	68·5	95·6	226·2	369·3
Hydraulic Res.	262·1	419·0	489·4	776·5
National Property	7·5	7·2	9·8	11·9
Investment	457·2	243·4	671·7	644·5
Sub-total	1,322·3	1,550·8	2,499·3	3,713·0
SOCIO-CULTURAL				
Public Education	314·0	427·8	711·8	1,153·2
Labour/Welfare	6·2	8·0	16·8	29·5
Agrarian	14·9	17·6	25·3	33·0
Health/Welfare	130·6	152·0	232·2	379·8
Sub-total	456·7	605·4	986·1	1,595·5
NATIONAL BUDGET ...	3,463·2	3,999·2	5,681·4	8,402·5

Sources: DGE, *Compendio estadístico, 1953,* table 312 (pp. 415–16) [1950, 1952]; *1956–7,* table 315 (pp. 449–50) [1955]; *1958,* table 281 (pp. 430–1) [1955–8]. Categories by author.

Appendix

TABLE XIV

Gross and Net National Products and Incomes, 1930–57

Sub-Table A. Estimated National Income, 1930–45

SECTORS	AMOUNTS (million pesos)				PER CENT.			
	1930	*1935*	*1940*	*1945*	*1930*	*1935*	*1940*	*1945*
Agriculture* ...	583	635	993	2,054	21·6	17·6	14·5	17·2
Mining	356	551	862	940	13·2	14·9	12·7	7·8
Petroleum ...	71	119	161	136	2·6	3·2	2·3	1·1
Manufacturing ...	315	605	1,648	3,020	12·8	16·3	24·2	25·2
Commerce ...	503	790	1,420	2,870	18·6	21·2	20·7	24·8
Construction ...	180	228	435	750	6·7	6·2	6·4	6·2
Other	693	786	1,283	2,218	24·5	20·6	19·2	17·7
Totals	2,701	3,714	6,802	11,988	100·0	100·0	100·0	100·0

* Includes stockraising, fishing, forestry, entered separately in source.
Source: Mosk, *Industrial Revolution*, pp. 314–15, based on Josué Sáenz, 'El Ingreso nacional neto de México', *Revista de Economía*, ix (28 Feb. 1946), 27–32. Percentages by author.

Sub-Table B. Net Domestic Product, 1939–45 compared with 1951–4

Activity	ANNUAL AVERAGE AMOUNTS 1939–45 | 1951–4 (million pesos)		PER CENT.	
	1939–45	*1951–4*	*1939–45*	*1951–4*
Commerce	2,944·5	16,939·1	28·0	29·1
Agriculture	2,136·7	11,519·4	19·9	19·8
Manufacturing	1,880·4	9,360·9	17·6	16·1
Mining	322·1	1,438·8	3·0	2·5
Construction	207·5	1,040·4	1·9	1·8
Petroleum	154·9	826·7	1·4	1·4
Electric power	54·5	293·4	0·5	0·5
All others	2,967·1	16,800·7	27·7	28·8
TOTALS	10,707·7	58,215·3	100·0	100·0

Source: Teichert, *Economic Policy Revolution*, table III–20, p. 155.

Appendix

(Table XIV continued)
Sub-Table C. *Net National Income, 1950 and 1957 (after Zamora M.)*

	AMOUNTS (million pesos)		PER CENT.	
	1950	*1957*	*1950*	*1957*
PRIMARY ACTIVITIES				
Agriculture	11, 864	19,665	21·5	24·2
SECONDARY ACTIVITIES				
Mining, petroleum industrial	15,375	21,646	28·8	27·1
TERTIARY ACTIVITIES				
Commerce, &c.	28,027	38,783	49·7	48·7
TOTALS	55,266	90,094	100·0	100·0

Source: SDE, *Diagnóstico económico regional*, p. 350. Percentage calculations by author.

Sub-Table D. *Gross National Product and National Income, 1948–59 ('000 million pesos)*

Year	GROSS NATIONAL PRODUCT			NATIONAL INCOME	
	Monetary terms	*Real terms*	*Rate of annual growth (real)*	*Monetary terms*	*Real terms*
1948	31·7	36·1	—	28·8	32·4
1949	35·2	37·6	4·0	31·7	33·9
1950	41·5	41·5	9·4	37·5	37·5
1951	51·8	44·5	6·8	46·8	40·2
1952	58·3	45·0	1·1	52·0	40·1
1953	56·3	44·4	—1·3	50·2	39·6
1954	66·5	47·8	7·1	59·2	42·6
1955	84·0	52·5	8·9	74·8	46·7
1956	94·0	56·0	6·3	84·0	50·0
1957	103·0	58·0	3·4	92·0	52·0
1958	114·0	60·6	4·3	101·8	54·3
1959	122·0	63·4	2·4	109·0	56·8

Source: DGE, *Compendio estadístico, 1958*, table 324 (pp. 456–7); rearranged; rates of annual growth by author. Data for 1959 by courtesy of Nacional Financiera.

349

TABLE XV

Mexico's Twenty-one Principal Crops, 1957

	AREA ('000 hectares)	PRODUCTION ('000 metric tons)	VALUE (million pesos)	PER CENT. Area	PER CENT. Value	RANKING 10 CROPS Rank Area	RANKING 10 CROPS Rank Value
Alfalfa ...	87·3	4,067·1	300·9	0·8	2·6		10
Bananas ...	52·3	538·2	266·7	0·5	2·3		
Barley ...	237·1	174·0	115·8	2·2	1·0	7	
Beans ...	1,151·9	410·0	511·5	11·2	4·3	2	6
Cacao ...	45·1	15·3	76·3	0·4	0·7		
Chickpeas ...	137·3	106·3	94·7	1·3	0·8	10	
Coffee ...	271·8	123·8	870·4	2·6	7·3	5	4
Copra ...	198·4	113·0	200·8	1·9	1·6	8	
Cotton ...	915·6	477·6	3,035·6	8·8	25·1	4	2
Henequen ...	157·2	118·8	209·7	1·5	1·7	9	
Limes ...	12·2	83·1	52·6	0·1	0·5		
Maize ...	5,391·8	4,500·0	3,148·1	52·4	25·8	1	1
Oranges ...	62·2	656·4	334·9	0·6	2·7		9
Peanuts ...	67·0	81·3	73·0	0·6	0·6		
Peppers ...	52·3	87·2	136·4	0·7	1·1		
Potatoes ...	40·9	196·6	112·4	0·4	0·9		
Rice ...	117·4	239·9	203·3	1·1	1·6		
Sugarcane ...	257·5	14,597·3	687·9	2·5	5·7	6	5
Tobacco ...	51·4	69·7	161·9	0·5	1·3		
Tomatoes ...	60·9	341·0	340·8	0·6	2·8		7
Wheat ...	957·9	1,376·5	1,166·7	9·3	9·6	3	3
Totals ...	10,325·5		12,100·4	100·0	100·0		

Metric ton = 2,204·6 lb.; hectare = 2.47 acres.

Source: DGE, *Compendio estadístico, 1958*, table 135 (pp. 223–25); totals, percentages, ranks, by author.

Five Leading Crops: Summary

Beans ...	1,151·9	511·5	11·2	4·3
Maize ...	5,391·8	3,148·1	52·4	25·8
Cotton ...	915·6	3,035·6	8·8	25·1
Wheat ...	957·9	1,166·7	9·3	9·6
Coffee ...	271·8	870·4	2·6	7·3
Total ...	8,689·0	8,732·3	84·3	72·1

TABLE XVI

Production of Principal Minerals, *1950–8*

(*'ooo metric tons*)

	Average Prod'n 1950–4	Prod'n. 1955	1958	
			Production	Value (m. pesos)
Antimony ...	5·0	3·8	2·7	24·8
Arsenic ...	5·8	2·9	3·1	4·7
Bismuth ...	0·3	0·3	0·2	11·7
Cadmium ...	0·8	1·3	0·8	32·9
Coal	1,218·6	1,342·1	1,470·7	99·5
Copper ...	60·5	54·7	64·9	418·0
Gold (a) ...	13·3	11·9	10·0	143·6
Graphite ...	26·8	29·3	19·6	12·1
Iron	316·6	429·2	619·5	267·1
Lead	229·3	210·8	201·9	678·3
Manganese ...	49·8	35·8	78·7	130·6
Mercury ...	0·1	1·0	0·8	65·2
Selenium (a) ...	2·8	60·2	0·1	9·8
Silver	1·4	1·5	1·5	529·7
Sulphur ...	42·9	518·4	1,284·9	
Tin	0·4	0·6	0·6	14·4
Tungsten ...	0·2	0·3	0·04	— ＼
Zinc	216·2	269·4	224·1	656·1

a. Metric tons; metric ton = 2,204·6 lb.
Sources: Rice, 'Basic Economic Data, 1959', table 7, p. 11; DGE, *Compendio estadístico, 1958*, tables 164–6.

TABLE XVII

Principal Classes of Mexican Manufactures, by Value, 1958–9
(Million pesos)

Rank		Class of Manufacture	1958	1959	
				Quarterly value	
			Year	2nd	3rd
1	...	Iron and steel	1,904·0	786·7	721·2
2	...	Beer	1,137·1	339·0	335·0
3	...	Rubber manufactures	916·5	270·6	265·0
4	...	Soaps and detergents	607·8	181·6	193·1
5	...	Flour mills	720·8	175·2	169·6
6	...	Paper and cellulose	622·5	171·3	170·6
7	...	Cotton goods	657·6	169·5	168·5
8	...	Cigars and cigarettes	614·4	167·7	167·8
9	...	Cement	521·5	146·7	151·9
10	...	Vegetable oils	542·3	136·7	127·0
11	...	Glass	256·1	64·8	84·9
12	...	Crackers, noodles, food pastes ...	272·4	73·6	70·4
13	...	Woollen goods	421·3	30·7	38·6
14	...	Preserved foods	150·9	65·4	30·5
15	...	Matches	105·4	29·4	28·3
16	...	Shoes	111·1	26·0	26·3
17	...	Knitted goods	68·2	21·5	24·1
18	...	Bricks, tiles, ceramic pipe ...	53·2	13·3	16·9
19	...	Artificial fibre goods	132·1	16·4	15·5
20	...	Stockings and socks	55·4	14·1	12·7
21	...	Mosaic and cement objects ...	44·8	9·0	9·3
22	...	Workmen's clothing	30·3	6·7	6·0
23	...	Wooden furniture	21·7	4·3	4·8

Source: Revista de estadística, xxii (May-June 1959), 305–29; (Nov.-Dec. 1959), 714–38; rearranged and ranked for 1959 by author.

TABLE XVIII

Foreign Trade, by Continents and Selected Countries, 1958
('ooo pesos)

CONTINENTS & Selected Countries	AMOUNT		PER CENT.	
	Exports	Imports	Exports	Imports
NORTH AMERICA ...	5,555·6	11,165·2	79·3	79·3
Canada	113·6	301·4	2·8	2·2
United States	5,442·0	10,861·6	76·5	77·1
CENTRAL AMERICA ...	194·5	76·4	2·7	0·5
SOUTH AMERICA	103·7	46·7	1·4	0·3
ANTILLES	100·8	13·5	1·3	0·1
EUROPE	792·3	2,471·5	11·5	17·6
Germany (W)	184·9	710·6	2·6	5·0
France	73·4	300·8	1·0	2·1
Great Britain...	149·1	456·7	2·1	3·2
Italy	29·1	267·7	0·4	1·9
Low Countries	142·6	143·7	2·0	1·0
ASIA	279·8	213·3	3·8	1·4
Japan	265·9	99·8	3·7	0·7
AFRICA	20·9	17·1		
OCEANIA	25·4	103·8		
TOTALS	7,073·0	14,107·5	100·0	100·0

Source: DGE, *Compendio estadístico, 1958*, tables 251, 252 (pp. 376–8), 267, 270 (pp. 406–8), consolidated, percentages by author.

Table XIX

Balances of Payments, Selected Years, 1953–8

(million dollars)

	1953	1955	1958*
ESTIMATED INCOMES			
Export of goods	561·3	760·3	709·0
Gold and silver production ...	57·6	47·8	52·0
Tourism, border transactions ...	313·6	349·9	559·6
Bracero remittances	33·7	25·0	35·7
Long-term credits	31·6	78·6	180·6
Other	6·5	5·1	25·0
Sub-totals	1,004·3	1,266·7	1,561·9
ESTIMATED EXPENDITURES			
Import of goods	811·0	883·8	1,128·6
National tourism, border	138·5	155·0	237·6
Amortization, long term credit ...	17·7	38·1	123·2
Amortization, foreign debt ...	13·5	20·3	13·2
Other	24·2	38·2	66·9
Sub-totals	—1,004·9	—1,125·5	—1,569·5
NET UNESTIMATED INCOMES AND EXPENDITURES† ...	27·0	15·0	—77·5
RESULT : NET SHORT-RUN CHANGE	25·6	116·3	—85·1

* In 1958 a much more detailed, different presentation was published, adapted here to earlier, more simplified versions of 1953 and 1955. All figures plus unless negative indicated.

† Interest and dividends on foreign investments; new investments; errors and omissions.

Source: Banco de México, in DGE, *Compendio estadístico, 1955*, table 302 (p. 373); *1958*, table 289 (pp. 437–8).

BIBLIOGRAPHY

THIS is a highly selective bibliography, omitting some items cited in earlier notes: short journalistic pieces of ephemeral utility, titles of works mentioned in the chapter on literature, official messages carried widely in the press, and several statistical and similar compilations of data, including Census publications. It does aim at recording those works which were especially useful in preparing the text and at offering suggestions for further reading on various topics. To that end some of the major recent titles have been included under a very loose subject classification below.

Much of the literature through 1952 has been discussed in the bibliographical essay of my own *United States and Mexico* (1953). For the English-reading audience, Professor Robin A. Humphreys, *Latin American History: a guide to the literature in English* (London, 1958) provides an excellent point of departure. Recently, to provide a general listing for the non-specialist interested in Mexico and Latin America, I prepared a bibliography, 'Latin America', issued by the American Universities Field Staff as part of *A Selective Bibliography: Asia, Africa, Eastern Europe, Latin America* (N.Y., 1960), pp. 357–414, and containing about 750 titles. Above all, however, the student and reader should consult the annual, selective, standard *Handbook of Latin American Studies* (23 v. to date, Cambridge, Mass. and Gainesville, Fla., 1936—), prepared co-operatively by leading scholars for the Hispanic Foundation in the Library of Congress, covering social sciences and humanities. It will provide information on periodicals, other bibliographies, and many other matters. Works listed below generally have specialized bibliographies and suggestions for pursuing questions further.

References to the First and Second Messages of President Adolfo López Mateos have followed the English versions appearing in the *Mexico City News* for 2 September of the respective years; references to his *2° Informe* refer to the official Spanish text which appears in nearly all the metropolitan newspapers on 2 September.

GENERAL

Cline, Howard F. 'Mexico, a Matured Latin American Revolution, 1910–1960', *Annals of the American Association of Political and Social Sciences*, v, 334 (Mar. 1961), 84–94.
A general survey, extending remarks read to the American Historical Association, 30 Dec. 1960.

Considine, John J. *New Horizons in Latin America* N.Y., 1958.
A temperate Catholic view, with useful chapter on Mexico.

Bibliography

Lewis, Oscar. 'México desde 1940', *Investigación económica*, xviii (1958), 185–256.
Briefer version as 'Mexico since Cárdenas', *Social Research*, xxvi (Spring 1958), 18–30. Brought up to *c.* 1959 the most recent version appears in Lyman Bryson, ed., *Social Change in Latin America Today*, N.Y., Council on Foreign Relations, 1960, pp. 285–345. Useful summary by a sociologist-anthropologist.

Loyo, Gilberto. 'Profile of Mexico Today', *Mexico This Month*, v/4 (Sept. 1960), 17, 21–23.
Summary of Mexican views of themselves.

Ross, Stanley R. 'Mexico: Golden Anniversary of the Revolution', *Current History*, xxxviii (Mar. 1960), 150–4, 180.
Short popular summary.

Simpson, Lesley Byrd. *Many Mexicos.* 3rd. ed. Berkeley and Los Angeles, 1952.
Readable, popular summary.

Tannenbaum, Frank. *Mexico: the Struggle for Peace and Bread.* N.Y., 1950.
Emotional plea for return to Cárdenas policies.

HISTORY

General

O'Gorman, Edmundo. *Breve historia de las divisiones territoriales; trabajos jurídicos de homenaje a la Escuela Libre de Derecho en su XXV aniversario.* ii/1. Mexico, 1937.
Summary of laws and decrees setting up colonial and national jurisdictions (states, territories, Federal District).

Parkes, Henry Bamford. *A History of Mexico.* 3rd ed. Boston, 1960.
A relatively brief, readable, but inadequate summary. Data for 1960.

Sepúlveda, César. 'Historia y problemas de los límites de México', *Historia Mexicana*, viii (1958), 1–34, 145–74.
Synthesis of diplomatic and other aspects of setting boundaries with the United States and with Guatemala, extensive bibliography.

Wolf, Eric R. *Sons of the Shaking Earth.* Chicago U.P., 1959.
Personalized synthesis of native Indian history from earliest times to the present.

Precolonial and Colonial

Bourne, Edward Gaylord. *Spain in America, 1450–1580.* N.Y., 1904 (ed. of 1906). (The American Nation: A history, iii.)
An historical classic.

Cook de Leonard, Carmen, ed. *Esplendor del México antiguo.* Mexico, Centro de Investigaciones Antropológicas de México, 1959. 2 v.
Uneven essays by many hands; magnificent illustrations.

Bibliography

Gibson, Charles. *The Colonial Period in Latin American History*. Washington, American Hist. Ass., Service Center for Teachers of History, 1958.
Summary of recent interpretations, with excellent bibliographical discussion.

Haring, Clarence H. *The Spanish Empire in America*. N.Y., 1947. Rev. ed. 1952.
Standard scholarly summary.

Howe, Walter. *The Mining Guild of New Spain and its Tribunal General*. Cambridge, Mass., 1949. (Harvard Historical Studies, 56.)

Parry, John H. *The Audiencia of New Galicia in the Sixteenth Century*. Cambridge U.P., 1948.
Historical, with much on western Mexico.

Peterson, F. *Ancient Mexico*. London, 1960.
A semi-popular summary in the Joyce tradition, with fine illustrations.

National

Bernstein, Harry. *Modern and Contemporary Latin America*. Chicago, 1952.
Chapters on Mexico are especially important, summarizing national trends to Alemán.

Bernstein, Harry. 'Some Regional Factors in the National History of Mexico', *Acta Americana*, ii (Oct.–Dec. 1944), 305–14.

Cosío Villegas, Daniel, ed. *Historia moderna de México*. Mexico, 1955–60. 5 v. [of projected 8].
A major historiographical achievement, tracing Mexican developments 1872–1910.

Scholes, Walter V. *Mexican Politics during the Juárez Regime, 1855–1872*. Columbia, Mo., 1957. (Univ. of Missouri Studies, 30.)
Summary, with extended bibliography, of a key period.

The 1910 Revolution

Brenner, Anita. *The Wind that Swept Mexico: the History of the Mexican Revolution, 1910–1942, [with] 184 historical photographs assembled by George R. Leighton*. N.Y., 1943.
Slanted Left text, with magnificent pictures.

Cline, Howard F. *The United States and Mexico*. Cambridge, Mass., Harvard U.P., 1953. (The American Foreign Policy Library, ed. Sumner Welles.)
Chiefly Mexican developments, 1910–50. Bibliog. and tables are helpful.

Quirk, Robert E. *The Mexican Revolution, 1914–1915; the Convention of Aguascalientes*. Bloomington, Indiana U.P., 1960.
Excellent treatment of the Revolution's crises following Madero's death.

Ross, Stanley R. 'Bibliography of Sources for Contemporary Mexican History', *HAHR*, xxxix (May 1959), 234–8.
An outline of the elaborate project at the Colegio de México, with helpful review of principal bibliographies (Ramos, al et.)

Bibliography

Ross, Stanley R. *Francisco I. Madero: Apostle of Mexican Democracy*. N.Y., Columbia U.P., 1955.
Standard biography.

Townsend, W. Cameron. *Lázaro Cárdenas, Mexican Democrat*. Ann Arbor, 1952.
Uncritical biography by an American adviser and admirer.

Weyl, Nathaniel and Sylvia. *The Reconquest of Mexico: the Years of Lázaro Cárdenas*. London, Oxford U.P., 1939.
Communist-slanted but useful survey of early Cárdenas programmes in all fields.

SOCIETY AND CULTURE

General

Beals, Ralph L., and Norman D. Humphrey. *No Frontier to Learning; the Mexican Student in the United States*. Minneapolis, Minnesota U.P., 1957.
An important cultural-sociological inquiry.

Bermúdez, María Elvira. *La Vida familiar del mexicano*. Mexico, 1955.
Reconstruction of family life from literary works from colonial to recent times.

Cline, Howard F. 'Mexican Community Studies', *HAHR*, xxxii (May 1952), 212–42.
A listing of all such studies through 1951, with analysis and critique, and related bibliography.

Edmondson, Munro S. *A Triangulation on the Culture of Mexico*. New Orleans, Tulane University, Middle American Research Inst., 1957. (Publication 17, pp. 201–40.)
An interpretative essay by an anthropologist.

Espinosa Olvera, René. 'Los Recursos humanos en el desarrollo económico de México', *Investigación económica*, xvi (1956), 335–49.

Iturriaga, José E. *La Estructura social y cultural de México*. Mexico, Fondo de Cultura Económica, 1951. (Estructura Económica y Social de México, 1.)
Helpful summary, based for modern times on 1940 Census, hence now slightly out of date, yet not replaced.

Lewis, Oscar. *Five Families: Mexican Case Studies in the Culture of Poverty*. N.Y. 1959.
A day in the life of five different social and cultural strata, four in Mexico City and including a newly arrived middle-class household.

—— 'Peasant culture in India and Mexico: a Comparative Analysis'. *In* McKim Marriott, *Village India*. Menasha, Wis., 1955, pp. 145–70. (American Anthropological Ass., *Memoir*, 83.)

—— 'Urbanization without Breakdown: a Case Study', *Scientific Monthly*, lxxv (July 1952), 31–41.
Migration of country-folk to Mexico City, to form sub-societies.

Bibliography

Whetten, Nathan L. 'The Rise of the Middle Class in Mexico', *In* Pan American Union, *Materiales para el estudio de la clase media en América Latina*. Washington, 1950–1, ii, 1–29.

Demography

Aguirre Beltrán, Gonzalo. *La Población negra de México, 1519–1810: Estudio etnohistórico*. Mexico, 1946.
Basic demographic study of the colonial period, broader than Negroes only.

Burnight, Robert G., and others. 'Differential Rural-Urban Fertility in Mexico', *American Sociological Review*, xxi (Feb. 1956), 3–8.
Technical, but quite important.

Flores de la Peña, Horacio. 'Crecemiento demográfico, desarrollo agrícola, y desarrollo económico', *Investigación económica*, xiv (1954), 519–36.

Glinstra-Bleeker, R. J. P. van. 'Algunos aspectos de la emigración y la inmigración', *Investigación económica*, xiii (1953), 27–40.

Moreno, Daniel. *Los Factores demográficos en la planeación económica*. Mexico, Cámara Nacional de la Industria de la Transformación, Comisión de la Planeación Económica, 1958.

U.N., Dept. de Asuntos Sociales, Divis. de Población. *La Población de la América Central y México en el período 1950 a 1980*. N.Y., 1958.

Indians

Aguirre Beltrán, Gonzalo. *Problemas de la población indígena de la Cuenca de Tepalcatepec*. Mexico, Instituto Indigenista Nacional, 1952. (*Memoria*, 3.)

Comas, Juan. *Bibliografía selectiva de las culturas indígenas de América*. Mexico, Pan American Institute of Geography and History, 1953. (Publ. 166.)

Comas, Juan. 'Indígenas de México', *Revista Población*, i (Aug. 1953), 36–44.
Analysis of 1940 Census returns re natives.

Instituto Nacional Indigenista. *Densidad de la población de habla indígena en la República Mexicana (por entidades federativas y municipios, conforme al Censo de 1940)*. Mexico, 1950. Introd. by Manuel Germán Parra. (*Memorias*, 1, No. 1.)
Analysis of 1940 data, with good maps; provides municipal data.

Lewis, Oscar. *Life in a Mexican Village: Tepoztlán Restudied*. Urbana, Illinois U.P., 1951.
A basic study, reappraising Redfield's earlier idealized findings on a modern Aztec community.

Marino Flores, Anselmo. *Bibliografía lingüística de la república mexicana*. Mexico, Inst. Indigenista Interamericano, 1957.
Arranged by language groups; helpful maps.

—— 'Indígenas de México; algunas consideraciones demográficas', *América indígena*, xvi (Jan. 1956), 41–48.
Synthesis of Census data of 1950, compared with 1940, on Mexican Indians.

Bibliography

Villoro, Luis. *Los Grandes momentos del indigenismo en Méx co.* Colegio de México, 1950.

Wagley, Charles, and Marvin Harris. 'The Indians of Mexico', *Minorities in the New World* (N.Y.), 1958, pp. 48–86.
Synthesis by social anthropologist.

Wolf, Eric R. 'The Indian in Mexican Society', *Alpha Kappa Delta: a Sociological Journal*, xxx (Winter 1960), 3–6.
Interpretative.

Education

Booth, George C. *Mexico's School-Made Society.* Stanford U.P., 1941.
Useful summary of schools in the Cárdenas era.

Bremauntz, Alberto. *La Educación socialist en México (antecedentes y fundamentos de la Reforma de 1934).* Mexico, 1943.
Radical view of school and society.

Johnston, Marjorie C. *Education in Mexico.* Washington, U.S. Dept. of Health, Education, and Welfare, Office of Education, [1956]. (U.S. Office of Ed., Bulletin 1956, No. 1.)
A summary pamphlet of high merit by a trained specialist.

Kneller, George F. *The Education of the Mexican Nation.* N.Y., Columbia U.P., 1951.
Excellent synthesis to about 1950; extended bibliography.

Navarrete, Ifigenia M. de. 'El Financiamiento de la educación pública en México', Mexico, UNAM, 1959. (Suplementos del Seminario de Problemas Científicos y Filosoficos, 2nd ser., No. 15.) Reprinted from *Investigación económica*, xviii (1958), 21–55.

Sánchez, George I. *Development of Higher Education in Mexico.* N.Y., 1944.
Now out of date.

—— *Mexico: a Revolution by Education.* N.Y., 1936.
Projects of the Cárdenas era.

The Press and Radio

Alisky, Marvin. 'Early Mexican Broadcasting', *HAHR*, xxxiv (Nov. 1954), 513–26.
—— 'Growth of Newspapers in Mexico's Provinces', *Journalism Quarterly*, xxxvii (Winter 1960) [unpaginated].

Castaño, Luis. *El Régimen legal de la prensa en México.* Mexico, 1958.
Discusses freedom of the press from several aspects, with important legislation in appendices.

Cosío Villegas, Daniel. 'The Press and Responsible Freedom in Mexico'. *In* Angel del Río, ed., *Responsible Freedom in the Americas.* N.Y., Garden City, 1955, pp. 272–90.

Bibliography

The Humanities

Crawford, W. Rex. *A Century of Latin American Thought*. Cambridge, Mass., Harvard U.P., 1945.
Ch. 9 sketches the Mexicans. Rev. ed. 1961.

'The eye of Mexico', *Evergreen Review*, vii (1959), pp. 22–213.
Translations of young and important Mexican writers.

González, Manuel Pedro. *Trajectoría de la novela en México*. Mexico, 1951.

González Peña, Carlos. *History of Mexican Literature*. Trans. Dallas, 1943.

Jiménez Rueda, Julio. *Historia de la literatura mexicana*. 4th ed. Mexico, 1946.

Martínez, José Luis. *Literatura mexicana del siglo XX, 1910–1949*. Mexico, 1949. 2 v.

Mead, Robert G., jr. 'Aspects of Mexican Literature Today', *Books Abroad*, xxxiv (Winter 1960), pp. 5–8.

Morton, R. Rand. *Los Novelistas de la revolución mexicana*. Mexico, 1949.

Rodman, Selden. *Mexican Journal*. N.Y., 1958.
Diary notes on art and culture by an avidly curious artist-intellectual.

ECONOMIC MATTERS

General

Alanís Patiño, Emilio. 'La Riqueza nacional', *Investigación económica*, xv (1955), 53–81.
National incomes and products to 1945, converted to 1955 values.

—— 'Los Problemas de desarrollo industrial de México', BNCE, *Comercio exterior*, vi (Aug.–Sept. 1956), 347–51, 418–21.

International Bank for Reconstruction and Development. *The Economic Development of Mexico*. Baltimore, Johns Hopkins U.P., 1953.
A now dated summary, as of *c.* 1950, with recommendations, many of which became official policy.

International Economic Consultants, Inc. *U.S.-Latin American Relations: Commodity Problems in Latin America*. A study prepared at the request of the Subcommittee on America Republics Affairs of the Cttee. on For. Rels., U.S. Senate . . . No. 2. Washington, 1959. (Country notes: Mexico, pp. 86–87.)

Jaffe, Abram J. *People, Jobs and Economic Development; a Case History of Puerto Rico supplemented by Recent Mexican Experiences*. Glencoe, Ill., Columbia Univ., Bureau of Applied Soc. Research, 1959.
More pessimistic about Mexico than other economists, basing findings on rather thin information.

James, Daniel. 'Sears, Roebuck's Mexican Revolution', *Harper's Magazine* (June 1959), 1–6.

Bibliography

Lichey, W. *Mexiko: Ein Weg zur wirtschaftlichen Entwicklung zwischen staatlicher Lenkung und privater Initiative: auf der Grundlage der Forschungsergebnisse von R. v. Gersdorff, C. Kapferer, I. Schaafhausen.* (Schriften des Hamburgischen Welt-Wirtschafts-Archivs, No. 8. Sonderreihe; Entwicklungsgebiete.) Hamburg, Verlag Weltarchiv. [1958].

A co-operative monograph, bringing data to about 1957. A very sound optimistic summary based on much data; important tabular statistical data; bibliography published separately.

Mosk, Sanford. *Industrial Revolution in Mexico.* Berkeley and Los Angeles, Calif. U.P., 1950. [rev. ed. 1954 not used].

Sound monograph, but now partially outmoded by developments 1950–60.

Mújica Montoya, Emilio. 'Los Salarios en la economía nacional', *Investigación económica*, xvi (1956), 565–81.

Nacional Financiera. *The Economic Development of Mexico during a Quarter of a Century.* Mexico, 1959.

Navarrete R[omero], Alfredo, jr. 'Los Programas revolucionarios y el futuro progreso económico de México', PRI, *Cuadernos de orientación política*, i/3 (Mar. 1956), 17–25.

Indicates that prosperity is not necessarily anti-Revolutionary.

Rodríguez Mata, Emilio. 'Evolución de la población de México y de algunas entidades típicas', *Investigación económica*, xiv (1954), 385–96.

Interesting study of selected regions.

Sarames, George N. 'Third system in Latin America; Mexico', *Interamerican Economic Affairs*, v/4 (Spring 1952), 59–72.

Discussion of Mexico's peculiar functional economic system that is neither capitalistic nor socialistic.

SDE and Inst. Mexicano de Investigaciones Económicas. *Diagnóstico económico regional, 1958.* Mexico, 1959.

Basic studies of national and regional developments, with recommendations; excellent statistics, maps, and charts.

Teichert, Pedro C. M. *Economic Policy Revolution and Industrialization in Latin America.* Univ. of Mississippi, Bureau of Business Research, 1959.

Ch. 12, 'Mexican Experience of Balanced Growth' espec. important.

USBFC, American Republics Division. *Investment in Mexico: Conditions and Outlook for United States Investors.* Washington, [1956].

Considerably broader than title implies: summary economic analysis with important appendices.

USBFC, WTIS, Statistical Reports, No. 59–35: 'Trade of the United States with Latin America: Years 1956–8 and Half-Years January 1958–June 1959'. Washington, Oct. 1959.

—— WTIS, pt. 1, Economic Reports, No. 59–5, 'Basic Data on the Economy of Mexico' [prepared by Katherine E. Rice. Jan. 1959].

Bibliography

USBFC, WTIS, Nos. 55–78, 56–24, 57–41, 58–36: 'Economic Developments in Mexico' [annually, 1954–8, prepared by Katherine E. Rice]. Washington, 1955–9.

—— WTIS, pt. 3, Statistical Reports, No. 59–35: 'Trade of the United States with Latin America: Years 1956–8 and Half-Years January 1958–June 1959'. Washington, Oct. 1959.

Wythe, George. *Industry in Latin America*. N.Y., Columbia U.P., 1945.
Pioneering treatment.

Fiscal

Aguilar, G. F. *Los Presupuestos mexicanos desde los tiempos de la colonia hasta nuestro días*. Mexico, 1947.

Bernstein, Marvin. 'Foreign Investments and Mineral Resources; a Few Observations', *Inter-American Economic Affairs*, xiii (Winter, 1959), 33–49.
Technical, but especially applicable to Mexico.

Espinosa de los Reyes, Jorge. 'La Distribución del ingreso nacional'. *In* UNAM, Escuela Nacional de Economía. *Problemas del desarrollo económico mexicano: cursos de invierno 1957*. Mexico, 1958, pp. 161–224.

Harvard Univ., Int. Program in Taxation. *Taxation in Mexico*. [Primarily the work of Henry J. Gumpel . . . and Hugo B. Margáin . . .] Boston, 1957. (World Tax Series.)
Basic and comprehensive coverage, with much history.

McCaleb, Walter F. *Present and Past Banking in Mexico*. N.Y., 1920.
Essentially a history through the early Revolution; conservative.

Navarrete R[omero], Alfredo, jr. 'Financiamiento del desarrollo económico de México'. *In* UNAM, Escuela de Economía. *Problemas del desarrollo económico mexicano: cursos de invierno 1957*. Mexico, 1958, pp. 135–39.
Major views of a present high official of N.F.

Scott, Robert E. 'Budget making in Mexico', *Inter-American Economic Affairs*, ix (Autumn, 1955), 3–20.

Urquidi, Víctor L. 'El Impuesto sobre la renta en el desarrollo económico de México', *Trimestre económico*, xxiii (Oct.–Dec. 1956), 424–37.

Communications and Transport

USBFC, WTIS, pt. 4, Economic Reports, No. 57–2: 'Civil Aviation in Mexico'. Washington, Jan. 1957.

—— —— No. 56–13: 'Highways of Mexico'. Washington, Sept. 1956.

Villafuerte, Carlos. *Ferrocarriles*. Mexico, Fondo de Cultura Económica, 1959. (Estructura económica y social de México, 7.)
Fundamental study of Mexico's railways.

Bibliography

Power

Guzmán, Eduardo J. '1958 Developments in Foreign Petroleum Fields: Mexico', American Ass. of Petroleum Geologists, *Bulletin*, xliii (July 1959), 1505–17.

Lara Beautell, Cristóbal. *La Industria de energía eléctrica*. Mexico, Fondo de Cultura Económica, 1953. (Estructura económica y social de México, 3.) Summary of data to beginning of the Ruíz Cortines term.

Powell, J. Richard. *The Mexican Petroleum Industry, 1938–1950*. Berkeley and Los Angeles, Univ. of Calif., Bureau of Business and Econ. Research, 1956.
Standard to point before industry recovered.

U.S. 80th Congr., 2nd Sess., House. *Fuel Investigation: Mexican Petroleum*. House Report 2470, Union Calendar 1220. Washington, 1949.

Labour

Banco de México, Dept. de Investigaciones Industriales. *El Empleo de personal técnico en la industria de transformación*. Mexico, 1959.

Chicago Univ., Research Center in Econ. Dev. and Cultural Change. *U.S.-Latin American Relations: United States Business and Labor in Latin America*. A study prepared at the request of the Subcommittee on America Republics Affairs of the Cttee. on For. Rels., U.S. Senate . . . No. 4. Washington, 1960.

Clark, Marjorie R. *Organized Labor in Mexico*, Chapel Hill, North Carolina UP., 1934.
Pre-CTM developments.

National Planning Ass. *U.S.-Latin American Relations: United States and Latin American Policies affecting their Economic Relations*. A study prepared at the request of the Subcommittee on America Republics Affairs of the Cttee. on For. Rels., U.S. Senate . . . No. 5. Washington, 1960.

Navarrete R[omero], Alfredo, jr. 'Productividad, ocupación y desocupación en México; 1940–1965', *Trimestre económico*, xxiii (Oct.–Dec. 1956), 415–23.

Rivera Marín, Guadalupe. *El Mercado de trabajo: relaciones obrero-patronales*. Mexico, Fondo de Cultura Económica, 1955. (Estructura económica y social de México, 4.)
Economic rather than historical analysis.

Salazar, Rosendo. *Historia de la CTM*. Mexico, 1956.
Like other works by author is patchy, but important.

—— *Líderes y sindicatos*. Mexico, 1953.

Stephansky, Ben F. 'The Mexican Labour Movement: an Interpretation of a Political Labour Movement'. Unpublished study, cleared for public use 12 July 1957. [U.S. Embassy, Mexico, 1956, typescript.]

Bibliography

LAND

Gill, Tom. *Land Hunger in Mexico.* Washington, C. L. Pack Forestry Foundation, 1951.
A conservationist's view.

González Santos, Armando. *La Agricultura: estructura y utilización de los recursos.* Mexico, Fondo de Cultura Económica, 1957. (Estructura económica y social de México, 6.)
Fundamental study and summary of a key complex problem.

McBride, George M. *The Land Systems of Mexico.* N.Y., 1923. (Amer. Geog. Soc., Research Series, 12.)
Classic pioneering work, now obsolete in many historical parts, but of continuing value.

Martín Echeverría, Leonardo. 'La Leyenda dorada sobre la riqueza de México', *Investigación económica*, xiv, 231–87.
Historical survey.

Mendieta y Núñez, Lucio. *El Problema agrario de México.* 5th ed. Mexico, 1946.
Pioneering sociological survey.

Senior, Clarence. *Land Reform and Democracy.* Gainesville, Florida U.P., 1958.
Chiefly a study of La Laguna and the ejido programmes to *c.* 1950, sympathetic but critical.

Silva Herzog, Jesús. *El Agrarianismo mexicano y la reforma agraria, exposición y crítica.* Mexico, Fondo de Cultura Económica, 1959.
Important statement deploring shift from Cárdenas's radical agrarianism.

Simpson, Eyler N. *The Ejido: Mexico's Way Out.* Chapel Hill, North Carolina U.P., 1937.
Classic account, at beginning of Cárdenas's agrarianism.

Tannenbaum, Frank. *The Mexican Agrarian Revolution.* N.Y., 1929.
Now of historical value; an early statement.

Whetten, Nathan L. *Rural Mexico.* Chicago U.P., 1948.
Massive compilation, now obsolescent, as based on 1940 figures.

Yáñez Pérez, Luis, assisted by Edmundo Moyo Porras. *Mecanización de la agricultura mexicana.* Mexico, Inst. Mex. de Investigaciones Económicas. 1957.
Elaborate analysis of Mexican agricultural problems *c.* 1950; a basic treatment.

GOVERNMENT AND POLITICS

General

Fitzgibbon, Russell H. 'Measurement of Latin American Political Phenomena: a Statistical Experiment', *American Political Science Review*, xlv (June 1951), 517–23.

Bibliography

Fitzgibbon, Russell H. 'A Statistical Evaluation of Latin-American Democracy', *Western Political Quarterly*, ix (Sept. 1956), 607–19.

García Valencia, Antonio. *Las Relaciones humanas en la administración pública mexicana*. Mexico, 1958.

Goodspeed, Stephen S. 'El Papel del jefe del ejecutivo en México', *Problemas industriales e agrícolas de México*, vii (Jan.–Mar. 1955), 13–208.
Spanish translation of a doctoral dissertation; biographies of Revolutionary Presidents.

Johnson, John J. *Political Change in Latin America; the Emergence of the Middle Sectors*. Stanford U.P., 1958. (Studies in History, Economics and Political Science, 15.)
Important general analysis, with ch. 7 specifically on Mexico.

Mecham, J. Lloyd. *Church and State in Latin America: a History of Politico-Ecclesiastical Relations*. Chapel Hill, North Carolina U.P., 1934.
Standard; juridical, with two chapters on Mexico.

—— 'Mexican Federalism: Fact or Fiction?', *A. Amer. Acad. Polit.*, ccviii (Mar. 1940), 23–38.
Answer: fiction.

Padgett, Leon V. 'Mexico's One Party System; a Re-evaluation', *American Political Science Review*, li (Dec. 1957), 995–1008.
Finds it less monolithic than earlier.

Scott, Robert E. *Mexican Government in Transition*. Urbana, Illinois U.P., 1959.
Important functional analysis.

Tucker, William P. *The Mexican Government Today*. Minneapolis, Minnesota U.P., 1957.
Descriptive compilation, with an extensive bibliog.

Recent Politics

Barrales V., José, ed. *El Pensamiento político del Licenciado Adolfo López Mateos*. Mexico, 1958.
Campaign and related pronouncements.

Cline, Howard F. 'Mexico: a Maturing Democracy', *Current History*, (Mar. 1953), pp. 136–42.
Detailed analysis of 1952 election.

Espinosa, Juan. *Presente y futuro de México*. Mexico, 1958.

González Luna, Efráin. *Humanismo político*. Mexico, 1955.
Statements by leader of the PAN.

Pineda, Salvador. *El Presidente Ruíz Cortines: itinerario de una conducta*. Mexico, 1952.
Eulogistic campaign biography.

Bibliography

Portes Gil, Emilio. *La Crisis política de la Revolución y la próxima elección presidencial.* Mexico, 1957.
Analysis and remarks by an ex-boss.

Taylor, Philip B. 'The Mexican Elections of 1958: Affirmation of Authoritarism?', *Western Political Science Quarterly,* xiii (Sept. 1960), 722–44.
Summary of political currents 1957; answers his query affirmatively.

Constitution of 1917

Bojórquez, Juan de Díos [pseud: Djed, Bórquez]. *Crónica del Constituyente.* Mexico, 1938.
Constitutional Convention of 1917 materials.

Lanz Duret, Miguel. *Derecho constitucional mexicano y consideraciones sobre la realidad política de nuestra régimen.* Mexico, 1947.
A basic treatment.

Palavicini, Félix F. *Historia de la Constitución de 1917.* Mexico, 1938. 2 v.

Rouaix, Pastor. *Genesis de los Artículos 27 y 123 de la Constitución Política de 1917.* Puebla, Gobierno del Estado de Puebla, 1945.
Account by a contemporary delegate.

Tena Ramírez, Felipe. *Derecho constitucional mexicano.* 3rd ed. Mexico, 1955.
Standard text.

Tena Ramírez, Felipe, comp. *Leyes fundamentales de México, 1808–1957.* Mexico, 1957.

Trueba Urbina, Alberto. *El Artículo 123.* Mexico, 1943.

Zamora Millán, Fernando. 'Fundamentos constitucionales de la intervención estatal en materia económica'. *In* UNAM, Escuela Nacional de Economía. *La Constitución de 1917 y la economía mexicana: cursos de invierno 1957.* Mexico, 1958, pp. 199–218.

Administration of Justice

Bayitch, S. A. *Guide to Inter-American Legal Studies: a Selective Bibliography of Works in English.* Coral Gables, Fla., Univ. of Miami Law Library, 1957.

Bremauntz, Alberto. *Por una justicia al servicio del Pueblo.* Mexico, 1955.
Recent trends in judiciary.

Burgoa, Ignacio. *Las garantías individuales.* 2nd ed. Mexico, 1954.
Legal text.

Cabrera A., Lucio. 'History of the Mexican Judiciary'. *In* David S. Stern, ed., *Mexico: a Symposium on Law and Government.* Coral Gables, Fla., Miami U.P., 1958, pp. 22–31. (Univ. of Miami School of Law, Interamerican Legal Studies, 3.)

Clagett, Helen. *Administration of Justice in Latin America.* N.Y., 1952.
—— 'Law and Courts'. *In* Harold E. Davis, ed. *Government and Politics in Latin America,* N.Y., 1958, pp. 333–67.

Bibliography

Vance, John T., and Helen Clagett. *A Guide to the Law and Legal Literature of Mexico.* Washington, Lib. of Congress, 1945. (Latin American Series, 6.)

Velasco, Gustavo R. 'The Rule of Law in Mexico'. *In* Stern, ed., *Mexico: a Symposium on Law and Government,* pp. 9–12.
Summary of concept of jurisprudence by a Mexican authority.

Militarism

Lieuwen, Edwin. *Arms and Politics in Latin America.* N.Y., Council on Foreign Relations, 1960.
A recent pioneering summary; Mexico is cited as a model, pp. 101–21.

Ross, Stanley R. 'Some Observations on Military Coups in the Caribbean'. *In* A. Curtis Wilgus, ed., *The Caribbean: Its Political Problems.* Gainesville, Univ. of Florida, School of Inter-American Affairs, 1956, pp. 110–28. (Series One, 6.)
Notes wane of Mexican militarism.

Communism

Alexander, Robert. *Communism in Latin America.* New Brunswick, N.J., Rutgers U.P., 1957.
Standard.

Allen, Robert L. *Soviet Influence in Latin America: the Role of Economic Relations.* Washington, Public Affairs Press, 1959.
Finds little Mexican-Soviet exchanges.

Corp. for Econ. and Indust. Research. *U.S.-Latin American Relations: Soviet Bloc Latin American Activities and their Implications for United States Foreign Policy.* A study prepared at the request of the Subcommittee on America Republics Affairs of the Cttee. on For. Rels., U.S. Senate . . . No. 7. Washington, 1960.

García Treviño. Rodrigo. *La Ingerencia rusa en México.* Mexico, 1959.
Former leader of CTM and presently head of Grupo de Socialistas Mexicanos sketches important aspects of the Communist party in Mexico.

Washington, S. Walter. 'Mexican Resistance to Communism', *Foreign Affairs,* xxxvi (Apr. 1958), 504–15.
Summary, attributing lack of Communist success to effectiveness of the PRI and the Mexican Revolution's own achievements.

INTERNATIONAL

General

Blanksten, George I. 'Foreign Policy of Mexico'. *In* Roy Macridis, ed., *Foreign Policy in World Politics.* N.Y., 1958, pp. 323–50.
In part based on outworn data.

Cline, Howard F. 'Mexico, Fidelismo and the United States', *Orbis: a Quarterly of World Affairs,* v (Summer 1961), 152–65.

Bibliography

Cronon, E. David. *Josephus Daniels in Mexico*. Madison, Wisconsin U.P., 1960.
U.S. ambassador during Cárdenas régime; much new and important diplomatic data on U.S.-Mexican relations.

Fabela, Isidro. *Buena y mala vecinidad*. Mexico, 1958.
Various articles by a respected former diplomat, praising U.S. relations 1934–53, but critical of present policies, as being a 'bad neighbour'.

MacKaye, Milton. 'Will Mexico go "Castro"?', *Saturday Evening Post* (29 Oct. 1960), pp. 25, 75–78.
Journalist's report on current Mexican views of Cuba; answers query negatively.

SRE, *La Política international de México, 1952–1956*. Mexico, 1957. (*Serie Problemas Nacionales y Internacionales*, 32.)
Foreign policies of the Ruíz Cortines regime.

——*Las Relaciones internacionales de México, 1935–1956 a través de los mensajes presidenciales*. Mexico, 1957. (Archivo histórico-diplomático, 2 ser, no. 9.)
Excerpts from annual presidential Messages from Cárdenas through Ruíz Cortines.

United Nations and OAS

Canyes, Manuel. *The Organization of American States and the United Nations*. 3rd ed., Washington, Pan American Union, Div. of Law and Treaties, 1955.
Legal analysis of relationships.

Castañeda, Jorge. *Mexico and the United Nations*. Prepared for El Colegio de México and the Carnegie Endowment for International Peace. N.Y., 1958. (National Studies on International Organization.)
Eng. trans. of *México y el orden internacional*. Colegio de México, [1956]. Nationalistic view of Mexico's foreign affairs, especially of its multilateral relations.

—— 'Pan Americanism and Regionalism: a Mexican View', *International Organization*, x (Aug. 1956), 373–89.
Suggests a Pan-Latin Americanism, to offset U.S. preponderance.

Cline, Howard F. 'The Inter-American System', *Current History*, v (Mar. 1955), 177–84.
Short, popular summary of OAS and its workings.

Houston, John A. *Latin America in the United Nations*. N.Y., Carnegie Endowment for Int. Peace, 1956. (U.N. Studies, 8.)

Maúrtua, Manuel Félix. 'El Grupo latino-americano en las Naciones Unidas y algunos problemas jurídicos', *Revista peruana de derecho internacional*, xvi (Jan.–June 1956), 10–43.

Bibliography

Braceros

Eldridge, Fred. 'Helping Hands from Mexico', *Saturday Evening Post* (10 Aug. 1957), pp. 28–29, 63–64.
Popular but useful information on *braceros*.

Galarza, Ernesto. 'Trabajadores mexicanos en tierra extraña', *Problemas agrícolas e industriales de México*, x (Jan.–June 1958), 1–84.
Summary of *bracero* matters, with illustrations and U.S.-Mexican treaty texts.

McWilliams, Carey. *Ill Fares the Land*. Boston, 1942.
Emotional treatment of the illegal 'wetbacks'.

ADDENDA

Alba, Victor. *Las Ideas sociales contemporáneas en México*. Mexico, Fondo de Cultura económica, 1960.
Labour-slanted history since 1910.

Dulles, John W. F. *Yesterday in Mexico; a chronicle of the Revolution, 1919–1936*. Texas, Austin U.P., 1961.
Day-today reconstruction, magnificently illustrated. Full bibliography.

Flores, Edmundo. *Tratado de economía agrícola*. Mexico-Buenos Aires, Fondo de Cultura Económico, 1961.
A basic treatise, linking Mexican with Latin American trends and problems; very recent (1959–60) data, and excellent technical bibliography.

Foster, George M. *Culture and Conquest: America's Spanish Heritage*. N.Y., Wenner-Gren Foundation, 1960. (Viking Fund Publications in Anthropology, 27.)
An important recent statement on the transfer of European culture.

González, Luis, and others. *Fuentes de la historia contemporánea de México* El Colegio de México, 1961.
The first of a 3-vol. bibliographical compilation, 1910–40, listing 6,873 books and pamphlets. Basic.

Lewis, Oscar. *The Children of Sánchez: Autobiography of a Mexican Family*. N.Y., 1961.
The self-portrait of one of the *Five Families* (1959), revealing much about lower-class Mexico City.

Tischendorf, Alfred. *Great Britain and Mexico in the era of Porfirio Díaz*. Durham, N.C., Duke U.P., 1961.
A study of British investment and enterprise, loss of economic hegemony 1876–1911.

INDEX

Agrarian Code, 214–15.

Agriculture : export and industrial crops, 266, 267–9; food supply, 86, 263–7; importance of in national economy, 48, 232–4, 253, 260, 265, 269; land potential, 45–48; see also Hydraulic schemes; Land reform; Physical features.

Alemán, Miguel, 24, 34, 68 f., 157–9, 160 ff., 176, 213 f., 238 f., 268, 275.

Alvárez, Luis H., 169.

Amparo, writ of, 138, 148, 215.

Anderson, Clayton & Co., 88.

Andreu Almazán, Gen. Juan, 169.

Army, 12, 17 ff., 142, 153, 155, 174–6, 307.

Art, 6, 12, 31, 129–31.

Aviation, 65–66.

Avila Camacho, Manuel, 34, 150, 153, 157 ff., 213, 232, 305.

Aztecs, 3, 6 f., 94.

Batista, Fulgencio, 314, 321, 322.

Bermúdez, Antonio J., 275, 279.

Bermúdez, María Elvira, 126.

Betancourt, Romulo, 314, 317.

Bourbon dynasty, 9, 12.

Braceros, see Labour force.

CNC (National Farm Federation), *see* Labour movement.

CTM (Confederation of Workers of Mexico), *see* Labour movement.

Calles, Plutarco Elías, 31 ff., 150–2, 223.

Camarena, González, 130.

Cárdenas, Lázaro, 85, 178, 207, 244; achievements as President, 33–34, 157, 231; anti-clericalism of, 176; expropriation of petroleum industry, 33, 274, 304; land reform policy, 88, 211–13; reform of Official Party and labour movement, 150–3, 155 f., 174, 223.

Carlotta, Empress, 20.

Carranza, Venustiano, 26, 28 ff., 209.

Carrington, Leonora, 130.

Castro, Fidel, 316 ff.

Castro, Raúl, 322.

Charles III (of Spain), 9.

Charles V, Emperor, 9.

Church, Protestant, 176, 177; journals, 184.

Church, Roman Catholic: journals, 184; Missionary and educational work, 7 ff., 192; relations with State, 18 ff., 24, 32 f., 156, 163–4, 174, 176–7, 192–3, 210; — with PAN, 168 f.

'Científicos', 21 ff.

Civil liberties, see *Amparo*, writ of.

Civil service, 142.

Communism and Communists, 32, 174, 177–80, 224 f., 301, 321, 324 ff.; discussed in OAS, 313, 316–20; *see also* Cuba; Soviet Union; United States.

Congress, powers and composition of, 139, 143–5; see also PRI; President.

Constitution: (1814), 17; (1824), 17, 39; (1857), 19, 23, 136; (1917), 30, 32, 135–9, 141 ff., 148, 179, 225, 234, 327; — Art. 3, 3, 148, 191, 194–5; — Art. 27, 137–8, 209–10, 214, 274; — Art. 123, 137–8.

Coolidge, Calvin, 32.

Coronel, Pedro, 130.

Cortés, Hernan, 3, 9–10, 271.

Creelman, James, 25.

'*Cristeros*', 32.

Cuba, relations with, 316 ff., 321–2, 324–8; *see also* United States.

Cuevas, José Luis, 131.

Díaz, Bernal, 10.

Díaz, Felix, 27.

Díaz, Porfirio, 16, 19, 20–22, 25 ff., 113, 136.

Dominican Republic, relations with, 315, 320.

Dorticós, Osvaldo, 324.

Dulles, John Foster, 314.

Economic and financial policy:
Federal expenditure, 194, 235, 237–41
GNP: and national income, 254–8; and labour force, 260; and manufacture, 281
Principles of, 232–4, 261.
Revenue and taxes, 241–3, 247.
State and private enterprise, 234–6, 244, 250, 275, 281, 283–4, 288.
See also Agriculture; Foreign investment; Foreign loans; Foreign trade; Hydraulic schemes; Industry; Nacional Financiera; Standard of Living.

Economic history, 12, 14 ff., 21–22, 159, 231–2, 270.

Education: development, objectives, and importance of, 31, 33, 191–6, 208; expenditure on, 191, 194, 239; schools in newly developed areas, 76, 77; see also Church, Roman Catholic; Illiteracy.

Educational system: basic structure, 196–7; primary, 198–202; university and technical, 202–7.

Index

Index